Near-Death Experience in
Indigenous Religions

T0347602

Near-Death Experience in Indigenous Religions

GREGORY SHUSHAN

OXFORD
UNIVERSITY PRESS

OXFORD
UNIVERSITY PRESS

Oxford University Press is a department of the University of Oxford. It furthers
the University's objective of excellence in research, scholarship, and education
by publishing worldwide. Oxford is a registered trade mark of Oxford University
Press in the UK and certain other countries.

Published in the United States of America by Oxford University Press
198 Madison Avenue, New York, NY 10016, United States of America.

© Oxford University Press 2018

First issued as an Oxford University Press paperback, 2023

CIP data is on file at the Library of Congress
ISBN 978-0-19-768543-3

Paperback printed by Marquis Book Printing, Canada

For the ancestors.

Contents

Foreword

GREGORY SHUSHAN HAS produced the most important scholarly work on near-death experiences (NDEs) in the last thirty years. Not since Carol Zaleski's landmark study (1987) comparing medieval NDEs and modern NDEs have we witnessed an academic study that is critical, interdisciplinary, and nonpartisan. So much of what we read about the NDE, even in the academic world, is limited by single-discipline thinking and an "unhealthy" obsession with material versus religious convictions. The work produced here in this book avoids this populist trap and by so doing provides us a resulting work that is nuanced, revealing, and original.

There is little doubt that a person's cultural background plays a role in what they might experience in a dream, an out-of-body experience, or an NDE. There is little doubt that such experiences will also be prompted or shaped by their physiology. Just as a smile must have physiological correlates so too must a thought, and logically, an NDE. But explaining a smile physiologically does not naturally extend itself to an explanation of happiness, not the least because happiness is only one of potentially dozens of reasons for a smile to cross one's face. Without doubt, culture, character, previous experience, and physiology, all play a role in how one encounters new experiences, especially experiences for which one has little preparation.

And the near-death experience is and has been an extraordinary novel experience in every human culture in which it has appeared. This evocative, consistent, but always reorienting "intrusion" into everyday assumptions about how reality works is the basis for Shushan's argument that NDEs have played a crucial role in the development of most, if not all, human religions. It is the show-stopping and disruptive role of the NDE that has generated the foundational force for religion, either creating its major direction and shape or redirecting or tempering its vision of possibilities. And it appears to have performed this role in widely dispersed cultures that have had little or no connection with one another. Shushan guides us through the early indigenous cultures of North America, Oceania, and Africa to establish this argument.

As part of his review, Shushan must navigate the counterarguments that come from those who believe that religions create the conditions for NDEs and not the reverse, that NDEs are merely physiological phenomena, or that NDEs are cultural and linguistic artifacts alone. Shushan resists the reductionist tendency to explain a complex and layered experience with a single explanation. He very quickly exposes the limitations of these single-discipline explanations. Whatever the mixture of possible explanations for the NDE one fact remains unshakeable. Near-death experiences are *experienced* as absolutely real, true to life, as empirical as your current experience of reading these words. Why then is there so much apparent diversity of images and symbols? Why, beneath all this diversity, is there yet a seemingly persistent core set of images and characteristics? Why are these experiences so extraordinary and yet so familiar? Why are they so life-changing both for the individuals who report them and also for those who hear of them?

Many of these academic questions occur largely because we are often struck by the novelty—the sheer jolting unusualness of the NDE as compared to our everyday experience. It is the unusual that attracts the unusual questions. This tendency has been exposed in the history of anthropology, where, in that discipline, there has been a long tradition of treating other human conduct unfamiliar to us as "exotic." We have asked questions about "others" that we rarely ask ourselves and are surprised that when we do so that the answers are just as weird and exotic. This was the message of the seminal 1956 *American Anthropologist* paper describing "Body Ritual among the Nacerima" by Horace Miner.

The "Nacerima" (Americans) were a "strange" tribe of people who indulged in seemingly odd body rituals including placing sticks in their mouths followed by gulping mouthfuls of water that was subsequently spewed out. This ritual was followed every morning and sometimes even again in the evenings. One could only speculate and debate the reasoning behind these behaviors. Was it related to food—to clarify and cleanse? Often the ritual appeared before eating, which made the "stick in mouth" ritual unlikely to be merely an oral bathing rite. Perhaps there were spirit beliefs associated with the rite after all. When asked about *not performing these daily rites* most of the members of this culture would declare that many catastrophes would befall them—"their teeth would fall out, their gums bleed, their jaws shrink, their friends desert them, and their lovers reject them" (504).

The purpose of Miner's paper was twofold. First, Miner showed the reader how the analytical style and language we use to describe the unfamiliar can actually help artificially construct, and therefore exaggerate, the unfamiliar. Second, he showed us that to the extent that we dismiss the experience of those we describe and fail to understand their knowledge of their own world *in their terms*, we risk creating theories that are more fantastic and misleading than the world we are trying to describe. To a very large extent that has been the fate of the NDE both by the major religions and also the scientific community.

The facts are that if any of us travel to a new country for the first time—one that is very different from our own—our experience of it will be very colored by our previous travel experiences; our personal values and preferences with respect to food, customs, sights, smells and sounds; what we have been led to expect from friends and colleagues or literature, television, or Internet coverage of that place; even by where and how much we see of that country. Our experience will also be colored by our physiology—our health during that time, whether we are colorblind or hearing impaired, whether we visit a place from the perspective of a wheelchair or with a guide dog by our side. These are such common, everyday assumptions that we scarcely mention them in our conversations and discussions when remembering that travel with friends and family. And the fact that these are crucial factors in understanding *what we saw and how we experienced it* makes none of these factors a basis for believing that our travels were hallucinatory or imaginary. The fantastic is a question we reserve for others, not ourselves.

The reason for much of this taken-for-granted comfort around travel tales is that so many have shared them. Incredulity and skepticism frequently come from little or no experience, and this is often the case with formal religious and scientific institutions. The regular but marginal occurrence of NDEs has made these experiences both a powerful driver of change and development within religion *and* a source of fear and suspicion. The widespread nature of even broader mystical experiences—such as out-of-body or shamanic experiences or deathbed and bereavement visions—has meant that they are not, strictly speaking, "anomalous." They have been part of the normal experience of cultures, but a disruptive—and therefore sometimes marginalized—part of that norm. This disruptive influence has always demanded change *or* accommodation from our different social institutions.

We have been slow to recognize this driving cultural and religious force in our lives, largely because of the popular tendency to exoticize or marginalize experiences to which we do not have ready or repeated access. Gregory Shushan carefully guides us toward the data and reasons why this has been so. He also describes the process by which, despite regular attempts to marginalize its power, the NDE has been perhaps the most important shaper of religious creativity in human history. This is a journey and an argument as fascinating and as engrossing as the social history of mankind itself.

Allan Kellehear, PhD, FAcSS
50th Anniversary Professor (End of Life Care)
University of Bradford

Acknowledgments

I AM EXTREMELY grateful to the Perrott-Warrick Fund, Trinity College Cambridge, for a generous grant that made this research possible; and to the Ian Ramsey Centre for Science and Religion, University of Oxford, for hosting the project and providing the necessary facilities and supportive environment. Finalization of the research and preparation of the manuscript were assisted by supplementary grants from the Cedar Creek Institute, the Society for Psychical Research, and the Alex Tanous Foundation for Scientific Research. Thanks also to the Oxford Center for Hindu Studies, the International Association for Near-Death Studies, the Afterlife Research Centre, and the Alister Hardy Trust and Religious Experience Research Centre, University of Wales Trinity Saint David. Finally, I would like to extend my gratitude to Paul Badham, Fiona Bowie, Giovanni Casadio, Wendy Dossett, Gavin Flood, Erlendur Haraldsson, Peter Harrison, Angela Hobart, Jan Holden, David Hufford, Allan Kellehear, Edward F. Kelly, James McClenon, Robert Mays, Peggy Morgan, Andrew Pinsent, Kenneth Ring, Shaunaka Rishi Das, Bettina Schmidt, Judith Shushan, Jenny Wade, and anonymous reviewers for thought-provoking discussions, suggestions, moral support, and other encouragements.

Near-Death Experience in Indigenous Religions

I

Exploring Near-Death Experiences
Across Cultures

Introduction

Regardless of their origin (biological, psychological, or metaphysical), near-death experiences (NDEs) are indisputably part of human experience, with accounts known from around the world and throughout history. They are commonly understood as collections of various kinds of spiritually interpreted episodes that individuals report having experienced during periods of clinical death or near-death. Though accounts vary greatly, typical features include sensations of leaving the body and existing in quasi-physical form; seeing one's own "corpse"; entering and emerging from darkness; bright light; visiting another realm; meeting deceased relatives; encountering beings that some associate with a particular religious figure; evaluation of one's earthly life; feelings of joy, peace, oneness, transcendence, or unity; impressions of having returned "home"; exceptionally vivid awareness; reaching barriers or limits; clairvoyance or precognition; a return to the body sometimes following instructions to do so; reluctance to return; and subsequent positive transformations of the revived individual (Greyson 1983, 1999; Fox 2003: 100f).

Unlike NDEs, which are spontaneous, shamanic experiences are deliberately generated through culturally particular practices, such as repetitive drumming, dancing, chanting, and drug use. In many cultures they involve individuals entering a trance state, which is said to enable them to temporarily leave their bodies in order to rescue the soul of a dangerously ill person, or to gain healing powers, wisdom, or other supernatural information from gods, spirits, or ancestors in realms of the dead.

Despite cultural differences, there are frequent basic similarities between afterlife conceptions, shamanic experiences, and NDEs cross-culturally. This book presents an explanation of the continuum of similarities and differences between these three strands of belief and experience in traditional indigenous societies in Africa, North America, and Oceania. It explores the role of culture in the experiencing, understanding, interpreting, and religious processing of NDEs, addressing some of the most problematic yet significant questions concerning extraordinary human experiences and religious beliefs:

- Do ideas about the afterlife commonly originate in NDEs?
- What role does culture play in how people experience and interpret NDEs?
- What is the relationship between shamanism and NDEs?
- How can we best account for both the cross-cultural similarities and differences between the afterlife beliefs of various cultures?
- In light of both religious and experiential diversity, what are the implications of the cross-cultural evidence for theories that NDEs indicate an actual afterlife?

My earlier book (Shushan 2009) demonstrated that in addition to expected culture-specific features, there were cross-culturally consistent themes in the afterlife beliefs of the world's earliest civilizations during periods of little or no cultural contact with each other (Old and Middle Kingdom Egypt, Sumerian and Old Babylonian Mesopotamia, Vedic India, pre-Buddhist China, Maya and Aztec Mesoamerica). These same themes corresponded to some of the most frequently reported features of NDEs, suggesting that the authors of the ancient texts were familiar with the phenomenon. All the civilizations also had mythological otherworld journey myths highly reminiscent of NDEs, and there were examples of actual historical NDEs in documentary contexts from China and Mesoamerica, and references to the phenomenon in India.

While that book focused largely on demonstrating and interpreting cross-cultural similarities, the present one deals more thoroughly with understanding cross-cultural differences. The primary sources for the indigenous societies are very different from ancient religious texts, and present new opportunities for analysis. Their documentary nature enables us to more clearly see the relationships between beliefs and experiences, and how and why they differ widely across cultures. Rather than interpreting beliefs in light of NDEs, we are here able to compare the varying ways in which NDEs were processed and assimilated into very different belief systems and ritual practices. How the experiences are regarded within their own cultural contexts is important to any discussion of the nature of NDEs.

Nevertheless, it is certainly significant that similarities of afterlife beliefs occur over such vast reaches of time, space, and culture, and that they often correspond to NDE phenomenology. Indeed, the high degree of cultural independence, along with the fact that the societies discussed in the present study had very different forms of social organization from the early civilizations previously examined, makes the existence of such similarities all the more significant. They will be demonstrated amply, as will the central argument that NDEs often influence or inspire afterlife beliefs, in combination with local sociocultural and environmental factors, and universal cognitive factors.

Understanding Cultural and Individual Variation in Near-Death Experiences

Rather than a single experience, the NDE is best regarded as a collection of typical subexperiences: a variable combination of a number of possible elements from an established repertoire, the details of which differ on a case-by-case basis according to individual circumstance. Any study concerning the content of NDEs (especially across cultures) must confront the problem of how accounts of an ostensibly universal experience can be subject to so much variation. We begin, therefore, with a particular set of premises derived from previous research that has engaged with these issues (e.g., Audette 1982; McClenon 1994; Kellehear 1996; Badham 1997; Belanti et al. 2008; Shushan 2009; Tassell-Matamua 2013, and many others), and which are further validated by the findings of the present study.

While accounts of NDEs share many common elements worldwide, those elements are embedded in matrices of clearly culture- and individual-specific material, and reflect established local beliefs. This suggests that NDEs originate in phenomena that are independent of culture. They begin as precultural *events* which cause experiences that are both culturally contextualized *and* cross-culturally thematically stable. Like any experience, NDEs are rooted in the contexts of those who have them. They are processed "live" by an enculturated individual, then recounted in socially, religiously, and linguistically idiosyncratic ways. In other words, how the *event* is *experienced* varies by individual, resulting in narratives being interpreted and expressed in highly symbolic local modes. It is a symbiotic relationship in which culture-specific beliefs and individual expectations influence universal experience, and vice versa. That the physical and conceptual contexts of NDEs are the same across cultures—an individual apparently dying for a period of time then returning to life—makes their other similarities all the more striking. These contexts also serve to define the NDE and reveal it as a discrete category of human experience—a culturally malleable but nevertheless pan-human phenomenon. Whether the prompting event is biological, psychological, and/or metaphysical in nature is aside from the fact that it triggers cross-culturally comparable experiences.

A further indication that NDEs are not entirely culturally created is that they can conflict with the expectations of individuals, with their religious beliefs, and with the theological conventions of their time and place. James McClenon (1994: ch. 9) cites examples from medieval China, Japan, and Europe. A study of Israeli NDEs found a "lack of a cultural model to help understand and process the experience" and that "confusion may arise when the actual experience of a person near death clashes with cultural expectations." One man who was previously unfamiliar with NDEs "was surprised to discover that other individuals had had experiences not entirely unlike his own," though was confused that it conflicted with Jewish mystical texts such as the Zohar (Abramovitch 1988: 175). Additional examples will be found in the succeeding chapters of the present book. Near-death experiences can also conflict with the expectations of those *with* prior knowledge of the phenomenon, who may wonder why their experience did not include a tunnel or life review, for example (e.g., Wren-Lewis n.d.; cf. Shushan 2014: 392).

For the purposes of the present study, an account qualifies as an NDE not according to how well it conforms to some hypothetical "typical" Western exemplar, but rather by indigenous context. The only criterion is whether the reported experience occurred in a return-from-death context (or in in the case of shamanic experiences, whether they were locally considered to involve afterlife themes). In other words, it is the individuals in the primary sources rather than the researcher who has decided what should be considered an NDE.

There is also evidence that the manner in which a person almost dies impacts the experience. Those who attempt suicide tend not to have a life review, for example (Ring 1980: 199). Stevenson and Greyson (1996: 203–4) suggested that the duration of an NDE might help account for such differences. The life review, for example, may come at a later stage in the dying process. This is supported by the findings of some researchers (Sartori 2008), though it conflicts with those of others (Grey 1985; van Lommel et al. 2001). The human tendency to organize events into coherent narratives makes it difficult to determine whether or not the sequence of the subexperiences is always consistent (Grey 1985).

Some scholars minimize the similarities between NDEs across cultures on the grounds that they do not live up to some ill-defined standard of being similar *enough*, or in sufficient combination, or that they are somehow negated by the differences (e.g., Zaleski 1987: 127; Augustine 2007: 106ff). The significance of the worldwide commonalities is largely ignored, inconvenient as they are for the thesis that NDEs are hallucinatory. The similarities are left unexplained, or even interpreted as differences where they are not *exactly* similar. With a less literal-minded approach, however, thematic similarities are clear. Moving through darkness need not be through a tunnel to count as moving through darkness; extraordinary light can have identity or otherwise; being instructed to return is an instruction to return regardless of the reason; and deceased relatives are deceased relatives whether they are parents, spouses, or siblings. Kellehear (2007: 148–9) also cautions against such literal readings of NDEs, and against minimizing cross-cultural similarities *or* differences. It is clear, in any case, that the *denial of similarity* argument is not supported by evidence. While there will be no one-to-one correspondence between every element of any two randomly selected NDEs (cross-cultural or otherwise), like any experience there is no reason to expect them to be precisely "the same" between any two individuals. As seen in the examples explored in the following chapters, the thematic consistencies are generally self-evident enough that the attentive reader will have no difficulty observing them.

Near-Death Experiences and the Experiential Source Hypothesis

Our beliefs and knowledge about the world are rooted in our experiences; and as experiences that are given religious import within their cultural contexts, NDEs are logical candidates to help us explain the origins of afterlife beliefs. It is unsurprising that a person would interpret an NDE as precisely what it appears to be, and henceforth believe that consciousness survives bodily death and undergoes various experiences in an afterlife state. The overwhelming majority of people who have NDEs believe in the reality of the experience—that they temporarily left their bodies, went to another realm, encountered other beings, and so forth. Indeed, one of the hallmarks of NDEs is that they alter spiritual or religious beliefs or orientation, "often leading to beneficial personal transformations" in both behavior and personal worldview (Greyson 2006: 401; cf. Sutherland 1990; Groth-Marnat & Summers 1998).

David Hufford (1995a: 28) originated the phrase "experiential source hypothesis" to describe this dynamic, developing the model from its nineteenth-century origins (e.g., Edward Burnett Tylor, Andrew Lang). He found that "There are classes of experience that give rise to spiritual beliefs among practically all who have them, regardless of their prior beliefs. The perception and interpretation of such experiences are similar among persons with very different backgrounds and expectations." Kellehear (1996), McClenon (1994; 2002), Shushan (2009), and others have reached similar conclusions and have provided a mass of cross-cultural evidence demonstrating that beliefs in the supernatural frequently result from near-death, out-of-body, shamanic, and other extraordinary experiences. The out-of-body experience (OBE) element appears to be particularly persuasive, for as Tassell-Matamua and Murray (2014: 23) summarized, "feelings of disembodiment during an NDE serve as experiential evidence to the individual that a soul survives bodily death" (cf. Tassell-Matamua 2013; van Lommel 2011; Metzinger 2005).

In addition to the historical examples found in this book, there is an important and perhaps foundational connection between NDEs and Pure Land Buddhism in both China and Japan, with many prominent figures in the traditions reporting having had such experiences. As McClenon (1994: 182) wrote, "Individuals separated by great distances and hundreds of years reported proceeding through a transition stage after death, being greeted at death by a being of light assumed to be Yama, Jizo, or Amida, and seeing similar images of Yama's hells or Amida's Pure Land. Pure Land proponents felt these accounts validated their faith." Afterlife narratives in religious contexts were often intended to prepare the individual for the experience, with NDE-like examples given of a particular individual who left the body, traveled to afterlife realms, and returned (e.g., the various accounts spanning the range of Vedic literature; Shushan 2009, 2011).

Cases of atheists who change their beliefs following an NDE are effectively microcosms of the experiential source hypothesis. Upon revival from his NDE in 1988, the materialist philosopher A. J. Ayer told his doctor, "I saw a Divine Being. I'm afraid I'm going to have to revise all my various books and opinions" (Foges 2010). As Fox (2003 117) remarked, it is difficult to conceive "how an existing cultural-linguistic system such as Ayer's could have produced an experience which ran so counter to itself." Similarly, the mathematical physicist, psychologist, and skeptic John Wren-Lewis (n.d.) had an NDE in 1983. Though he did have knowledge of the phenomenon, his experience did not conform to his expectations, challenged his view that mysticism is a form of neurosis, and led him to believe in the perennial philosophy.

There is much precedent for the NDE experiential source hypothesis. Stanley Krippner (2012) provides a great deal of historical, cross-cultural evidence for the importance of various extraordinary experiences on transforming individual spirituality and religious beliefs. Caroline Franks Davis (1989: 162–3) gives examples of individuals who were wholly bewildered by their experiences, and only able to make sense of them upon later exposure to religious ideas that allowed them to culturally process what had happened to them. Kelly Bulkeley's (2008: 19) cross-cultural comparison of dreams led him to conclude "that prototypical dreams have played a creative role in virtually all the world's religious and spiritual traditions." In his study of experiences of "unusual light phenomena," Fox (2008: 34) observed that they regularly lead "to spiritual, mystical or religious transformation, [and] have been reported virtually throughout recorded history in a wide variety of different cultures, religions and spiritual traditions." Members of Spiritualist churches actively seek experiential evidence for belief in an afterlife, and often claim that mystical and paranormal experiences are directly responsible for changing preexisting beliefs (Brown 2003: 137–8). Hufford (2005: 13–6, 33) demonstrated that the neurophysiological phenomenon of sleep paralysis is commonly interpreted in local supernatural terms cross-culturally, and can lead to new beliefs or validate existing ones. It occurs when REM sleep is disrupted, and is characterized by a sense of being immobilized by a malevolent presence, to which is ascribed different identities (e.g., ghosts, demons, witches, extraterrestrials) according to cultural orientation.

Also relevant are the reports of anthropologists whose materialist worldviews were challenged by inexplicable phenomena they encountered during fieldwork. Evans-Pritchard (1937: 34) and Edith Turner (1992: 149), for example, could not explain "spirit events" they witnessed in Africa. So prevalent are such cases that there have been two collections of scholarly articles on the subject (Goulet & Miller 2007; Young & Goulet 1994; cf. Bowie 2013; Hunter 2015; McClenon & Nooney 2002). The experiences may be entirely culturally alien to the anthropologist, and that in itself is a factor that leads to the questioning of reductionist paradigms. Such cases further demonstrate that spontaneous, unexpected, extraordinary experiences occur in transcultural contexts; and that they can transform the beliefs of highly educated, skeptical, rational, Western academics as well as the beliefs of the "others" they study.

There is, in any case, an undeniable link between extraordinary experiences and religious beliefs and practices. In a survey of 488 societies worldwide, Erika Bourguignon (1973: 11) found that 90 percent of them had "one or more institutionalized, culturally patterned forms of altered states of consciousness" that occurred within religious or ritual contexts. She concluded that such experiences have been known throughout human history, and she regarded them as "raw materials" which through a process of "cultural interpretation" can be integrated into an "institutional, often ritual, framework . . . [and] within a world view and a value system" (Bourguignon 1974: 234). Weston Le Barre (1972: 265–6) went so far as to argue that religious beliefs per se came entirely from the "inner world" accessed through such experiences: "Every religion, in historical fact, began in one man's 'revelation'—his dream or fugue or ecstatic trance." Indeed, accounts of prophecies; supernatural healings; transubstantiations; unusual births; encounters and communications with divine, demonic, deceased, or otherwise spiritual beings; journeys to other realms; returning from or otherwise transcending physical death; and other "miracles" are key features in nearly every religious tradition worldwide, both ancient and modern. Rare would be the religion that does not have some kind of experiential event, understood emically to be extraordinary, as a key feature of its foundational beliefs. These experiences are often associated with particular individuals whose status is elevated by virtue of having had them.

Reasoning, Skepticism, and the Hermeneutics
of Religious Experience

There is much scholarly opposition in the study of religions to the concept of "religious experience" (Shushan 2014, 2016a), and to cross-cultural comparison (Shushan 2009, 2013)—particularly when concerned with the question of cross-cultural similarities. All experience and all belief are said to result entirely from linguistic and cultural particularities, so that the idea of a panhuman experience type in which religious beliefs are grounded would be unintelligible (e.g., Cupitt 1998; Sharf 1998; Proudfoot 1985). Any solid evidence in support of these "hard" cultural-linguistic constructivist assumptions is lacking, and they appear to rest entirely on a particular set of culturally situated philosophical commitments. This is in contrast to the abundant evidence for NDEs and the experiential source hypothesis.

As outlined previously, part of our purpose here is to explore the varying ways in which NDEs are culturally interpreted. There is no claim that they or any other experiences are not culturally situated. This does not mean, however, that experiences are wholly incommensurable across cultures. Culture, after all, is simply what overlays the universal experiences involved in being biologically human. Whether we use qualifying terms such as "religiously interpreted states of consciousness" (Segal 2004: 323) or "experiences deemed religious" (Taves 2009), NDEs are by definition interpreted as revealing what happens after physical death. Examining afterlife beliefs in relation to those experiences is to therefore examine them in their proper context. Assuming a constructivist explanation for a belief not only decontextualizes the experiences from indigenous understandings of them but also denies the testimonies of the very people whose religions we study.

Assumptions that extraordinary experiences, and indigenous claims about them, are imaginative, entirely cultural, or otherwise false[1] have less in common with the scientific method than with the dismissive and hostile attitudes of certain early Christian missionaries. For example, when Mi'kmaq Native Americans stated that their afterlife beliefs arose from NDEs, Chrétien Le Clercq (1691: 207) called the claim "ridiculous" and stated that it was due to "error and imposture." Jean de Brébeuf (1636: 141) derided Wyandot beliefs as simply "ignorance and stupidity!" Early anthropologists also displayed lapses in ethnographic objectivity. Despite indigenous claims that they were the source of knowledge about the afterlife, Elsdon Best (1905: 232) dismissed Maori NDE accounts as "childish tales," and ignored descriptions of the other world as a realm of light, instead choosing to describe it as a "gloomy underworld" (ibid. 234). Robert W. Williamson (1933: 373) dismissed a Polynesian NDE as "only the dream or story of an old woman who had been in a state in insensibility," despite the presence of similar narratives elsewhere in the Pacific that he himself recounted.

Suggesting that NDEs are entirely imaginary implicitly seeks to elevate scholars to a superior position to those who report having had such experiences, characterizing them as uncritical products of their belief systems (cf. Barnard 1992). If we refuse to accept testimonies of extraordinary experiences, on what grounds do we accept anything an individual says about his or her culture? If we accept a description of an afterlife belief as representing the beliefs of a community, we must also accept the reasons given for those beliefs.

In fact, extraordinary experiences provide perfectly rational grounds for beliefs, and help to demonstrate the cross-cultural process of reasoning based on evidence (cf. Flood 2012: 126ff, 136, 139). Donald E. Brown (1991: 130–40) argues that conjectural reasoning and abstract thought are among the various human universals, alongside magical and divinatory practices, ritual, folklore, dream interpretation, and belief in "something beyond the visible and palpable."

Time and again, experiential validation is shown to be a prerequisite for belief, with distinctions being made between extraordinary experiences that seem genuine and those that do not. The Saulteaux Ojibwe distinguished genuine NDEs from dreams and shamanic visits to the land of the dead "based on the direct observation of the bodily condition of the persons involved" (Hallowell 1940: 29). A Dakota Sioux shaman's account of the "Land of Spirits" was only accepted because his predictions about war and hunting were invariably correct (Jones 1829: 225). Following a Maori woman's NDE, "it was a general source of regret" that she did not return with tangible evidence of her journey (Shortland 1856: 155). Trobriand Islanders showed skepticism about individuals who claimed to have visited the spirit world, and some even believed that any claims of interaction with spirits were "downright lies" (Malinowski 1916: 162). The Gitksan, Wet'suwet'en, Beaver (Mills 1988: 408), Tillamook (Boas 1923: 12), and Tlingit (De Laguna 1972: 776ff) all had systems to empirically validate reincarnation cases, including evidential dreams, past-life memories, and birthmarks and personality traits consistent with the earlier personality.

Skepticism and reasoning were also employed in response to claims of both local religious leaders and foreign missionaries. The early eighteenth-century Innu, for example, frustrated the French Jesuit missionary Joseph Jouvency when they expressed disbelief at the doctrine of eternal fire on the grounds that no forest could be large enough to provide an endless supply of fuel, and that "there could be no fire where there was no wood". Jouvency lamented, "This absurd reasoning had so much influence over the minds of the savages, that they could not be persuaded of the truth of the gospel" (Kenton 1927 I: 17). Similarly, missionaries in Tahiti in 1803 encountered resistance to the doctrine of resurrection on the grounds of a lack of evidence and because bodies observably rot into the earth (Oliver 1974: 488). In South Africa, a Sotho man would not convert to Christianity because no dream or other "supernatural occurrence" had persuaded him to do so (Keable 1921: 523).

The Kwakwaka'wakw sometimes had individuals pose undercover as shamanic initiates in order to unmask the fraudulent or deceptive activities of other shamans (Boas 1930: 1ff). When the Wanapum prophet Smohalla went into trance, skeptics stuck him with needles and cut him with knives to ensure he was not faking. Only when he did not react—and indeed not bleed—did they accept what they were seeing (Mooney 1896: 719). Skeptics in the Marquesas Islands believed that mediumistic spirit communications "were made by means of ventriloquism" (Frazer 1922: 370).

The most common reason for the decline of Native American religious revitalization movements was the lack of evidential validation: the prophecies made by the leaders failed to come true (du Bois 1939: 39–40, 106; Mooney 1896: 700–2). The teachings of a Pomo prophet were abandoned when his method of having dreams of the dead proved unsuccessful (du Bois 1939: 106). A member of the Indian Shaker Church was ridiculed when he claimed to be Christ (ibid. 749). A failed prophecy in New Guinea similarly led to the prophet's downfall (Seligman 1910: 655–7).

Thus, across cultures, distinctions are made between "ordinary" and "nonordinary" experiences, with the latter requiring some form of evidential validation before being incorporated into belief systems. The experiential source hypothesis itself indicates a kind of personal logical positivism: through direct observation, the evidently empirical reality of NDEs convinces those who have them of their veridicality. Bulkeley (2008: 276) goes a step further, arguing that dreams actually stimulated the "capacity for rational thought and critical reflection," allowing "the power of reason to become increasingly aware of deceptive appearances, hidden connections, subtle perceptions, and cognitively impactful emotions." The same might also apply to NDEs and other extraordinary experiences, for the drastic differences between ordinary and extraordinary states of being necessitate the engagement of rational thought in order to explain each state and differentiate between them in meaningful ways.

In summary, for a number of reasons NDEs present a major challenge to the types of criticisms discussed above:

1. Their existence is accepted by researchers from the most reductionist to the most theological of orientations. Their occurrence is not in dispute, only their origins and meanings; and they are reported throughout history and in all parts of the world. This demonstrates that:
2. NDEs are phenomenologically classifiable. The common characteristics of NDE reports distinguish them as a particular type of extraordinary experience.

3. They typically occur under similar, generally *physical* circumstances: an individual is close to death, apparently dies, subsequently revives, and reports having undergone particular unusual experiences. This means they have an objectively cross-culturally stable *context*.

4. The fundamental *interpretation* of NDEs is apparently universal—not simply in general "religious," "spiritual," or otherwise "supernatural" terms, but specifically the belief that "this is what happens when we die."

Indigenous Religions and the Nature of the Sources

The societies under consideration here did not produce written religious texts or accounts of their belief systems, and our primary sources are thus the records of missionaries and explorers beginning in the sixteenth century, and materials written or compiled by predominantly Western ethnographers from the nineteenth to early twentieth centuries. This means that all the accounts have been filtered through the lenses of individuals who have varying ideologies, biases, levels and types of ethnographic and linguistic skills, and powers of insight and interpretation. Much of it lacks context, detail, or sufficient background knowledge, and overgeneralizations are common. In the case of some missionaries and early explorers, there are value judgements, disdain, and even ridicule.

Unfortunately, however, we are limited to the available evidence, regardless of how flawed. Given the number of sources used, it is not possible to evaluate the credentials or methodological rigor of each and every author, though the professions of those who were not trained ethnologists are specified. In any case, there is no reason to assume that most of our sources are wholly untrustworthy, or that individuals with missionary or economic motives were by definition incapable of accurate recording. Indeed, there is no way to account for the independent evidence for the cross-cultural existence of NDEs and related beliefs than to accept a degree of reliable reporting. The material taken as a whole in each chapter reveals distinct patterns for each geographic area, adding a cumulative weight to the arguments made here. In better-represented societies we can compare the information from more than one source, and it is often the case that even the poorest sources generally agree in descriptions if not interpretations.

It is also important to remember that there were diverse beliefs within single cultures, changes in beliefs over time, and different understandings and ideas between individual informants. Concepts of orthodoxy or canonical narratives are largely irrelevant. Furthermore, indigenous informants themselves may have modified accounts of their beliefs, denied having any in order to avoid discussing them, or even invented beliefs, particularly when speaking to inquirers with an overtly Christian stance or in a position of power. In general, the societies were first studied during periods of religious, cultural, social, and/or physical crises due to multipronged colonialist assaults on their land, resources, bodies, and souls— which partly entailed the destruction or transformation of traditional beliefs and practices.

Ultimately, despite concerns about the reliability of some sources, a careful ethnohistorical reading of them is the only way to try to understand the experiences and beliefs of people in these past societies. Attempts to extract "original" beliefs from modern converted societies are almost entirely speculative, relying on a priori assumptions of what was and was not indigenous in the first place. Such assumptions are frequently made when postmortem reward and punishment are found in "unexpected places"—as if the concept itself is enough to show borrowing or influence from Christianity.[2] Of course, such concepts can also be found in most ancient civilizations, Eastern religions, and many other non-Christian contexts. Similarity is not in itself evidence of borrowing (cf. Shushan 2009: 9–24; 2013).

While I have focused on accounts prior to significant external influence or conversion to a foreign religion (in our cases, Christianity or Islam), borrowed elements and syncretizations are certainly evident in some of the narratives. Strict cultural purity (if such a thing ever existed) is not required in order to explore indigenous ways of processing and integrating NDEs and related experiences. Indeed, how societies responded to Christianity is an important consideration in the relationship between NDEs and religious revitalization movements. In many cases, however, the beliefs and the experiences they embody can also be found in earlier sources, prior to conversion. With few exceptions, when more recent NDEs provide an opportunity for comparison with earlier accounts from the same region, I have excluded most material from fully converted societies.

Most of the material under consideration here comes from low-population, village-based or nomadic small-scale societies with hunter-gatherer and/or herding/limited horticultural subsistence patterns. They are characterized by a lack of industrialization, urbanization, complex economies, political systems, and literacy, though not all groups share all these characteristics. While some cultures or ethnicities themselves cannot be considered "small-scale" (e.g., in Africa the Igbo and Yoruba numbered in the millions), societies were organized into smaller communities in scattered villages or homesteads.

Rather than strict guidelines of scale, however, the more important criteria are (1) indigeneity of belief, and (2) the fact that the societies in the three world regions that are the subject of this book—Africa, Oceania, and Native America— were wholly independent of each other. Their distribution across the globe in culturally and geographically discrete groups means that any similarities between these premodern societies cannot be due to diffusion of beliefs across oceans and continents.[3] These are important considerations when testing constructivist theories that claim religious beliefs are simply reflections of local social phenomena.

It should be noted that there is no evolutionist stance here behind the limitation to traditional indigenous societies. There is no implication that they are to be considered as "survivals" of hypothetical religions of early humans, and there is no value judgement concerning their conceptual or ritual sophistication, effectiveness, or "truth" in relation to each other or indeed to any belief system. The past tense is used to emphasize the ethnohistorical nature of the study, and simply because the sources are mostly a century old or more. There is no implication that present people in the societies do or do not maintain beliefs consistent with their forebears. Indigenously preferred culture names are used throughout except in direct quotes, where the current accepted usage is provided parenthetically.

In addition to scouring hundreds of primary sources, I have also performed searches in the Human Relations Area Files (HRAF) World Cultures Database—a collection of ethnographic materials representing over four hundred societies. Its categories include terms such as "notions of the temporary departure of the soul from the body," "conception of the survival of the soul," "career of the soul after death," "mode of departure from the body," "indefinite sojourn as a disembodied soul or ghost," and "journey to a realm of the dead." Older syntheses (e.g., Frazer 1913–24; Moss 1925; Hultkrantz 1957) have been invaluable in locating relevant accounts, though wherever possible I have gone to the original text rather than relying on summaries.

As well as being an ethnohistorical comparison, this book also has historiographical dimensions. Beyond the necessity of relying on older sources for their ethnographic content, some early scholars also reached conclusions and developed theories that, though largely disparaged or simply ignored in the contemporary anthropological study of religions, nevertheless prove relevant, innovative, and astute. Because academic trends have ensured that very few more recent scholarly works in this area have been produced, a critical engagement with and reevaluation of these earlier theories proves highly constructive. The work of Mircea Eliade (1964), for example, is notoriously flawed for unfounded universalizing and overgeneralizing, ignoring differences, an overreliance on diffusion, speculation in the guise of theory, and so forth. However, almost despite himself, some of Eliade's conclusions are proven correct by the present study, and some of his speculations contain much useful insight. My use of his work, or any given source, does not imply my wholesale endorsement of it. However, he took seriously reports of extraordinary experiences where more recent scholars in the study of religions focus almost exclusively on social functionalist and postcolonialist theories with scarcely a consideration of individual experiences.

Myths, Legends, Near-Death Experiences, and Shamanism

While indigenous distinctions were sometimes made between documentary NDEs and legends or myths with NDE themes (e.g., Hallowell 1940: 29), this was by no means the rule. How to classify an account is thus not always obvious. For the purposes of this study, narratives are considered NDEs if they concern subjects who were either alive at the time the account was related, who existed within living memory of the community, or were otherwise indigenously considered to be historical. Legends have many of the hallmarks of NDEs, though the subject is normally a culture hero ostensibly from the remote past. They are often lengthier and with greater detail, and frequently serve to teach lessons or morals. Myths feature deity protagonists, or culture heroes who interact with deities prior to the otherworld journey, and typically explain the origin of some belief, practice, or knowledge (e.g., the origin of agriculture, funerary practices, details about the afterlife, etc.). They are often elaborately detailed and contain numerous story-like episodes, with the afterlife journey forming only a part of a longer narrative. These distinctions do blur, and some legends and myths are likely elaborated versions of some historical NDE. The further distant in the past the original experience occurred, the greater degree of cultural and narrative accretion it would display. Of course, many may have resulted from intertextuality or borrowing from neighboring communities; or they may be fictitious—pure inventions inspired by general awareness of NDE or shamanic phenomena, and/or existing local afterlife beliefs.

One of the most frequently recurring narrative types is the so-called Orpheus myth, involving protagonists who travel to an afterlife realm while still alive in order to retrieve a loved one (spouse, lover, parent, child, sibling, or friend). Such myths generally involve a prohibition on some activity (e.g., eating, sex), which if broken results in the protagonist being forced to remain in the other world, or the loved one having to return to the realm of the dead after a period of time on Earth. The term "Orpheus myth" is used here as a convenient descriptive shorthand (following Hultkrantz and others), and does not imply any genetic relation to the ancient Greek model.

Though a generally accepted part of the academic lexicon, the term "shamanism" is controversial because it is commonly applied to a wide variety of practices in unrelated societies (Kehoe 2000: 4, 37ff; Rock & Krippner 2011: ch. 1).

It is perhaps technically appropriate to confine the term to the linguistically and historically related societies of Central Asia and the Subarctic rim who use the Evenki word "shaman"—although even this usage is challenged by the fact that the word has earlier roots in the Sanskrit *sramana*, meaning a religious mendicant or monk (Shirokogoroff 1935: 3). Eliade's (1964: 5) definition of shamanism was restricted to practices involving an individual entering a trance state "during which his soul is believed to leave his body and ascend to the sky or descend to the underworld." In contrast, I. M. Lewis's definition (2003: xviii) privileges possession over "mystical flight" as the "defining feature" of shamanism on the dubious grounds that focusing on the latter is "old-fashioned" (ibid. xix). The term is used here with the implicit qualification of "shamanic-*type*"; and in a much more general sense to include various kinds of indigenous healers, prophets, diviners, mediums, and so forth, who use culturally situated ritual techniques involving altered states of consciousness to effect healing, soul-retrieval, protection, exorcism, or knowledge acquisition. This is largely consistent with Jakobsen (1999: 1ff), Johansen (1999: 40–1), Thorpe (1993: 5–6), Winkelman (2013: 57), and encompasses both Eliade's and Lewis's definitions.

Ideas and terms for "soul" or "spirit" also differ widely, though in any belief in an afterlife there is always by definition the concept of individual consciousness surviving death. The terms are used interchangeably here, as per the primary sources. As Michael Winkelman (2013: 50) argued concerning "shamanism," "When similar concepts are found cross-culturally, terminology must be developed to convey the similarity found in diverse places." This applies equally to the other generalizing terms discussed previously.

Analysis, Contexts, and Organization

Although cultural and regional tendencies are key themes of this book, it is important to move the study of cross-cultural NDEs beyond the classificatory, beyond the search for universals, and beyond debates surrounding the notion of an actual afterlife. Rather, this book incorporates discussions of all these approaches and others in order to present an interdisciplinary means of understanding NDEs in both their cultural diversity and worldwide similarity.

Previous considerations of cross-cultural NDEs have been concerned primarily with the quantitative tabulation of each subexperience (i.e., life review, tunnel, being of light, etc.) within a particular culture. The tabulation is then compared to a hypothetical "typical Western" model in order to identify which NDE features can be considered universal. While a justifiable and valid pursuit, there are various problems and limitations with such an approach. First, because so few examples were known from a particular region, they could not be considered representative. Second, while it is true that certain NDE elements occur more frequently in some areas than others—and it will be seen that some tend to correspond to social scale—it is also true that there are nearly always exceptions. This means that attempting to systematically disentangle the universal from the cultural in order to make general statements about NDE phenomenology is of questionable ultimate value.

Though we may speak of cultural tendencies, instead of attempting to establish rules of universality the present book seeks to understand the experiences in local as well as cross-cultural terms. This is best served through a deeper, more contextualized consideration of the evidence than a strictly quantitative study allows. Though the sheer number of narratives makes a fully detailed analysis and comparison of each and every example impossible, particularly relevant cases are given fuller attention in respect to their wider cultural, historical, and religious contexts where the evidence allows. On the other hand, the large number of examples helps to reveal both local and panregional patterns, and lends quantitative weight to the generalizations and conclusions. This approach helps to avoid some of the main criticisms of comparative studies: decontextualization (extracting religious beliefs from their social, cultural, and historical matrices) and unfounded universalizing (making gross generalizations based on inadequate sample sizes).

Each of the following three chapters is devoted to a single world area, with their first sections being primarily phenomenological descriptions and summaries of accounts, followed by analyses and conclusions. The chapters are presented in the order in which I undertook the primary research. This, I believe, makes for a more interesting "narrative arc" enabling the reader to more clearly follow the journey from data to conclusions. For example, I half-expected the African material to defy existing scholarly generalizations,[4] and to discover much similarity with North America. That it actually revealed very different afterlife beliefs and attitudes towards NDEs shaped the research and helped it evolve from focusing mostly on similarity and the problem of universalism, to featuring a more nuanced exploration of differences in the ways NDEs are received in particular societies. In the concluding chapter, an interdisciplinary interpretive strategy is employed to explore the implications of the findings in the three area-specific chapters, and to develop a general theory on the relationships between NDEs and afterlife beliefs. A theoretically eclectic approach that evaluates and incorporates elements of theories from various disciplines leads to a more comprehensive set of explanations.

The question of whether or not human consciousness survives bodily death (the "survival hypothesis") is largely incidental to the analysis of NDEs within their religious, cultural, and historical contexts. Nevertheless, the role of culture is very much relevant to the idea that NDEs constitute evidence for survival, and must certainly be taken into account by those making claims to that effect. While this book does not aim to prove or disprove the survival hypothesis by virtue of the evidence from cross-cultural NDEs, the implications for the hypothesis are discussed in the Conclusions. Specifically, I examine the philosophical problem of whether the notion of an afterlife can be intelligible or not, given cultural and religious diversity.

We do not *know* what will happen to us when we die, and the nature and limits of human consciousness are not fully understood by modern science. I am skeptical in the traditional sense of being critical about claims on both sides of an argument, but not dismissive of that which is unknown or unproven. Though I remain agnostic on the subject, some of the evidence is certainly interesting if not compelling. Furthermore, as will be seen, claims of evidential occurrences during NDEs (e.g., the anomalous attainment of information that proves to be accurate) are themselves cross-cultural, and often contribute to beliefs that the experiences are "real." The study would be inadequate if it ignored the existence of such claims. I do not, however, seek to validate or invalidate whether any individual was clinically dead prior to revival, if they truly gained supernatural powers, and so on. It would be tedious to qualify every truth-claim of extraordinary events in the narratives with terms such as "alleged" and "ostensible", though such qualifiers should be seen as implicit in my summaries of the accounts.

As well as allowing informed philosophical speculation regarding what *kind* of survival the evidence could suggest if taken at face value, examining metaphysical and ontological dimensions alongside other interdisciplinary factors provides methodological balance. As David Hufford (1995b: 60) wrote, "the tendency to count disbelief as the 'objective' stance is a serious, systematic bias that runs through most academic studies of spiritual belief." Instead, he argues, "We must learn to tolerate uncertainty and ambiguity, while holding the reduction of uncertainty and ambiguity in our knowledge as primary goals." This is best achieved through the interdisciplinary theoretical eclecticism adopted here—or in Hufford's words, "a multiplication of perspectives" for "the more views we consider, the more reason we have to be hopeful about our conclusions."

This is the first book dedicated to NDEs in indigenous societies, and one of the very few on the phenomenon in historical, cross-cultural contexts. Because dying is obviously a universal human experience, identifying potentially universal aspects of the experience in relation to cross-culturally parallel themes in afterlife beliefs and shamanic experiences is of universal concern. It is also a potentially unifying force, discovering that which underlies and transcends culturally particular manifestations. At the same time, engaging with cross-cultural differences respects the uniqueness of each society and underscores the wide diversity of the ways in which humans negotiate their extraordinary experiences and religious beliefs. Analyzing the local responses to the universal phenomenon offers insight into the role of NDEs in human thought concerning fundamental existential problems surrounding death, dying, and postmortem survival—and indeed into the construction of culture and identity in general.

2

North America

Introduction

Native American beliefs were first recorded by European explorers beginning in the sixteenth century, and Christian missionaries in seventeenth. Their accounts rarely approached anything like modern ethnographic standards, and it was not until the nineteenth century that a more systematic and objective kind of reporting began.

Though precise dating of oral traditions is not possible, the beliefs of Native American peoples certainly originated far earlier than our earliest records. While shared mythical forms across the continent could conceivably indicate a common source, attempts to trace their origins or diffusion patterns are speculative. It is possible that some beliefs traveled with the earliest settlers from Siberia across the Bering Strait land bridge, c. 10,000–15,000 BP, and/or from the civilizations of Mesoamerica, to be gradually modified and elaborated as cultural identities diversified. However, there are numerous and vast differences between the various Siberian, Mesoamerican, and Native American religious traditions.

Drawing on many early primary sources, the ethnologist Hubert Howe Bancroft (1875: 511–29) generalized about continent-wide afterlife beliefs, and on a general, thematic level his findings are borne out here. The main recurring themes he identified include postmortem existence in a spiritual "body," and often a soul of component elements; darkness and light; barriers, obstacles, and perils; meeting deceased relatives; encounters with and assistance from deities; afterlife fates being determined by some evaluation of worth (e.g., social status, mode of death, earthly behavior and morality, proper funerary ritual); an afterlife realm described as an idealized mirror image of Earth; intermediate states; reincarnation and/or numerous types of transformations (e.g., into heavenly bodies); return to the creation or origin point; and feelings of joy and bliss. The anthropologist Åke Hultkrantz (1953: 473) identified the additional themes of the Milky Way as a path for souls to the land of the dead, or alternatively one path to a heavenly realm and another to annihilation (Hultkrantz 1967: 133); afterlife destinations in the sky or underground, reached through the horizon; and the maintenance of social status divisions (Hultkrantz 1992: 167–8). The other realm was frequently characterized as a place of dancing, music, and happiness, with unlimited supplies of food and drink. The dead possessed supernatural, even god-like powers such as shape-changing and affecting people on Earth. Underworlds could be positive places, though they could alternatively be gloomy and nega-tive with earthly conditions inverted. In such instances, the dead feared living "visitors" (e.g., NDErs and shamans) as if they were ghosts, and found them to be offensive-smelling. Time was distorted, and food was unsavory or would be inedible to the living (e.g., thorns, dirt) (Hultkrantz 1957: 91–2, 107–12, 115). In some cultures with reincarnation beliefs, souls must wait for a new life to be assigned to them. More often, they were given the choice of whether or not to reincarnate, and the ability to choose their new parents. When there were beliefs in souls made up of different components, it was the nonconscious soul that was reincarnated, suggesting that the conscious soul remained in afterlife realm(s) (Hultkrantz 1953: 421, 477).[1] Concerning tribes that did not believe in an after-life, Bancroft (1875: 522) argued that they were rare exceptions, and that most claims of disbelief were due to scholarly error.[2]

Native American narratives "of living persons who in dreams, trance or coma have journeyed to the other world and succeeded in returning to the living" are "innumerable" (Hultkrantz 1957: 19, 236–7). Indeed, the majority of ethnohis-torical sources relating Native American beliefs consulted in the course of this research yielded at least one such narrative. One of the most common types is the Orpheus myth, involving a living individual who travels to an afterlife realm in order to retrieve a loved one (spouse, lover, parent, child, sibling, or friend), as discussed earlier. Taboos on eating or sexual relations in the otherworld, or on relating the experience to others upon return, are typically imposed on the indi-vidual by a deity or spirit, and are ultimately broken. This results in the deceased being unable to return to Earth, or dying again (i.e., returning to the realm of the dead) after a period of time back on Earth. Hultkrantz (1957: 7, 19, 57–8, 115, 140, 313ff) found approximately 120 examples from 79 widely distributed societies. While many are discussed here, so abundant and structurally consistent are these narratives that there is neither space nor purpose to review them all.

A key function of shamans around the continent was to travel to the other world in spirit-form to retrieve the soul of a sick or dying person. This was achieved by deliberately inducing altered states of consciousness through prac-tices such as smoking, fasting, extended graveside vigils, and continuous, repeti-tive drumming, dancing, and singing. Testimonies of deliberately-induced personal experiences of both shamans and ordinary individuals often correspond to Orpheus myth themes, and share similarities with NDEs.

Nevertheless, regardless of the common theme of visiting the realm of the dead and returning, neither Orpheus myths nor shamanic narratives should be confused with documentary accounts of ostensibly historical, spontaneous NDEs. Indeed, the greater similarity among Orpheus myths than among the more idiosyncratic NDE accounts helps to distinguish both as discrete narrative types. While there is fluidity between the categories—indeed, sometimes narratives that might seem highly mythologized were regarded indigenously as being true—some indigenous peoples made distinctions between NDE narratives and their mythological and shamanic counterparts. Earlier scholars (e.g., Franz Boas, Cora du Bois, Irving Hallowell, Åke Hultkrantz, Leslie Spier) also recognized such distinctions despite structural similarities across the genres and the fact that NDEs had yet to be named and codified at the time of their research.[3]

Notwithstanding numerous differences in details, the main recurring elements in the NDE accounts are leaving the body in spirit form and seeing one's "corpse"; attempts to interact with living people on earth; journeys on a spirit road to another realm; guides and guardians; obstacles, barriers, and perils; transitions from darkness to light; heavenly realms and underworlds described as idealized mirror images of Earth (though sometimes experienced as reversals by visiting spirits); meeting predeceased others; feelings of happiness, or the afterlife being joyful and beatific; encountering a deity; being instructed or choosing to return (either because it was not yet time to die, or for a specific positive purpose, such as bringing information about the afterlife to people on Earth); reluctance to return; reentering the body; spiritual renewal or transformation with a change in values or purpose upon return (e.g., becoming a healer or spiritual teacher); and continuing vivid recall of the experience.[4]

Eastern Woodlands
Algonquin

The earliest recorded Native American NDEs are found in Thomas Hariot's (1588: 37–8) account of the first voyage to Virginia in 1585–6. They were related to Hariot (a fluent Algonquin speaker) when he asked about the tribe's afterlife beliefs. The first, which was said to have occurred a few years prior to Hariot's arrival, involved a "wicked man" who had been "dead and buried," then revived. He claimed that his soul had journeyed westward toward the hellish realm of Popogusso, but was saved by a deity who made him return to his body in order to teach his people how to avoid such negative fates. The second, contemporary with Hariot's visit, described a man who left his body during his own funeral. He walked along a path lined with houses and abundant fruit trees, and met his deceased father who sent him back to his body to tell his people about the happiness of the other realm (cf. Wade 2003: 85–6).[5] These accounts indicate Algonquin belief in two separate, morally determined realms at least twenty-five years prior to missionary activity,[6] though the notion coexisted alongside beliefs in a single realm for all.

The idea of separate realms for different cultures is evident in a 1636 report in which the French Jesuit missionary Paul Le Jeune was told by a local that he was welcome to go to his own European afterlife realm, because "each loves his own people; for my part, I shall go and find mine" (Hultkrantz 1980: 167). Another French Jesuit missionary, Paul Ragueneau (1646: 25ff), was told of Algonquins who had traveled to the land of souls and "heard wonders." The dead had renewed bodies and lived a blissful existence in populous cities. The accounts led the local people to conclude that the Christian heaven and hell were "fables."

The French explorer Nicolas Perrot was "a keen and shrewd observer" who spent most of his life among Algonquin tribes, and was the first European visitor to several of them (Blair 1911: I, 13–5). Sometime between 1680 and 1717, peoples of the Great Lakes and Mississippi Valley told Perrot that their afterlife realm was different from that of Europeans, and that this information came from ancestors who had chanced upon it while on a military expedition. When discovered by the dead, they were escorted back to the border between worlds and told not to return until they die. Though war and death are obviously inextricably linked, there is no overt NDE or shamanic context. Nevertheless, the claim of an experiential basis for the belief should be noted, as should the thematic NDE elements of the narrative (border crossings, encountering spirits, being instructed to return), and the beliefs that reportedly arose from it: the realm of the dead was reached by crossing an unsteady log over rapids. Souls of the young and healthy could cross easily, but children and the elderly were in danger of drowning. Fish from the river sustained them on the journey. At a mountain that blocked their path, two giant pestles rose and fell alternately, threatening to crush the traveler and presumably result in annihilation. Those who passed successfully entered a "beautiful and fertile land" "beyond this Earth," with a fine climate, abundant birds and animals, and so many fruits and flowers that "it delights their hearts and charms their imaginations." Proceeding onward as drums pounded in time to their steps, they were greeted by joyous, dancing spirits who welcomed them with a large feast. Souls could then "dance and make merry forever," without sorrow or other unpleasant elements of earthly life (ibid. 89–92).

Wyandot (Huron)

The French Jesuit missionary Jean de Brébeuf (1636: 141–53) lived with the Wyandot for fifteen years, learned their language fluently, and was a careful chronicler of their culture. He was told that their afterlife beliefs originated in reports of individuals who had died and were "brought back to life,"[7] and were maintained by the retelling of such narratives. Brébeuf also recorded an Orpheus myth in which a man followed his sister to the other world after prolonged mourning. He traveled toward the sunset, fasting all the while, though his sister appeared each day and gave him a small quantity of food. After more than three months, he came to a river. On the other side was a clearing with a cabin, and he felt joyful upon seeing an old man go inside. He successfully crossed the river on shaky fallen trees, and reached the cabin. The old man asked him where he was going and why, and after hearing the answer he told the visitor where to find his sister in the spirit village, and gave him a pumpkin in which to carry her soul. When the brother found his sister, he startled her and the other spirits, and they fled. He followed, and in the struggle to restrain her she shrank small enough that he managed to trap her in the pumpkin. He then returned to the old man, who gave him a second pumpkin containing his sister's brains, along with instructions on how to resuscitate her: return to Earth and exhume her body, then hold up the two pumpkins. The brother did as he was instructed, but because he was observed by people in the village, his sister's soul escaped and he was left only with her decaying corpse.

Another French missionary, Francois le Mercier (1638: 51), related the experience of an Arendahronon Wyandot man who died and went to another world. There he met two English women "who warned him that he should not yet go into the land of souls," and that he should burn his robe upon his return to life in order to cure an infectious disease. They gave him a prophecy that French missionaries would carry out a genocide on the native peoples.

Le Jeune (1640: 199–201; Kenton 1927: 389) related two Wyandot NDEs. In the first, a dying man went to the other world, where he was welcomed by his deceased relatives. They told him of the "fine dances and feasts" they would have when he ultimately joined them. When the man revived he prepared for his death, and died shortly thereafter. In the second account, a sick man found himself at the border of "the most delightful place imaginable," and saw a recently deceased Frenchman of his acquaintance. Though he wanted to enter this realm, he was turned away because he had not been baptized. When he revived, he told his people of Heaven and its baptism prerequisite. Interestingly, this man disbelieved a contemporary Algonquin NDE on the grounds that the experiencer had seen no Frenchmen in the other world. The Algonquin had revived just as he was being buried, and described having been to the land of the dead, located at the setting sun, and seeing only indigenous people there. When he returned to his body he claimed that he had the power to stay alive but preferred to return to the other world, and so "he lay down and died again."

A partly distressing NDE led to perhaps the earliest indigenous religious revitalization movement, when a converted Wyandot woman rose from her burial in a Christian cemetery and told of her experiences in the heaven of the French—a realm of fire where Christians burned souls in order to possess them. She was greeted "with firebrands and burning torches, with cruelties and torments inconceivable." Though she was dead only one day, it seemed like years. She was finally assisted by "a certain person, moved with compassion for her," who released her from her chains and showed her a valley that led to the afterlife realm of indigenous people who had not converted to Christianity—a place of delights and goodness, without evil. She could see the realm's villages and fields, and hear people dancing and feasting, though because she wanted to warn her people of the dangers of converting to Christianity, she decided to "return into her body." The news of her experience "soon spread everywhere" and became "an article of faith" among indigenous people. Additional new beliefs also stemmed from the experience, such as that the sky is a fiery realm since it is closer to the sun (Ragueneau 1646: 29–33). The beliefs were still current eleven years later, as reported by Jean de Quen (1657: 289–91), who complained that missionaries were often being accused of luring native souls to heaven in order to burn them.

The Wyandot cited further individuals "who say that they have risen from the dead and have witnessed all that." One was another woman who died and returned to tell of her journey to the border of the land of French souls, where she similarly witnessed her people being burned by the French. She broke free of her guides and returned to her body, partly to avoid the same fate, and partly to warn her people. While such narratives were quite possibly based on the original, De Quen noted the difficulty of convincing the people that they were untrue, for they "allege their own experience in confirmation" of their beliefs—including that conversion brought misfortune.

The Wyandot believed that the soul retained human form after death, and that after leaving the body it stayed by the grave until the next Feast of the Dead (every twelve years). While some thought the dead became turtledoves after the feast, most believed that they traveled on a wide road toward the setting sun. An entity named Pierce-Head removed their brains, a motif interpreted by Hultkrantz (1957: 97) as symbolizing loss of "the memory-soul" or "ego-soul," forgetting one's previous life and shedding the desire to return to Earth. Souls then crossed a log over a river guarded by a snapping dog. Those who fell were carried away by the rushing waters (ibid. 141–7), while the rest reached a "great

Village"—a mirror image of Earth, where souls "do nothing but groan and complain" until "Captains" interfere and "moderate." Rivalries between tribal groups in separate spirit villages persisted in the other world. Suicides, those who died in battle, the very young, and the very old also had separate villages.

Mi'kmaq

Roman Catholic French missionary Chrétien Le Clercq (1691: 207-8) lived with the Mi'kmaq of the Gulf of St. Lawrence and Nova Scotia for twelve years beginning in 1675, and was fluent in their language. He reported that they based their afterlife beliefs on the NDE of "one of the most prominent men of the nation." When the man revived from apparent death, he described meeting the ruler of the realm of the dead, Papkootparout. He gave the man "certain fruits" which the dead eat, and allowed him to return to Earth in order to tell his people about the Land of Souls, "which had been up to that time unknown to them." The man died soon after relating his experiences, and his testimony was taken by his people as "indubitable truth, [and] was more than enough to persuade them that souls, after departure from their bodies, had a place to which they went to remain." The narrative directly inspired other members of the tribe to attempt to undergo similar experiences, demonstrating that NDEs and shamanism were considered related types of experience with similar meanings. It also suggests that beliefs derived from NDEs were subsequently validated, perpetuated, and elaborated on through attempts at replication via individual shamanic experiences. In disbelief, Le Clercq reiterated that such experiences—and only such experiences—are responsible for the indigenous beliefs in the soul and afterlife (ibid. 212, 213).

Iroquois

The Latvian missionary Henry George Loskiel (1794: 34–5) wrote that Iroquois afterlife beliefs were based on

> the testimony of two Indians, who were dead for several days; and had meanwhile been in the habitation of the good spirits. When they revived, they related that this place was to the south of heaven, and that the bright track called the milky way, was the road to it. This led to a most glorious city, the inhabitants of which enjoyed every possible good in great abundance.

Though they had separate roads to the other world, Europeans had blocked the way for Natives, who as a result had to make a long detour.

Some believed that the land of the dead was to be found "over a great rock, upon which the heavens reel to and fro with stupendous noise." Two men claimed to have traveled to the other world this way, but refused to discuss it upon their return.

Loskiel also wrote of the origins of syncretistic religious movements of the 1760s, when certain "preachers" (i.e., shamans or healers) "pretended to have received revelations from above, to have travelled into heaven, and conversed with God." Though their descriptions of their journeys differed, all said it was perilous, particularly in avoiding being ambushed by "the Devil." Those who passed successfully met "the Son of God," then proceeded "to God himself," who commanded them "to instruct the Indians in the way to heaven," and about God and the Devil. Some, however, only reached the entrance to the other world, where they saw smoking chimneys and heard cocks crowing.

French missionary Joseph-François Lafitau (1724: 253–8) described an Orpheus myth almost identical to the Wyandot version related by Brébeuf over a hundred years earlier. It differs mainly in that the protagonist is protected and assisted on his quest by Tharonhiaouagon, goddess of the other world. The point is also made that despite his failure to "rescue" his sister, the man succeeded in bringing back knowledge of the other world. Lafitau also recorded beliefs that the land of the dead was in the west, and was reached via a "Path of Souls" in the Milky Way. It was a realm of happiness, plenty, and joy, though fates were ethically determined.

Lenape (Delaware)

In 1762, the prophet Neolin sought an encounter with the creator deity, the Master of Life. Following prolonged "fasting, dreaming and magical incantations," he set off on his "journey to the spirit world." After eight days he reached a brook at the edge of a meadow, and three paths cutting through a forest. The first two were blocked by the "wonderful phenomena" of a "bright flame" leaping from the ground. He walked for a day on the third path before coming to "a vast mountain, of dazzling whiteness." From the summit, a beautiful woman told him that if wished to proceed he must rid himself of his guns, ammunition, supplies, and clothing, then wash himself in the stream. He obeyed, ascended, and at the summit he found a "rich and beautiful plain" with three fine villages in the distance. A "gorgeously attired" man appeared, welcomed him to the "celestial abode," and took him to the Master of Life, who was surrounded by "unspeakable splendor." He told Neolin that the indigenous people must fight the British; cease using European weapons, tools, food, and alcohol; adopt monogamy; cease sorcerous practices; and return to traditional ways of life. He gave Neolin a stick carved with a prayer summarizing the new teachings, and Neolin carried it back to Earth with him as evidence of his experience (Parkman 1870: 205–7). A map

Neolin drew of the afterlife regions showed that the main path there was held by Europeans, though another had been created by the Master of Life for indigenous people. Souls risked perils such as an "evil spirit" who would take them to hellish, barren, hot realms, and enslave them as horses or hunting dogs (Mooney 1896: 667).[8] Neolin's vision was clearly a culturally situated, deliberately sought shamanic-type one, rooted in political-historical circumstances, and with Christian-influenced puritanical elements. Nevertheless, the religious changes Neolin espoused were grounded in the authority of the experience, which implicitly looks to NDEs as well as to the long tradition of shamanic visionary narratives and Orpheus myths for validation.

Shamanic otherworld journey narratives were also central to the foundation of Lenape Peyotism, a religion rooted in experiences that result from ingesting the hallucinogenic peyote cactus. While on the brink of death in 1880, Chief Elk Hair received visions from the deified form of Peyote about right thinking, compassion, empathy, and "how to study our existence." He was cured by the drug and started a branch of the religion after reviving. Around the same time, Nishkû'ntu ("John Wilson") went on a "journey to the sky realm," and returned to his people with highly detailed new religious and ceremonial teachings given to him by Peyote (Petrullo 1934: 34–46, 81).

Cherokee

In 1789, the American naturalist William Bartram (1853: 27) wrote that all Native people he had encountered (primarily Cherokee and Muscogee) believed in the existence of an immortal soul that survives physical death in an afterlife of rewards and punishments as determined by earthly behavior. In addition, they related an

> abundance of stories of men that have been dead or thought dead for many hours and days, who have revived again, giving an account of their transit to and from the world of souls, and describing the condition and situation of the place and spirits residing there. And these people have always returned to life with doctrines and admonitions tending to encourage and enforce virtue and morality.

In an NDE from roughly a century later, a woman died of smallpox and traveled to a land of spirits where she met a chief she had known in life. In consultation with other spirits, it was decided that "she could not come and live with them yet." She returned to her body and recovered from her illness. The woman's daughter recounted the event, and emphasized that "it was not a dream" (Mooney & Olbrechts 1932: 142).

Around the same time, a shaman died as a result of an illness and revived after half an hour. He described how he had risen from his bed, walked along a road, and climbed a mountain to a beautiful meadow. He passed through a building filled with children, then two more with adults. In a fourth he met an officious European man with a long white beard, sitting at a desk. "Well, have you come to live with us?" the man asked, not bothering to look up at the shaman when they shook hands. He was about to write the shaman's name in a ledger, but stopped and said, "I think you had better go back home again," adding that he would return permanently in thirty-three days. He gave the shaman a tin coin that would assist him in finding his way back. A trapdoor opened and he fell "at a terrific speed, the air rushing past him as if it were a windstorm." He landed on a mountain, threw the coin, and followed it back to where his body lay (Mooney & Olbrechts 1932: 142–4).

Such accounts were considered to be key sources of knowledge about the afterlife for the Cherokee (Hultkrantz 1957: 294). They bear thematic similarity to local myths concerning creation and the origins of death and the afterlife, in which the sun (or her daughter) dies, goes to the other realm, and returns (Mooney 1900: 252ff, 436–7).

Ojibwe (Chippewa)

Near-death experiences were also integrated into Ojibwe afterlife conceptions. According to the geologist William H. Keating (1825: 154–5), the Ojibwe believed that when the soul (*Ochechag*) left the body at death, it reached a stream spanned by a giant snake. It refused passage to those "in lethargy or trance" (i.e., not actually dead) and threatened to devour them. "These souls return to their bodies and reanimate them." Those who successfully crossed the stream could visit Earth in order to give warnings of imminent dangers, or to invite the living to the other world. People who died from drowning would fall into the river and remain there. The good proceeded to a southern coastal region called Cheke Chekchekame to live a life of dancing, singing, and eating mushrooms, without work, worry, or pain. The bad were "haunted by the phantoms of the persons or things that they have injured."

The American geographer and ethnologist Henry Schoolcraft (1825: 404–9) recorded the NDE of an Ojibwe chief who died in battle. According to custom, his body was dressed in ceremonial garb and leaned against a tree facing the direction his enemies had fled. The chief remained conscious inside his lifeless body, and when his companions departed, his spirit followed them. Back at their village he watched them tell his people of his death and bravery. No one could see or hear him, however, which led to the realization that he was out of his body.

He resolved to return to it, and after four days he came upon a "mysterious fire" blocking his way. He told the fire that he was trying to return to his body, then leapt through. Suddenly he found himself back in his body, leaning against the tree. He told his people of his experiences, and instituted a new funerary ritual of burning fires for four nights following burial in order to comfort the soul on its journey.[9] Out-of-body experiences as catalysts for realizing one is dead (e.g., bewilderment at seeing one's own corpse, failing to communicate with the living) is a common NDE feature (cf. Wade 2003: 88–9; Shushan 2009: 143–5).

Roughly contemporary is the NDE of a hunter named Gitshee Gauzinee, who died after an illness. His wife and others suspected he was not actually dead, however, and delayed burial. After four days he revived and related how he had traveled on "the path of the dead" for three days. He grew hungry, and when he saw game animals regretted that he did not have his gun with him. He decided to return for it, and on his way back he met spirits on their way to the land of the dead, overburdened with supplies such as kettles, weapons, and food. They assisted him by sharing their belongings, but he was determined to return home. As he approached his lodge, he found a "line of waving fire" encircling it. He leapt through the fire, and returned to his body. His account led to a change in the funerary practices of his people, reducing the grave goods interred with the dead so that they would have an easier journey with less to carry (Schoolcraft 1825: 410–412; cf. Wade 2003: 88–90; Kellehear 1996: 29; Schorer 1985).[10] While a simple functionalist interpretation is compelling (the change he suggested would reduce wasted resources), we nevertheless have a case of a personal experience narrative directly impacting religious belief.

Schoolcraft (1839: 31ff) also related a myth in which the eponymous culture hero, Ojibwe, descended through an opening in the ground while searching for his family's magic arrows. He found himself in a vast and beautiful realm of spirits, where he encountered buffalo that could speak like humans. They questioned him about his presence there, and when he explained, they told him that he was the first living human ever to visit the realm. Back on Earth, Ojibwe's brothers were attempting to "dishonor" his wife, so the buffalo instructed him to return to live a long and happy life. Ojibwe then saw a bright light, "as if the sun was shining in its splendour but he saw no sun." A buffalo told him that the light was "where those who were good dwell," and that a dark cloud was the place of "wickedness." The guardians then helped return him to Earth.

In 1790, a ten-year-old boy named John Tanner (1830: 290–1) was captured by a Shawnee warrior and sold to the Ojibwe. He lived with them for thirty years and became culturally assimilated, speaking only their language. He recounted local beliefs in individuals dying, traveling to the other world, and returning to life. They described following a path to a river, and a giant, inedible strawberry which turned into rock when one tried to eat it. The river was traversable only by a "swinging log," and a giant dog waited on the other side. Some souls were subjected to "taunts, and gibes, and insults" from their predeceased friends, or given ashes and bark to eat; though some men described a world filled with women eager to become their wives. Tanner concluded that "the dreams all have been tinged with some shade of colour, drawn from their own peculiar situation," though assumed Ojibwe beliefs were responsible for the experiences rather than vice versa.

However, the historian and geographer Johann Georg Kohl (1860: 214–26) was told by the Ojibwe that they knew about the afterlife because "many of our tribe have been there and returned." In one example, a hunter died of an illness, "and his soul went on the great wandering." His experience features elements found in Schoolcraft's and Tanner's accounts. At the giant strawberry he was interrogated by a man dressed as a raven. He refused to rest or taste the strawberry, and continued to the river. At the village of souls he heard drums, and saw people playing sports and games. He met his deceased parents and though his mother was happy and tried to feed him, his father asked why he had come and tried to send him away, reminding him that he had a wife and son at home. The hunter's uncles arrived and agreed that he should go back to care for his family. He relented, but before he left his mother gave him a packet of red powder. He returned the way he had come, though when he reached the river he found that it had become fierce and turbulent, the log had become a snake, and the strawberry "a red-hot mass" with "a great savage man" wielding a hammer next to it. The hunter successfully passed these obstacles, then saw his cousin walking toward the land of the dead. He tried to convince the cousin to return to Earth with him, but he "was really dead, and must go to the land of souls." After advising his cousin on what to expect on the journey, the hunter continued on his way until he became lost, surrounded by smoke on a burning prairie. He leapt through flames, and awoke in his body surrounded by his grieving family. He told them of his experience and produced the packet his spirit mother had given him. Inside was "a pretty little blood-red sponge." He ate a piece of it, and lived a long life.

Some of these features were elaborated upon in explanations of afterlife beliefs. Those who tasted the strawberry were "lost." Those who fell into the river became toads or fishes. The giant dog made sure spirits traveled only westward, barring them from returning to Earth. The souls of children were often helped on the journey by a kind adult soul. The paradise of the god Menaboju was reached after three or four days, and spirits there lived a life of happiness, music, and dancing, eating mushrooms and a kind of phosphorescent wood. All indigenous people shared the same paradise, though the Christian realm was separate. Shamans (*jossakids*) could visit the other world during "convulsions" after funerary feasts: "They manage to deceive the attention of the great dog, and when they return they make a speech, and tell us all they have seen." As Kohl (1860: 90) noted, Catholic traditions are not evident in these narratives despite having been introduced two hundred years earlier.

There are numerous Ojibwe NDE-type narratives from the early twentieth century. Indeed, according to "the people of old," "whenever anyone died, it was common for him to rise from the dead; and so he would give an account of what it was like at the place where the dead go." In the other world, a "great ghostly person who watched over the ghosts" sometimes sent people back to Earth, telling them, "Not yet is your time up to come to this place," at which point the individual would return to life[11] (Jones 1917: 311–3, collected 1903–5). The narratives are largely consistent with earlier accounts and beliefs, though each with additional idiosyncratic elements, such as substituting a cucumber tree or a raspberry for the giant strawberry. One youth died and journeyed along a road, following a small child to a beautiful place. Noticing that the child was crying and still attached to its cradleboard, the youth tried to pick it up but somehow he could not reach it. He continued onward, experiencing sparkling lights, the river, log, and guardian dogs. In the spirit village he met his deceased grandmother, who explained where he was and told him to "go back" because "It is not yet your time to come here." He also met his aunts, who took him to a dance where everyone was merry, though some of his relatives and companions were missing heads or limbs. The grandmother explained that they had been slain that way, and that the sparkling lights he had seen were ghosts. The youth then had to return, because his body was about to be buried. After following various paths he came to the fire, flung himself in, and reentered his body. His experience served to teach his people not to bury children attached to their cradleboards, as that is how they would remain in the next world (ibid. 3–23).

Another boy was sent home from the spirit world just as his body was about to be buried. He leapt through the fire, returned to consciousness just in time, and described the afterlife to his people, explaining that the Northern Lights were souls playing games (Gayton 1935: 275). In an example from the beginning of the 20th century, a man returned to life just before his own burial, and told how he had been sent back from the other world "for his time had not yet come." His experience led to a practice of delaying burial for four days in case the soul returned and the person revived. Various addenda were added to afterlife beliefs around this time, such as different obstacles for every sin committed, and members of the Grand Medicine Society possessing a formula to say to the snake which would make their journey easier than others (Landes 1968: 198–9).

In a somewhat hallucinatory account of 1913, an old woman with smallpox was accompanied on her journey to the spirit world by a woman with a dog. In addition to various familiar elements, she encountered a pair of oxen breath-ing fire, a village of invisible dogs, "a big light," and dancing spirits who were offended at her smell because she is "a body not dead." Everything suddenly vanished, and after several months in a coma she saw "a little star shining," which gradually grew bigger. She heard the voice of her husband telling her children that she was dead, and she revived soon after (Knight 1913: 92–5).

In 1929, the Ojibwe of Queen Elizabeth Islands stated that their knowledge of the afterlife came from a woman named Gizikkwedanjiani, who followed her dead husband there. Though he told her to go back and take care of their child, she per-sisted. She encountered a bloody-mouthed canine "that devours the souls of those who have tormented dogs." At the "river of death" she paid her passage by sprin-kling tobacco on the water, causing phosphorescent logs to remain still for her to cross. Those who could not pay became crayfish, though witches would burn on the log. At "the storehouse of brains" Gizikkwedanjiani was interrogated and asked what she was doing there. When she explained her intention of retrieving her husband's soul, she was told to go ask Djibweabuth, brother of the underworld ruler Nanibush. Djibweabuth agreed to give Gizikkwedanjiani her husband's soul and brains. Though the husband did not wish to return with her, she took him anyway, and succeeded in reanimating him back on Earth (Jenness 1935: 109).[12]

In the 1930s, the Ojibwe of northwest Minnesota and western Ontario told the anthropologist Ruth Landes (1968: 189–91) that they "learned about after-death at first hand, usually from old or sick Indians who 'died' temporarily, their souls being released to the after-death sphere." According to one informant, when a person dies "his shadow leaves this sphere and body for another sphere and body, feeling its way through a tortuous dark unknown tunnel, emerging into a ghostly land through which it must race so madly, to elude ghostly terrors, that the wind whistles in its ears." The deceased then met various ancestors, and were given the knowledge to overcome a series of evils and to cross the river. A Grandfather then provided a bow, and the newly arrived soul shot and followed an arrow to the village of the dead, an idealized mirror image of Earth "beyond the western hori-zon" where all were happy, equal, and young. Women were greeted by a female ghost named Shell Woman, and men by her male counterpart. The souls of chil-dren, however, went to a realm reserved primarily for white people. Those who drowned or burned to death would continue to do so in the afterlife.

Hallowell (1940: 29) found that the afterlife beliefs of the Berens River Saulteaux Ojibwe

are supported by the testimony of individuals who are said to have trav-elled beyond the bourne and returned to tell their fellows about it; by the testimony of those who have approached the land of the dead in dreams; the resurrection, or resuscitation, of persons reputed to be dead; by the invocation of the spirits of the dead in the conjuring lodge, and in other ways.

In response to Hallowell's queries about their afterlife beliefs, the Saulteaux described the NDE of a man named Flat-Stone, who was dead for two days. After traveling down a road, he came to a wigwam, where he met an old man who asked him where he was going. Flat-Stone refused to eat when the old man offered him food, and was then led to his parents in a vast village. He met other villagers (some of whom "had moss growing on their foreheads, they died so long ago")[13] who wanted news about their people on Earth. When Flat-Stone heard "three or four beats of a drumstick," he suddenly thought of his children and decided to go back, returning along the road he had come. When he revived it was daylight, "But even daylight here is not so bright as it is in the country I had visited," he said. He taught his people "not to be scared about dying" and that the dead "are in a good place."

In another Saulteaux NDE, a man traveled along a road lined with straw-berries, including an enormous one that had fed previous travelers. He heard shouting and laughing as he approached a town and saw someone he knew, but was stopped and told "You're not wanted yet." Another man claimed to have left his body during an illness, and traveled along a road to a rocky hill. A disem-bodied voice said it would show him what was beyond, and he saw a beautiful place that was "very bright," and full of grass, flowers, and trees. When the man complained that he could not get there, the voice told him he was not ready yet and to "go back and prepare yourself." He was directed to a different road, then passed through a fire to reenter his body. An unusual Saulteaux narrative tells of a man named Mud-Turtle who revived after being buried alive. Afterward he often acted strangely at night, making movements and exclamations as if he were in the middle of a lacrosse game. It emerged that he had visited the realm of the dead where night and day are reversed, had played lacrosse with spirits there, and was reliving the experience in his dreams.

It is also worth mentioning a 1914 narrative, in which the spirit of a man com-municated to his son through a shamanic medium. The father reassured the son that he and the boy's deceased sister were in "a beautiful country . . . always happy, and without pain, hunger, or thirst," and that if he leads a good life he would be able to join them. A child then communicated essentially the same information, adding that it is "very bright" in the other world, and that there are flowers, gar-dens, and singers (Hallowell 1940: 44).

Shawnee

In 1805, the Shawnee prophet Tenskwatawa died suddenly, then revived at his own funeral, claiming that two young men had shown him the spirit world. He was not permitted to enter, but only to observe from the border. As with Neolin, he was given instructions to abandon European ways of life, reassert traditional culture, and impose puritanical moral strictures. Tenskwatawa also claimed to have received revelation from the Master of Life, and to be an incarnation of the culture hero/deity Manabozho, who was punishing the Natives for abandoning their "purity." If they returned to indigenous ways, Manabozho would reward them with plentiful game and the return of deceased loved ones. Tenskwatawa's testimony had a profound effect on various tribes, leading to overzealous bans on alcohol and sorcery, which sometimes resulted in witch-hunts and immolations. In addition to these immediate doctrinal changes, Tenskwatawa's power and authority were sustained by his regular dreams and visions (Mooney 1896: 672–4).

Ho-Chunk (Winnebago)

In the early 1850s, a prophet named Wabokieshiek visited the other world after days of fasting. He saw a group of spirits there doing "the friendship dance", which he instituted among his people when he returned. An Orpheus narrative also reinforced the link between extraordinary experience and religion, serving to explain the origin of the local Ghost Dance—a form of religious revitalization movement characterized by ritual dances that led to visionary experiences, and concerned with restoring traditional ways of life, rejecting European colonists, and the dead returning from the spirit world. The Ho-Chunk version incorporated elements from a shamanic experience with established mythical themes, and was indigenously categorized as a combination of "that which is old" (myth) and "that which has happened" (tale) (Radin 1923: 18, 22, 34–7).

In his 1909 autobiography, a shaman named Sam Blowsnake (1909: 5–7) related memories of states between lives. After dying on a battlefied, his spirit traveled home, unaware that he was dead. Ignored by his family, he floated back to the battlefield and saw his corpse below. He was then taken to the western horizon, to the spirit world where one can travel anywhere by thought alone. Blowsnake tried to return home for four years, until the spirit village chief allowed him to be reincarnated so he could take revenge on the enemies who had killed him and his relatives. Blowsnake also remembered watching the burial of his body from above in his next incarnation, going to a joyful spirit realm, and then to "the place where Earthmaker lived" where he stayed another four years before being reincarnated again. During a later Peyote-influenced "death", he again encountered the Earthmaker—whom he seemed to identify with his own soul. During the experience he conveyed Christian-influenced messages about "God's Son" to others in the Peyote cult (Blowsnake 1909: 198f).

In a shamanic-themed Orpheus legend recounted by Blowsnake, a man named Wakisha followed his deceased wife to the spirit land. Assisted by an old man covered in hair, he overcame various obstacles on his journey, only to face a series of taunts and humiliations from his deceased relatives for attempting to rescue his wife. He succeeded, however, and returned with her to Earth. He also brought back a drum given to him by the old man, which had the power to restore souls of the sick and dying (ibid. 49–55).

The Ho-Chunk believed that the dead do not know they are dead until they actually see their own body. A narrative concerning what to expect in the other world described souls of the dead traveling on a wide road at sunrise, overcoming obstacles, and being met by their grandmother. She interrogated the deceased, confirmed their identity, then offered some rice. Those who ate it would get a headache, and the grandmother would break open their skulls and remove their brains, causing them to forget Earth and those left behind. Their souls became "like a holy spirit." When the rice turned out actually to be lice, this resulted in the deceased being "finished with everything evil." After following four footsteps "imprinted with blue earth," souls were greeted by more relatives before arriving at a river of fire with a perilous swinging bridge spanning it. Assisted by guides, souls crossed to the spirit village, an idealized mirror image of Earth. Members of a Medicine Lodge, and those who died in battle or led a good life, reincarnated on Earth (Radin 1923: 95–6, 266; collected c. 1908–13).

Meskwaki (Fox)

In a narrative collected c. 1901–2, a man named Painter fell from a tree and was unconscious for three days. His grandson stressed that he "really had been dead at the time." Following a well-trodden path, Painter went to another world which "seemed in his heart" to be "home." He met various others on the way and eventually arrived at a beautiful river. He heard drumming from the other side, and saw pleasant countryside and a distant town with buildings similar in style to earthly graves. Painter crossed a bridge to the town, and saw people dancing, playing games, and racing horses. His deceased parents and siblings were there, and they told him to return to Earth because his children would be sorrowful at his death. Painter was reluctant, however, and continued on the path. He then met a deceased former girlfriend, who commented on the decline in his appearance over the years. Painter decided to return to Earth for some better clothes, then he suddenly revived. The narrative conflicted with certain local afterlife expectations, such as encountering "the One-who-cracks-open-the-Skulls," and the deity of the spirit world, Tcipaiyaposw (Jones 1907: 207–11, 383). Nor is there mention of the afterlife beliefs reported by US Major Morrell Marston in 1820, such as morally determined fates of rewards and punishments (Blair 1911: II, 174–5). This may, however, be due simply to a diversity of local traditions rather than actual contradiction.

Seneca

In 1799, the missionary Henry Simmons recorded the NDE of a youth who was expected to die after being stabbed. He ascended to a well-trodden path then arrived at a house, which he entered. An extraordinarily beautiful man invited him to sit, but the youth was so restless that he could neither sit nor speak. He continued onward to another house where he was ushered in by a gloomy-looking official, whose mouth moved "in different shapes" and side-to-side. The house was filled with noisy, drunken, distressed people, some of whom he recognized and who were long dead. An old woman was dying, and he was told that the world would end when she did. He was then subjected to punishments which corresponded to specific sins: being forced to drink molten metal for drinking alcohol, being chained for pursuing married women, and losing his arms for striking his wife. The official sent him home, and told him that if he ceased such "evil practices" he would be able to dwell in the first house. The youth awoke sobbing and was so profoundly affected that he was unable to relate the experience for some time. He ultimately resolved to become a better person (Swatzler 2000: 51–2).

In the same year, the prophet Sganyadiyo (Handsome Lake) journeyed to "heaven and hell" during a serious illness. He told his people not to bury him, that he was going to see his deceased son and niece, but would return. He ascended on the Milky Way, the stars of which were footprints of the previously dead, and "a more brilliant light than the light of earth appeared." The long, elaborately detailed narrative includes many scenes of judgment, reward, and punishment (some of which appear to be have been borrowed from the above account). Sganyadiyo encountered George Washington and Jesus, who told him that his people "will become lost when they follow the ways of the white man." Before sending him back to Earth, a guide encouraged Sganyadiyo to tell his people about his visions, and gave him a warning that he must conduct a particular ceremony upon his return or a "great sickness" would befall them. The guide also issued strictures against alcohol, witchcraft, and belief in dreams sent by the Devil. This experience followed Sganyadiyo's earlier deathbed "wondrous visions," visits from supernatural beings, and instructions from the creator god to teach his people a new set of strictures. Together, these experiences led directly to Sganyadiyo founding Gaihwi:io ("Longhouse Religion"), with the "moral plan of the cosmos" revealed in his NDE becoming "the core of the new religion's theology" (Wallace 1970: 242–4; Parker 1913: 11, 24).

A Seneca Orpheus legend tells of a woman who traveled to the "land of the Mother of Ghosts" to retrieve her dead husband, Djengo'se. After following him for four days, she was stopped at a "narrow passageway" and interrogated by two men. They asked what she was doing there since she was not dead, and after hearing her story they decided to help her. They warned her that the next passageway would be guarded by panthers and gave her two pheasants as a toll for them. At a third passageway she was again interrogated. The warder gave her a gourd containing "the fat or oil of a man," with a tendon as a stopper. The woman was told that upon reaching a strawberry field she should rub the oil on her hands, at which point the Mother of Ghosts would appear. After interrogating the widow, the Mother of Ghosts helped to hide her until evening, when Djengo'se and the other spirits arrived for a dance. When they smelled the widow, the spirits became suspicious, but the Mother of Ghosts succeeded in trapping Djengo'se in the gourd. She told the widow to hurry back to the first passage, where she would be given further instructions. Retracing her path, the widow eventually reached home and prepared her husband's body as she had been directed, by stopping every orifice except the mouth with a mixture of deer fat, human fat, and clay. When she released the soul from the gourd, it entered her husband's body and he returned to life. Djengo'se was then "invulnerable to the spells and incantations of sorcerers and wizards" (Curtin & Hewitt 1918: 570–3).

Miami

Concerning the NDE of a young Miami (Indiana) man who lived "very many ages ago," the interpreter and ethnologist Charles Christopher Trowbridge (1938: 51–3) wrote, "Upon this vision they rest their belief of a future state." The man described taking a journey westward on a well-used path. At a fork he met an old man, who told him which path led to a house of fiery punishment for murderers, thieves, adulterers, and other criminals. The man took the other path and came upon a giant dog, which would devour those who had been cruel to animals. After crossing rapids on fallen trees, another old man directed him onto a further road. The NDEr met others who wanted to play a game with him, but he declined and continued on. At "a place prepared for dancing," he was interrogated by four elderly male singers. When he told the men where he had come from, they informed him that many of his relatives were already there, dancing, "abundantly supplied with everything necessary to eat and to wear." They invited him to join them, and though he wished to, he realized he had left his bow on the road, and decided to go back for it. He retraced his steps, and when he found his bow it was enveloped in flames. When he reached for it, he returned to his body.

Arctic and Subarctic
Innu (Montagnais)

In 1634, the Innu told Le Jeune that they gained their knowledge about the afterlife from two of their people who been there and returned. On the basis of that evidence, they contended that Le Jeune's statements about heaven and hell were incorrect, for all "go to the same country, at least, ours do" (Kenton 1927: 111–2).[14] They resisted his teachings despite the fact that they had already been exposed to Christianity by Basque whalers, and referred to the sun as "Jesus" (according to another missionary, Gabriel L'Alemant in 1626; ibid. 57).

The Innu conceived of the soul as an immortal "shadow" of the individual, possessing a subtle body that consumed funerary offerings. The realm of the dead was located in the "great village" in the eastern horizon. It was reached by ascent through the Milky Way, or on foot over water crossings. Day and night were reversed, and the dead ate bark and wood. In the daytime they sat with elbows rested on knees and head in hands as if they were sick, and at night they hunted souls of animals.

Greenlandic Inuit

In a mid-eighteenth-century report by the Norwegian missionary Niels Egede, a shaman (*angakkut*) claimed to have been to heaven, where he "talked with God" who was "big and shiny as the sun" and made thunder and wind sounds. Because the *angakkut* had gained firsthand experience of the other world, he was skeptical about Egede's description of heaven, since it excluded the presence of seals (Jakobsen 1999: 31). Not long after Egede's report, the German missionary David Cranz (1767: 200–203) described Greenlandic Inuit beliefs in souls that could leave the body and travel on voyages, particularly in dreams and via shamanic activity. Shamans could retrieve the souls of those in danger of dying and restore them to health, or exchange a sick soul for a healthy animal one. While some believed the soul was made of a physical substance, *angakkuts* "who pretend to have visited frequently the realm of souls, describe the soul as pale and soft" and immaterial. Great hunters, women who died in childbirth, and people who drowned went to an afterlife realm under the sea or underground, where immortal souls lived a happy existence in a land of abundance, eternal sun, and streams flowing with easily caught fish. The other realm was reached by sliding down a dangerous, rocky slope covered in "blood and gore." In cold weather especially this could lead to "perfect extinction." Another possible fate was "to soar beyond the rainbow" to a lunar paradise where souls transformed into the Northern Lights and lived an eternity of dance and play. Some, however, believed that the sky world was for witches and for lazy, wicked, worthless people who would suffer a meager existence and be constantly plagued by ravens. Some held transmigration beliefs, including that the souls of dead children took up residence in one of their siblings.

The Danish geologist Hinrich Johannes Rink (1875: 36–8) spent many years in Greenland beginning in 1848. He confirmed such beliefs, adding that some spirits in the sky-world played ball with a walrus head, "which gives rise to the aurora borealis." It was sometimes visited by "souls temporarily delivered from their bodies," and reached variously by sky, road, or kayak. The soul was seen as a mirror image of the body, "able to leave it temporarily and return to it", or to visit Earth after death in the form of a ghost (ibid. 42, 44). In one narrative, a couple accidentally revived their newly deceased son, though he soon returned to the underworld (ibid. 298–300).

On shamanic travels to the Mother of the Sea, the soul passed through the "mansion of all souls deceased, which look as well, if not better, than ever they did in this world, and want for nothing." One shaman named Kunigseq undertook a journey to the underworld by descending through the floor, assisted by "helping spirits." He reached a place of sunshine and heather-covered hills, saw children by a river, and met his brother and mother who had been gathering berries. When she tried to kiss him, a helping spirit pushed her away and said, "He is only here on a visit." The spirit warned Kunigseq that if he ate any of the berries he would not be able to return home. His mother tried to convince him to stay, pointing out that his family was already there and describing the life of abundance in the underworld, with smooth seas, good hunting, and no snow. He could see newly dead men on kayaks, and hear their laughter. "I will come again when I die," he told his mother. Soon after Kunigseq returned to Earth, his son died. Remembering the pleasant life in the underworld, Kunigseq committed suicide in order to return there (Rasmussen 1921: 38–9).

To become an *angakkut*, initiates invoked Torngarsuk, the deity of the undersea realm. When he appeared, the initiate would die of fright and be taken on a tour of "heaven and hell." After being taught the "wisdom and skill" of the *angakkut* profession for three days in these other realms, he would return to life (ibid. 210–1). Despite contact with European whaling ships "for decades" prior to such reports, Jakobsen (1999: x) describes Greenlandic shamanism as "untouched by other religions."

A nineteenth-century account of the initiation of an East Greenlandic shaman, Sanimuinak, involves transformation through dying and returning to life (among other trials and spirit communications) (Jakobsen 1999: 53–5). A female initiate, Teemiartissaq, reported a dream in which she descended to an underground realm and met a spirit who guided her through the ocean to a village of the dead. The spirit's assistant told Teemiartissaq that she could leave if she would later summon souls via drumming. She met her deceased brother, then returned to Earth and helped a soul to ascend from a grave. While such accounts share similarities (names of spirits, initiates being devoured, and returning to life naked), there are enough differences that Jakobsen (1999: 56–8) concludes that "the *angakkut* is very much a creator of his own spiritual world."

Bering Strait

In a Yupik or Inupiat NDE, a shaman died and his soul traveled to the other world on a path well-beaten by souls of the dead who had gone before him. He arrived at a village similar to those on Earth, and was led to a house by two spirits. Inside, meat was roasting on a fire, and in the meat were eyes that followed the shaman's movements. He was instructed not to eat the meat because "it would be bad for him." He continued onward and traveled to the Milky Way, then returned to his body in its grave, revived, and told his people about his experience. The shaman who related this narrative also remembered having died while in a previous incarnation. He visited the land of spirits, then reincarnated on Earth in the body of an unborn child. Shamans of this region had a tradition of inducing NDEs by apparently being burned alive (Nelson 1900: 433-4).

Deg Hit'an (Ingilik)

The Episcopal missionary John W. Chapman (1912: 66–7) lived among the Deg Hit'an for nearly twenty-five years before they would discuss their afterlife beliefs. In 1887 they told him of a girl who was lost while out hunting with her family. She was taken by two strange men, and after losing consciousness found herself in front of a house. Though confused that there were no footprints in the snow leading to the house, she went inside. It was so dark that nothing was visible "except one little ray of light, that came from a long way through the darkness overhead." She heard voices discussing why she was there, then an old woman appeared and illuminated the room by waving a wand over the girl. Feeling embarrassed, the girl hid herself in a corner, away from the various women she could now see. Instructed to look outside, she saw a vast village filled with people. When given food she felt nauseated and could not eat, and grew weak with hunger as the days passed. Eventually good food and water appeared when her parents on Earth made funerary offerings to her. When winter came six months later, the girl followed a hunting party to a precipice. The old woman told her that she could only ascend it if she were to die; otherwise she must return to her people. She remained through the spring, and in the summer she floated some distance down the river on a log, then walked along the bank. One day she saw her father floating in the direction from which she had come, and though she shouted and waved he did not notice her. The girl transformed into a bird, then "resumed her own shape" and returned home. Her mother could not see or hear her until she rubbed fish-eggs on her clothing. When she told of her experiences, her mother revealed that her father had died in her absence, providing evidential confirmation of the girl's experience of seeing her father in the spirit world (the so-called "Peak in Darien" element of some NDEs, of seeing people not known to have died; see Greyson 2010). As a direct result of the girl's narrative, new feasts and funerary offering traditions were instituted, indicating a change in religious beliefs.

Gilgulim Inuit

In the early twentieth century, the Danish explorer Knud Rasmussen (1929: 99) asked an *angakkut* named Aua about Gilgulim afterlife beliefs. In response, Aua described shamanic experiences in which the soul ascended through a hole in the roof of the hut, assisted on its flight to "heaven" by the souls of the dead who had become stars. Though spirits in the other world greeted shamans excitedly, they were disappointed that their stay was temporary. After enjoying themselves for a time, the shamans returned to Earth and related the experiences to their people.

An *angakut* named Anaituarjuk was said to have frequently visited an undersea realm for those who died by violence or sucide. Life there was similar to that on Earth, with hunting, fishing, and preparations for winter. To enjoy their pleasures and obtain blessings for the community, shamans also visited the eastern heavens in the Land of the Moon Spirit, a realm for those who died natural deaths or of disease. Some believed that the dead were judged by the sea-spirit Takanakapsaluk. Good people who did not break taboos were sent to the eastern heavens, while those who "failed to observe the ancient rules of life" were detained by Takanakapsaluk "to expiate their misdeeds" before proceeding to the undersea realm. Both were pleasant places without hardship, though in the heavenly realms "pleasures appear to be without limit". In one narrative, a man returned from the undersea realm to tell his people that he had been killed by his hunting companion. Souls that had been "lost or stolen" could be retrieved by *angakkuts* (ibid. 94–5, 109, 129–30).

Southwest
Tewa

In 1680, the Tewa religious leader Po'pay of Ohkay Owingeh journeyed to "the magic lagoon of Shipapu, whence his people traced their origin and to which the souls of the dead returned after leaving this life." The ancestors endowed Po'pay with supernatural powers, and instructed him to return to Earth to lead his people in revolt against the Spanish. Back on Earth, the ancestors appeared to him "as shapes of fire" and helped coordinate the rebellion (Mooney 1896: 659). Whether deliberate or spontaneous, Po'pay's experience helped inspire a reassertion and revitalization of indigenous culture, reinforcing the fact that traditional foundational contexts for cultural and religious innovations were frequently grounded in claims of religious experiences—particularly those characterized by visiting the realm of the dead and returning with new power and knowledge.

Apache

The famous Chiricahua chief Geronimo recounted the NDE of a man who had died in battle. He traveled westward through a cave, where guards allowed him to pass because he was "without fear." Arriving at a cliff, he swung himself onto a sand hill below and slid through the dark, narrow passages of a "canyon which gradually grew lighter until he could see as if it had been daylight; but there was no sun." He encountered serpents, bears, and lions, which he passed safely because he spoke fearlessly to them. After negotiating walls that clashed together repeatedly, he entered a forest and a verdant valley with "plenty of game" and people he had known in life. He was disappointed at having to return to life in his body. (Barrett 1906: 208–9; cf. Wade 2003: 92–3).

Three further relevant Chiricahua narratives were collected in 1931–5. In the first, a woman returned from unconsciousness during a serious illness and told of how "her ghost had gone from her body." She saw cottonwood trees and a stream, traveled to a high bluff, then jumped into the darkness below. She landed on a mound, and slid down to a village filled with light, where people lived "just as we live here." Relatives took her to her parents' camp, warning her that if she ate anything she would have to remain in the spirit world. When her two previous husbands started fighting over her, her relatives advised her to return to Earth. "Her ghost came back to her body and she opened her eyes."

The second narrative tells of a woman who was visted by a boy and girl, who told her she was "wanted in the other world." She followed them through "a sort of trap door with tall grass" concealing a mound. They slid down to a mirror image of Earth, with white people and towns, where spirits remained the age they were when they died. The spirits asked the woman why she was there, and when she explained they told her that the children had made up the story, that she was not wanted after all. Shortly after returning to life, the woman died.

In a myth intended to explain "How the Antelope Got His Name," a man wounded in battle "was between life and death". He started for "the after-world", but knew that he must return to Earth or he would die and remain in the other world forever. He suddenly transformed into an antelope, and dashed back to Earth. When he recovered, the antelope was named *zilahe*—"he who is becoming" (i.e., transformation from man to animal and back again) (Opler 1942: 82ff).

In a Lipan Apache NDE from 1935, a man was shot and left for dead. Everything went black, then became extremely bright. He followed a steep path to a beautiful place with green grass, trees, and a stream. In the distance was a village between hills. A group of men were playing "hoop and pole," and he hid in some bushes to watch. When a score needed to be settled, the players called in the man's father. When he saw his son, he had another man instruct him to return to Earth because his time had not yet come. He wanted to reassure his son, however, that the realm was "a good place, and that only those who have been good when on Earth belong here." An impassable hill separated this realm from a dark, misty one to the north, reserved for witches and people "who shoot things into others." They ate only what the living would not, such as lizards, snakes, and horned toads. Obeying his father, the man ran back to Earth. He saw "some awful object" ahead, which turned out to be his own body surrounded by blood. He tried to avoid it but was somehow impelled back inside. He revived and reported his experience to his people, and "That is what the Lipan believe about the place where they go at death."

Three further examples were related by Lipan elders. In the first, a woman died while riding a horse and traveled past a prickly pear tree. An old woman gave the fruits to new souls of the dead, though souls who were "not really dead" were merely told about life in the other realm. The woman then arrived at a tree hung with the various body parts missing from wounded people who were still alive, which they would later reclaim to become whole again. She proceeded to a ledge and saw a group of people sitting in a circle below, then slipped and fell down the slope. One of the men advised her where to find her parents and sister, and her father told her it was not yet her time to die. She angrily took a different path back to her body, reentered, and revived.

A narrative with an Orpheus theme involves a man who "died or fainted" while grieving deeply for his lost daughter. He found her in the other world and saw that she was happy there, but did not recognize him. His experiences were otherwise nearly identical to the above. When he revived, he told of how the other world was a good, happy place, where "everything is fine" and people "live better than we do," adding, "Now I'm not afraid to die."

Another man who was killed in battle saw on the trail to the other world three companions who had been killed with him. They urged him to follow, though he could see nothing ahead. When he looked back the way he had come, he saw something disturbing that he did not recognize, which turned out to be his own body. Because "it was not his turn to die," he went back into his body and revived (Opler 1940: 97–101, 104–5).[15]

Recurring features such as sliding down mounds and food taboos demonstrate intertextuality, and/or experiences conforming to some degree to cultural expectation, and/or being interpreted according to standard cultural modes.

Hopi

Near death from pneumonia in a government boarding school hospital in 1907, seventeen-year-old Don Talayesva (1942: 120–9, 134) had the defining experience of his life (recounted in extraordinary detail in his autobiography). His Guardian Spirit appeared and said to him, "You shall travel to the House of the Dead and learn that life is important. The path is already made for you. You had better hurry; and perhaps you will get back before they bury your body." His soul flew on the wind to a mountain where a cornmeal path led to a dimly lit tunnel. A voice said, "Don't be afraid, walk right in." He did so and found himself on a mesa near his village. He went home, but none of his relatives could see him except for his deceased grandmother, who was making her way to the Skeleton House at the pace of one step per year. Talayesva then floated up a long flight of stairs. He heard a bell ringing and met a Kwanitaka (member of a Warrior society) who "was now a spirit god and doing police duty directing good people over the smooth highway and bad people over the rough road to the House of the Dead." The rough road was "full of rocks, thorns, and thistles," with "naked, suffering people" being threatened by snakes and struggling "with heavy burdens and other handicaps such as thorny cactus plants fastened to their bodies in tender places." Talayesva took the smooth road, "sprinkled with corn meal and pollen," and rose to the top of a mesa where flowers were blooming and birds were singing, even though it was midwinter. He saw black-and-white striped clowns "joking and teasing one another." They told him, "you must hurry back to your body," but he proceeded to ancient cliff dwellings of the ancestors. A Kwanitaka scolded him for not believing "in the Skeleton House where your people go when they die. You think that people, dogs, burros, and other animals just die and that's all there is to it. Come with us. We shall teach you a lesson on life." They took him to a house where he had to choose between two pots of suds from which to be washed, one red and one white. Talayesva chose the white one, which ensured he would be able to return to his body.[16] The spirits washed his hair, then led him to a fire pit into which murderers were being pushed by their victims before becoming beetles. As the Kwanitakas escorted Talayesva back to life, Maasaw (Skeleton Man, creator deity associated with the sun) came after him wielding a club. Talayesva fled to the top of a canyon where the clowns encouraged him to jump. He did so, landing on another clown who told him,

> you have learned your lesson. Be careful, wise, and good, and treat every-body fairly. . . . Go back to the hospital and to your bed. You will see an ugly person lying there [i.e., his own body]; but don't be afraid. Put your arms around his neck and warm yourself, and you'll soon come to life. But hurry, before the people put your body in a coffin and nail down the lid, for then it will be too late.

Talayesva returned to his body, which had been prepared by the hospital staff for burial. His Guardian Spirit appeared and told him that he will become "an important man in the ceremonies." Talayesva then recounted his "death journey" to a visiting chief (Tewaquaptewa) who "said it was true, for those were the same things that the old people said they saw when they visited the House of the Dead." Talayesva's "death experience," as he called it, led directly to a spiritual renewal in which he rejected ten years of Christianization, and embraced indigenous Hopi tradition and beliefs (cf. Green 2008).

Such experiences were fundamental to Hopi afterlife beliefs per se, for

> it is widely believed that many people die . . . and visit the other world, only to be returned to life . . . if their time has not yet come. Quite often, persons who have had these experiences "remember what they saw while they were dead," and the Hopi regard their accounts as accurate descriptions of conditions in the realm of the dead. In general, these stories verify the notion that the behavior of the deceased is a replica of life on earth.

According to a First Mesa myth, NDEs would have been more common had Coyote not sealed off the return entrance from the other world. The dead would have revived after a temporary four-day visit there (Titiev 1944: 107).

In 1934, the experiences of "people who had 'died' . . . gone to Maski [the underworld] prematurely, returned to life, and told of their adventures in the other world" accounted for the belief that "while horses, burros, and sheep (all useful animals economically) went to Maski at death, dogs did not" (Titiev

1972: 104). In the same year, a man with influenza "dreamed he was dead and that he visited the Skeleton House where he saw some of his friends whom he knew were still alive in the village."[17] Another example demonstrates "the way in which tradition, myth, and custom may receive confirmation and support by dream experience." A man died after falling from a horse, then traveled on a path to a fork. One branch was for Hopi who "were mean" in life. It led them to bread ovens, which would turn them into "large black beetles." The path for the good led to a mesa, where "married men flew from the cliff on their wedding plaques; the married women wrapped in their wedding blankets. They went to a place of constant happy activity, of life as on earth." Children ascended to the sun, while infants were reborn on Earth. The man had to return at the fork, otherwise "his breath would not have returned to his lifeless body" (Beaglehole & Beaglehole 1935: 15–6).

While the Hopi practiced communication with the dead (Titiev 1944: 135, 172), it was not to seek knowledge about the afterlife. Nor did they have vision quests or other trance practices, "and did not believe in illness caused by soul loss" (Levy 1992: 127). Therefore, NDEs appear to be the primary source of Hopi knowledge about the afterlife. While the Hopi did have related myths, they lacked the typical Orpheus plot.

In one example, an Oraibi boy was curious about the afterlife, so his father arranged for a shamanic figure to give the boy "medicine" to make him die temporarily.[18] On a westward road, the boy was interrogated about what he was doing there. When he replied that he wanted to learn about the other realm, he was told that he had taken the wrong path. He was forced to wait a few days, then proceeded on a path through cactus and agave plants to a cliff where he met a chief. After asking why the boy was there, the chief showed him a particular house, just discernable through dense smoke. He arranged the boy's kilt as a parachute, and threw him over the cliff. The boy descended slowly then walked until he met Skeleton Woman. She warned him about a road leading to annihilation, and told him that the smoke was from "the wicked" being burned. Proceeding to Skeleton House, the boy was greeted by villagers who perceived *him* as a skeleton. They asked who he was, then led him to the house of his ancestors. He could not ascend the ladder to the house, however, because it was made of sunflower stalks. The spirits laughed at him when he ate, for the dead only consume the essence of food. The boy observed that the other world was "not as light" as Earth, and with poor living conditions. There were temporary punishments that were particularly bad for those who mistreated women, such as carrying bundles of cactus while naked. Good chiefs kept their *tiponis* (sacred ceremonial object) in the spirit land, and benefited from funerary offerings on Earth. The spirits gave the boy instructions on rituals to perform for their benefit when he returned to

Earth, in exchange for "rain and crops." They then sent him back, telling him it was not his time to be there. He successfully found his body, reentered it, and came back to life, convinced that people survive bodily death and that their fates are determined by their earthly behavior (Voth 1905: 114–9).[19]

Maski was a realm of creation and fertility, and could be reached via the Grand Canyon, or through graves. Earthly order was reversed, for it is day in the underworld when the sun passes through during Earth's night. Seasons were also reversed, and underworld spirits walked backward in the kiva (ritual meeting room) and wore reversed face markings. Otherwise, life was similar to that on Earth, with continued traditions, religion, and agriculture. As well as being associated with the sun (and hence a being of light), Maasaw was a fertility deity who helped humans emerge from the underworld at the time of creation (Titiev 1944: 107, 171–4; Tyler 1964: 3–6, 8). Kwanitakas became Kachinas (spirit beings) who assisted humans at the emergence, guarded the underworld gate, and directed souls onto the correct path after reading their minds (Colton 1959: 79).

In the Tusayan Hopi afterlife, a spirit named Tokonaka conducted judgments. Depending on the degree of purification achieved in afterlife fires, a "bad" soul would proceed to "Sipapû, the Underworld from which it came," be "transformed into a prayer-beetle" or an ant, or be annihilated (Fewkes 1899: 647). Members of societies other than the Kwanitaka went to lakes, springs, mountains, or the center of the Earth, while deceased chiefs became flowers and plants (Titiev 1944: 136 n.48; Tyler 1964: 14–5, 59). Some ascended a stick placed in their graves, and became clouds. There were also different fates depending on marital or tribal status (Beaglehole & Beaglehole 1935: 12, 13; Titiev 1944: 36, 177, 230). The soul was seen as a weightless "breath-body" (*hik'si*), which could remain in communication with the living. They could even "leave the underworld in vaporous forms and, becoming cloud-people, pass over their former villages to bring rain." They could also revisit Earth in the form of masked, painted Kachinas (Fewkes 1924: 381; Titiev 1944: 108).

Cochiti

A 1924 narrative concerns a man who was habitually cruel to animals and who disbelieved in life after death. He died while sucking snake eggs, when a snake flew down his throat to retrieve them. He was taken by "chief priests" on the road to Shipap, where he saw melons that could only be eaten by those who "have a good heart and believe in everything." They entered Shipap through a door and encountered men sitting in a smoke-filled room, unhappy about the man's deeds. The chief instructed his messengers to "take him back to his own body or they will bury it," and advised the man to "believe in everything." The man knelt and asked forgiveness, and the messengers returned him to his body. He subsequently became a better person, ceasing to mistreat animals, and believing "in all the kachinas and medicine men."

When an acting chief died, he was returned to this world because it was not yet his time to die. He had to first become a full chief, and learn "how to take care of his people." On his return journey, he was shown various types of afterlife punishments for "bad" people, as well as happy spirits and reunited couples. Messengers took him back to his body, which was being prepared for burial. He was afraid of it, however, and reluctant to reenter, so the messengers had to push him back in. When he revived, he "gave the people all that he had been told and he cared for them."

In a narrative with Orpheus themes, a woman's prolonged mourning prevented her daughter from progressing in the other world. Her refusal to bathe made her daughter dirty, so the spirits convinced her to wash, then took her to the other world to see that her daughter was well. When she returned, her body was about to be buried. The spirit chief told her "Don't be afraid of your own body," and when her daughter threw her into it she returned to life.

A shaman who was close to death was taken to the other world, and shown rewards and punishments. "People who committed evil deeds" were placed under an iceberg, tied to a post and starved, or kept in a corral. Those "who have done good deeds on the earth" went to a beautiful realm of dancing and plenty. Good shamans had a separate place, and the man recognized spirits of fellow shamans he had known in life. Bad shamans were burned or suffered other punishments. The man's guide instructed him to tell his people what he saw, in order to renew their faith (Benedict 1931: 128–32; 255–6).

Zuni

In 1928, a woman died of measles, saw "a bright light in the room," and left her body. She traveled westward to meet her deceased grandfather and aunts "still living the way we do." The experience not only resulted in a change in the woman's own beliefs ("I never believed that could happen but it really did"), but she was thereafter made a healer as a member of a medicine society (Bunzel 1932: 481–2; cf. Wade 2003: 94–5; Kalweit 1988: 204). Furthermore, her experience was inconsistent with Zuni afterlife conceptions[20] in which the dead remain near the body for four days, change shape, become the wind, or enter the "lake of the kachinas" (Wade 2003: 95). This suggests that the experience was largely independent of its cultural context. Indeed, the Zuni saw "all visionary states" as "dangerous individualism" (Hultkrantz 1953: 146).

Great Plains and Great Basin
Sioux

Anna Gayton (1935: 277) observed that "supposed actual visits to the land of the dead are not uncommon or unnatural experiences in the Plains." According to the amateur ethnologist James Athearn Jones (1829: 225), the Dakota Sioux learned about the afterlife from a shaman named Akkeewaisee. While in a trance state "for many moons," he was led by the "Manitou of Dreams" through a cave and over mountains, rivers, forests, and regions of intense heat and cold, until finally reaching a precipice. There he saw many people, including some he had known on Earth, preparing for the "dangerous test of their good or bad deeds, the unerring trial of their guilt or purity." A man too lazy to hunt fell "into the depths below, where the Evil Spirit received him into his arms, and condemned him to . . . a life of labour and fatigue." A man who had deserted in battle fought eternally with the tribe he had fled, and a liar who disbelieved in the powers of shamans met a similar fate. A man who had struck his mother and spat at his father was chained to a wheel rolling on the floor. Akkeewaisee then took the path of good spirits, following the encampments and fires they made on their journey to the next world. Eventually he reached Wanare-tebe, the realm of Waktan Tanka (Great Spirit). There were streams, flowers, groves, buffalo on a prairie, fine hunting, and villages "blissful and happy beyond measure." Akkeewaisee met the spirits of his mother and father, and proceeded to the village where his people dwelled. He asked if the dead could visit Earth, and they explained that they could do so only when dying children needed guides to take them to Wanare-tebe. Akkeewaisee's soul then "reanimated his body, and he awoke. He related to the people of the tribe his dream of the Land of departed Spirits," and it was recounted through the generations.

In 1849, a man named Male Elk died then revived on his funeral-scaffold two days later. He told of how his soul had traveled along the "path of braves" and through a land of idyllic natural beauty. He swam across a river to the village of his ancestors, and met his uncle. The uncle would not allow him to eat, for doing so would prevent him from returning to Earth (Tylor 1871 52, n. 1).

One day when White Bull was nine years old (1858), he "fell asleep and 'died.' His soul seemed to leave his body, and was in another place." A naked man, painted with zigzag stripes and riding a black horse, told him to pay close attention so he could later accurately tell his people about the experience. He then transformed White Bull into a plant by piercing him through the heart with a lance, and instructed him to kill a painted cow when he returned to Earth. After additional dreamlike encounters, White Bull was given the "power to look in four directions and kill a man in all four," and "victory when riding horses" of four particular colors. The experience "made him brave," and he grew up to become a warrior. Later in life, White Bull became "so ill that he went out of his head. His soul left his body." A man dressed in white approached from the west and took him to Cherry Creek (an earthly location). Four other men approached from the north, wishing to befriend White Bull. A living buffalo skeleton then emerged from underground and grew flesh, hide, and hair. He said he had been appointed to help White Bull, and told him to eat some particular roots. When they located them on the prairie, White Bull awoke in his bed. His wife procured the same roots, fed them to White Bull, and he was cured (Vestal 1934: 12–5, 249–50; DeMallie 1984: 85–6). These accounts contain many detailed, perhaps hallucinatory idiosyncrasies alongside familiar NDE elements such as OBE, another realm, precognitive information, and transformation upon return.

When Black Elk was just five years old (1868), he had a spontaneous experience in which two men descended from the sky, singing to him, "a sacred voice is calling you" (DeMallie 1984: 109). Four years later, he had an NDE in which the same men appeared and took him into the clouds, where his grandfather called for him. He could see his parents below, looking at his body, and he felt sad to be leaving them as he ascended on a cloud. The men showed him a vision of many different horses in all directions, one of which carried him through a rainbow gate to a lodge where his "six grandfathers" were "having a council." The first four represented the cardinal points, the fifth "the Great Spirit above," and the sixth was himself, aging in reverse from an old man to his nine-year-old self. He was given curing water, herbs, and "the power of the four quarters," and was instructed to use his new powers to help his people. Black Elk's account of this twelve-day experience runs to thirty pages (ibid. 111–42), and features (1) typical NDE thematic elements such as OBE and seeing one's own corpse, a positive and transcendent place of bright light, deceased ancestors, intermediate states, prophetic visions, reentering the body, and positive fruits of the experience (cf. Wade 2003: 99–100); (2) clear cultural elements, including human-animal/plant transformations, sacred sticks, acquiring powers, and references to particular indigenous people, dress, places, and shelters; and (3) individual, idiosyncratic elements such as multiple ascents, a man of fire in the center of the Earth, flaming rainbows, drinking a little blue man in a cup, and a horse's life review. The narrative also features correspondences to Ghost Dance teachings and practices, such as a sacred tree, dancing in a circle, and themes of vanquishing whites and reestablishing traditional culture and lifestyle. As such, the account functioned to legitimize Black Elk's authority as the famous, powerful Oglala Lakota Sioux Ghost Dance leader he became (DeMallie 1984: 259).

Indeed, Black Elk's deliberately sought Ghost Dance visions were very much like his ostensibly spontaneous NDE, and all included the attainment of divine knowledge and instructions through spiritual means. In one he was met by two men who told him told it was not yet his time to meet his Father, then showed him a Ghost Dance shirt to reproduce on Earth for his people (DeMallie 1984: 261–2). In another, a Native Christ-like figure[21] radiating light stated that "earthly things that grow" belong to him as decreed by the Father, then instructed Black Elk to preach the message to his people. Twelve women taught Black Elk a song, and twelve men gave him special sticks to take back with him. He returned by crossing a perilous river (ibid. 266).

Black Elk had a second NDE while in Paris in 1889, again ascending on a cloud, then traveling to his home and family. He awoke in a doctor's office, having been pronounced dead. Black Elk's mother later corroborated his OBE visit, claiming that she had seen him returning home on a cloud in a dream (ibid. 252, 255).[22]

Black Elk himself referred to all his experiences as "visions," and did not seem to place greater empirical value on one type over another. He did, however, emphasize that they were not dreams, and that they "actually happened" (ibid. 109). Seeking such experiences through a "vision quest" was integral to Lakota tradition. They "invested a man with a supernatural aura," and gave him "special knowledge and power." Though considered "special," childhood visionary experiences were not uncommon, particularly among individuals who later became religious leaders or warriors (ibid. 83–4).

Ute

The Mormon missionary and interpreter Dimick Huntington (1919: 317–8) reported the NDE of a man named Wah-ker. Around 1840, he "died and his spirit went to heaven." He met "the Lord sitting upon a throne dressed in white," and though he wanted to stay, "the Lord told him that he must return to earth." He gave Wah-ker a new name, and prophetic information about the coming of the white people "who would be his friends, and he must treat them kindly."

Cheyenne

Of the Cheyenne afterlife realm, Grinnell (1928: 91–3) wrote that "Occasionally people who have been very sick believe that they have died and have gone to this country, and then have returned again." Picking Bones Woman vividly recalled her NDE of 1848, fifty-four years after its occurrence. While she was seriously ill, a voice called to her that she was wanted by her deceased mother. Feeling "as if she were flying," she floated northward to a door in a large bluff. She crashed through to the other side and was met by old men in buffalo robes, including one she recognized who had been long dead. They told her that her mother had "gone back," and that she must return to Earth with her husband's baby. She did so, and back in her lodge she noticed her body lying lifeless on her bed. Somehow finding herself back in her body, she realized that no baby was there and that her body had never left the lodge.

Cree

The Geologist and explorer Henry Youle Hind (1860: 129–31) reported an NDE he had heard on a 1858 expedition. A Plains Cree man "was sick and fell asleep," then awoke surrounded by heavy mists "on the bank of a deep river, whose waters were flowing swiftly and black". On the southern side of the river were the "bright and glorious" "happy hunting grounds," and to the north were the "dark and gloomy ... hunting grounds of bad Indians." The man tried to cross to the southern side, but "the recollection of bad deeds prevented [him] from stemming the current," and he was swept onto the north bank instead. He "spent many moons" in this "dreary land," trying to hunt but always near starvation, "hurt by enemies, or wet and cold and miserable." He eventually reached another river crossing, and because he had been good during his time in the dreary land, he was able to swim against the current and successfully reached the happy side. All his sorrows vanished when he saw the people, buffalo, and clear sky, and he felt "a warm, fresh, scented, happy breeze." He fell asleep then woke up in his body, which lay inside a tent.

In a 1913 narrative, an old man named Loud-Voice died and followed a trail "to a fine place where everything was pleasant." After returning to life he repeated the journey on later occasions, until the spirits tried to keep him in the other world. He escaped by transforming into a snake, then a fly, and finally an owl (Skinner 1916: 363).

Paiute

In 1870, the Commissioner of Indian Affairs witnessed the Northern Paiute shaman Wodziwob in a trance while others in his tribe sang "a song that was to guide the spirit back to the body." When he revived, Wodziwob initiated a new dance, and related how spirits of the dead and the Supreme Ruler were on their way from the spirit realms to transform Earth "into a paradise" (Mooney 1896: 702–3). After one dance, Wodziwob claimed to have died and met the dead (du Bois 1939: 5). A roughly contemporary prophet named Winawitu went "to the spirit land in a four-hour trance," and saw "spirits generally enjoying themselves." He returned from his experience with newfound clairvoyant and prophetic powers, and preached "rejuvenation by dancing," and peace with the Europeans (ibid. 3).

In 1888, Wovoka (Jack Wilson) was ill with a serious fever. He lost conscious-ness and was taken to the spirit world where he saw deceased ancestors, "all happy and forever young" in an idealized mirror image of Earth. God told him he must return to his people to preach a message of love, universal peace, hard work, and no fighting, lying, or stealing. As a reward they would attain a positive afterlife among their friends, without illness or death. Wovoka became a religious leader who claimed he could control the weather, and taught a Christian-influenced prophecy of eschatological regeneration: Jesus in cloud-form would resurrect the dead, ushering in a new golden age, and the dead should therefore not be mourned. Wovoka also brought the Ghost Dance back from the other world, which would accelerate the prophecy's fulfillment and help devotees glimpse the afterlife in dreams. He subsequently underwent further trance-visits to the other world (Mooney 1896: 701–2, 772–4, 778, 781). The religion, with local variation, spread far and wide across the continent to tens of thousands of people in 30–35 tribes, even uniting previously warring peoples. It was maintained through expe-riential validation in dream cults, and through deliberately sought trance-visions of the dead brought about by prolonged dancing (ibid. 784ff, 926–7).[23]

Tsuu T'ina (Sarcee)

In 1875, a woman named Katie Dodginghorse recounted "a true story" she had heard from her great-grandparents, about a man who left his body and went to "a beautiful place." An official sitting at a desk writing in the "Book of Life" did not turn to greet the man, but merely told him it was not his time to die. He was sent back to Earth with precognitive abilities and various other miraculous skills, and became a prophet. "So the Indians believed there is a better place for them," Dodginghorse concluded.

In the second half of the nineteenth century, the Tsuu T'ina Ghost Dance was explained by an Orpheus myth in which a man told his wife in anger, "I wish you were a ghost!" The next day he found that both she and their child had been reduced to bones. In mourning, he traveled to the spirit world to find her. The spirits taught him a dance that enabled him to bring her back, and when he returned to Earth he introduced it to his people as a mode of healing and curing (Jenness 1938: 97–8).

Shoshone

During a prolonged illness c. 1890, a Shoshone man named Enga-gwacu (Red-shirt) Jim had a vision in which the sun told him he was going to die, but that he could come back to life if he wished. His soul, which was ten inches tall, left through his thigh. He looked back at his body and saw that it was still breathing, but after three paces it "dropped, cold and dead." Something passed suddenly through his soul, then he descended and found himself in "another world." He encountered a helper of the sun-god A'po who was "making some dead men over again." A'po, described as "a handsome Indian," told him, "You don't look very ill," then withdrew a "thin wire" from a leather bag and tapped it three times. Enga-gwacu Jim was suddenly able to see A'po's hands, which were "as small and clean as a baby's."

> Then the whole world opened up and I could see the Earth plainly. I saw everything there. I saw my own body lying there dead. The Sun told me I would be restored to life (Lowie 1909: 301–2).

Enga-gwacu Jim had a later experience in which he ascended to the clouds and met skeleton people, including some friends, in a world filled with sagebrush. After these experiences, he "questioned Shoshone medicine-men concerning a hereafter; but mistrusts both their statements and those of the missionaries, because they fail to tally with his personal experiences" (ibid. 229).

In 1910, a shaman died temporarily by going into a trance and sending his soul to the land of the dead in order to rescue a young boy who was ill. The boy was playing with dead children across a mountain, and was reluctant to return. The shaman persuaded him, and the boy regained consciousness and was cured (Hultkrantz 1992: 78, 92). In the mid-twentieth century, it was still maintained that "some living persons are said to have gone over to the other side in a state of coma, and they have reported a life of 'happy hunting grounds.'" The soul could also leave the body in dreams and through disease or witchcraft, during which time it could wander to the spirit land (ibid. 83).

Blackfoot

An 1896 narrative tells of how "Old Person once died for a day and a night, but his spirit returned to his body." He reported that he had traveled to the afterlife realm (Sand Hills), but was not admitted because "his time to die had not yet come." Sand Hills was located "far east on the plains," and was surrounded by quicksand to keep out the living. The dead spent their days hunting buffalo, and eating berries and other earthly foods (McClintock 1923: 115).

In an Orpheus myth, a man dreamed that an old woman gave him the power to travel to the land of the dead to retrieve his wife. One of his deceased relatives acted as guide, but only after first trying to frighten the man away with "fearful noises" and "strange and terrible things," then interrogating him: "Where are you going, and who told you to come here?" A ghost warned the man to be careful, or risk dying in the other world. On his arrival, a feast was held in his honor, though his relatives refused to attend because of his bad smell until the host masked it with burning pinewood. The host then persuaded the relatives to allow the man to take his wife back to Earth. They gave him "a medicine pipe, the Worm Pipe," then escorted the couple on the four-day journey. During this time, the man could not look at his wife or she would disappear forever. Back at their village, the couple underwent purification in a sweat lodge to be reintegrated into earthly life. However, one night when the wife did not immediately do as the man asked, he picked up a firebrand as if to strike her, and she disappeared (Grinnell 1892: 127–31). The narrative functioned, in part, as an origin myth of the sacred Worm Pipe; and as a spirit-sanctioned condemnation of wife beating.

Pawnee

According to the oldest members of a Pawnee community in 1892, their afterlife beliefs originated in dreams of dwelling with the creator deity Tirawa, in communications with souls of the dead, and in experiences "of being dead ourselves, and of meeting these people and talking with them, and going to war with them" (Grinnell 1893: 355). Concluding an Orpheus narrative, one informant remarked, "Then people were convinced that there must be a life after this one" (ibid. 194). A chief named Secret Pipe related his own NDE:

> I was dead once. Just as I died, I found my way leading to an Indian village. I entered it, and went straight to the lodge of my friends and my relations. . . . I even knew my old relations, whom I had never looked on when I was alive. I went into a lodge, but I was not offered a seat, and I thought that I was not welcome. I came out of the lodge, and went out of the village toward the west. Then I came to life again. In the morning I had died, and I came to life in the afternoon. That must be the reason I still live, and am getting old. I was not welcome yet. They did not receive me. From this I am convinced that there is life after we are dead. (ibid. 356–7)

A Skidi Pawnee narrative tells of a young man who died and had an OBE, during which he saw his body and his grave being dug. As he headed east along a well-trodden path, a voice told him to stop and get inside a black brass kettle that descended on a rope from above. The man did so, and ascended in the kettle to another realm, where he was met by four men, painted red and wearing buffalo robes. They directed him to some swans, which explained that one path was for warriors and another was "bloody." Not being a warrior, he took the latter and saw many flowers growing, and he was crowned with garlands. Ahead was a knoll with a fire that "increased" as he approached, until it enveloped him. He continued westward until the fire waned, and in its place sat Tirawa in the form of a golden eagle (an idiosyncratic notion conflicting with usual Skidi belief; Dorsey 1904c: 342, n.127). Tirawa directed him to the path of chiefs, which took him to the village of his relatives where he saw children playing, young men practicing shooting arrows, women skinning buffalo, and ponies which he had known in life. His uncle emerged from a new, white tipi and told him that he smelled bad, then explained that he was too young to be in the Spirit Land and must return to Earth to become a warrior and chief. He gave his nephew a new robe, beads, the title of "chief," and strings of feathers associated with a mystery he must learn. The man reentered his body just as it was being lowered into the grave. As predicted, he subsequently became a great warrior, shaman, and chief. He only related the experience when he was an old man, deciding that his people should know the fates of their relatives (ibid. 69–70).

In a Pitahauirat Pawnee Orpheus narrative similar to the Blackfoot example above, in keeping with Pawnee mourning ritual a young man spent several days on the grave of his sweetheart, crying, fasting, and losing weight (ibid. 341, n. 125). Eventually he went to a village to seek food, and found the girl surrounded by the grave goods that had been buried with her. She told him that her relatives would help them return to Earth together, but that he could not touch her. They proceeded back to her grave, but when she saw her uncles mourning there she tried to get away, for she was tired of their visits and offerings. The man attracted the attention of the uncles, and together they succeeded in restraining the girl. She remained a ghost, however, for her bones were still buried. The couple had a son and lived happily for many years, but during an argument he beat her until she disappeared in a whirlwind, which spiraled out the roof opening. The next day their child died and was buried with her. The man mourned for four days until his ghost-wife reappeared, and reminded him that "when we die we live again." She told him that because of his abuse, the living could no longer visit the land of the dead (Dorsey 1906: 13, 126–35, collected 1899–1903).[24] The narrative was classed as "true" by the Pawnee, and was believed to have actually taken place. Its condemnation of wife beating, explanation of the barrier between realms, and implied precepts of limiting offerings and extending mourning at graves would thus have been seen as having experiential authority.

In a Kitkehahki Pawnee version intended to educate about the afterlife, the Wind told the man to cease his mourning, then guided him to other world. An old woman seated on a sage carpet told him that he must journey through darkness and cross a log over a black stream. In the Spirit Land "all was light" and people were dancing, including the man's wife. He was instructed to throw mud balls at her, which brought about her return to Earth, though she again departed due to his abuse. Like the Pitahauirat narrative, it was considered factual and served to explain certain rites or ceremonies—in this case, the origin of the Elk dance, which the man learned in the Spirit Land. Such narratives also included shamanic themes such as extreme stress leading to the experience, assistance from supernatural entities, a perilous journey, soul retrieval, and acquisition of knowledge in spirit realms (Dorsey 1906: 411–3). Elements such as entering darkness, emerging into light, deceased relatives, encountering other entities, barriers or limits, and reluctance to return are also consistent with NDEs.

Kiowa

Through fasting and prayer, the Kiowa prophet Bi'anki (who became known as Asa'tito'la, "The Messenger") undertook "frequent visits to the spirit world" in order to obtain knowledge and information for his people. In a narrative of one such experience, he described traveling across a plain of buffalo and ponies until he reached the spirit village. He met four women he had known in life, who arrived on horseback with sacks of wild plums. They told him where to find his deceased brothers, and he went to greet them as they arrived in the village from a buffalo hunt. He then returned the way he had come, meeting "two curious beings" on the way, which he depicted as green triangular figures with crosses at their tops. They told him to continue, and he came upon a large Ghost Dance circle where he saw another woman he had known on Earth. He then sought the rest of his relatives and was directed to a tipi on the other side of the village. There he found his father, siblings, chidren and others. They offered him meat, and shortly after refusing it, he woke up on the mountain where he had gone into his trance (Mooney 1896: 909–11). Bi'anki illustrated this vision (ibid. pl. CVII), depicting the spirit village, his peoples' tipi, his female friends and deceased brothers on horseback, the Ghost Dance circle, and the path he took through the spirit world. The cover of the present book features another of Bi'anki illustrations, and is labeled "drawing of his vision to the spirit world" without further elucidation. With some speculative imagination, perhaps we can see themes such as radiant light, darkness, paths, tunnel, spirit beings, and a deity. It was drawn originally on separate sheets, which presumably indicate different stages of the experience. In a photograph of Bi'anki, he displays the drawing while explaining its meaning—giving religious teachings based on his experiences (ibid. 910; pl. CVI) which conflicted in part with Kiowa beliefs (Martin 2013: 112).

A'aninin (Gros Ventre)

In 1901, an elderly man reported a frightening and apparently hallucinatory NDE he had when young. While his body was being prepared for burial, he headed north to Cypress Hills. He was chased and caught by a small bear, which clung to his leg. At an enormous camp along a creek, naked men and women caught the boy in order to eat him. He escaped and returned to his body. As is often the case with negative NDEs (Greyson and Bush 1992), the man awoke in a distressed, confusional state (believing he had brought the bear with him, unable to recognize his people, losing his senses, relapsing; Kroeber 1908: 276–7).

Arikara

White Owl fainted while tending his ponies, and died shortly thereafter. He traveled on a path heading east, then found himself in some kind of enclosure with "a little hole" through which he could see people in a village. He wanted to join them but was stopped by a man who instead directed him to a lodge on a hill, telling him that only the dead could enter the village. Inside the lodge were many people, painted red and playing black drums. They danced with willow sticks that represented living relatives, and called for their deaths so that they would come to the spirit world. They wanted White Owl to stay, but a man told him he must return to his own land (Dorsey 1904b: 152–3).

Wichita

In a Wichita Orpheus narrative reminiscent of Pawnee versions, a man in deep mourning for his wife traveled to the land of the dead, assisted by the spirit of a deceased friend. To bring her back, he had to throw mud balls at his dancing wife, and was not allowed to touch her. He also had to join war parties, and to hunt and kill a buffalo then return it to life by kicking it and rubbing its fat all over his own body. Back on Earth, everyone was glad to see him, having believed he had died; but when he slept with another woman, his wife returned to the spirit world. The man described the otherworld as an idealized version of Earth, and explained that those who died in battle went to a happier realm than those who died of illness. This led to a change in belief, and from that time forward men fought with increased bravery (Dorsey 1904a: 301–4). In an alternate version, the man is referred to as the one "who told that there is such a thing as death and life again after death" (ibid. 310).

Crow

According to Lowie (1922: 383–4), the Crow were generally unconcerned with the afterlife, often lacking such beliefs altogether. For some, however, NDEs generated personal beliefs, filling a void left by the lack of culturally sanctioned ideas about the afterlife: "Those who had any conceptions based them on the reports of tribesmen who are believed to have died and returned to consciousness." One man who revived after being killed by a gunshot wound "told the people that all the dead were camped together and had a better way of living than the Crow; hence he said, 'Don't be afraid to die.'" Another "died and came to life again. He said that all who had died were still living and that they were better people than the Crow. The Crow believed it." Despite being insulted in the other world, one man who returned to life "was eager to go back to the dead again and died once more soon after." Another returned after arguing with his deceased brother, and reported "that the dead had a camp like ours and a good way of living."

These four brief examples dating from 1907–16 show clear cultural influence, such as westward travel on a road, river crossings, horse riding, tipi camps, and local earthly features. Typical NDE elements include traveling toward light, deceased relatives, a land of joy and happiness, barriers and limits, being instructed to return to the body by a spirit authority, reluctance to return, and loss of fear of death after reviving. Corresponding to a general disinterest in the afterlife, Crow traditions of dreams, visions, and shamanic activity lack afterlife-related themes (Lowie 1922: 323–73), and NDEs thus appear to have been a separate category from these other types of phenomena.

Northwest
Dakelh (Carrier)

Early in the nineteenth century, a Wet'suwet'en man named Bini wandered off during a grave illness. His "cold and half desiccated" corpse was discovered months later in nearby woods (Barbeau 1923: 19ff). During his funerary ritual, he came to life, singing. He could no longer speak Wet'suwet'en, and knew only the language of the Sky-beings. Through a ritual, he enabled a youth to understand and interpret for him, and described how his "mind embraced the whole world" when he died. A voice called him, and he spiritually ascended a ladder that appeared from above: "It was only my shade that was climbing, for my body was left behind." He "pierced the sky vault slowly" as if being born into it, and saw "the four corners of Heaven." To the west was "a very old man, as tall as a tree, as white as snow," and many white people were sitting motionless. To the east were spirits dressed in white, dancing, drumming, and singing. After relating the experience, Bini died then revived again. This time he told of encountering "the two head-chiefs of the Sky," the Father and his son, Zazeekry ("Jesus Christ" in corrupted French pronunciation [Lanoue 1993: 455]). They told Bini of an impending plague and apocalypse, which would be brought about by the sins and traditional customs of his people, and by their ignorance of the Cross and baptism. Bini was baptized, and instructed to preach repentance, baptism, and the sign of the cross to his people. A week later, he again died and returned, this time preaching Christian strictures and displaying items brought back from Heaven—a prayer calendar, a cross, and a white cloth with curative properties. He also had new supernatural powers, including telepathy, precognitive dreaming, and causing dead twigs to blossom (Barbeau 1923: 38–40). The experience was said to have occurred prior to missionary influence, and "even the appearance of the earliest white men" in the region. Bini prophesied their arrival, their animals and technology, and that "they will make life easy for us." Regardless of whether Bini had prior knowledge of Europeans, or whether the narrative was elaborated over time to lend it more credence, or indeed whether it was genuine clairvoyance, it is evident that his experience led directly to new religious beliefs for himself, his people, and other tribes. His system "became the law of the country," combining indigenous traditions with Christianity, together with the new experiential element of the Prophet Dance, which participants hoped would enable them to ascend to Heaven. Bini's experience also resulted in a change in afterlife conceptions: "Instead of the Cave-of-the-Dead our home shall be the Sky where the white spirits sing and dance near the gate of sunrise" (ibid. 33, 42, 48–9, 57).

In the 1920s, the Wet'suwet'en stated that many of their people had seen the road to the afterlife realm "when at the point of death." In one example, a man followed his wife there by being buried alive with her. The road was lined with berries, but the husband could neither eat nor drink since he was still alive. They reached a precipice and a river, with a black town for the dead on one side, and a red town for robins on the other. Both sent canoes for the wife, and though she wanted to take the black one, her husband convinced her to take the red one so he could eat. However, an old woman appeared and warned them that eating would make them unable to return to Earth. When spirits offered them frogs, snakes, lizards, and huckleberries which were really the eyes of dead men, the couple gave them to the old woman. The next day she told them how to return to the precipice in order to ascend back to Earth. Rather than a filthy road for dead dogs, they chose a barely visible path, and had to cross an undulating snake spanning the "river of death." They finally reached the summit, arrived at their graves, and reentered their bodies. An attending shaman called to his people and they joyfully exhumed the couple. The wife, however, was unhappy because she experienced everything in reverse: eating tree bark instead of berries, feeling cold in summer and hot in winter. When she died again, her husband did not follow. "It was from this medicine-man, and from the salmon boy,[25] that the Indians learned where people go when they die. They alone of all living beings have visited the land of the dead" (Jenness 1934: 143–5).

Tenino and Santiam

Sometime before the 1850s, a Tenino boy named Dla'upac died and went to heaven, then revived after five days. He claimed that he had met God, who told him about the impending destruction of the world and the resurrection of the dead (Spier 1935: 21–2; cf. Ruby & Brown 1989: 6).

A Santiam man c. 1928–36 explained ho\w "long ago" individuals sometimes died then returned to life, and told of how their spirits had traveled to the other realm but were sent back because it was not their time to die. The spirits in the other world would say, "We do not want you to come here yet. When we want you to come, we will tell you" (Jacobs 1945: 74).

Makah

In 1858, a man named Harshlah died of an illness. He revived in his grave but managed to free himself. After convincing his people that he was not a ghost, he recounted his journey to the underworld, where he saw friends and relatives living an enjoyable life. They had no bones, only the skin and flesh that had rotted from their physical bodies. They told Harshlah that he smelled bad, and made him return to Earth. The event led to a change in Makah funerary practices, for "Since then they have been very particular to secure all bodies so firmly that a revival is hopeless." The information Harshlah gave about the afterlife validated "their ancient ideas," which made it impossible for missionaries "to teach them our views of a future state." The Makah concluded that the European afterlife was in heaven and that theirs was in the center of the Earth, though they also believed in reincarnation. Nevertheless, the Makah had little concern for the afterlife (Swan 1869: 62–4, 83–4).

Wanapum

Around 1860, Smohalla was killed in a fight with a rival shaman. He revived and proclaimed that he had been "in the spirit world and had now returned by divine command to guide his people." Having witnessed his death, his people believed him and accepted his teachings on the authority of his experience. Smohalla's message was consistent with other revitalization movement prophets. His new "Dreamer" religion (Washani) combined local belief and ritual with elements of Catholicism and perhaps Mormonism, though he himself claimed unfamiliarity with Christianity (Ruby & Brown 1989: 37). Washani spread to many neighboring tribes, introducing a system of hereditary priests, and new dances and ceremonies. The religion was sustained, in part, by further experiences in which

Smohalla apparently died, left his body, went to the spirit world, and returned with additional revelations; and by the trance-visions of his followers via repetitive ceremonial singing and drumming. Smohalla taught that the greatest wisdom came from dreams, and from participating in Dreamer rituals (Mooney 1896: 718–9, 723, 726–8).

Sanpoil and Syilx

Contemporary with Smohalla, Skolaskin (born c. 1839) died after a prolonged illness, and revived while his body was being prepared for burial. He awoke singing a new song, and described how he had reached a gate on his journey to the land of the dead. A man asked Skolaskin where he was going, then told him that he could not proceed and must return to his body. Before doing so, a previously unknown creator deity, Quilentsuten, gave Skolaskin new moral strictures for his people, and instructed him to teach a seventh day of rest, devotion to Quilentsuten, and that the good and faithful would have a positive afterlife reunited with their loved ones (ibid. 148). Skolaskin's power and authority were cemented when he successfully predicted an earthquake (Ray 1936: 68–9, 71–3; Ruby & Brown 1989: 135, 148, 225 n.11).

A woman of the nearby Syilx people explained how "Some dead Indians come alive" and tell of their experiences in the other world. Her grandfather recounted having traveled on a road to a place of singing, dancing, and games, meeting deceased relatives, seeing souls being rewarded and punished, and being sent back to "work off your sins." Around 1872, a young man named Qwelasken died of an illness, then returned to life five days later. He claimed to have met God in the other world, who warned him of the end of the world. Qwelasken correctly predicted an earthquake, preached Christianity, and had revelatory divine dreams (Cline 1930: 172–3).

Tsimshian and Nisga'a

The Anglican missionary William Duncan recounted how most Tsimshian shamans were selected:

> if a man or woman is taken in a fit, and remains motionless for so long that they are concluded dead, should such a one ultimately recover, that is the person who is regarded as competent to deal with diseases; for it is believed, that, during the period of unconsciousness, supernatural power and skill were vouchsafed them.

Their afterlife beliefs involved a heavenly realm for the good, and an underworld for the bad (Mayne 1862: 289). The ruler of the dead was himself a shaman, who assisted others in soul retrieval (Hultkrantz 1957: 95). Franz Boas (1916: 323–4) recounted a shamanic initiation myth involving retrieving souls from the other world and bringing the dead and dying back to life (cf. ibid. 473).

A Nisga'a narrative "explains the ideas of the ... tribe regarding the future life" (ibid. 544). While his friends washed and dressed his lifeless body in preparation for his funeral, a man's soul was carried by a ghost to the other world. They followed a trail to a river, then a canoe ferried them to a town. There they met a chief who instructed a group of shamans to remove the man's heart. He was protected by an amulet worn around his neck, however, and was able to return to Earth and reenter his body.

Nuu-chah-nulth (Nootka)

The Scottish businessman G. M. Sproat (1868: 209, 212–4, 269, 273) lived with the Nuu-chah-nulth for two years, and described their beliefs in NDEs and shamanic soul retrieval. When a person was very ill,

> his soul (*Kouts-mah*) leaves his body and goes down into the country of Chay-her, but does not enter a house. If it enters a house, that is a sign that it has taken up its abode below for good, and the sick man dies.

If a shaman followed the soul to the other world and succeeded in rescuing it, he deposited it back in the patient's head and they recovered.

It was believed that souls had human shape and could "wander forth from the body and return at pleasure" (e.g., in dreams), and pass into other bodies (including animals). At death, chiefs and those killed in battle went to the realm of the deity Quawteaht to live a life of abundance, beauty, sunshine, and happiness. Others descended to Chay-her, which resembled an inferior version of Earth, with smaller game, no salmon, and inadequate blankets. Chay-her was sometimes personified as a boneless, bearded old man who would steal the souls of the living unless shamans intervened.

Kwakwaka'wakw (Kwakiutl)

In a late nineteenth-century narrative, a man named Lebid[26] died but could not be buried because the snow was too deep. Three days later, his people found him "singing his sacred song," surrounded by howling wolves. He awoke and described how he had left his body, and had seen it lying dead. A man came for him and he followed him into the woods until they arrived at a house. A "great sha-man" named Naualakume told Lebid that he must return to Earth so "that he may cure the sick in his tribe." Naualakume then vomited a quartz crystal and threw it into Lebid's sternum, which gave him "shamanistic power." Lebid, Naualakume, and other shamans wearing wolf masks went to sit by his corpse. Naualakume took the breath from the spirit-Lebid, and "blew it into the mouth" of his body. The sur-rounding wolves began licking the body, and Naualakume pressed on both Lebid's spirit head and his physical head, until his soul shrank to "the size of a large fly." Naualakume blew the soul into the body, and when Lebid revived he became a shaman, known for having come back to life (Boas 1930: 46–8).

Vomited quartz crystals, being licked by wolves, sacred songs, and other ele-ments of the narrative are known Kwakwaka'wakw shamanic initiatory motifs (ibid. 7, 44, 271; Boas 1966: 135). The shamanic context of the narrative may account for inconsistencies with Kwakwaka'wakw afterlife beliefs, in which the deceased ascends to an upper world as a bird, on a ladder, or on a "chain of arrows" through a windy doorway; or travels via canoe into the western horizon through a passage under the sea to finally reach the world of the ancestors (who may choose to be reborn on Earth), presided over by the Chief of the Sky (Boas 1935: 125). In any case, the narrative demonstrates an association between NDEs, afterlife beliefs, shamanism, and the elevation of certain experiencers to positions of religious importance.

Likewise, the narrative of a woman named Xu'ngwid tells of how she died during an illness, and went to "a very good place" with "a large, shining house." A man emerged and led her into the house where she met "our Lord." He told her "Your body is dead," and that her people back on Earth were mourning for her. Out of pity for them, he decided, "Now you will go back to your body." He called a shaman to "take the sickness out of the soul of Xu'ngwid." The shaman sang sacred songs, made the sign of the cross, and pressed on her head, neck, and stomach. The Lord then told her, "go into your body. Then immediately sing the sacred song sung by my shaman who set you right again. Now you will be a sha-man and you will have mercy and cure your people." Xu'ngwid did as instructed, and concluded, "Now I was a shaman after that" (Boas 1930: 54-6).

Kathlamet

In 1891, "one of the last survivors of the Chinook" related how his grandfather had died of a disease, but revived and told of his visit to the land of ghosts. He went to a house with crossbeams that he initially mistook for people; then encoun-tered a man who appeared to be dragging his own entrails, but they turned out to be a reed mat. There were people building canoes on the other side of a river, and the tall grass in which he stood made a bell-like sound that communicated his identity to them. He was greeted by a relative, who brought him a recently deceased girl he had desired on Earth. The man decided he no longer liked her, however, because she resembled her mother. His uncle then appeared and offered him seal meat, which he did not swallow because it tasted bad. Feeling insulted, he turned to leave "and at once the sun struck my right side." He "fell in a swoon" and found himself back with his people on Earth. The narrator added that before his grandfather's experience, shamans did not know about the afterlife, "but when he had been dead they learned about it" (Boas 1901: 247–51). When a person was ill and in danger of death, shamans were sent to retrieve their souls from the spirit world, and the sick person would revive. If the soul had taken the left-hand trail or entered the house of ghosts, however, return was impossible.

An Orpheus myth tells of Blue Jay's visit to the spirit land to look for his sister, who had been taken as a wife by ghosts. A bird told him the way, and when he arrived his sister asked if he was dead. Next to her were the bones of her husband, and at night the skeletons in the village came alive. Blue Jay went fishing with a boy, catching only leaves, branches, and logs. Though instructed by his sister to speak softly, when he heard singing coming from another canoe he joined in and the boy became a skeleton. When he stopped singing, the boy returned to normal. Blue Jay amused himself by trying the same trick with others, and by switching around the heads of adult and children skeletons. For this he was sent back to Earth, though because he did not follow all his sister's instructions, he died and returned to the land of spirits where things then seemed real (Boas 1893: 42–3).

Tlingit

As a source for Tlingit afterlife beliefs, Boas (1890: 843–4) was told of the NDEs of two shamans who had lived 150–200 years earlier (i.e., as early as 1690). The first died after a long illness, then revived some days later. He described sitting next to his body, feeling no pain, while his mother performed his funerary rituals. He tried to tell her that he was not dead, and to ask her for food, but she did not hear. When his people made funerary offerings to him, it satisfied his hunger. He then realized he was dead and decided to proceed to the "land of souls." At a fork in a road he took the well-trodden path, for by then he "longed to die" and go to the "country of the deceased." He reached a steep ledge at "the end of the world," with a river rushing below "formed by the tears shed by the women over the dead." Across the river in a village of the dead he saw people he recognized, including his deceased grandmother and uncle, and children he had tried to cure but failed. The dead could not hear him, and ignored his pleas to be taken across.

He went to sleep, and when he woke up someone finally came to ferry him to the other side. He was treated kindly, though forbidden from speaking of things on Earth. The spirits wanted him stay, but when he discovered that the food was inedible, the water undrinkable, and that "the spirits lead a miserable life" he decided to leave. Following a path beyond the river, he eventually "saw many hands growing out of the ground, and moving towards me, as though they were asking something." He then came to "a great fire" with "a sword swinging around" behind it, and "many eyes" were watching him. Though he hated the spirit world, he did not wish to return to Earth because his mother couldn't hear him. He thus decided to die a violent death in order to go to the realm of the deity Tahit. But when he thrust his head into the fire where the sword revolved, he returned to his body with a feeling of coldness. The reason more people do not return from the otherworld, he explained, was that they feared "the hands, the eyes, and the fire."

The other shaman, Ky'itl'a'c, committed suicide and ascended a ladder to the realm of Tahit. He was interrogated by "an old watchman, who was all black, and had curly hair," and was allowed to pass when he explained that he had killed himself. At the house of Tahit, the deity instructed two spirits to give Ky'itl'a'c a tour of "the whole country." They took him to a lake in the Milky Way, and gave him a pebble to try to throw at white geese floating there. The spirits sang when Ky'itl'a'c succeeded, making him laugh and feel like he was being tickled. They then took him "through the cloud door" to see Tahit's daughters. When Ky'itl'a'c saw Earth below he decided to return, so he pulled a blanket over his head and jumped. He made his way to a house where a baby was crying and effectively reincarnated into himself, for "He himself was the child, and when he came to be grown up he told the people of Tahit" and his realm—including that those who had been beheaded in this world "had their eyes between their shoulders in the upper world" (Boas 1890: 844–5). Tlingit afterlife fates were determined by mode of death, and the otherworld mirrored Earth. Those who died violently went to Tahit's heavenly realm, while women who died in childbirth and those who died of illness went "to a country beyond the borders of the earth." The dead in both realms joined together during daylight (ibid. 843).

In a late nineteenth-century narrative, a man named Mustak died for two days. When he revived he told of his perilous journey to a river, past thorny bushes and "beasts of the forest." A boatman took him to "spirit-land," where he met his uncle. He was unhappy to see Mustak, warned him not to eat anything, and told him to "hurry back, as fast as ever you can." Mustak instead decided to explore the village, which was a miserable place. Those who had not been cremated could not use fireplaces, so Mustak kindly gave them blankets. Others were starving, and they urged him to return to life and tell his people that they required more offerings of food, water, and blankets. His mother also instructed him to return, and to tell his people what he had experienced. She taught him a ritual to prevent further deaths "when a dead body is in the house," and Mustak finally left when the spirits grew so insistent "that they commenced beating me and clubbing me, until I was glad to run away."

Around the same time, a woman was said to have died and returned twice, and her claims similarly reinforced beliefs about offerings to the dead. A Sitka man also died and returned in order to tell his people that the dead required more offerings, "and that all who adhered to the traditions of their fathers were the favored ones in the next life . . . while those who follow the new Christ-religion were their slaves and sat back in the dark, cold corners" (Knapp & Childe 1896: 157–8, 160). Another man had no fewer than three NDEs, so that "In spiritual matters he is considered an authority." In a further nineteenth-century example, a man died and traveled on "a wide and pretty path that led to the other side of the mountains where the ghosts of the dead stay." At a river he encountered stranded souls who "had no friends among the dead who could take them across in their canoes." They had no food and could not drink the bitter green river water. More fortunate souls were greeted by friends who would ferry them across "and ask about news from the other world." They remained dependent on the offerings of the living for their food and drink. The man was told that once he crossed the river "he could not return and that he should return while he still could, before his corpse was cremated." He "came back to life and told his tribesmen what he experienced and saw" (Krause 1956: 191–2).

Swanton (1908: 461–3) stressed that Tlingit afterlife beliefs derived "from men who had died and come to life again." One man died but returned because the path to the ghost world was too difficult, with thorns, wolves, and bears. He told his people about life in the other world, gave them instructions on funerary offering practices, and explained that houses will fill with spirits when someone is about to die.[27] His people then equipped him with moccasins, gloves, and protection against the wild animals so he could reach the ghost world successfully.

When one Sitka man fell sick, spirits came to welcome him and he died. He returned and told of his visit to "an everlasting place" where spirits sat "outside on the porches of grave houses." A "chief who had died long ago" reprimanded him for his anger about spirits not having to work for their offerings, and sent him back to Earth because he carried a war spear. The man explained to his people that the offerings make the spirits happy. He subsequently died and returned four more times, and only died permanently when his war spear was taken away (ibid.).

In an Orpheus myth, a man suffered prolonged grief and sleeplessness following his wife's death. After her body was buried, he followed her spirit to the other world, walking day and night through woods and valleys. He emerged into light, at a lake with a large flat stone. Across the water was the ghost village, and he shouted for someone to come for him. Only when he whispered, however, could the spirits hear this man who "has come up from dreamland." They ferried him across in a canoe and led him to his wife, who warned him not to eat or he would "never get back." She said they should make haste in their departure, and they returned the way he had come. When they arrived home she did not return to her body, and the family could only see her shadow and hear her voice. She decided to revert to how "she used to be," though when her jealous cousin spied on her and her husband, they disappeared back to Ghost Land amid the sound of rattling bones (Swanton 1909: 249–50).

Information about the other world also came from individuals who remembered intermediate experiences prior to reincarnation, for the Tlingit believed that souls could decide to be reborn on Earth and choose their new parents and sex (Knapp & Childe 1896: 163; De Laguna 1972: 777, 779). In one example, a child revealed that he had recently been a man killed in battle. He taught his people what he had learned during his intermediate experience: that there was a particular realm for those who died by violence, and that spirits of the dead appeared on Earth in the form of St. Elmo's fire when a murder was about to be committed (Swanton 1908: 463).[28]

According to Swanton (1909: 81), the Tlingit believed that fates of the dead were decided by the creator deity, Raven-at-the-head-of-Nass. Those who died natural deaths went to the upper afterlife realm of Kiwa'a, a happy mirror image of Earth. Those who died violent deaths went to a higher realm called the Sleep House, via a ladder guarded by a spirit being. New arrivals were interrogated about how they were killed before they could proceed. Those who died of illness undertook a long, perilous journey "through a dense forest and across a river to a big city." Those who died with "the greatest number of blankets and slaves" became high-ranking chiefs. White people occupied "a very inferior position" and wandered about cold and hungry, dressed only in thin sheets. Witches and thieves "had to pass through a deep hole in the Earth to an underground Hades," and risked annihilation (Knapp & Childe 1896: 155–7, 161–2). Those who died unavenged drifted "on the wind with the clouds," while those who drowned went to an underworld. Bad people went to "Raven's Home" (Swanton 1908: 461), and "are to be dogs and such low animals hereafter." Some spirits could go to the sun, moon, or stars (Swanton 1909: 81).

That Tlingit afterlife beliefs were sustained by subsequent experiential validation is shown by Frederica De Laguna's (1972: 767, 772–6) findings from Yakutat as late as 1949–1954: "Knowledge of the afterlife is supposed to have come from the reports of those who either visited the land of the dead in a deep faint, or who died and could remember their experiences after their reincarnation." By evidence and example, De Laguna was told of various individuals who traveled to the otherworld and returned. While most are largely consistent with those already summarized, others are more idiosyncratic. For example, a Sitka man named 'Askadut died and found himself outside his body, unable to reenter. His family could not hear or see him, and he attended his own funerary feast and cremation. He found that he could not leave his ashes "until he began to think of the place where the dead people go." Because he had waited so long, his journey was difficult, plagued by thorn bushes, rain, and sleet. He arrived at a muddy riverbank, and could see people on the other side. He called to them, but they could not hear, and it was only when he grew tired and yawned that they heard and came for him. In some versions of the narrative 'Askadut returned to Earth because "he wanted to come back to his family so bad"; though in others it was upon his deceased aunt's instruction. Nine days after his return, he reincarnated as his own wife's baby. He told her he was 'Askadut, and she recognized him "by a cut or scar on his foot." De Laguna concluded, "So it was from 'Askadut that they learned about the dead, and what to do when people die."

In another narrative of intermediate state memories, two men were killed and found themselves walking in a "strange land." One stopped to rest, though the other continued until he came to a river, where he rested beneath a tree. The riverbank started to erode over the course of nine days, and the man could not move. On the tenth night he fell into the river, and woke up in his new body—his sister's baby. His companion was reborn at the same time, and they were raised together (De Laguna 1972: 775; cf. 774). The practice of holding wakes for as long as eight days was to ensure "that a comatose person would not be mistaken for a dead one and prematurely cremated" (Kan 1989: 127).

Salish

In 1881, a Squaxin man named Squ-sacht-un (John Slocum) was confirmed dead by "all present." As he recounted ten years later:

> My breath was out and I died. All at once I saw a shining light—great light—trying my soul. I looked and saw my body had no soul—looked at my own body—it was dead.

He revived temporarily, then died again:

> Angels told me to look back and see my body. I did, and saw it lying down. When I saw it, it was pretty poor. My soul left my body and went up to the

judgment place of God. . . . I have seen a great light in my soul from that good land; I have understand [*sic*] all Christ wants us to do. Before I came alive I saw I was sinner. Angel in heaven said to me, "You must go back and turn alive again on earth . . . ." When I came alive, I tell my friends, "Good thing in heaven. God is kind to us. If you all try hard and help me we will be better men on earth." And now we all feel that is so (Mooney 1896: 752).

Further details of Squ-sacht-un's experience were provided by Charles D. Rakestraw, supervisor at a nearby Native school. While in the other world, Squ-sacht-un entered a house where a well-dressed man asked him if he believed in God, then led him into another room. On the wall was a photograph of Squ-sacht-un on which he could see "all the bad deeds of his life." In a third room he saw people he recognized being burned in a furnace. He then met God, and angels gave him the choice of either going to hell or going back to Earth to preach the Christian life. Before returning to his body, Squ-sacht-un was taken to a higher room and shown "a bright land of beauty and comfort, and experienced a sense of deep tranquility" (Ruby & Brown 1996: 4).

Squ-sacht-un's subsequent teachings combined Christian and indigenous beliefs, and had a strong experiential character. In addition to miraculous healings, as the missionary Myron Eells wrote, followers of the resulting Shaker religion "dreamed dreams, saw visions . . . and were taken with a kind of shaking" of their arms and heads, sometimes uncontrollably, while in a "hypnotic condition." The Shakers distinguished themselves from Ghost Dance and Dreamer religions, and considered themselves Christians. However, as conveyed by the contemporary historian James Wickersham, the Bible was not valued

as a book of revelation. They do not need it, for John Slocum personally came back from a conference with the angels at the gates of heaven, and has imparted to them the actual facts and the angelic words of the means of salvation. . . . They know there is a heaven, for John Slocum was there, and believe in a hell of fire for the punishment of sinners, because the angels in heaven told John Slocum about it.

Squ-sacht-un's authority was also considered superior to that of the Bible because he was Native, 1,800 years more recent than Jesus, and was able to give his testimony in person and in the local language. Louis Yowaluch, the Church's head in 1893, confirmed that Squ-sacht-un's experience was directly responsible for the foundation of the religion, and that the account was not regarded locally as being part of any preexisting indigenous tradition:

We heard there was a God from John Slocum—we could see it. Same time we heard God, we believe it. . . . John Slocum came alive, and I remember God and felt frightened. We never heard such a thing as a man dying and bring word that there was a God (Mooney 1896: 752–5).

Certain modern historians also see the experience in such terms: Ruby and Brown (1996: 9, 34) concluded, "this one event in John Slocum's life gave rise to the Indian Shaker Church," and "most important for his credibility was his near-death experience." Jay Miller (1988: 194) summarized, "By dying and reviving, John gave personal expression to the concern of the Christian god for Indians, as ancient shamans had died and returned to announce other religious reforms."

A young Nuxálk (Bella Coola) girl traveled to the other realm and described seeing a river beneath a hill covered in sharp stones. Both time and space were reversals of Earth: day was night, winter was summer, and people walked upside-down, spoke a different language, and had different names. A rope ladder led to a house overseen by two men, and those who entered could not return to Earth but eventually died again to "sink to the second lower world, from which there is no return." Those who did not enter were sent back to Earth by the gods, and were reborn in their previous family. In another narrative, a man went to the other world in a canoe. He encountered deceased relatives who wept and pleaded, "Don't come here. We don't want to see you so soon." A spirit of shamanic initiation known as Lalaiail or Kleklatieil, told the man to return to his body or he would have to remain in the other world forever. When the man revived, he became a shaman himself. Descriptions of the land of the dead were "principally obtained from shamans who believe they have visited that country during a trance" (Boas 1898: 37–8).

Near-death experiences were integrated into the Nespelem creation myth, where the deity Old One explained how the living will learn about the afterlife:

I will send messages to Earth by the souls of people that reach me, but whose time to die has not come. They will carry messages to you from time to time; and when their souls return to their bodies, they will revive, and tell you their experiences. (Teit 1917: 83)

The Snohomish Lushootseed Salish believed that people who died could "come to life again in a few days." A shaman named Little Sam died when he was a boy, and while his body was being prepared for burial, his soul traveled to a river. There were ghosts on the opposite bank, and Little Sam called for his deceased brother. A canoe came for him and the ghosts asked if his mother knew he was there. When he replied that she did not, they sent him back because "they did not want him now, but he could come back when he was older." He awoke to hear his mother calling him (Haeberlin & Gunther 1924: 81–2; collected 1916–7).

The Puyallup-Nisqually Coast Salish "postulated the existence" of an afterlife "from the fact that souls were brought back from there by shamans" (Smith 1940: 98). In accounts of soul-retrieval, the soul headed westward to a stream that had to be crossed on a fallen tree. A second stream was crossed by canoe, and led to the village of the dead. Seasons, day and night, and tides were reversed, though in all other respects life mirrored that on Earth (Haeberlin 1918: 253–5). Shamanic initiates on the Northwest Coast were ritually clubbed "to death" to bring about "inner experiences of a tradition-bound content." The initiate returned to the body with supernatural power, and the experience was seen as "proof that the new shaman is able to visit the dead and to return from them," and to retrieve souls of people who are in danger of death (Hultkrantz 1992: 64–5).

The Tillamook "learned about the country of the dead" when a man died for five days and was brought back to life through shamanic rituals. He described a long journey to a river where he sat for ten days, as "bad" people must do. A canoe then ferried him over to a house where "all the souls were gathered," and they celebrated his arrival with dancing. The realm was ruled by Tsaai'yahatl, and had an abundance of fish and game. Most souls were eventually reincarnated on Earth. Bad people would get lost for a time before being guided to the correct path; though the "very bad" ended up being boiled in a pot, thrown into a fire, fed "snakes and vermin," and enslaved forever (Boas 1923: 11–2).

In a 1920s report, a Quinault man returned to life five days after his burial. He reported that he had traveled to the spirit world "but the dead failed to take good care of him so he returned." His report was consistent with Quinault beliefs in a "good" and "bright" mirror image of Earth, intermediate states, river crossings, reason for return, and other features. The dead eventually died a second death, after which they became immortal guardian spirits. The Quinault also practiced soul retrieval via shamanic journey (Olson 1936: 159–63).

Coos

In a narrative from 1901, a sick man asked his sons not to disturb his corpse for five days in the event of his death. His soul left his body and eventually found a path that had red-painted sticks lying about. He heard eagles and seagulls, then descended a slope to a village. His father, brother, "and many other people whom he knew" greeted him in canoes. Instead of landing, however, his father told him to go see his grandparents, and the man did so. The grandfather gave him a dish of lice to eat, explaining that it was the custom for new arrivals. The man refused, and threw the plate in the fire. The grandfather later explained that had he eaten the lice, he would have been unable to return to Earth. The man then wanted to swim in the river, though his grandfather warned him against it. He went anyway, and returned with his legs covered in eels, which they cooked and ate. That night, as his grandparents slept, he crossed the river and went to a dance, where he saw a woman he knew. The dancers shouted when they realized that he was alive, and the man ran back to his grandparents. He then returned to the dance and saw the girl distributing grave goods that had been buried with her, as instructed by a living relative. The man again fled to his grandparents when he was noticed, and decided to return to Earth because his children were waiting for him. Though his body had started to decompose, he successfully revived. He brought his sons two invisible fish, one cooked and one raw, and the next morning there were many fish in the river, "some half cooked, and others half fresh." After that, the man never aged (St. Clair & Frachtenberg 1909: 37ff).

Ktunaxa (Kutenai)

Despite being dead for seven days and already in a state of decomposition, another man's spirit also returned his body. When his people unwrapped his funerary cloths, he related how he had been to "the land of the dead." He was told to return to teach his people about what he had seen there, along with "more songs and prayers" and the Black-Tail Deer dance, which became a common hunting ritual. "I know all about power," he explained. "I saw it in my dream. You can believe that there is such a place." A contemporary narrative involved a spirit helping a woman to retrieve her husband from the other world by singing and dancing. The songs became part of the Black-Tail Deer dance (Wissler & Duvall 1908: 157–9).

California
Karok

Around 1840–50, "a doctor woman" was killed by two men. She revived after ten days, and remained silent for a month before relating her experience. She described finding herself at the top of a hill, above a pine tree stump that "all the dead people brushed against" as they passed. At a red mountain were two trails. The one leading downriver went to a place for "men without sense," where people lived poorly. The downhill trail for good people led to a flat, yellow country across the river, with abundant fish and birds. Spirits were dancing, gambling, and shooting targets with bows and arrows. Some crossed the river to greet the woman, laden with "valuables," but a man struck her with a stick, told her not to cross, and to "go back." The woman protested, saying "I like this place," but when the man insisted, she returned to Earth (Kroeber 1946: 17–8). This "'actual' account of return from the land of the dead" (ibid. 13) is markedly different from the elaborate plot, descriptiveness, and literary character of a Karok Orpheus myth (ibid. 14–7), in which "two women follow a man and fail completely to bring him back."

Achowami, Maidu, Modoc, Shasta, and Klamath

The Achowami were reportedly uninterested in the afterlife until the introduction of the Earth Lodge dance and the Wintu cult (c. 1875), which involved individuals receiving songs from ancestors during dreams and sharing them with the rest of the tribe in dance ceremonies. These practices had significant and lasting impact on traditional shamanism, resulting in a change in the way shamans received their power: experiential contact with deceased relatives superseded group initiation (du Bois 1939: 47, 57–9).

In the early 1870s, the prophet Widunduni of the nearby Maidu people visited the spirit world in dreams, learned a new dance that was supposed to bring back the dead, and taught it to his people (ibid. 39–40). In a Modoc Orpheus narrative, a man who followed his deceased daughter to the other world "was not dead but his spirit left his body" (Hultkrantz 1957: 69). Despite having similar myths, the neighboring Shasta knew little about the afterlife "up to the time the Ghost dance was introduced" (Voegelin 1947: 53). Similarly, the Klamath had an Orpheus myth much like those of the Modoc and Shasta,[29] though their afterlife beliefs had "solely a folkloristic existence, for it little concerns the actions of the living." Nor do Klamath return-from-death narratives feature descriptions of another world or a journey there. In one example, a woman had a deathbed vision of ghosts who "caught her" before she revived (Spier 1930: 93, 102). Relatives of newly deceased individuals had dreams about the arrival of their loved ones in the spirit world, and would "express in songs what they have seen during their slumbers" (Gatschet 1890: xcvi–xcvii).

Yurok

The Yurok had a word for people who "returned to life from coma" (*kemmeihtso*), and a special song and dance for them. In an Orpheus myth reported c. 1900–1908, a man saw an apparition of his lover while fetching a doctor for her. When he returned to the village he found that she had died. Accompanied by Weasel, he followed her to Tsorrek, the land of the dead, where he saw people dancing and having "every kind of enjoyment." They succeeded in bringing the woman back, though she returned to Tsorrek when someone mentioned that she had died and returned to life. In an alternate version, the man returned to life during his own burial. He explained that rather than taking "the ghost's trail" from which there is no return, he took the ferryman's boat down a river. He struck a bank and broke the boat, and saw many houses with fires and people dancing. After that, no one died for ten years for "there was no boat to ferry them across" (Kroeber 1976: 382–4, 422).

Cahuilla and Serrano

The Desert Cahuilla believed that the spirit realm (*Telmekishis*) was reached by a road leading eastward to a gate guarded by Montakwet, "a man who never dies." He interrogated the deceased and tested them with the string-game, cat's cradle. Those allowed to proceed had to then pass through two constantly shifting mountains. The "wicked" were crushed before transforming into "bats, butterflies, rocks, or trees." The good (those who were generous, considerate of old people, and devoted to the creator deity Mukat) proceeded safely "into the regions beyond." Some people arrived in Telmekishis too soon and were sent back: "This is evidenced by the fact that a person who has apparently died, in a minute begins to breathe again." Such individuals could not relate the experience until three years had passed, or they would die and be crushed between the shifting mountains (Hooper 1920: 321, 342).

The neighboring Serrano claimed to have no afterlife beliefs, though nevertheless had a detailed Orpheus narrative. This led Hultkrantz (1957: 274–6, 280) to conclude that their indigenous religion had been "degraded" by Christianity, and that their own myths had become denigrated to the class of "fairy tale."

Patwin, Pomo, Yokut, and Miwok

One day while hunting in the 1870s, Lame Bill fainted and went into a trance state for four days. When he revived, he told his people about spirits of the dead living in heaven, and instructed them to build a special house for performing a dance the spirits had taught him. This was the foundation of Bole-Maru, the Dreamer Religion. Prior to his experience, Lame Bill did not believe in his dreams, and the Patwin did not believe in an afterlife: "It was the first time these people had heard such things. He was the first man who saw all this." His people were initially skeptical, until "they started dreaming themselves." Bole Maru prophets in other tribes preached messages consistent with Lame Bill's, and also derived them from afterlife visions. The movement instituted religious and ritual changes to symbolism, feasts, dances, songs, regalia, and funerary practices (e.g., waiting four days before burial) (du Bois 1939: 67–9). Believed to be divinely inspired, the dreams

> dealt not only with ethical and eschatological material, but also furnished the authority to give certain dances. The details of the dances, the costumes and the songs were all contained in dreams. During the ceremonies, Bole-Maru leaders imparted to the people the content of their revelations and preached a moralistic code. . . . Reward for faith was life in an afterworld of flowers, plenty, and peace (ibid. 133).

While drawing on elements of Christianity, the movement was rooted in existing local beliefs in the abilities of shamans to communicate with the dead, and in healing through soul-retrieval (ibid. 137).

Jim Batci of the neighboring Pomo dreamed that he went up a mountain and found his deceased sister. She told him he had to return since he was not yet dead, and instructed him to preach to their people that a coming flood was going to destroy the world, detailing the type of structure to build in order to protect them (ibid. 96).

An Orpheus myth was the main source of afterlife knowledge for the nearby Yokut (Gayton 1935: 269). Central to the mythology of the neighboring Miwok was a belief in "The tendency of the dead to rise and return to life on the third or fourth day after death" (Merriam 1910: 19).

Tolowa

Tolowa dreamers deliberately induced deathlike comas through some unspecified means. They would revive after ten days, mirroring the claims of the prophet Depot Charlie, who prophesied the return of the dead and brought back a dance from the spirit world. Upon returning, prophets would relate information about their journeys to the land of the dead. According to Du Bois (1939 19–20), "their prophetic and moralistic discourses elaborated primarily the concept of a Supreme Being and crystallized ideas of an afterlife." In one example from c. 1871–81, Welthnesat revived from his "coma" and reported that he had been in heaven, where he saw the dead. Everything was "clean and white," and there were "clouds filled with angels." The experience transformed him, for "Before he dreamed he had been a mean man, but afterwards he was as nice as could be."

Analysis and Conclusions
The Experiential Dimension of Native American Afterlife Beliefs

Cultural and individual diversity notwithstanding, Native American afterlife beliefs generally correspond to local reports of NDEs and shamanic journeys to realms of the dead. The experiences were widely regarded as having preceded the beliefs, as evident by the multiple overt indigenous statements to that effect. Many of the examples reviewed here feature claims that knowledge about the afterlife came from such experiences. Where such statements are lacking, the experiences nevertheless commonly gave rise to other new religious beliefs or customs.

That the valorization of afterlife journeys was a widespread Native American cultural trait was not lost on previous researchers. Extrapolating from his field-work in the Pacific Northwest, Boas (1896: 8) wrote,

> All myths describing the future life set forth how a certain individual died, how his soul went to the world of the ghosts, but returned for one reason or the other. The experiences which the man told after his recovery are the basis of the belief in a future life.

More recently, Miller (1988: 142–4) compared historical Lushootseed Salish sha-manic journeys to the realm of the dead with similar phenomena in twenty-one tribes across the continent. He observed that individuals reviving from apparent death gave "proof to the independence of body and soul, while also supporting the reality of another plane of existence," and that together with funerary prac-tices, "temporary visits to the afterworld gave people a set of expectations about life after death."

The phenomenon was explored in the greatest depth by Hultkrantz (1992: 27–8), who over his long career stressed the importance of such experiences in Native American afterlife beliefs. He wrote that for "medicine men, some visionar-ies, [and] sick persons in a coma" who have visited the other world, "this other life has been a palpable reality." In general, he added, a Native American believed only "in what he has himself experienced or what a reputed visionary has experienced. There is always a doubt in his mind as long as he has not had a visionary glimpse of the world of the dead." Such was the authority of experience that for some (e.g., Algonquin, Saulteaux), it actually took precedence over preexisting beliefs when it came to knowledge about the afterlife. Individuals such as the Greenlandic *angakkut* and the Shoshone NDEr Enga-gwacu Jim believed the evidence of their own experiences over the statements of missionaries or even local shamans. Furthermore, where eschatological systems were absent, experiences were the *sole authority* for belief (e.g., the Great Basin Washo, and the Southwestern Hualapai; Hultkrantz 1957: 295). These experiences revealed not only the fate of the dead, but also addressed "the skeptic's request to know how man came by this knowledge" (Hultkrantz 1980: 285). Hultkrantz (1957: 290, 293–4) took seriously experiencer testimony, pointing out many indigenous statements that afterlife beliefs were rooted in experiential phenomena (or supplemented by them), and that individuals referred to such narratives when asked about their beliefs.

While writing that "these transcendent voyages have stimulated the growth of eschatological conceptions" (ibid. 69), Hultkrantz (1967: 28–9) was particularly astute in considering cultural factors alongside the experiential source hypothesis, taking into account "An integral view of the world and of life, the weight of inherited traditions, and the repeated evidence of visionaries who have looked beyond death." While narratives of afterlife journeys may have originated in experiential phenomena, their "colourful contents are folkloristic motifs that have migrated over wide areas," and descriptions of the land of the dead itself mirror "existing cultural, social, and natural premises in the tribal unit" (Hultkrantz 1980: 173). At a more fundamental level, Hultkrantz (1967: 28–9) argued that the belief that souls were separable from the body "is at once the result of and the basis for these remarkable experiences," indicating a symbiotic relationship of belief and experience.

A few exceptions prove the rule. Being more concerned with survival in extreme conditions than with metaphysical problems, the Copper Inuit generally stated that they did not know the fate of the soul after death, and had only vague notions that it survived the body, perhaps through reincarnation. Such uncertainty reflects the fact that NDEs, Orpheus myths, and indeed any other afterlife journey narratives are absent from the Copper Inuit ethnographic literature.[30] Furthermore, while it was accepted that shamans could rise from the dead (Pryde 1972: 115) and retrieve souls (Jenness 1959: 49), the Copper Inuit had "no tradition of shamans having visited . . . the Land of the Dead" (Rasmussen 1932: 33). Thus, without experiences to corroborate the claims they heard from neighboring peoples or missionaries, the Copper Inuit did not firmly adopt any clear afterlife conceptions. As seen above, the case was similar with the Klamath, though to a lesser extent; while the Shasta and Patwin reportedly had little or no afterlife beliefs until the experiences of the founders of local Ghost Dance movements in the nineteenth century. In 1820 when a Sauk chief was asked if he believed "that the soul lives after the body is dead" he answered, "How should we know, none of our people who have died, have ever returned to inform us" (Blair 1911: II, 145). Without experiential evidence, the chief remained agnostic about the afterlife. There is a clear correlation between agnosticism, disbelief, or unconcern about the afterlife on the one hand, and a dearth of NDE and related narratives on the other (as will be further seen on a comparative level in the following chapters).

Afterlife Myths, Shamanism, and NDEs:
A Reciprocal Relationship

As seen, the phenomenon of apparently dying, undergoing certain types of experiences, and returning to life is common to NDEs, Orpheus and other afterlife myths, and some visionary, soul retrieval, initiation, and reincarnation narratives. While most are clearly categorizable, it is sometimes difficult to make such distinctions, for all share return-from-death themes and typical NDE features, alongside cultural characteristics, and individual idiosyncratic elements (cf. Hallowell 1940: 30, n.1). Nevertheless, such category distinctions are sometimes indigenous as well as scholarly, and many Native American peoples (e.g., Saulteaux, Ho-Chunk, Pawnee, Karok, Klamath) distinguished between fact, legend, tale, and myth. While such information does not often accompany specific narratives, categories are usually evident by context: NDEs are spontaneous and allegedly historical; Orpheus myths involve an individual following a loved one to the spirit world; and shamanic narratives occur in ritual/healing contexts of soul retrieval, initiation, or knowledge acquisition. Not all afterlife myths have specifically Orpheus themes, however, and both myths and NDEs often possess a shamanic character (e.g., individuals being considered shamans by virtue of having had an NDE).

Forty years prior to the popular recognition and codification of the NDE, Spier (1935: 13–4) put shamanic experiences in a different category from "actual happenings" by virtue of the fact that the shamans did not "die." He also distinguished between "purely mythical" narratives and those "couched as historical happenings". Hultkrantz (1957: 235–7) similarly distinguished between individuals who appeared "lifeless," were taken for dead, and returned to life unexpectedly, versus shamans who were fully expected to return from their deliberate afterlife journeys. Hultkrantz (1980: 233–4) attempted to clarify the varying contexts and phenomenological features that characterize "the experiences which have taken place in sleep, comatose states of different kinds (fainting fits, deep unconsciousness, temporary cessation of respiration, 'suspended animation') and shamanistic trance." While he found that ordinary dreams rarely involved journeys to the land of the dead (as per Hallowell 1940: 29), they may have led to (or at least reinforced) concepts of dualism. The dream-image of the self and of others, and the apparent realness of dreams "bear incontrovertible witness to the fact that the dreamer can journey independently of his body." Indeed, "The Indians themselves emphasize how the dream-experience has helped them to the belief in a soul separable from the body" (Hultkrantz 1953: 243–4). Afterlife journey experiences, however, more typically occurred during serious illness or physical/ mental stress. The numerous examples of NDE-type narratives in which individuals are met on the journey by inhabitants of the afterlife realm and sent back to their bodies indicate a distinct experience type. Thus, the afterlife realm can be approached in dreams, but not entered; those who are ill can go there, but risk staying permanently; and shamans have the ability to travel freely between the two realms.

The shaman often encountered "difficulties that the sick person is not always subjected to since his soul is magnetically drawn there." This could suggest that the origins of beliefs in "nightmarish obstacles" on the afterlife journey lie in shamanic experiences rather than in NDEs. Shamanic experiences were also said to "underlie the conceptions of the road to the realm of the dead" (Hultkrantz 1967: 132–4). While there may be some truth in these perceptions, distressing NDEs with "nightmarish obstacles" do sometimes occur; and more problematically, many of the narratives with ostensibly documentary contexts actually contain these supposedly typically shamanic features. Indeed, despite his attempts at a more precise classification, Hultkrantz may be conflating the two kinds of narratives when he states, "The frequently recurring Indian pronouncements to the effect that the shamans knew the realm of the dead best—or that only they knew the realm—are probably to be interpreted to mean that shamans had, in the last analysis, given the eschatological belief its exact form" (ibid. 238). This is not fully supported by the evidence presented above, in which many of the narratives that were said to have given rise to afterlife beliefs—and indeed to the creation of new shamans—did not have shamanic origins. Claims that afterlife beliefs originated in shamanic experiences came primarily from the Northwest (Nuxálk and Puyallup-Nisqually Salish, Tlingit, Wet'suwet'en), with one from the Arctic (Gilgulim Inuit), and one from the Plains (Sioux). Of these, the Tlingit and Wet'suwet'en shamans actually had NDEs, while Puyallup-Nisqually shamans practiced ritual clubbing to "death." Only the Gilgulim, Nuxálk, and Sioux examples lacked return-from-death themes, and only the latter referred to a specific individual rather than being a general statement that afterlife knowledge came from shamans.

Conversely, Hultkrantz (1957: 121, citing Ottowa and Lipan examples) saw the theme of individuals being sent back to Earth because it is not yet their time to die, as being typical of NDEs. He also suggested that postmortem reward and retribution were "related both to local mythology and individual Indians' personal experiences during death-like states." As in this world, social order in the other world was preserved by exclusion of criminals, witches, and other undesirables, and this is reflected in NDE narratives in which "dangers of the journey function as mechanisms for weeding out untrustworthy people" (Hultkrantz 1980: 182).

Gayton (1935: 280–2) argued that Orpheus myths were "invariably" seen as historical, and that though afterlife beliefs derived from them, the "psychic experiences" themselves "follow the myth pattern to some extent, varying, of course, from individual to individual." Similarly, Hultkrantz (1957: 68) argued that the very fact that Orpheus narratives often held the elevated status of myth, or "seriously intended explanatory legend" with an "authorizing function," indicates that they must "be based upon a foundation in a reality accepted as genuine." Indeed, it is "precisely this empirical background that has assured the popularity of the Orpheus tradition." Furthermore, Hultkrantz believed that the "uniformity" and "fixed order" of the narratives strengthens the idea that they originated in "actual events, the subjective experiences of particular individuals." The "Orpheus tradition" was thus inspired by "events which once occurred in a certain context, and which have passed into tradition, even if a tradition that has in the course of time been transformed through many elaborations." The resulting narratives present "a romanticized version" of the actual experience (ibid. 225–7, 229). In addition, "these basic experiences have been constantly renewed within the frame of the religious life" (ibid. 220), that is, through subsequent NDEs and shamanic journeys.

As confirmed in various Orpheus narratives reviewed in this chapter, it "can in some cases be definitely established" that they "changed earlier existing eschatological notions in accordance with [their] own eschatological standards"—specifically, Hultkrantz (1957: 282–3) argued, conceptions of a gloomy, negative afterlife changing to a more positive "brighter atmosphere."

While largely consistent in plot and structure across the continent, there are also numerous differences between Orpheus narratives. These usually consist of additional or altered incidents that reflect "social customs and values," or local details such as "canoes on the Northwest Coast, tipis in the Plains, prayer sticks in the Southwest—so much stage property," as Gayton (1935: 283–4) wrote. The narratives also show influence from local literary forms, including creation myths and animal tales. Varying socioreligious factors between Native American cultures meant that different morals or lessons were emphasized in the various versions, from the breaking of taboos to the origins of certain rituals and strictures. The key teachings, however, were *what happens when a person dies*, and *what to expect in the other world* (Hultkrantz 1980: 285).

The theme of traveling to the spirit land to retrieve souls is obviously a shamanic one, leading Hultkrantz (1957: 233–4) to argue that Orpheus narratives were based on shamanic experiences rather than NDEs. In going after the soul, the protagonist's role is closer to that of the shaman than to the loved one. The shamanic character of the myths is also evident in the means by which the protagonists embark on their journeys, such as fasting, prayers, and self-imposed hardships brought about by extreme grief (Hultkrantz 1957: 60–4). Other common shamanic themes in these myths include references to ceremonial structures (sweat lodges, kivas; ibid. 159), animal protagonists (e.g., the Kathlamet Blue Jay) that may refer to shamans in animal-spirit form, the presence of spirit-shamans in the land of the dead, and returning with spiritual knowledge, prophecies, new religious teachings, and even ceremonial objects (e.g., drums, prayer sticks).

The widespread distribution of Orpheus myths suggests a degree of borrowing and intertextualization. Indeed, the "storylike" structure and overall consistencies across the continent suggest that this should be seen as a literary genre. Along with various culture-specific details, the theme of "mourner seeking deceased loved one" is a literary device, adding a universally relatable poignancy that would facilitate transmission (ibid. 260–1). Depending on degree of literary elaboration, some of these narratives were likely not seen as "historical" at all, but were rather primarily didactic, intended to impart particular teachings through an engaging, entertaining tale. In any case, the basic plotline of Orpheus myths is itself part of the main underlying lesson common to all such narratives: the mutual contextualization of NDEs (i.e., of the beloved) and shamanic soul retrieval journeys (i.e., of the protagonist) as sources for knowledge about the afterlife.

Despite any intertextualiztion, however, the consistency of the narratives is likely due more to the consistency of the experiences rather than entirely to diffusion. As Hultkrantz (1957: 307, 312) concluded, the "Orpheus tradition" arose in different cultures "on the basis of an extraordinary ecstatic experience, which, via memorates, has been transformed to tradition." In a symbiotic relationship between belief and experience, the "tradition" itself was accepted as describing shamanic experience, and even became "the origin tale" of certain shamanic practices and spiritual knowledge. This illustrates the process by which extraordinary experiences can be elaborated into cultural narrative forms, and integrated into religious beliefs and practices.

The Ghost Dance and Other Near-Death Experiential Religious Movements

Near-death and shamanic experiences were crucial to Native American religious revitalization movements of the seventeenth to nineteenth centuries. These cases provide rare glimpses into the process of the formation of new religious beliefs and practices, and the experiential contribution to them.

With but few exceptions, the individuals who founded these new religions or brought back new teachings "gained their positions as Prophets by trance-induced otherworldly experiences," and by virtue of the belief that they had "died, gone to heaven, and returned" with divine wisdom (Ruby & Brown 1989: 13, 30; cf.

Kroeber 1904: 32; Mooney 1896: 922–4).[31] It is significant that the major move-ments reviewed in du Bois's (1939) exhaustive survey primarily had NDE founda-tional contexts, while the lesser movements were more often grounded in dreams and visions.[32] That NDEs held greater evidential force is unsurprising considering that unlike these other phenomena, they are rare, spontaneous, outwardly dra-matic, emotionally charged, and difficult to convincingly fake. Furthermore, the teachings of cultural renewal and promises of resurrection or a heavenly future life, were uniquely relevant to and consistent with NDEs, sharing the conceptual themes of "rebirth" and revitalization.

Many of these foundational NDE narratives had a distinctly shamanic char-acter (e.g., that of Black Elk; cf. Wade 2003: 112). This, too, is unsurprising when we consider their cultural contexts. While the founders of prophetic religions grounded their teachings in the authority of ostensibly spontaneous afterlife experiences, the experiences themselves were interpreted through the lenses of local shamanic traditions. Indeed, while most shamans and prophets discussed in this chapter gained their status as a result of their NDEs, a few already held it prior to the experience.

To varying degrees, then, the experiences conformed to cultural expecta-tions (i.e., established beliefs, Orpheus myths, and prior shamanic and NDE narratives), and the movements themselves were clearly rooted in existing indig-enous traditions. As one Paiute informant stated, Ghost Dance leaders "didn't start anything new. They just learned from the old people" (du Bois 1939: 4). As outgrowths of existing dreamer-prophet/shamanic-visionary traditions, cer-tain experiential narratives do not simply show signs of intertextuality, but were likely wholly invented or plagiarized for personal gain. Skolaskin, for example, exploited his status to fulfill his self-professed divine vision of marrying six virgins (Ruby & Brown 1989: 136), and later admitted that "the whole scheme had been a hoax to gain power" (Ray 1936: 75). Nevertheless, given the consistency between these foundational accounts and other NDEs, it is both unlikely and groundless to believe that they were all due to invention or diffusion. Indeed, no historical lineage can be drawn to account for them all.

Some of the founders of these movements had a prior history of extraordinary experiences, and subsequent leaders were chosen for their trance-journey abilities. Among other extraordinary experiences, Smohalla, for example, had undergone a traditional spirit quest prior to his NDE (Ruby & Brown 1989: 20). Mooney (1896: 774) believed that Wovoka's "frequent trances would indicate that, like so many other religious ecstatics, he is subject to cataleptic attacks." Black Elk was also susceptible to such experiences, leading Wade (2003: 112) to suggest that he may have been "predisposed . . . to have unique NDEs with richer and more varied content than most." Sganyadiyo also had visions and revelations prior to his NDE. This is consistent with McClenon's (2002, 2006b) theory that shamans and prophets have a higher degree of hypnotizability (as is discussed in the final chapter).

Of course, none of this is to deny the sociopolitical factors involved in these revitalization movements, or their role in asserting cultural identities. They certainly reflect anxieties about European dominance, and carry messages of either resistance or greater integration. They served community-binding functions and constituted efforts at cultural, and indeed physical, survival against the threat of annihilation. Christian elements (ideas of salvation and resurrection, baptism, the abandonment of indigenous practices, moral precepts, acceptance of Jesus) were incorporated to appeal to Christianized Natives, to appear less threatening to the Europeans, perhaps to simply capitulate in some cases, and/or out of genuine religious feeling (cf. Shushan 2016b).

While the sociopolitical dimensions have been amply covered in the scholarly literature (e.g. Andersson 2008, Smoak 2006, Cave 2006), however, the importance of the experiential element has been widely ignored in recent decades, resulting in an implicit denial of emic voices through the negation of indigenous testimony. Much of the indigenous meanings of these movements and experiences have been sidelined. The experiential source hypothesis is thus not a competing theory, but a supplementary and corrective one. The fact that the experiences occurred in particular historical contexts and were used to certain social-religious-political ends does not invalidate the experiences themselves, for functionality does not indicate functionalist origins. Given the abundant evidence for these types of experiences over hundreds of years, it is clearly a case of a particular experience type being interpreted in light of a particular situation, and adapted and utilized for cultural/political needs and empowerment. It is worth noting that at least one movement, that of the Wet'suwet'en prophet Bini, was alleged to have come about prior to any existential threat from Europeans (Lanoue 1993: 7, 19). Nor are these religions entirely defined by their historical contexts, for some are still practiced today (e.g., Gaihwi:io, Indian Shaker Church).

The importance of the experiential dimension is further reinforced by the fact that the movements were maintained and periodically revalidated by individuals having similar experiences: "From time to time, men 'died' and returned to life with renewed assurances of the truth of the doctrine" (Spier 1935: 5). Over the course of four years, Mooney (1896: 924) found that even while the "original religious excitement" was waning, participation in the dances and other practices was on the rise. Indeed, these movements can be seen as democratizations of shamanism—the shamanization of the entire people in order to increase spiritual and political power. The process of the transmission of the newfound religious knowledge lay (1) in the telling and retelling of the narratives, resulting in greater elaboration and gradual mythologization, and (2) in attempts by adherents to undergo similar experiences.

Conclusions

There is a symbiotic relationship between Native American afterlife beliefs and related extraordinary experiences. The different narrative types (accounts of local beliefs, Orpheus myths, near-death and shamanic experiences) are intertwined. The experiences both generate and modify beliefs, and are themselves rooted in existing traditions. In other words, experience influences belief, and belief influences experience as well as its interpretation and expression – which in turn influence subsequent experiences. The beliefs are "deepened and confirmed by subjective experiences occurring *in conformity with* the tradition handed down" (Hultkrantz 1957: 295), and the experiences "become incorporated into the expectations of the faithful and their anticipations of life after death" (Hultkrantz 1967: 132–4).

As self-induced attempts to replicate NDEs, or at least access the same spiritual "reality," shamanic afterlife journey experiences mimic NDEs. The shamanic state is, to some degree, a near-death state, brought about by practices that compromise one's physical and psychological stability leading to a loss of consciousness—including being clubbed unconscious, burned alive, and "imitative interment" in which the shaman lies in a grave to facilitate transference to the world of the dead (Hultkrantz 1957: 62–4).[33] Stemming from culturally situated practices and traditions, and being rooted in expectation, shamanic afterlife narratives show deeper cultural elaboration than narratives of spontaneous NDEs, as well as imagery of a more surreal, hallucinatory character (meat with eyes, lunar and undersea realms, being devoured). Orpheus myths show even greater literary elaboration, mythologization, and intertextuality, and are best seen as an accessible means of conveying the ritual and spiritual teachings deriving from the afterlife-related experiences.

Arbitrarily placing the chicken before the egg, Boas (1896: 8–9) concluded that "the visions of the sick person" [i.e., NDEs] were "caused entirely by the tales which he had heard of the world of the ghosts," adding that widespread recurrence of the narrative type "proves that one vision was always suggested by the other." However, given the evidence for NDEs being a universal phenomenon, his argument is an untenable alternative to accepting an extraordinary experience type that can lead to belief.

Nor is there anything to suggest a European origin of Native American afterlife beliefs per se (notwithstanding Christian influence, particularly in religious revitalization movements). This is evidenced by the early primary sources which make clear that the local people had not yet been exposed to Christianity, by the overall consistency of indigenous beliefs and afterlife narratives preceding widespread missionization, and by the use of archaic, untranslatable terms and references to ancient times found in many narratives (Hultkrantz 1957: 208). Diffusionist claims often rest on preconceived assumptions about what was and what was not an indigenous belief to begin with. This is repeatedly the case with conceptions of postmortem reward and punishment (e.g., Tylor 1871: 68; Hultkrantz 1957: 283; Rasmussen 1932: 33; and Courlander 1971: 213), though such ideas are found in differing forms in the earliest pre-Christian reports (around the world as well as in North America).

Obviously, not every manifestation or detail of every afterlife belief is rooted in direct personal experience, nor is every religious revitalization movement. Nor is it possible to determine definitively which narratives (and therefore which beliefs) were the result of genuine extraordinary experiences, and which were wholly part of tradition. Some were likley to have been merely imaginative or even technically "fraudulent" on the part of the shaman or NDEr, but with deep roots in mythologized historical experiences that formed the bases of certain traditions. Nevertheless, given (1) the quantity of experiential narratives that are thematically consistent with the cross-cultural model of NDEs, (2) the repeated examples of these experiences leading to innovations in religious beliefs and practices, and (3) the numerous indigenous statements that beliefs arose from such experiences, it is clear that Native American afterlife beliefs were typically grounded in such experiences, which were culturally and individually processed, interpreted, shared, and elaborated over time.

3

Africa

Introduction

Despite acknowledgment of the great diversity of African cultures and beliefs, most scholars nevertheless allow for some general pan-Africa commonalities. The anthropologist George C. Bond (1992: 3) writes that, notwithstanding "differences in environment, population density, technology, economic activity, history, political systems, social and cultural arrangements, and languages" across the "hundreds of different ethnic populations with their own beliefs and practices and customs related to death and burial," there are nevertheless "broad currents or intellectual streams surrounding birth, death, and notions of an afterlife." From a theological perspective, John Mbiti (1971) and Bolaji Idowu (1973) identified a "unified African traditional religion" on which Christianity could be built (Ray 2000: xii). Idowu (1973: 78) emphasized that while "It is foolhardy to generalize about Africa," there is nevertheless "a basically more or less homogenous system." He refers to "African religion" (singular), and stresses that all African groups "originated from a few common cultural roots."

Cross-cultural contact is attested from the earliest times, however. The ancient Egyptian civilization had increasingly complex relationships with Sudan and Ethiopia beginning in the fifth millennium, and there was substantial interaction with North Africa by the ancient Phoenician, Hellenistic, and especially Roman civilizations. In sub-Saharan Africa, however, interaction was limited to trading posts in the southeast, and Roman expeditions beginning in the first century CE. Christianity entered Africa as far back as the first century, with missionary activity beginning in the late fifteenth century. Muslim influence began in the eighth century, expanding greatly in the sixteenth and nineteenth centuries (P'Bitek 1970 53–4; Ray 2000: 143–4, 169). The lack of a section on northern Africa in this chapter reflects an absence of relevant pre-Islamic accounts from the entire region, meaning that effectively we are concerned only with sub-Saharan Africa.

European colonialism and exploitation, including the slave trade, led to entire African populations being "wiped out" or fragmented, resettled, and merged with other groups, so that "their identities have now been lost or at least confused with those of the peoples with whom they have merged" (Idowu 1973: 78–9). As early as 1877, the British missionary Henry Rowley (1877: 15) wrote that information on African religions

is derived almost entirely from such tribes as have been brought under the influence of missionaries, or who have lived for some length of time in the neighborhood of European colonists.

Generalizing about Bantu peoples, the missionary Dudley Kidd (1904: 81) wrote:

It is well-nigh impossible to be quite sure what the natives believed before white men visited them; the early writers asked them far too many leading questions for their evidence to be of much value.

Informants would often tell Kidd what they thought he wanted to hear, and he found a "Great uncertainty and diversity of opinion" regarding the afterlife, including "garbled" versions of what had been learned from other missionaries (ibid. 79).

The "systematic study of African religions through fieldwork" lagged behind serious ethnographic research in other parts of the world, beginning as late as 1930 then swiftly declining (P'Bitek 1971: 105). Attempts at scholarly, unbiased recording prior to that time are rare, and some early reports were wildly inaccurate, deeply colored by intolerant Christian worldviews and imperialist agendas. The missionary context of many such reports means that the sole or primary interest in understanding a culture was to better facilitate its conversion (ibid. 52). While a few early explorers were more sympathetic, the common discourse in Europe was that Africans were a species of semimythical "wild men"—a notion that helped to justify the slave trade (ibid. 35–6).

Ethnohistorical approaches to African religions are also scarce, partly due to a dearth of sources and partly to an academic disciplinary boundary between anthropology and history (Ikenga-Metuh 1987: 9). There are precious few general reviews of afterlife beliefs in Africa, and none of any great historical sweep, depth, or focus. Most are chapters in general surveys of African religions, which are less concerned specifically with indigenous preconversion beliefs than with emphasizing change due to exposure to Christianity. In most such cases, the grounds for determining whether beliefs were preconversion or not are not given. Ikenga-Metuh (1987: 279), for example, wrote of beliefs "unaffected by forces of change from outside Africa," though he does not provide evidence or rationale for the claim.

Ethnographic study on the subject of death in African societies has been more concerned with ritual than with conceptions of the postmortem fates of individuals and the origins of those conceptions. There is scant material on the afterlife even in early missionary and explorer works, and accounts of near-death experiences (NDEs) are comparatively few. This is partly due to the inadequacy of sources, though it also reflects the general lack of preoccupation with such themes in indigenous African religions. It is widely agreed that the afterlife was not typically a major concern, and that ethics were not grounded in prospects of postmortem judgement (Ikenga-Metuh 1987: 263; P'Bitek 1971: 85). Where such beliefs *were* a significant focus of an indigenous religion, rather than spiritual experiences in other realms, "the idea of immortal ancestors dominates African thought about death and the afterlife" (Wiredu 1992: 148).[1] It is revealing that when asking informants about the nature of the afterlife, one of the most frequent responses to both missionaries and ethnographers was simply, "we do not know." Some actively disbelieved in life after death. The Hadza, for example, believed "that the corpse rots in the ground, and that is the end of the person" (Bond 1992: 6).

Nevertheless, there are many examples of beliefs in a spirit that leaves the body after death, remains nearby for a number of days, then departs after burial (Ikenga-Metuh 1987: 264) "to another state of existence" (Mbiti 1990: 153). Indeed, Mbiti (1971: 131–2) went so far as to write that the idea of postmortem survival "is a universal belief among all African peoples as far as one's evidence shows," citing the Luhya, Akamba (Kenya), Bachwa, Mbuti (Congo Kinshasa), Lugbara (Uganda), and Lozi (Zambia). The spirit was seen as a sort of "psychophysical . . . analogue of a body" that could appear to the living as an apparition (Wiredu 1992: 139). According to Mbiti (1990: 156), souls were often believed to consist of four components: the Breath, or animating life-force that dissipates at death; an Ancestral Guardian Spirit that simultaneously inhabits the individual on Earth while remaining in the spirit-land of the ancestors; the Destiny Spirit, a "spark of the Creator" that returns to the deity at death; and the Self, Personality Spirit, or "Real Man," which survives consciously and becomes either an ancestor spirit or a ghost.

The journey to the other world was sometimes described as being "long and arduous," or as crossing a dark, cold river. Funerary ceremonies allowed souls to integrate into the community of deceased ancestors in the other realm, and offerings were made so that the deceased would have food on the journey and gifts for the spirits (Mbiti 1990: 78–9, 156). By virtue of their closer proximity to the divine, ancestor spirits had increased power, which they could use to help the living on Earth (Ikenga-Metuh 1987: 263–6).

It was often the case that certain conditions had to be met in order to become an ancestor spirit, including "good moral conduct," living to old age and dying a natural death, having offspring, and most especially receiving proper funerary rites (Ikenga-Metuh 1987: 263–6). Certain individuals, as determined by the judgment of the deity or the "court of the ancestors," achieved a divine-like state though the absorption of "the attributes of the original deity" and by living in a "spirit mode of existence." Except for a few kings or heroes, however, the deceased rarely became actual gods. Neither judgment nor reward were generally expected or hoped for, however, for it was believed that most had the same fate (Mbiti 1990: 79, 156, 158–60). Because spirits continued to serve the community, a heavenly afterlife "in which people endlessly just enjoyed themselves (in however "spiritual" a fashion) without any responsibilities would be viewed as glorified idleness. . . . There are, of course, no temptations or tribulations in that life, but neither are there any excitements" (Wiredu 1992: 143).

Less common was a perception of the ancestral realm as a heavenly paradise "in which they have a happy, unending reunion with their folk who are waiting for them on the other side" (Idowu 1973: 188). Parrinder (1974: 136–7) wrote that such beliefs were limited to Nigerian peoples, who held them alongside conceptions of a cold, dark underworld where the deceased were judged by "God." Mbiti (1990: 78–9) cites examples of beliefs in deceased spirits going variously to an underworld (Luhya, Banyarwanda, and Igbo), living "in the air, the sun, moon, or stars" (San, Mamvu-Mangutu), and in "woods, bush, forest, rivers, mountains, or just around villages." Some believed the spirit realm was near their homes, but that it was invisible.

The other world was commonly seen as a mirror image of this one (Rowley 1877: 90), to the extent that characterizing this world as "earthly" in distinction to afterlife realms is "metaphysically inappropriate" (Wiredu 1992: 137). Status, professions, environment, hierarchies, and general activities were maintained (Mbiti 1990: 157), and going to the other realm was often seen as a return home after visiting Earth.

A primary fear was to become an aimless, homeless spirit, for this meant not only being cut off from one's community and kinship group but also actually causing them harm. While beliefs in postmortem judgment and retribution were rarely stressed, it was the fate of criminals, witches, sorcerers, those who broke taboos, and those who died of particular diseases to become such wandering spirits (Ikenga-Metuh 1987: 271). Idowu (1973: 186–7) also cited beliefs that bad people go to a hellish rubbish dump.

The personal identity and community membership of spirits faded after four or five generations, at which point they were seen no longer as "people" but as "things." They then entered a state of "collective immortality," losing their "humanness" while gaining "full spiritness" (Mbiti 1990: 78, 158–9).

Belief in a form of reincarnation within one's kinship group was also common, and children were often given the names of their deceased former selves. Rather than actually being the reincarnated ancestor, however, it is perhaps more accurate to characterize the belief as a form of partial possession: the new individual was merely guided by the ancestor who could be simultaneously present in more than one incarnation, in the spirit world, and in the ancestral shrine (Ikenga-Metuh 1987: 267–69; Mbiti 1990: 160). Some considered it a punishment to remain in the otherworld rather than being reborn, and many believed that souls reincarnated in animals, particularly snakes (Parrinder 1974: 138). Reincarnations ceased once "collective immortality" was achieved (Mbiti 1990: 160).

While the extensive survey of primary sources conducted here has not led to a contradiction of these generalizations, it has indicated that otherworldly afterlife beliefs were comparatively rare. That is, when such beliefs were expressed at all, they largely corresponded to the above outline. However, concerns about the continued actions and influence of ancestor spirits on Earth were more commonly the focus of beliefs related to life after death.

Despite the scarcity of documentary NDE narratives, there are further indications of knowledge of the phenomenon in the form of return-from-death accounts, which describe the outward occurrence itself though without reference to the subjective experiences of the soul's temporary journey outside the body (e.g., in the Tiv culture of West Africa; Downes 1933: 32). While deathbed visions, spirit possession, and mediumship are all widely attested, accounts of afterlife experiences or descriptions of conditions in the other world being communicated by ancestors or other spirits appear nonexistent. Nor are there accounts of memories of intermediate realms prior to reincarnation.

Western
Tshi

In general, Tshi-speaking people of Ghana reached their conclusions about the afterlife "partly through dreams, and partly through the condition of man during sleep, trances and states of syncope" (Ellis 1890: 15). They believed that humans have "a second individuality, an indwelling spirit residing in the body" which "will, after death, continue his present experience in a ghostly shape" in the spirit world (Srahmunadzi). Some souls lingered for a time before going to there, and for them the path was "dark and gloomy" and the destination "difficult to find." Those who died when their time on Earth was complete went directly to Srahmunadzi, but sometimes needed two to three years to recover. It was conceived of as an idealized mirror image of Earth, where natural cycles were reversed, and where everyone was at the prime age of their lives. (Ellis 1887: 187).

The Ashanti of southern Ghana (who had a tradition of firm resistance to European influence) told of a shamanic healer who went into a trance state seeking a remedy for death. He warned his people that it would appear as if he were dead, but that they should not conduct his funerary rites. Six days later, however, they did just that, and the healer therefore did not return with the secret of immortality (Ray 2000: 97). Ashanti afterlife beliefs involved a temporary stay in the spirit world while awaiting reincarnation within one's own clan (Rattray 1927: 319).

Ga

A myth from the Accra region of Ghana (related c. 1858) tells of how Ananute, the son of Anansi (the Spider), followed a rolling palm-nut into a rat hole, and encountered three dirty spirits who had not bathed or shaved since creation. The first was black, the second red, and the third white. They asked the boy why he was there, then gave him yams and told him to cook only the peels and discard the rest. The peels became whole yams, and the spirits gave him some to take back home with him. Before he left, they taught him a song but forbade him from ever singing it. Ananute made further trips to the underworld for more yams, until one day Anansi followed. Ananute sang the forbidden song and "burst from above, and broke down, then his head was cut off, and he also died, but still he went on singing!" The spirits brought him back to life, but when he resumed singing they beat him. When he told his village what had happened to him, he was exiled (Werner 1925: 208ff).

Ewe

Afterlife beliefs from Ghana and Togo indicate that NDEs impacted funerary ritual practices. It was believed that the soul (*edsieto*) could depart from the body, leaving it in

> a condition of suspended animation; it is cold, pulseless, and apparently lifeless. Sometimes, though rarely, the soul returns after such an absence, and then the man has been in a swoon or trance; more generally it does not return, and then the man is dead. It is in consequence of the belief that the soul does occasionally return after leaving the body, that appeals to the dead to come back are always made immediately after death; and, generally speaking, it is only when the corpse begins to become corrupt,

and the relatives thereby become certain that the soul does not intend to return, that it is buried.

It was also believed that shamans could leave their bodies and visit Ghost-Land (*edsie*) as well as earthly places. The shaman could assist the dying by stopping the ancestral spirit in the other world from making them ill. The other world was a seen as a mirror image of Earth, reached by crossing the Volta River (Ellis 1890: 106–7).

Akan

The Dutch West India Company merchant and slave trader Willem Bosman (1704: 384–5) related an account from the kingdom of Whydah (Benin) in which "an old Sorceress" told of "strange things concerning Hell" after claiming "to have been there in person." She saw "several of her acquaintance there," along with a previously deceased "Captain of the Blacks," being "miserably tormented." This served to confirm her people's beliefs in an underworld where souls of "the wicked and damned are punished with fire," which they reportedly held prior to conversion to Christianity.

A German missionary told the explorer William Winwood Reade (1874: 361–2) of the experience of a funerary human sacrifice victim he witnessed at Akropong. According to the ritual custom, a woman was stripped naked, but was only "stunned, not killed." She awoke surrounded by corpses, then proceeded to the council elders to explain that "she had been to the Land of the Dead and had been sent back because she was naked." She therefore asked them if she could go and dress before the sacrifice was consummated.

Fon

The famous explorer Sir Richard Burton (1864: 104) described how the Fon of the kingdom of Dahomey (Benin) would hire shamanic healers when they believed they were in danger of death. The shaman would go into a trance, descend to the underworld to "deliver their excuses," and upon returning would describe what he saw. The British entomologist J. A. Skertchley (1874: 463–4) also wrote of Fon "medicine men" who claimed to have visited the afterlife realm of Kutomen to rescue the souls of the dying. According to the French anthropologist Dominique Zahan (1979: 131–2), in traditional Fon ceremonies for "apprenticeship in mystical life," the initiate danced wildly until he collapsed and was believed by attendees to be dead. After eight days, a "resurrection" ceremony was held and the initiate was reborn with godlike powers.

The Fon believed that souls of the deceased traveled over three rivers and up a mountain to the realm of the ancestors. There they waited until burial rituals on

Earth had been conducted, at which point they would become fully integrated into the afterlife community (Idowu 1973: 189). The supreme deity Mau judged the deceased's body (whether the physical body or a new spiritual one is unclear), assisted by a spirit who kept records of everyone's good and evil deeds, notched on opposite ends of a stick. Those who were judged positively went to Kutomen, where they retained their earthly social status and lived a life similar to that on Earth. Those who were judged negatively were destroyed and reincarnated (Skertchley 1874: 461).

Yoruba

In a Yoruba (Nigeria and Benin) myth, a boy went to "Deadland" to ask his deceased mother where he could find her necklace. Upon arriving he had to pay a doorkeeper and was not allowed to touch anyone. He found his mother by a spring with other dead people, and she asked him why he had come. When he explained, she told him where to find the necklace, and asked him to make "frequent offerings" to her when he returned to Earth. The boy returned, and found the necklace where his mother said it would be (Ellis 1894: 139).

Yoruba shamanic figures in secret societies (e.g., Egungun, Oro) were chosen by virtue of the belief that they had "risen from the dead" (ibid. 107). Individuals in these societies would impersonate the deceased and visit their families to assure them that their loved ones would watch over them. In earlier times, the shaman was "thought to be the dead man himself temporarily returned to life" (Talbot 1926: 476–7), which suggests knowledge of past NDEs and their impact on religious beliefs and practices.

Yoruba afterlife beliefs involved the deceased's soul remaining on Earth for seven days. Victims of accidents or witchcraft, and those who lacked proper funerary rituals, remained on Earth to "wander in the forests, mountains and rivers." While those who were struck by lightning initially shared the same fate, they "may eventually enter into animals, reptiles, and trees" and through them cause misfortune to the living (Ikenga-Metuh 1987: 272–3). Those who died old became ancestors of high status, with power to "bless, protect, warn, and punish their living relatives." Those who died young became "fairies" and wandered aimlessly, without respect for living or dead. Everyone else was judged by the deities Olorun and Obatala (the creator) after giving them an account of their lives on Earth (Mbiti 1990: 156). The bad were sent to a place of broken potsherds that is eternally hot and dry; while the good were reunited with family and clan in a place "without sorrow or suffering" (Ray 2000: 102–4), where life was a continuation of that on Earth (Ikenga-Metuh 1987: 273). There one could choose to be reincarnated, sometimes into more than one person at once (Ray 2000: 102–4).

Ekoi

The Ekoi of southeastern Nigeria believed that the soul is immortal, and separable from the body during trance states when it can travel to other worlds. This was proven, in part, by a woman whose body was buried alive while her soul was away. Her spirit appeared to the people and admonished them:

> It was a great pity that my kin were in such a hurry to lay me in the grave . . .
> for my soul had but gone away for a time, and I only died after its return,
> because I could no longer breathe in the Earth (Talbot 1912: 231).

A number of Ekoi myths are thematically related to NDEs, and evidently reveal distant cultural memories of the phenomenon. One tells of how

> in the beginning of the world when men died, they were carried in a sort
> of dream to the dwelling place of Obassi Osaw [creator and sky deity]. If
> Obassi thought it would be a good thing he would bid the dead man wake,
> and stand up before him. Then he would make him alive again and send
> him back to Earth, but such men on their return could never tell what
> had happened to them. One day Obassi thought, "Men fear to die. They
> do not know that perhaps they may come to life again. I will tell them
> that sometimes such a thing may happen, then they will have less dread
> of death."

For whatever reason, he sent a duck and a frog to Earth, each with a different message. The frog arrived first and explained to humans that death is simply the end of existence. The duck, however, was not only late but forgot to deliver the message that people "may come to life again." "That is the reason why, when a man dies, we cannot see him again, because Duck lost the message, and we must go according to the one which Frog brought us" (ibid. 229).

In an Orpheus myth, a boy named Mkpaw wanted to follow his father to the Ghost Town (Mfam Akabansi). Facing the sun, he offered a pair of eggs to the "Male God and Female God." Chicks hatched from them and accompanied Mkpaw into the sky, where he met an old woman covered in sores. She asked Mkpaw why he had traveled there, then offered to give him something valuable if he would wash her sores. He agreed, and in return she told him how to identify Obassi Osaw at the house where he "sits in judgement" (Red Fly would land on him). When Mkpaw found Obassi, the god told him to stay long enough to see the ghosts passing on their way to market. Mkpaw did so, and saw his parents and a friend. Obassi then instructed Mkpaw to return to Earth, and gave him a magic box that would make anything he wished for appear, but warned him to never leave it open or allow a woman to touch it. When Mkpaw returned, a friend's wife touched the box and both Mkpaw and the friend died. The myth functioned as a lesson in the proscribed handling of religious articles (Talbot 1912: 18–20).

In another narrative, Obassi Osaw disliked one of his sons, Agbo, and gave him increasingly difficult tasks. He ultimately ordered the boy to go to "the Thunder Town" to retrieve an elephant tusk. On his way, Agbo met "the Chief of the ghost people," Ita Ebat Ane. She was "bathing in a spring" though she smelled bad, and her body was covered in such terrible boils that she could not use her hands. Agbo helped her bathe and fed her, then she disappeared. He continued on his way, and again met her at a river. She told him that Obassi had sent him on this journey so that he would die. She tapped her belly, which caused a town to appear, then she transformed into a beautiful woman. After bathing Agbo, she told him how to make his way safely through the ghost town, and warned him against eating anything there. Red Fly guided and protected Agbo, and helped him find Obassi's tusk. Ita Ebat Ane then gave Agbo a machete and had him cut a thunderbolt in two, which he could use to kill his father (ibid. 209–11).

In a myth that explains "Why Living Men Can No Longer See the Road to the Ghost Town," two women went there separately and met Ita Ebat Ane, who again offered to exchange information for help with bathing. The first woman treated her kindly and was rewarded with a song, instructions on what to say to the ghosts when she is questioned, and eggplants to distribute to her village. The second woman cruelly poked at Ita Ebat Ane's sores, causing her to transform into a beautiful woman. Ita Ebat Ane mercifully allowed the woman to go on her way, but she was killed and eaten by ghosts when she was unkind to them. Ita Ebat Ane then decreed "that no live person should ever again come to Mfam Akabansi, and, from that day, hid the road from mortal eyes" (ibid. 233–8).

A number of additional Ekoi myths explain the origins of religious beliefs and ritual practices in terms of an individual who dies, visits the spirit world, and returns. In one example, a boy followed a drumming sound to the other world. He was told how to make sacrifices to cottonwood trees, before being reanimated and returning to Earth (ibid. 34). Animal myths involving tortoises, cocks, and dormice traveling to the spirit world explained sacrifices to ghosts, and the origins of animal sacrifices (ibid. 7–9, 58–9, 62–4). One example told of a dormouse who followed a palm nut down a hole to the other world, and returned with a magic drum that contained sacred spirit images used in the Egbo secret society (ibid. 46–8).

Other kinds of knowledge were also believed to have originated in the other world. One myth told of a man who followed an antelope "down a great hole" to the spirit realm, where he was captured by ghosts but was freed after showing kindness to their children. He returned with the secret of the language of animals, though he died instantly after telling his wife of it (Talbot 1912: 100–101). Another myth explained how tomatoes were brought to Earth from the spirit village: a woman went there after inadvertently marrying a ghost, and was saved when her deceased sister gave her tomatoes to eat before sending her back to Earth (ibid. 238–41).

The Ekoi believed that souls of the dead who led a fulfilled life would journey to the other world, and that they rarely returned. Those who died violently, however, "wander about in this world and trouble people until the time comes when they are set free to join those who have gone before" (ibid. 232).

Igbo

Generalizing about the Niger Delta region, Talbot (1932: 261) wrote that beliefs in the soul leaving the body at death, and sometimes in dreams, were common. "Powerful wizards" were thought to have the ability "to bring the dead to life again after the soul has gone forth," drawing the soul back into the body by use of "medicine." Talbot (1926: 269, 299) also cited phenomena such as communication with the dead by various means, "luminous forms and faces," and deathbed visions of deceased ancestors.

An Igbo (southeastern Nigeria) folktale told of a girl who revived her mother by means of prolonged graveside mourning and four days of "persistent weeping." The girl's half-sister later tried the same with her own mother, but through her impatience, accidentally pulled the head off the body as it emerged from the grave. The tale explained the origin of a certain kind of palm fruit which resembled a human head, for when the girl was told by her angry father to rebury her mother's head, such a tree grew on the spot (Dayrell 1913: 9–10).

The Igbo believed that the soul of the deceased left the body and remained on Earth until proper funerary ceremonies were conducted. They then crossed a river to the "sky realm" with the assistance of a ferrywoman, Ase Sei-Ba. She was paid with whatever was placed in the corpse's hand at burial, or with some part of the grave goods. Those who were "harsh and cruel to others in this life" had a long wait, and risked being overturned in the ferryboat, or some other peril. Most eventually reached the other side, with the exception of "those who are bad too much." Once the deceased arrived in the sky realm and joined their people, the soul was "summoned before Chi [creator deity] to give an account of its earth life," and to ask the deity for a wealthy, healthy reincarnation on Earth. As with the Indian doctrine of Karma, the Igbo believed "that rewards or punishment will follow in the next life" (Talbot 1932: 265–6). According to the archdeacon of the Niger, George Thomas Basden (1921: 118–9), a second burial was required to prevent the deceased from returning to Earth and haunting the living. The Igbo characterized departing for the afterlife as "going home," and spirits remained there for "as long as they behave themselves" or until their designated reincarnation. Bad behavior resulted in banishment into a limbo-like state of "lost souls."

Kagoro, Hausa, Ibibio, Batanga, and Dogon

The Kagoro of central Nigeria had a clear NDE context for their afterlife beliefs:

> If a person was likely to die, the soul left its bodily case and traveled towards the stream that divides this world from the next; and if the ghosts of the departed ancestors on the other side thought it was time for the person to die, the soul was allowed to cross; but if not, they drove it back to the body, and the sick person recovered. (Tremearne 1912: 170)

Certain narratives of the Hausa of northern Nigeria concerned individuals visiting the "house of Death," though they lack any clear near-death context (Tremearne 1913: 157, 441ff).

In the Idiong secret society of the Ibibio of southern Nigeria, initiates were "killed" so that they would "journey to the town of the dead and there learn the future" (Talbot 1926: I.192).

The American missionary R. H. Nassau (1904: 328–9) recounted a narrative of the Batanga of Cameroon, concerning a witch who left her body "to attend a witchcraft play." While she was away, her husband smeared cayenne pepper all over her lifeless form, barring her reentry. Unable to return to her body, she soon died.

Beyond the coastal region and to the northwest, according to fieldwork carried out in the 1930s, the Dogon of Mali worshipped Lébé, "an immortal ancestor who suffered temporary death and was returned to life" (Griaule 1938: 46).

Central
Fang

The Bwiti religion combined traditional ancestor-based traditions, both Christian and indigenous revitalization elements, and the use of the hallucinogenic drug iboga. The effects of the drug are said to correspond to NDEs to such an extent that Süster Strubelt (2008: 33) equates the two experiences, categorizing them as "ibogaine-induced" and "natural" NDEs, and hypothesizing at length about "a common neuronal mechanism" responsible for both states.[2] The consumption of massive amounts of iboga during initiation was potentially dangerous, sometimes resulting in death (Fernandez 1982: 475). This suggests that, at least in some cases, the individual was indeed undergoing an actual NDE, both caused and enhanced by the drug. One initiate stated, "All the Banzie [initiates] thought I had gone too far and was dead." However, the Fang differentiated between experiences generated by iboga and those that occurred during illness: the former had "fruits" in the form of a "therapeutic result" (Fernandez 1982: 478).

In 1958–60, Fernandez (1982: 14) studied Bwiti in a Fang village in a Gabon rainforest. Though converted twenty years earlier, the Fang practiced a marginal form of Christianity alongside traditional religion. The syncretistic Bwiti allowed initiates to "be born into the unseen and thence come to know death and the land beyond" (ibid. 381), and to continue contact with the ancestors (ibid. 486). Iboga was taken "to swell the soul on the tendons and veins of the body so that it could break free and journey off to Bwiti" (ibid. 471). According to the Fang, all their "rites, songs, and dances have come to Bwiti in visions received from the land of the dead," although in some cases it was clear that they "were invented by leaders without benefit of vision" or had derived from Christianity (ibid. 649, n.3). Chapels were decorated to reflect how "things are really done in the land of the dead" (ibid. 382), and the iboga experience was seen as an "authentic source of moral code" (ibid. 302–3). In particular, the encounter with deceased ancestors "conclusively convinces them of the worth of their religion" (ibid. 540).

In the twenty-one "fully reported visions" Fernandez (1982: 427) collected, all featured encounters with deceased relatives, fifteen involved excursions along paths by floating or flying, and twelve included encounters with "greater powers." Among the seventy-eight brief accounts he collected, there were eighty-six instances of contact with deceased relatives among forty-two people (some seeing more than one), and thirty-six with deities and other spirits. In typical iboga experiences, after leaving the body the soul traveled through the forest, ascended into the sky, and met deities, spirits, and deceased ancestors who instructed the individual to "change his lifeway, to join Bwiti, or to work harder" (ibid. 303). Some reported traveling along paths, river crossings, and going to places of unusual brightness; and there are accounts of individuals meeting their deceased parents, grandparents, and siblings. One woman was sent back to her body by a man with a spear who asked her, "Where are you going? You are not dead." A man saw the body of his living brother lying on a road, which turned out to be premonitory because the brother died shortly after. The man followed the road to a vast desert, and his father appeared to him "in the form of a bird", reassured him that he would be his guardian spirit, and led him back to his body. On his return, the man saw "Christians dressed in animal skins," with "heavy crosses around their necks" (ibid. 478–9). When another man went to the spirit world, he saw the chicken sacrificed during his Bwiti initiation (ibid. 482), then encountered Eyen Zame (the indigenized Jesus) "shining on a cross." The man "passed beneath the cross to a house of glass on a hill," which belonged to the goddess Nyingwan Mebege (deity identified with the Virgin Mary). Inside was the man's brother with two other men dressed in white, writing the man's history and his new Banzie name.

Another initiate reported that he was told by his deceased grandfather to look into the sun, which revealed the path to Eyen Zame. When he arrived, however, Eyen Zame told him he could not enter because his skin was black, and "all the dead are white." Similarly, another encountered "a barrier of black iron," which black people could not pass. In the distance "it was very bright" and there were "colors in the air." The initiate's father descended "in the form of a bird" and gave him his iboga name along with the ability to fly. They crossed a river where people dressed in white shouted in recognition, then met a man with hair "piled up in the form of a bishop's hat," a long beard, a red cross tattooed on his neck, and his beating heart visible in his chest. The initiate then "looked up and saw a woman in the moon—a bayonet was piercing her heart, from which a bright light was pouring forth." The spirit of his father then told him to return to Earth (Fernandez 1982: 479–82).

Initiates emerged from their experiences with new understanding, joy, patience, tranquility, conviction (ibid. 462–3), and reorientation "toward the land of the dead" (ibid. 382–3)—the "original and final place," where one was purified and restored to "pristine conditions" (ibid. 491). Iboga experiences purportedly gave the Banzi miraculous powers, which were demonstrated during ceremonies. These included healings, spirit communication, levitations of objects, and elaborately stage-managed displays of magic such as manifestations of individuals and falling to one's death from a tree then reappearing in a different place (ibid. 437–8). Those who frequently undertook iboga journeys were seen as being more of the spirit world than of Earth. A founder of one branch of the religion became Bekone, or "Man of the Dead" following his experience, and gained the ability to facilitate "resuscitations by ecstatic alienation" (ibid. 293, 302).

Though some afterlife conceptions were disputed, it was generally held that the realm of the dead was also the realm of creation (ibid. 491), located in the western sky (ibid. 217) "beyond the sea to the great light" (ibid. 461) and reached via "the path of birth and death" (ibid. 460). Alternatively, it was said to be below a river (ibid. 103). Individuals were punished for misdeeds during their earthly life rather than in the spirit world, though improper funerary ritual would result in the soul of the deceased wandering in the forest. Some, however, believed that there were three judges of the dead: the Scrutinizer, Partitioner, and Classifier, who damn souls to an eternal second death in a hellish realm (ibid. 236 n.5, 237). Belief in a cyclical afterlife and rebirth was more common, with souls being reborn in the other world, eventually dying there, then being reborn again on Earth (ibid. 343). Spirits could continue to interact with the living, in both helpful and dangerous ways (ibid. 253–4).

Like Bwiti, initiation into the Fang ancestor cult also had a drug-induced experiential afterlife element. While villagers danced and sang songs about death and the soul leaving the body, initiates would eventually collapse into unconsciousness and the ancestors would take them "up the road of death." Initiates were believed to go "only half the trip to the land of the dead" in order to gain knowledge of the "miracles" there, and they returned with the ability to communicate with the ancestors (Fernandez 1982: 259–63). Eyen Zame was considered to be "the first of the dead," the ruler of the spirit world, and "the one who showed men and women how the spirit could leave the physical body . . . and still return to it. That is, he showed men that they could know death and still be living" (ibid. 457). His experiences served as a model for drug-induced journeys to the realm of the dead, and his return or "resurrection" symbolized "the knowledge of life in death and death in life" (ibid. 517). He was also the creator, and a being of light identified with the rising sun.

The concept of temporarily dying and visiting the spirit world was thus instrumental to Fang traditions, as were more specific NDE themes such as OBEs, meeting deceased ancestors and other spiritual entities, returning to the "home" or origin state, beings and realms radiating light, obstacles and barriers, being instructed to return for a specific purpose, returning to the body, and subsequent positive transformations. Indeed, even before the introduction of Bwiti, such themes were important elements of Fang religion. In sharp contrast to many African cultures, early missionaries found that the Fang were particularly interested in matters concerning death and resurrection (ibid. 486).

While Fernandez (1982: 485) correctly noted that descriptions of such experiences often showed signs of intertextuality and expectation, some of his structuralist assumptions do not withstand scrutiny. He argued, for example, that the experiences mirrored ritual action and migration legends (ibid. 490), and concluded that belief in their validity can be accounted for by preexisting ideas about the soul and afterlife (ibid. 486). However, this conflicts with Fernandez's own acceptance of the experience itself as a source of knowledge, as per the Banzie themselves. Nor does it account for themes and features consistent with NDEs (Fernandez was apparently unfamiliar with the phenomenon per se). Furthermore, it begs the question of what those "original" experiencers were experiencing (i.e., before there were any accounts to intertextualize). Nor does it explain the numerous idiosyncratic differences between reports, nor their similarities with thematically similar reports in unrelated cultures. Thus, while there is certainly a strong element of cultural uniqueness and secondary elaboration to the accounts, local structural factors alone cannot account for the NDE-like phenomenology of the experiences, or their interpretation in an afterlife context.

Teke

According to Fernandez (1982: 486), "The claim to have died, to have known and to have mastered death, and to have the power to resuscitate the dead, is very old among would-be religious leaders in western Equatorial Africa." He cited a 1938 "account of the visionary death of one Jacques Ngoya . . . who journeyed several days to the land of the dead" and returned with new ritual and moral strictures. He encountered his deceased brother, who taught him dances that he was instructed to introduce to his people on Earth "for their salvation and well-being." He was also given a new set of rules that they should obey, combining traditional and Christian ideas, including helping the sick, feeding the poor, not committing murder or theft, and celibacy for four months (ibid. 302–3).

Mbuti

In the 1920s, a Mbuti shaman (*ischumu*) of the Congo Ituri rainforest said he learned about the afterlife from his father, another *ischumu*. It was believed that as the soul (*Bukahema*) left the body, it was surrounded by spirits (*Baketi*) who would "pounce" on the deceased. The "wicked" would be thrown into a fire "which burns somewhere in the bowels of the earth," while the good would go to live with the creator-god Mungu, who "looked like a man" but was also identified with rainbows and snakes. Despite the conceptions of reward and punishment in a fiery hell, the Ituri were particularly resistant to outside influence, and reportedly had no contact with nearby Muslim peoples (Schebesta 1933: 164–6).

Turnbull's (1965: 249ff) 1950s fieldwork found that the Mbuti speculated little on the afterlife, explaining that since the living have not been there they do not know what it might be like. Nevertheless, they held beliefs that after death the soul ascended into the sky, returned to the god Tore, and became a star. The animating life force became the ancestral totem. Alternatively, according to the northern archer group, Tore's realm was located in caves and ravines. One soul component became a mischievous forest spirit who served Tore, while another became a star with the celestial deity (ibid. 191). Among the net hunter group was the belief that life "continues in some form or another, in much the same way that it is lived by the living," either in a mortal state dwelling in a forest, or as an immortal spirit in the other world (ibid. 238).

Efé

In a legend of the nearby Efé, a man followed an animal into a cave while out hunting game for a funerary ritual. The wounded animal led him through a "side passage" to a river and a large banana field. Confused, the man was about to cry out when he heard the sound of wood chopping. The woodcutter was a woman from his village who had been put to death for sorcery. She recognized him and asked if he was there because he had "fallen asleep." He explained that he was lost, and she offered to take him to the village of spirits (Lodi). The man asked how that would be possible since he was not dead. The woman's husband joined them, and together they went to Lodi. The spirits there also asked if the man had "fallen asleep," and the husband replied that he was "only on a journey." The man told his story and they all danced together. After three months, the spirits told him that they had visited his village and had seen his wife mourning him, believing him to be dead. This upset the man, and after another month the spirits allowed him to return to Earth. They gave him gifts and sacrificial goats, instructed him to return the way he had come, then accompanied him to the outskirts of his village before disappearing "into their holes." A feast was held in the man's honor upon his return. The narrative was recounted in order to explain afterlife beliefs, demonstrating that it was accepted as factual (Schebesta 1936: 194–5).

In another Efé myth, a man ascended to a heavenly realm to be with the deity Baatsi, leaving his family to believe he was dead. The realm he visited does not seem to normally have been a land of the dead, and the ascent appears to have been bodily (ibid. 184–5).

The Efé believed that the soul (*Bopuri*) went to Tore "in the sky. . . . things are good up there and they are bad down here." The soul was carried there by flies, though it could also ascend on lightning (ibid. 236).

Bakongo (Kongo)

The prophet Dona Beatriz Kimpa Vita was a Kongolese Catholic as well as being a medium in the local Kimpasi healing cult. Initiation into the cult involved a ritual death and resurrection, brought about by cutting off the circulation with tight bonds. Upon revival, or "rebirth," initiates were believed to be possessed by a friendly spirit who would stay with them throughout their lives (Thornton 1998: 57).

In 1704, as a contemporary recounted, Kimpa Vita died during a weeklong illness "and has been revived from the dead" (ibid. 119). She claimed to have met Saint Anthony, who told her he had "been sent from God to your head to preach to the people." He gave her religious and political instructions, then entered her body and remained in her thereafter, just as spirits did with members of the Kimpasi cult. Subsequently, Kimpa Vita died each Friday in order to commune with God in heaven over the weekend. Her possession gave her the ability to perform miracles such as healings (Thornton 1998: 132) and controlling nature and the weather (ibid. 136–7), and led to the foundation of a syncretized religious revitalization movement called Antonianism. During a time of European religious and ethnic persecution, slavery, and political turmoil, she taught a message of peace along with an indigenized Christianity that relocated the origin story of Jesus to the Kongo (ibid. 160). The religion was also characterized by claims of an impending apocalypse (ibid. 131), which alongside the NDE context and localization of foreign themes are all common with religious revitalization movements across cultures. The movement had its own missionaries, some of whom replicated Kimpa Vita's experiences: "Saint Isabel" and "Saint Lucy," for example, were dead for seven days before reviving, then repeated the process weekly (ibid. 148). Two years after her experience, by order of the Kongolese Roman Catholic King Pedro IV (Nusamu a Mvemba), Kimpa Vita was burned at the stake on suspicion of being a witch possessed by a demon.

Like Kimpasi and Antonianism, a Bakongo secret society practiced a form of simulated resurrection, in which individuals went to a healer to ritually "die." The community considered initiates to be dead for a period of six months to three years, during which time they were supposed to decompose until only a single bone remained. When "brought back to life" they were reintegrated into society (Weeks 1914: 159–64).

In 1921, the prophet Simon Kimbangu died and after three days returned to life with the power to raise the dead. Descriptions of associated NDE phenomena are lacking, but the very fact of his return seems to have been foundational to his movement, the Kimbanguist Church (Janzen and MacGaffey 1974: 60).

A nineteenth-century NDE was reported by the English trader Richard Edward Dennett (1898: 133–4). A man who died after being struck by lightning reported that he had been carried up to the realm of the god Nzambi Mpungu. He was fed and shown a land of plenty, with "great plantations and rivers full of fish." After a few weeks, Nzambi Mpungu asked him if he wanted to stay, but the man decided to return. Dennett (ibid. 60ff) also reported a myth in which a man journeyed to the other world in order to find his brother, who wanted to go there after seeing it reflected in a mirror. They returned together to Earth, along with other dead people.

The missionary G. Cyril Claridge (1922: 288–9), who spent twelve years among the Bakongo, stated that their ideas of the afterlife originated in OBE phenomena, in which there was widespread belief. He referred to reports of being outside the body and seeing it "as though stark dead", to souls visiting their own funerals, and to travels to earthly and supernatural places. One narrative related the adventures of a "common man" who followed a "wizard" to "the country of the dead," where he witnessed a cannibalistic witchcraft ceremony that gave the wizard renewed power (Claridge 1922: 152–3). The Bakongo also believed in ghosts and mediumship (ibid. 144, 146), and had a secret brotherhood called the Death and Resurrection Society in which people with physical disabilities would undergo a simulated death before being "raised from the dead" fully healed (ibid. 190).

According to Abbot Proyart (1776: 596), missionaries in the Kongo were particularly interested in discovering local beliefs about the soul. They were consistently told that "all believed the soul to be spiritual and that it survived the body." Though informants did not know in what state the soul survived, "whether joy or pain," they believed that "it flies from the towns and villages, and flutters in the air above the woods and forests, in the way which the Deity pleases." Proyart stressed that even those "who never had any connection with foreigners" consistently held such beliefs.

Focusing primarily on nineteenth-century material, Wyatt MacGaffey (1986: 73) found that the Bakongo believed that individuals who were suffering a prolonged death were "being interrogated on the threshold" of the next world about possible witchcraft offenses. He also recounted a case in which a man was "sent back for his identity card." MacGaffey (1986: 53) suggested that the Bakongo word for "death" (*lufwa*) is more accurately translated as "catalepsy" because it is "reversible and may happen several times to one individual." Returning from the dead, and healers restoring souls to bodies, were thus seen only as "remarkable rather than miraculous."

Though rather recent for the present purposes, a later twentieth-century non-Christian Bakongo NDE should also be mentioned. A man "died" and found himself "at the bank of the Zaire River. . . . Across the river several people appeared and said, 'you must not die; there are too many orphans to care for.'" They told the man about three plants, which would cure infertility in women, and he returned to his body with the knowledge (Janzen 1978: 196; McClenon 2006a: 24).

According to missionary John H. Weeks (1914: 267–8), the Bakongo of the Lower Congo believed that it was possible for a corpse to return to life until it had been fully desiccated. Despite such notions and beliefs in OBEs during dreams (ibid. 282), it was also stated that the living could not visit the land of the dead. The other world was sometimes conceived of as a town in a forest where life mirrored that on Earth. Alternatively (or simultaneously), it was believed that at death the deceased traveled to a forked road. The bad took a path to the sun, and the good took a path to the moon. Judgment was held at a "court," and "confirmed . . . by the Supreme Deity (*Nzambi*)." These conceptions existed alongside beliefs in reincarnation (Weeks 1914: 278–9), and that shooting stars were spirits of the dead (ibid. 282).

The validation—if not origin—of Bakongo new religious movements was commonly grounded more in prophetic visions than in NDEs. As McClenon (2006a: 25) explained, "Such experiences trigger profound beliefs—sufficient to launch the visionary's career as a prophet." Concerning Bakongo religious texts from Lower Zaire, Janzen and MacGaffey (1974: 56) wrote that narratives of "supernatural" experiences "become the organizing myth or charter of a religious movement." In the Bakongo case, however, such experiences and beliefs had more to do with possession and witchcraft than with the afterlife and NDEs.

Boloki, Kaonde, Sanga, and Lunda

The Boloki of the Congo believed that the living could temporarily leave their bodies. After death the soul traveled to the netherworld, where it was greeted by "departed spirits." The good remained there while the bad were subject to punishment before being sent back to torment people on Earth. The Boloki also practiced possession mediumship (Weeks 1913: 264, 321).

The Kaonde, Sanga, Lunda and neighboring Congo Zambesi groups believed that certain men would rise from the dead and become "another human being" who was immortal (*wusangu*). As with the Ashanti shamanic healer mentioned earlier, in certain cases a man would tell his wife that he was going to die so that the villagers would expect his resurrection. Instead of conducting his burial, they would place him where he could rise "and start on his new existence without trouble." The predominant afterlife belief, however, was that the soul left the body and reincarnated into another human or animal, according to choice (Melland 1923: 151–2, 166).

Nuer

The Nuer of south Sudan were particularly resistant to Christianity and were subject to little missionary influence until the 1940s. In an NDE from the 1950s, a man named Gik Cam Jok died and returned. He described how he had met the prophet Ngundeng Bong (1830–1906), who told him it was not yet his time to die, and that he would return to the other world "when things were finished." The man died shortly after the end of the decades-long civil war (Johnson 1994: 317).

Though belief in life after death was common, in his 1930s fieldwork Evans-Pritchard (1956: 154) found that the Nuer did not claim to know the location of the other world or what life was like there, and indeed seemed uninterested in "what happens to them after death." He nevertheless recorded beliefs both in an Earth-like underworld, and in a heavenly realm where souls rejoined the creator deity Kwoth, for "Life comes from God and to him it returns." That it was a spiritual realm is attested by the explanation, "his soul has gone above, his flesh was buried". Spirits of the dead could influence Kwoth for their friends and relatives, return as ghosts to haunt the living, or even carry off family members and cattle (Evans-Pritchard 1956: 146, 174). The Nuer also had spirit possession beliefs and practiced mediumship (ibid. 35ff).

Eastern
Baganda (Ganda)

In a Baganda (Uganda) myth, a hunter named Mpobe followed his dog through a tunnel to the land of the dead, where he saw "people, a large garden, and many houses." The dog led him to Walumbe, god of death, who asked him where he had come from and what he had experienced so far in the netherworld. Mpobe explained that he was lost and had not had time to look around, being focused on following his dog. Walumbe told him to return to his home, but warned him never to tell anyone that he had been to the other world, on punishment of death. When Mpobe returned, he told his mother of his journey and was subsequently killed (Roscoe 1911: 465–67).[3]

Lango

The Lango of Uganda believed that the soul could leave the body and interact with the ancestors during dreams and in shamanic trance states. The soul was identified as Orongo, "the universal spirit form" of the omnipresent invisible spiritual essence, Jok. The individual soul (*tipo*) was a "separate, though not entirely independent" form of Orongo, which was absorbed into Jok after the funeral; though it could also be dangerous to the living (Driberg 1923: 220, 229–31). Shamans (*abanwa*) could visit Jok Orongo to obtain advice and information, then return to their bodies (ibid. 239). In order to prevent premature burial, cold water was thrown on apparently dead individuals in order to revive them in case they were only in a trance (ibid. 166). The Lango were notably reticent about discussing their beliefs, and banned their members from religious activities if they had been "contaminated by white influence" (ibid. 216).

Lotuko

A Lotuko (Uganda) myth explained why people no longer return from the dead. A woman was in deep mourning after her child died, and she appealed to the supreme deity Majok to restore the child to life. When the god did so, this angered the father who then killed the child for good. This, in return, angered Majok, who vowed that he would not bring the dead to life anymore, and that henceforth when any Lotuko die they must remain dead (Cunningham 1905: 370).

Chaga

In a Chaga (Kenya) narrative from c. 1914, a girl named Marwe committed suicide in order to escape her parents' wrath at her neglect of the family crop. She jumped into a pool, entered another world, and met an old woman and some children in a hut. Though she was told she could rest, Marwe helped the children in their work and refused to eat anything. Eventually she decided to return home, and the old woman asked her, "Shall I hit you with the cold or with the hot?" The girl chose cold, and the woman had her dip her arms and legs into a pot. When she pulled them out, they were covered in bangles. The old woman gave Marwe a beaded petticoat and told her who her future husband would be. When Marwe returned to life, she married the man after curing his disease, and later brought him back from death. She thus received a prophetic vision that turned out to be accurate, and returned with supernatural healing powers as fruits of her experience (Werner 1933: 93).

A similar narrative involved a girl named Maruwa being given jewelry in the other world, and having to choose between returning to Earth via "the manure" or "the burning." She chose the former, was thrown into a manure pit, and returned home unharmed. When a neighbor's daughter became jealous of the jewelry, she also drowned herself but chose "the burning." She returned to Earth with "fire hidden in her body," then burst into flames and died (Werner 1925: 206–7). In another narrative, a man went through a gateway to the other world and saw his two deceased children. An old woman asked him if he wanted to return to Earth via the "sewage-door" or the "sugar-cane door." The latter would result in his arriving in his home through the fireplace, getting burned, and dying soon. The former ensured he would return safely to his house and have a long life (ibid. 196).

In a narrative first published in 1909, a man lost his sons and went to kill the sun god Iruwu in revenge. As he waited for sunrise to take the path to the other world, a noisy procession of people approached, "shining like fire" and clearing the way for "the Shining One" to pass. Though the man tried to hide in fear, the radiant people discovered him and took him to Iruwu, who asked where he was from and why he was there. When he explained, Iruwu offered to let the man shoot him with his arrow, but the man declined. Iruwu then told him he could take his sons back, "but they were so beautiful and radiant that he scarcely knew them," so he decided they should stay in the other world. Iruwu sent the man back to Earth, rewarding him with riches, more sons, and a long life. Werner (1933: 51-3) found it "remarkable" that the sons were dwelling with the sun god, "for as a rule the Bantu think of their dead as living underground." Such unique elements, which run contrary to local beliefs, may suggest that the narrative was rooted in an actual NDE. Other Chaga ascent myths do not involve deceased ancestors, and though they portrayed the heavenly realm as an idealized mirror image of Earth populated with people, it was not overtly described as an afterlife realm.[4]

The Chaga believed that people taken to the underworld by ghosts could later return (Werner 1925: 187). The journey there took nine days and involved a perilous desert crossing leading to a gateway. To be admitted, the deceased had to give a bull to the Spirit Chief and his warriors (presumably provided in the form of a sacrifice by the deceased's living relatives as part of the funerary ritual). The deceased's grandfather and other relatives then greeted the new arrival, and told "him the reason why he had to die." Afterlife conditions were dependent on sacrifices made to the Spirit Chief by the dying, meaning that the rich remained rich and the poor remained poor: "Chiefs and Headmen" dined well, while most other people had to eat "ants, crabs, frogs and insects." Overall, however, the other realm was seen as a less appealing version of Earth (Dundas 1924: 124–5).

Nandi

In a widespread Nandi (Kenya) account, a man died after falling into a river. He found himself in "a strange country" similar to Earth. Spirits came to him and said: "Young man, your time has not yet come when you should join us. Go back to the earth." With that they struck the ground, the man lost consciousness again, and woke up near the place where he had fallen into the river.

The Nandi believed that souls of the deceased descended to an underworld, but only after the body had been eaten by a hyena. It was a mirror image of Earth, where positive or negative existence was dependent on one's earthly wealth. Status, age, and activities persisted. Ancestor spirits generally acted as guardians of the living, but could also be fearsome ghosts (Hollis 1909: 41, 70–1; Huntingford 1953: 137–8). It was also believed that the soul left the body during sleep, trance, or faints, and that people could communicate with spirits of the dead during dreams (Hollis 1909: 81-2; Huntingford 1953: 158).

A Nandi myth told of how a dog gave the first humans the opportunity to return from death. In exchange for some milk and beer, they would be able to "go to the river" and "come to life again on the third day." The people insulted the dog, however, by not giving him the milk and beer in their own drinking vessels, thus dooming themselves to physical mortality (Hollis 1909: 98).

Elgeyo

In 1920, the district commander of Kenya, J. A. Massam (1927: 195), recorded an Elgeyo narrative in which a man died, left his body, then returned to it as it was about to be buried. He claimed "that he had been up above, and had seen wonderful herds of stock belonging to the sun, 'Assis' [supreme deity], and lesser herds belonging to the rain god 'Elat'." He was told by the inhabitants of the other world that his only hope of ever remaining there permanently was to kill a man back on Earth. He did so a month after his return to life, then died in jail. The account conflicts with Elgeyo afterlife beliefs in intra-clan reincarnation and the continued existence of ancestors on Earth.

Luhya

A Luhya narrative of "Why people never rise from death" explained how in the distant past, people used to return from the dead after four days. One day when a boy returned, he was rejected by his mother, "who told him that he had died and should stay in the grave." The boy did as he was told, but placed a curse on the people ensuring that henceforth the dead would stay dead (Wagner 1954: 44). The Luhya also believed in prophecy through dreams, and that powers could be gained directly from the ancestors (ibid. 46).

Akamba

The Akamba of Kenya had myths in which entire groups of people were resurrected, of ancestor spirits (*aimu*) resurrecting a single individual multiple times, and of distant times when people were immortal and could be resurrected or rejuvenated (Mbiti 1971: 157–8). The *aimu* appeared to the living as "inexplicable light" (Hobley 1910: 86), and sent visions to children who were destined to become healers. It was believed that the deceased went to join the ancestors in the other world, in a new body identical to the one left behind. The other world was located underground, or was conceived of as being "everywhere," though invisible. It was an idealized mirror image of Earth, where souls had spiritual powers and were able to interact with the creator deity. They could also communicate via mediums, warn the living of dangers, and assist with agricultural activities. They also posed a potential threat, however, due to their abilities to cause madness and to possess the living, and they were thus propitiated with offerings. Once souls became *aimu*, they were no longer considered to be part of the community, though were still present in areas of "hills, rocks, and large ponds." They were considered to be something between human and divine, and their abilities included flying, shapeshifting, moving with extraordinary speed, "and even dying several times" (Mbiti 1971: 134–5).

Kikuyu

When asked about local afterlife beliefs, a Kikuyu (Kenya) informant in "pre-missionary days" related an otherworld journey narrative that recalls the Zulu and Mbuti descent myths discussed elsewhere in this chapter (all three were Bantu-speaking people). A friend of the informant's brother followed a porcupine to a realm of "bad people" who had much livestock but lived in "very cold" conditions without clothing, with only a scrap of hide to cover their faces at night. They bound the man and kept him in the underworld for "many years." He eventually escaped by jumping into a hole beneath a tree and following a tunnel, though he was pursued "until he came to a fire, and then the bad people could not seize him." The man returned to his village and told his people what he had experienced, then died a few days later. In contrast, when another Kikuyu informant was asked about the realm of the dead, he replied, "How can I, a living man, tell you about the dead?" (Routledge & Routledge 1910: 243–4).

Maasai

The Maasai (southern Kenya and northern Tanzania) told British administrator Alfred Claud Hollis (1905: 307–8) that when a man dies, "his soul dies with him ... [and he] does not come to life again." They did, however, believe that OBEs could happen during dreams, and if a dreamer was awakened too suddenly his soul might not return. Hollis also reported beliefs that the souls of medicine-men became snakes once their bodies decayed, and that certain prominent individuals went to "heaven." The German military officer Moritz Merker (1910: 170), who spent more than eight years with the Maasai (1895–1908), described their "religious doctrine as it is handed down and taught by the old men." They believed in a "guardian angel" psychopomp who took all souls regardless of status or behavior to a "cloud land." There the soul was judged by the creator deity 'Ngai. The good joined their deceased relatives in an idealized Earth-like paradise—a realm of abundance where spirits dwelled without worries or work. The bad were "driven into a barren, waterless desert," while borderline cases were allowed into paradise but had to work (ibid. 269).[5]

Nyakyusa

According to the missionary D. R. Mackenzie (1925: 298), who lived with the Nyakyusa (southern Tanzania and northern Malawi) for twenty-four years, they believed that those who committed suicide had to explain to the spirits in the other world why they did so. Their reasons did not determine their fate, however, for all were told to "come and rest." According to Mackenzie, "This information comes from persons who 'died' and returned, though a more common belief is that the dead do not return." Mackenzie was not clear whether other Nyakyusa afterlife beliefs originated in NDE phenomena, though they included descending through the grave to an underground Land of Spirits, meeting deceased ancestors, acquiring great power, dwelling with the deity, and the ability to visit Earth (including in animal forms). The underworld was an idealization of Earth where one's status was maintained, cattle and fruits did not need tending, and there was plentiful hunting and fishing, even though "everything is small . . . [and] insubstantial." If the spirit's family died out, it would become a frog (Mackenzie 1925: 190–5).

Tumbuka

In the early days of missionary activity among the Tumbuka (Malawi), a man's body was being prepared for burial when it suddenly revived. As the missionary Donald Fraser (1914: 126) reported:

> On his recovery he told how he had gone by a narrow road until he came to a great village where the people lived without marriage. He had spoken to them, but none would hold conversation with him. They told him to be gone, for he was not wanted there. He tried to tell his story, but no one would listen to him. They beat irons together and tried to drown his words, for he was too uncanny.

The Tumbuka believed in out-of-body travel to visit the realm of the dead and other faraway places, during dreams and otherwise. The dead lived in an underworld "great valley where everything is good." There was no death or sorrow, and people regained their youth and spent their time dancing and grinding "their heavenly corn" among "beautiful domestic fowls." Those who "lived selfish and cruel lives" were greeted with disdain in the underworld, and spirits would slap them and "dance about them in derision." Spirits of the dead could also also enter into animals, or remain on Earth and "are everywhere," living among the people or in sacred groves. The after-death existence of the soul was temporary, with the individual gradually fading "into oblivion after a few generations" (ibid. 124–7).

Tanala

The phenomenon of individuals returning from death was known to the Tanala of Madagascar, though apparently not NDEs. This was perhaps due to the fact that when a "corpse" began to revive, "it is quietly strangled" for it was believed

that the soul (*angatra*) had not returned, but that the body had only been ani-
mated by the breath or life force (*aina*). It was, nevertheless, believed that souls
of the living could visit villages of the dead, but they risked staying there permanently. They were sometimes assisted in their return by shamans (*ombiasy*), but all
memory of their afterlife experiences was eradicated upon revival. Out-of-body
experiences could occur otherwise in the living, and it was believed that the soul
"leaves the body during sleep, unconsciousness or insanity, and dreams and hallucinations are its actual experiences" (Linton 1933: 165). Considered spirit duplicates of physical bodies, souls of the living and the dead could appear visibly to
each other, and meet in dreams and under trance (ibid. 166–7).

After death, "a person who has been formally disowned, a notorious sorcerer,
or a man of extremely evil life" would be rejected by the ancestors and denied
admittance into the afterlife community. Such souls became "vagabonds" who
hung around the earthly village, disrupted rituals, tried to negatively influence
other ancestor spirits against the living, or became "malevolent human spirits"
who lived in rivers and caused drownings (ibid. 160). Otherwise, the afterlife
was the same as life on Earth. It was variously believed that the other realm was
located in a nearby sacred mountain, forest, or hilltop, in abandoned villages or
tombs, in villages among the living, or that it was in the sky with the creator
deity Zanahary. Some believed that souls were drawn back to the burial place
of their placenta. If the umbilical cord was not thrown into a sacred river after
birth, the soul could not go to the realm of the ancestors. People of the Menabe
area believed that those who were killed with spears and those whose bodies were
denied burial in the village tomb (e.g., thieves, sorcerers, and those who died of
certain diseases) became bird-like beings called *ziny*, with fire under their wings
(possibly "derived from the Arab djinns") (ibid. 167–8).

Southern
Mbundu

In the mid-seventeenth century, the missionary Giovanni Antonio Cavazzi wrote
of a Mbundu (Angola) woman who returned from death after being sacrificed
because "her services in the Other World were not needed." In 1922, the Mbundu
told the Swedish-American historian Amandus Johnson about individuals
who had "risen from the dead." They described having visited the spirit world
(Kalunga) which was reserved for "those judged worthy," and was ruled by the
creator deity Soba Kalunga. John Thornton (2002: 75) considers these narratives
to be explanations for Mbundu afterlife beliefs, and McClenon (2006a: 23) likewise sees them in the context of the experiential source hypothesis.

In a myth reported in 1894, a man named Ngunza was upset that his brother had died, so he captured Kalunga-ngombe, Lord of the Netherworld. Kalunga-ngombe explained that he was not responsible for death, but that it was due to human action. The two went together to the other world for four days, and Ngunza found his brother living as he had on Earth, "much happier where he was" and not wishing to return. Ngunza returned with the gift of seeds for cultivation. When Kalunga-ngombe later came for him, Ngunza avoided him by transforming into a water spirit (*Kituta*) (Chatelain 1894: 249–50).

In another Mbundu narrative, a doctor and his little boy followed a deceased queen through her grave to an underworld village. When they found her, she pointed out Kalunga-ngombe in the distance, then showed them a chained man who looked like the king, Kitamba. She prophesied that Kitamba would die within a few years, then gave the doctor and his son an armlet. Upon returning, they presented the armlet to Kitamba as evidence of their encounter with his wife. The king died a few years later as prophesied (ibid. 225–7).

The Mbundu also had beliefs in the transmigration of souls after death. A seventeenth-century ruler told Portuguese missionary Manuel Ribeiro that souls of men passed into their wives or children. Ribeiro also mentioned a funeral in which guns were fired to frighten the soul away and prevent it from entering a family member. Some, however, believed that the soul died with the body (Thornton 2002: 74).

Lamba

The Lamba (Zambia) recounted to the missionary-ethnographer Clement Martyn Doke (1931: 258) incidents of people who were ill and in danger of death, and who "speak in a weird way, using the most extravagant language, telling of wonderful things" they have seen. Such experiences were not interpreted as the individual having visited the afterlife realm, however, but were instead attributed to spirit possession. The Lamba also believed in other extraordinary occurrences involving the dead, including spiritualistic communication (ibid. 232), ghosts (ibid. 241), contact during dreams (ibid. 248), and corpses being haunted by demons (ibid. 249).

Ila

Though "any notion of a general bodily resurrection appears very ridiculous to them," the Ila of Zambia nevertheless had "vague tales . . . of people who have actually returned in the flesh." This was achieved by virtue of a powerful drug that would make a dead person rise again after three days, at which time they would travel eastward to a land called Chundu, to live a new life there (Dale 1920: 103).

The Ila had at least three myths explaining why people do not return from death, including one similar to the Ekoi myth of the duck and frog: a chameleon was sent by a deity to tell people that they "shall die and pass away for ever," while a hare was sent with the conflicting message "that they shall die and return." The deity ultimately sided with the chameleon.

Spirits of the dead were feared and afterlife beliefs were extremely varied, but most had little to do with NDE phenomenology: traveling to an underworld or someplace in the east similar to Earth; remaining at the grave, in the village of the living, or in a tree, a rock, or anthill; becoming an animal, an evil spirit, or a deity; possession of a living person, and eventual reincarnation (ibid. 118–9). Prophets gained their status through possession experiences, rather than through NDEs or shamanic afterlife journeys (ibid. 142ff).

Tswana (Bechuana)

The British missionary William Charles Willoughby (1928: 99) recounted four Tswana (Botswana) NDEs. In the first, his "house-boy" was depressed with grief to the point of physical illness following the death of his brother. He claimed that he "went away" and saw the brother as well as his father and uncle. The latter told him that he should not leave his mother, and that he therefore must return. The boy concluded, "they sent me back with great peace," and he revived with "new life" transformed by his NDE.

A Tswana elder recounted an NDE from his youth. He had been declared dead, and while his grave was being prepared he left his body and traveled to

> a very lovely city, full of strange people, white[6] and glistening. The town, also, was radiant with splendour, and there was not a stump in it, nor any-thing that could cause stumbling or disaster. A superb man whom he met there told him to arise and depart, and so he returned to Earth.

The man had a second NDE later in life, again while his body was being prepared for burial. He claimed he was not delirious either time, and denied the possibility that the content of his experience could have been influenced by Christianity. He declared, moreover, that in every generation there were individuals who were thought to be dead but had recovered before burial; and that many of them had seen what he had seen, though they, too, knew nothing of Christianity. He further stated that the existence of the kind of afterlife he described was common knowl-edge among the Tswana, as was "the radiance of the town and its inhabitants." He also noted "that it was not a rare thing" for people to have deathbed visions of deceased relatives who told them to "arise and depart" (i.e., to return to Earth) (Willoughby 1928: 100–1). The neighboring Shona likewise believed "that when a man is dying he sees in a vision the spirits of his dead relatives" (Bullock 1950: 175).

A lapsed Christian convert reported a distressing NDE, in which she died and went to the spirit realm where "she felt a flame of fire burning in her breast, and causing her such distress as she had never experienced on earth." She saw a deceased aunt and cried out for water, but was given none. Then she saw Jesus "and the flame was quenched within her." He explained that the fire was an inevitable punishment for those who drink alcohol ("Kafir-beer"), for it drives away the Holy Spirit. On her return journey, the woman was shown a rock painted yellow, black, and white, though she was not told the meaning of it. She was, however, told "that she would die before sunset; and she did." Willoughby (1928: 101–2) suggested that much of the imagery of the experience was a result of pain cause by the woman's inflamed lungs, her own predilection for drink, and from a sermon she had attended.

The missionary/anthropologist Samuel Shaw Dornan (1925: 280) was for some reason unconvinced that the Tswana definitely believed in "the persistence of individual personality after death," despite hearing firsthand reports to that effect. He recorded beliefs that souls went to an afterlife world that mirrored Earth, located to the east in the rising sun, where they joined their deceased relatives. Alternatively, it was believed that souls remained on Earth, and that they could communicate with the living and affect them in both negative and positive ways. British missionary J. Tom Brown (1926: 69–71) also attested to Tswana afterlife beliefs, including in a heavenly realm for the good and a hellish one for the bad. This was alongside myths explaining why people do not normally return from death (similar to those of the Ekoi, involving delayed messages between humans and deities; ibid. 163–4, 167). Dornan (1925: 280) claimed that such conceptions were "colored by Christian belief". This may have been the case, considering that around a century earlier, Moffat (1951: 253) wrote that "Death and a future state are subjects they do not like to contemplate, and when they are introduced it frequently operates like an imperative order for them to depart." Perhaps the occurrence of NDEs, alongside a Christian framework for their interpretation, and in combination with existing indigenous traditions, led to the development of Tswana afterlife beliefs.

Zulu

Traveler and businessman Henry Francis Fynn (1824–36: 32–4) related a narrative from Natal about a man named Bandla who was taken by a lion to an underworld of abundance and joy, where people contiuned the same roles they had on Earth. He met deceased relatives and kings, spirits who sang and danced, and his former wives who "had been kept as they were . . . till the death of the husband." The spirits questioned Bandla about why he was there, then instructed him to report back to his people "that death was only a sleep from which they again rise to live in happiness." A relative scratched his eye as a sign to convince people back on Earth of the truth of his story. He was also told where he would find a goat to sacrifice on his way back, and the information turned out to be accurate. Bandla's account was believed by his people and by local tribes, and he became a favorite of his chief Magaye and of the famous king Shaka (1787–1828). According to Fynn, Bandla was "peculiar" and "his account of the world below is still believed by his countrymen as an undoubted truth."

In what is perhaps an alternate version of the same narrative, reported by the British missionary Joseph Shooter (1857: 270–1), an old man was carried off by a lion to its den, "sank into the earth," and found himself in the spirit land. It was a fine place, where he saw spirits of his own people who "are much smaller than we are," including Umbia, a great chief and doctor of the previous generation who had recently appeared to the king in a dream. In a version reported by the American missionary Lewis Grout (1864: 136) the lion took the man through a "long and narrow" passage. The man was not allowed to stay in the other world, and was sent back to Earth after being given food. Upon his return, he described the spirit realm as a happy place with plenty of cattle, though everything and everyone was in miniature.

One of the British missionary Henry Callaway's (1868: 317–20) informants told him of a man he knew named Uncama, who had followed a porcupine to the underworld. He passed a pool, crossed a river, and entered a dark tunnel. It gradually grew light, and Uncama eventually emerged in an underground village—a "great country" with "mountains, precipices and rivers" just like in the upper world. He saw smoke rising and there were dogs and people, including children. Suddenly afraid, Uncama decided to return. He found his wife in mourning for him and preparing his funeral.[7]

David Leslie (1875: 120–1) was a trader, hunter, and Zulu-speaking court interpreter who spent most of his life in the Colony of Natal (South Africa). He reported that in addition to beliefs that "witches" could bring the dead back to life, according to one informant there were also "people who have died and come back again in the proper way." As an example, the man told of a brother who returned from death after his own funeral: "He told us that he had been in a fine country, where the corn and sugar-cane grew thick and tall, and the cattle were as fat as fat could be; and that he met a cousin of his, who had died a long time before, who told him to go back immediately." Otherwise, another spirit would give him food, and he would have to remain in the other world. The brother woke up in his body, thinking "ah! what a delightful country I have been in." He then "seemed continually to mourn for the good things he had left; would speak to no one, and wandered about as if he did not belong to us." Interestingly, the informant interpreted his brother's experience as explaining why so few people ever return from the dead: the chances of meeting a relative are slim, so it is more likely that one will meet a stranger and be given food.

The American missionary Josiah Tyler (1891: 97) wrote that "the manner in which [the Zulu] obtained a knowledge of Hades" was through the narrative of a hunter who followed a deer through a deep hole in the ground. It led to the realm of the ancestors, who lived a good life with an abundance of food and cattle. The Zulu also believed in precognitive dreams, and practiced spirit mediumship (ibid. 107).

Grout (1864: 158–9) reported that shamans undertook visionary journeys to visit the ancestor spirits. They generally attained their status following a prolonged illness and being thrown into the sea. According to Willoughby (1928: 126), in the "olden days" Zulu prophets usually became so after a diviner or other religious practitioner would revive following "a comatose condition . . . and when the person regains consciousness he is wont to declare that he died, went to the spirit-world and was sent back with a message to men."

The Zulu believed in a particular type of possession called *ukuthwasa*, or "emergence," indicating rebirth "as a 'new' person" following possession by an ancestor spirit (Lee 1969: 134–5, citing examples as early as 1833). In a 1951 account, a woman was suffering a prolonged illness due to possession by angry ancestors. Following sacrifices made on her behalf, she went into "a very deep sleep" and saw her grandfathers and great-grandfathers coming to her. She awoke strong and healthy, and became a professional diviner. The account is consistent with other deathbed visions in that the ancestors went to her rather than vice versa.

The Zulu were notably resistant to Christianity, and their afterlife beliefs involved the dead becoming ghosts and going to live underground with the ancestors. They attained "great power" in the other world, though they retained their earthly social status (Shooter 1857: 161–2). They could visit Earth, take the form of snakes, and influence the lives of the living. Grout (1864: 136), however, wrote that beliefs varied widely and there was little agreement between individuals. Beliefs in reincarnation as snakes were also attested, with different species assigned to particular social roles, age, or sex (Bryant 1917: 40).

Sotho (Basuto)

The British missionary Robert Keable (1921: 527–9; cf. McClenon 2006a: 30) recounted a distressing Sotho NDE in which a man died and traveled along a road until he came to a fork. Uncertain which way to go, he hesitated until a guide appeared and led him onto one of the paths. Struck by the guide's "villainous countenance," the man grew afraid and demanded to know where they were going, then called for help when the guide refused to tell him. A man with a cross on his head scared the guide away, told the NDEr that he was on the path to hell, and instructed him to go back the way he had come. When the man returned to life, he immediately went to a catechist to convert to Christianity. Because the catechist was not supposed to baptize except "in extremis," he instead put the sign of the cross on the man's head. That night, the man died again and traveled to the same crossroads, but took the other path. He was sent back, however, because he did not have a cross on his head. Although the catechist had made one, it was not a sign of complete conversion via baptism. The man persuaded the catechist to baptize him, then died a third and final time. Keable regarded this case as evidential, arguing that the NDEr did "not know enough of Christianity" to have understood that he was not "officially" a Christian after being given the initial sign, and only learned this through paranormal means during his NDE.

Keable (1921: 529–30) also described the experiences of a man whose conversion to Christianity and authority as a prophet both lay in an NDE. He died during an illness and returned after his funerary preparations had been made three days later, though he felt he had been away many years. He recounted how he had traveled to a river he could not cross, where many other souls were gathered on the bank. Spirits from the other side made regular trips to select new souls to join them, but they told him that only when his knees had hardened from kneeling in prayer would he be selected. He learned to pray, finally crossed the river, and arrived at "God's throne," where he was "ordered to return to earth" in order to teach repentance. Though the man was previously illiterate, God gave him the power to read the Bible, which he demonstrated once he returned to life. He also had newfound healing and prophetic powers, and knowledge of many prayers. As a prophet who "died and rose again from the dead," he drew large crowds and effected the conversion of many people. Others, however, refused to convert because they themselves had experienced no "dream" or other "supernatural occurrence" persuading them that they should do so (ibid. 522–3).

Keable (1921: 525) found that the Sotho otherwise had "no definite theology at all as to departed spirits," and no conclusions regarding the nature of an afterlife realm. Nor did they fear NDE incidents, and were "not commonly fearful of dead bodies." They believed in apparitions of the dead, and despite seventy-five years of missionary activity, they continued to have faith in dreams and to "believe of a man unconscious that he is dead" (Keable 1921: 522). However, earlier afterlife beliefs were reported by the French Protestant missionary Eugène Casalis (1861: 242), who lived among the Sotho for twenty-three years beginning in 1833. He described widespread beliefs in an underworld where "shades wander about in silent calm, experiencing neither joy nor sorrow." Less common were beliefs in an underworld happy hunting ground for immortal souls. Casalis (1861: 242) also recounted a version of the myth explaining why people no longer return to life when they die, featuring a chameleon and a lizard.

Khoikhoi

In a Khoikhoi (South Africa) myth, the culture hero Heitsi-Eibib returned from the dead and climbed out of his grave (Kidd 1904: 413–4). He was, in fact, said to have died and returned multiple times. In one narrative he was flung repeatedly into the cavern of ancestors, but escaped each time. In another, he died from eating poison grapes but returned "healthy and well," though nevertheless afraid that as a dead man he might poison his family. Some considered him to be the supreme deity Tsui-goa, and he was said to possess the abilities to shape-shift and read the future (Quatrefages 1895: 205, 212–6).

According to the Swedish naturalist Carl Thunberg (1788: 141–2), the Khoikhoi believed in "the immortality of the soul and its separation from the body," though were not interested in concepts of "afterlife fates such as reward and punishment." Instead, they were more concerned with the potential malevolent influences of an "evil spirit." Over 120 years later, Theal (1910: 84) wrote that they "had not the faintest conception of their own resurrection, or conception of a heaven or hell."

Analysis and Conclusions
African Afterlife Beliefs, Shamanism, and NDEs: An Uneasy Relationship

While the NDE-like themes evident in various afterlife conceptions, otherworld journey myths, and shamanic experiences may hint at actual NDEs, ostensibly historical, unambiguous examples of the phenomenon are scarce in the African material. There are scarcely a dozen such narratives, and some lack detailed description of the experience (Mbundu, Akan). Two additional examples demonstrate general knowledge of NDEs (Ewe, Lamba). There are few indigenous statements that afterlife conceptions originated in NDEs (Efé, Bakongo, Mbundu, Zulu), and two statements that they arose from drug-induced or other altered states of consciousness (Fang and Tshi, respectively). Some derived only certain elements of afterlife beliefs from NDE phenomena (Ekoi and OBEs, Nyakusa and the fate of suicides, Kagoro and why some return from death, Teke and new teachings and rituals), or merely had preexisting beliefs confirmed (Akan ideas of a hellish underworld). Others pointed to afterlife journey myths (i.e., involving animals, deities, or culture heroes) as sources of afterlife conceptions (Kikuyu, Ekoi). The authority of only a few prophets and religious leaders lay in NDEs (Bakongo, Sotho, Zulu). Accounts from the Yoruba, Nuer, Chaga, Mbundu, Ekoi, Fang, Bakongo, Tswana, Zulu, and Sotho show concern for NDE accounts to be taken seriously, featuring claims of prophecies, miracles, or physical items brought back from the other world as evidence for the veracity of the narrative.

Of the dozen or so ostensibly documentary NDEs, two were overtly hellish (Akan, Tswana), while some others featured negative elements. The Tumbuka man was ignored in the other world then sent away because "he was not wanted there" (Fraser 1914: 126). Similarly, the Mbundu sacrificial victim was sent back because her services were not required, and the Akan woman was sent back because she was naked. In the Elgeyo example, the man was told he must commit a murder back on Earth if he wished ever to remain in the other world. Those that read most like NDEs familiar from other cultures, and with positive spiritual elements and interpretations, are from the Bakongo, Nuer, Nandi, Tswana, Zulu, and Fang (if we allow that some iboga experiences qualify as NDEs).

Among the Ashanti, Ewe, Fon, Mbuti, and Lango, leaving the body and traveling to the other world to interact with spirits was the preserve of select qualified shamanic figures, though detailed narratives of such experiences are lacking. Shamans impersonated deceased spirits through possession practices among the Bakongo, and in the Yoruba Egungun, Oro, and other secret societies of southern Nigeria. The most relevant shamanic practices, however, were those of the Fang's Bwiti religion, with iboga-induced visions that share basic phenomenologies with NDEs, as well the essential meanings of spiritual knowledge, rebirth, and joy gained through afterlife journeys. Indeed, given the dangers of ingesting large quantities of the drug, some Banzie may actually have had NDEs. The Idiong Ibibio society "killed" initiates so they would travel to the other world and obtain precognitive information.

Though NDEs are certainly attested in the primary sources, there is a tension between the phenomenon, afterlife conceptions, and shamanic practices. To some extent, this can be accounted for by the more predominant beliefs in the continued presence of ancestor spirits on Earth, whose malevolent or benevolent powers gave them a more immediate significance than speculation about life in other worlds. This in itself is likely related to the relative lack of concern about the afterlife as mentioned in the introduction to the present chapter. Statements such as those of the Kikuyu and Mbuti, to the effect that no one knows what the other world is like because none have been there, further reinforce the fact that NDEs and related experiences were not typically sources of knowledge about the afterlife for African peoples.

However, a deeper understanding of this tension between afterlife conceptions and related experiences is to be found in certain attitudes toward death per se, and toward the very notion that the dead can return to life—particularly when viewed in the contexts of witchcraft, possession, and malevolent ancestor spirits.

Returning from Death as Aberration: NDEs and Otherworld Journey Myths

The idea of an individual returning from the dead was widely regarded as a frightening aberration, and NDE narratives often conflicted with the focus of local afterlife beliefs. Rather than being seen as positive, enlightening, spiritual experiences that brought benefits to the individual and thus to the community, they were rather more often seen in terms of other unwelcome extraordinary phenomena such as possession and evil spirits.

There are various examples of mistrust and hostility toward those who apparently revived from death. Among the Tanala, if a dead or dying person revived and returned to the village they were immediately stoned to death or strangled (Sibree 1880: 291). Kimpa Vita was killed on suspicion of being a witch possessed by a demon. After the Zulu NDE reported by Leslie (1875: 122–3), the man was almost put to death due to fears among his people that he had been revived by witches. When the Akan human sacrifice victim returned from unconsciousness, her request to be killed again after she dressed was readily granted (Reade 1874: 362). When one of Kidd's (1904: 247) acquaintances revived as he was being placed into a grave, everyone in attendance at the funeral fled in terror. According to the Dutch missionary Johannes van der Kemp (1747–1811), among the Khoikhoi if a person revived from apparent death, he or she was sent away to "die again," effectively denied the chance of recovery (Lichtenstein 1812: 319). Alongside the Congo Zambesi belief that certain men would be resurrected as new individuals, steps were taken to ensure that the people were forewarned so the man could begin his "new existence without trouble" (Melland 1923: 151–2). The Tumbuka NDEr met so much resistance when trying to relate his experience that his people drowned his words out by making noise "for he was too uncanny" (Fraser 1914: 126). In South Africa there was said to be an "unspeakable horror of a dead body" (Kidd 1904: 76), and presumably a reanimated "dead" body would have been considered even more horrific.

The dynamic has continued into more recent times. In a Bakongo example from the 1960s/70s, the NDEr reported that upon reviving, the mourners gathered around him "began to quickly move away from me. It took them hours to accept me again as a member of the living community." He added, "You will never find anyone who is willing to associate or be in the same company with the dead." Another Bakongo NDEr reported that his wife was "terrified" by his return, and was afraid of him (Bockie 1993: 89–90). Likewise, in a study of fifteen Zambian NDEs reported by the physician Nsama Mumbwe (Morse & Perry 1992: 120–4), the phenomenon was locally interpreted as resulting from witchcraft, "bad omens," or other malign forces. Despite the presence of some familiar NDE structural features (darkness and tunnel-like sensations, encounters with entities dressed in white robes, reaching a border or limit, and being told to return to the body), many of the subjects "interpreted the event as somewhat evil." Half the participants "thought that the NDE signified that they were 'bewitched' or about to be" (ibid. 121).

Such negative perceptions were reinforced by return-from-death and other-world journey myths. Rather than acting as didactic narratives that purported to reveal what to expect after death or what kind of behavior would ensure a positive afterlife, the myths remarkably served to justify the stigmatization of NDEs by characterizing them as aberrational, against divine authority, or otherwise unnatural and unwelcome. Indeed, as with some NDErs, the protagonists of these narratives were often punished or even "killed again" for the transgression of returning from death. In the Baganda myth, for example, Mpobe was killed for revealing to his mother that he had inadvertently visited the netherworld (Roscoe 1911: 467). In the Lotuko myth explaining why people no longer return from the dead, the child was killed by his angry father after returning to life (Cunningham 1905: 370). In the Luhya narrative of similar function, the boy's mother drove him away when he revived because "he had died and should stay in the grave" (Wagner 1954: 44). Ananute, the protagonist of the Ga myth, was expelled from his village when he related his experiences in the underworld (Werner 1925: 208ff). In the Ekoi myth of the frog and duck, when the deity Obassi Osaw allowed certain people to return from the dead, they "could never tell what had happened to them" (Talbot 1912: 231). While the reason for this is obscure (cultural restriction, divine edict, or something else), it nevertheless demonstrates that relating an NDE was considered problematic. The Tanala believed that any experiences of otherworld journeys would be forgotten upon revival.

In addition, the myths featured proscriptions on relating knowledge obtained in the afterlife. Ananute was forbidden from singing a song he had learned from spirits there (Werner 1925: 208ff). In the Ekoi myths, the woman was instructed in the ghost world not to tell anyone what she had experienced; Mkpaw died after his return to life when a woman touched the magic box he was given in the spirit world; and the man who learned the language of animals in the ghost town died after revealing it to his wife. That the Ekoi otherworld was a dangerous, inhospitable place for visitors is further evidenced by Obassi sending his son there with the intention of killing him; and the woman who was killed for being unkind to spirits, in the myth explaining why living people no longer visit the land of ghosts (Talbot 1912: 233–8). The local significance of a Zulu NDE was that it was considered evidence of why the dead do not normally return to life (the risk of being given food by a spirit in the otherworld). Willoughby (1928: 2–5) also recognized these dynamics among Bantu peoples (which includes the Baganda, Luhya, and Ekoi), writing that attitudes toward the afterlife were commonly rooted in myths of garbled messages from a deity via animal protagonists. Rather than revealing what one may expect in the next world, such myths served to explain why people do not come back to life, for there is "very little speculation concerning the nature of the soul and its afterlife" because there "is no earthly use" for such questions.

While such narratives may nevertheless point to historical NDEs, perhaps sometime in the remote past, the myths that grew around them served to reinforce the notion that returning from the dead is aberrational and unacceptable. Thus, while certain beliefs (e.g., that people should not return from the dead) were grounded in such accounts, the impact of actual narratives of NDEs on African afterlife conceptions was minimal and limited to only a few cases. Narratives of documentary NDEs conflicted with established attitudes toward the notion of returning from death. As such, they were not of sufficient interest or significance to fundamentally reorient attitudes toward beliefs in postmortem survival in positive other worlds, benevolent beings of light, happy reunions with deceased relatives, positive spiritual transformation, and so forth. Indeed, such were the conceptual prohibitions on NDEs that the few examples we do have often lack detail, or the phenomenon is mentioned only in a general sense.

In summary, NDEs were enlisted more to reinforce negative beliefs about returning from death than to introduce new positive ones. Otherworld journey myths gave religious justification for *not* valorizing NDEs, and a culturally sanctioned context for actively denying or marginalizing them. Conversely, when NDEs were seen in a more positive light, there were correspondingly more positive afterlife journey myths, as seen with the Mbundu and Fang.

Funerary Deterrents to Resurrection

Corpse disposal methods sometimes served as deterrents to revival from near-death states, involving deliberate measures to prevent the dead from returning.

In other cases they were designed to ward off some other misfortune caused by the presence of the body. Regardless of intentions, however, many African funerary practices all but precluded the possibility of NDEs occurring. The Baka of Cameroon, for example, practiced immediate burial after fully binding the body and sewing it into a skin sack (Rowley 1877: 92), leaving no chance of a return. The Ovaherero of southern Africa broke the back of the deceased before burial to "prevent mischief" (Theal 1910: 186). Concerning southern Africans, the Scottish missionary Robert Moffat (1842: 306–8) wrote,

> When they see any indications of approaching dissolution in fainting fits or convulsive throes, they throw a net over the body, and hold it in a sitting posture, with the knees brought in contact with the chin, till life is gone.

One unnamed West African culture would break every bone in a corpse's body to ensure that it was dead (Nassau 1904: 234). The Lozi of Zambia conducted burial immediately after apparent death, while the body was still warm (ibid. 228–9), as did other Bantu peoples in South Africa (Kidd 1904: 244). Indeed, such was the hurry to be rid of the body among the Bantu that premature burials are attested (Kidd 1904: 247). According to the French Protestant missionaries Thomas Arbousset and François Daumas (1852: 364), tribes neighboring the San also sometimes interred people alive in their haste to bury the dead. This was evidenced by individuals who recovered and "succeeded in getting out of their sepulchre." The Igbo also practiced immediate burial, as well as a symbolic second burial to ensure that the deceased would not become a malevolent, haunting ghost (Basden 1921: 120–1).

Attitudes toward the dying are also relevant, often demonstrating an acceptance of the inevitability of death which would preclude efforts to facilitate an individual's recovery. Some sources stressed that when death seemed certain, there was a uniquely African resignation and acceptance characterized by "remarkable composure" (Fernandez 1982: 236). Basden (1921: 118) reported that in earlier times the Ibo would sell elderly women to cannibals in order to pay for the women's funerals, which were "considered much more important than her latter end on earth." The Ibo and Ibibio would poison the elderly if they survived while the younger generation died, believing they were sapping their youthful strength (Talbot 1926: 511). Among the Elgeyo, the elderly were barely fed and their deaths were not greatly mourned. Massam (1927: 213–4, 218) encountered a man who was apparently unmoved at the death of his wife and two children, and believed that Elgeyo men in general did not mourn their wives. When the missionary Ruth B. Fisher (1911: 54) inquired about a sick Baganda girl who was being neglected despite the fact that she was at risk of death, she was told that the girl's fate was for the deity to decide. Nor was such acceptance reserved only for others. Moffat (1842: 135) encountered an old woman in southern Africa whose children had left her alone to die, as dictated by local tradition. She resisted his attempts to "rescue" her, explaining, "It is not our custom; I am nearly dead; I do not want to die again." In some reports, such was the degree of fatalism that even minor illnesses could convince individuals that they were going to die, and that nothing could save them. Mackenzie (1925: 298) found that the Nyakyusa would commit suicide for any number of what other societies might consider to be trivial reasons, such as quarrelling at home, loss of a lawsuit, or minor financial troubles. Likewise, Fisher (1911: 54) wrote that "human life is regarded so lightly" by the Baganda that "a man will readily kill himself at the death of a favorite cow." The Romanian anthropologist Dominique Zahan (1979: 46) went so far as to write of a general African "indifference to death and . . . contempt for life," citing examples of individuals volunteering for human sacrifice and cheerfully awaiting execution, and of the fairly common practice of abandoning the elderly to die of starvation or to be eaten by wild animals.

The Dangers of the Dead

Many early scholars stressed a commonality of fearful beliefs surrounding death and the dead across Africa. Death itself was widely seen as unnatural, caused either by a malign spirit or deity, or by witchcraft. Nassau (1904: 231) wrote that the "apparently heartless ceremonies" surrounding death and burial were best explained by "belief in witchcraft" and "fear of spirits." Generalizing about the continent, Rowley (1877: 89) wrote, "any allusion to death jars gratingly on the feelings of all who hear it" (cf. Fernandez 1982: 236). The San were particularly reticent about discussing death and held a great fear of it (Dornan 1925: 144), while "death inspires [the Lozi] with a mortal terror" (Nassau 1904: 228–9). Kidd (1904: 244) reported that the Bantu fear of death was so pronounced that they would "flee in terror" from one who was dying. Their practice of abandoning the dying was "in order to avert the danger of the presence of the dreaded something that could not be explained" which surrounded death (Theal 1910: 186). In 1777, the German Moravian missionary Christian Georg Andreas Oldendorp described a Loango (Congo) belief that if an individual appeared to the living three days after death, "it is a proof that he is not gone to God" and has ill intent (Prichard 1836: 209). The Khoikhoi would not rescue a person who was in danger of death, for misfortune was considered to be contagious. Indeed, those who witnessed the event would "always run away from him, nay, he will even turn and throw stones at him" (Lichtenstein 1812: 319). Corpses were often seen as sources of pollution and contamination, and in southern Africa they were dragged by ropes to prevent them from coming into physical contact with the living (Moffat 1842: 135). The Sotho attributed all illness to spirits of the dead, and believed that they could return as fearsome ghosts (Casalis 1861: 246, 249). Death was seen as "the greatest of all defilements," and anyone who had come into contact with a corpse or grave—or even with a sick person—was deemed impure (ibid. 255). It is interesting to note that the Sotho NDEs reported nearly 60 years after Casalis both led to conversions to Christianity, perhaps indicating that local beliefs were unable to philosophically accommodate the experience (as may also have been the case with the Tswana, as stated earlier). Though the corpse-fear and negative attitudes toward the dead had vanished since Casalis, Keable (1921: 525, 527– 30) reported a lack of any definite, clear indigenous afterlife beliefs.

Attitudes surrounding the very idea of souls leaving their bodies were also sometimes negative. The Ibo reportedly had a deep terror of disembodiment—"a haunting fear that lives with them always" (Leonard 1906: 152). One informant stated that "when the soul leaves the body it is finished with this world, as far as its original body is concerned, and nothing can be done to bring it back again to the same body" (ibid. 141). Unsurprisingly, there are no attested Ibo NDEs or afterlife journey myths. Such perspectives are consistent with Ikenga-Methu's (1987: 263) statement that the worst possible afterlife fate in African religions was to become "a wandering spirit, cut off from the community and communion with one's family and kinship groups." Beliefs that witches could leave their bodies and harm people, either in invisible form or by possessing an animal or bird, were also common (Idowu 1973: 175–6). There are numerous accounts of "phantasms" of dying individuals appearing to relatives (cf. Parrinder 1974: 137), and these apparitions were often seen as fearsome or menacing. Deathbed visions of deceased relatives among the Boloki of the Congo were considered to be the "witch-souls" of the departed, coming "to throttle the life out of" those to whom they appeared (Weeks 1913: 262). While deathbed visions and apparitions of the dying are attested in the modern West and elsewhere in the world, they are less usually seen in such a threatening light (e.g., Gurney et al. 1886; Osis & Haraldsson 1986: 54ff).

Certain shamanic beliefs and practices also reinforced that fear and danger surrounded returning from death. The Yoruba Egungun, for example, were viewed with trepidation due to the belief that they had risen from the dead in order to surveil the living and punish them if necessary (Ellis 1894: 107). Generally speaking, transgressing the finality of death was acceptable only in particular types of religious or ritual leaders who were believed to have supernatural powers. This is evident among the Ashanti, Ewe, Fon, Fang, Mbuti, and Lango, all of whom had shamanic figures who left their bodies to travel to the other world and interact with spirits. Because such activities were the preserve of select professionals (with few exceptions, such as the Bwiti religion), when NDEs occurred spontaneously in "ordinary" people, they were greeted with mistrust. This was likely due to beliefs that those who were unequipped to deal with such experiences risked unwittingly bringing danger to the community (i.e., malevolent spirits, through possession or otherwise). On the societal level, it may also have been that a democratization of such experiences was perceived as a threat to the authority of shamanic leaders.

As seen in the case of Antonianism, possession held greater religious import and significance than any possible NDE content of Kimpa Vita's return-from-death experience. Indeed, while the fact of her return was one of the foundational elements of the religious movement that grew around her, it is significant that her experiences while dead were not recorded at all. Likewise, when Lamba individuals apparently died and returned to life, it was interpreted as the more culturally familiar spirit possession rather than NDE (Doke 1931: 258). Given their beliefs in other extraordinary phenomena related to spirits of the dead, it is significant that the Lamba showed no interest in reports of individuals who claimed to have been to afterlife realms and returned. This corresponds to the facts that they had "very hazy ideas" about the afterlife, and that many of the beliefs they did have were not typical of NDEs, such as resting in a subterranean realm unlike Earth until the creator deity Lesa gathers everyone up and takes them to his heavenly abode (ibid. 231–2). Likewise, the Ila attributed return-from-death occurrences to a drug that could bring the dead to life, and had only "vague tales" of such occurrences with no details of any actual experience (Dale 1920: 103). Correspondingly, they had inconsistent afterlife beliefs lacking NDE themes, and multiple myths explaining why the dead do not return to life. The Tswana, Sotho, and Lotuko had similar myths.

Interpretations of apparition experiences also reveal more concern with possession than with an afterlife. Instead of conveying information relating to the other world, a Lozi new religious movement called The Twelve Society (founded in 1944) originated when a visiting spirit gave instructions on curing people possessed by European spirits (Reynolds 1963: 133–4). Such orientations have persisted over time, as evidenced by the 1970s Zulu shaman (*sangoma*) Dorcas, whose OBEs during an illness were not considered nearly as important as her decision to allow possession by her deceased grandfather. It was her possession experience rather than her OBE that led to her becoming a shaman (Kalweit 1984: 88–9). Even reincarnation was sometimes seen in terms of possession, with ancestor spirits inhabiting new individuals.

The African focus on possession shamanism may also be related to slavery. Lenora Greenbaum (1973: 54) discovered a correlation between possession trance practices and the occurrence of slavery. In her cross-cultural survey of trance state types, Erika Bourguignon (1973: 11) found that sub-Saharan Africa—where slavery was known in 78 percent of societies—had the highest percentage of possession trance worldwide. Slavery has also been linked to beliefs in zombies. The notion that sorcerers can remove a person's soul and then reanimate and enslave the corpse is known from Benin, Nigeria, Cameroon, Zambia (Lozi, Cewa, Ila), Tanzania (Zinza, Kaguru), the Transvaal (Lovedu), and among the Zulu. While such beliefs are thought to reflect fears and memories of slavery (Ackermann & Gauthier 1991: 478), they are also overtly associated with witchcraft and thus conform to the overall pattern of "return-from-death" occurrences being seen in negative, aberrant, fearful terms. Such attitudes likely strengthened resistance to Christian ideas of resurrection despite widespread conversion over centuries (Thornton 2002: 80).

Exceptions that Illustrate the Tendency

There are, of course, exceptions, and while they may not prove an actual rule, they do help to evince general tendencies while also highlighting great diversities. While again it is problematic to generalize based on limited and inadequate sources, it seems no coincidence that the African cultures with narratives of more positive NDEs, or more accepting attitudes toward them, had generally more positive, optimistic views of the afterlife, along with less precipitous corpse disposal practices. Their beliefs appear to have been less focused on malevolent spirits, and less characterized by fear of the dead, and of the dead returning to life.

For example, prior to burial the Ewe people would appeal to souls of the recently deceased, asking them to return to the body. Burial was conducted only once bodies had begun to decompose in case the soul wished to return (Ellis 1890: 106). As seen above, knowledge of NDEs was incorporated into Ewe beliefs, and the form of shamanism they practiced involved both journeys to the Ghost-Land and soul-retrieval. The Ewe also had detailed, NDE-like conceptions of an afterlife, including leaving the body, traveling to another realm, meeting ancestor spirits, reaching a border, and the possibility of returning to life after temporarily dying. There is thus a direct correlation between Ewe afterlife beliefs and NDEs, which in turn impacted their funerary ritual and shamanistic practices.

Similarly, the Fang expended great effort on survival (Fernandez 1982: 236ff), and this corresponds to an overall stress on experiential knowledge about the afterlife. In both Bwiti and in ancestor cults, they valorized drug-induced afterlife journey experiences—at least some of which appear to have been actual NDEs—and many religious teachings derived from them. Even before the advent of Bwiti they held much interest in the afterlife, particularly concerning death and resurrection. Afterlife beliefs were said to have originated in the other world, and it is significant that they correspond so clearly to NDE phenomenology. Those beliefs existed alongside other positive and altogether more "spiritual" ideas, such as a cyclical afterlife of sequential deaths and rebirths, which is a striking contrast to the focus on malevolent ancestor spirits as found in many other African cultures. While there were corpse taboos and fears of malevolent spirits, these were not central concerns; and an "insouciance in the face of death" resulted from faith in a positive afterlife as derived from extraordinary experiences.

The Bakongo had a comparatively high degree of interest in the afterlife, and it is surely significant that they had a correspondingly greater number of NDEs and related narratives. Indeed, Bakongo informants themselves stated clearly that their afterlife and soul beliefs originated in NDEs and other extraordinary experiences. Prolonged funerary practices in which corpses were not buried until full desiccation or decomposition had occurred (Dennett 1898: 133–4; Weeks 1914: 267–8; Claridge 1922: 273) would have increased the possibility of revival from a comatose state. While there is no record of afterlife journey experiences of Kimpa Vita or Simon Kimbangu, they both apparently died and returned to life, and the very fact of their return was deemed religiously significant as evidenced by the religious movements that grew around them. That invited possession by benevolent spirits was also practiced is revealing, and suggests at least some openness to NDEs and other death-related spirit phenomena.

The Tswana similarly had a relatively high number of NDE narratives alongside a more accepting attitude toward the phenomenon, and positive beliefs in a radiant otherworld in the sun. Ancestors were more usually seen as benevolent forces than as potential threats (Brown 1926: 98). Tswana funerary practices were meant to better preserve the body, laying it in a hidden niche concealed alongside false graves. While they alternatively bound corpses and buried them in the fetal position soon after death, fears of the dead returning to life are not attested (ibid. 67–8).

The Lango would throw water on the body to confirm death prior to burial. Their beliefs in OBEs, in souls of the dead traveling to the place of the ancestors, in the ability of shamans to visit there to gain knowledge, and their mystical conceptions of the soul merging with the universal spirit are all themes that indicate experiential influence. Such beliefs, combined with efforts to prevent premature burial, demonstrate greater acceptance of ideas of the dead returning to life, more willingness to listen to those who had had such experiences, and an interdependence of experience and belief.

Unsurprisingly, there are also exceptions to these generalizations, and some cultures had more fluid, complex, ambiguous, and/or evolving attitudes toward death, the dead, and the afterlife. While the Zulu had a comparatively greater number of NDE-related narratives, both positive and negative attitudes to them are attested (e.g., the account of Bandla following the lion vs. the man suspected of sorcery). Shamanic practices involved travel to the spirit world as well as other forms of communication with the dead. Grout (1864: 137–48) described lengthy, elaborate rituals to prevent the ancestors from taking the soul of a sick person, as well as intense public mourning. Shooter (1857: 238–9) reported that while the sick and dying would sometimes be abandoned, this was to avoid touching the eventual corpse rather than out of fear of it reviving. In any case, Grout (1864: 165) stated that abandonment was practiced only with strangers rather than with members of the local community. While Tyler (1891: 211) described Zulu burial practices as hasty, this did not preclude revival. He cited a case in which a woman who had been barely covered by earth in her grave startled her son when she sat up and said, "How do you do, my child?" It was believed that "wizards" (*abatakati*) would sometimes exhume bodies in order to transform them into enslaved animals, and that if they were interrupted in their work the body would be left "half restored" to go "wandering about the country, a fool or an idiot" (ibid. 151). Such notions, however, do not seem to have led to generally negative feelings about the dead returning to life. On the contrary, Callaway (1868: 52 n.53) reported that if a missing individual believed to be dead returned unexpectedly, there was a great celebration. A myth involving a young girl who "had risen from the dead" reinforces this notion, for her return was greeting with rejoicing and feasting (ibid. 246–7).

While Nandi funerary practices involved leaving corpses to be eaten by hyenas, this was due not to fear of pollution, possession, or reanimation, but to the belief that it was the means by which the deceased would be conveyed to the spirit world (i.e., via the body of the hyena). Though brief, the Nandi NDE is one of the most typical in content of the African examples, and their ideas of the other world are not inconsistent with it. It is significant that the narrative was widely known among the Nandi people.

The Nuer buried the dead quickly, practiced strict corpse avoidance (Evans-Pritchard 1956: 144ff), were focused on malevolent spirits, had an intense "horror of death" in general (ibid. 154), and an overall lack of interest in the afterlife. Nevertheless, some Nuer practiced mediumship, and believed in a heavenly afterlife with the creator, or an underworld that mirrored Earth. That such beliefs existed prior to Gik Cam Jok's NDE summarized above may suggests that a more open attitude toward afterlife ideas enabled a more positive interpretation of the NDE, allowing it to be placed in a politically useful prophetic context (i.e., concering the end of the civil war). Alternatively, perhaps it was increasing Christian influence and the political situation itself that led to the acceptance of the NDE.

Conclusions

Given the generally negative attitudes toward death, and particularly the notion of the dead returning to life, it is not surprising that accounts of NDEs in the

African material are comparatively rare. As we have seen, it was often the case that due to local cultural factors, little or no effort was expended on reviving an individual who showed signs of returning from apparent death. This was sometimes the case not only on a community level, but on an individual one as well, where local custom was given precedence over self-preservation (e.g., in the case of the Akan woman who asked to be killed again after dressing, or the southern African woman who refused to be "rescued"). The lack of effort in resuscitation, and the deliberate measures taken to prevent revival, correlate with the fact that NDEs were rare. Furthermore, in some societies, those who revived from apparent death risked being killed or otherwise persecuted. The danger inherent in discussing such experiences likely resulted in many going unrecorded. As seen in the more recent Kongolese and Zambian studies, such dynamics have continued in more recent times, demonstrating that hostility to the notion of revival from death is a specific, culturally continuous phenomenon that impacted the reception of NDEs in various African traditions.

Such attitudes are also consistent with the relative dearth of afterlife journey myths and speculation about an afterlife per se. This suggests a direct correlation between receptivity to NDEs, and active interest and belief in conceptions of life after death with NDE-like features (e.g., leaving the body, traveling to another realm, encountering deceased relatives and other spirits, darkness and preternatural light, positive fruits upon return, and so on). The suspicions of sorcery, witchcraft, possession, and general malevolence surrounding those who appeared to return from death meant that their accounts of their experiences would not have been welcomed, or accepted as evidence of what happens when people die. As such, in the rare instances when such experiences were expressed, they would have been unlikely to lead to significant changes in religious beliefs in general. On the contrary, the apparent return from death itself would have validated existing beliefs in possession or witchcraft, again inhibiting NDE narratives from being expressed in the first place. The content of the experiences themselves was not only considered to be theologically irrelevant, but also would have been potentially threatening to the status quo of the religious hierarchy. While the authority of some healers or shamans was grounded in the *fact* of their return from death, claims to have brought new beliefs, strictures, or other kinds of teachings back from the other world were comparatively uncommon.

It is true that a very different interpretation could be spun from the data in this chapter, selectively highlighting similarities between NDE phenomenology and the afterlife beliefs and related myths to which it corresponds.[8] Two factors prevent such an approach, however. The first is simply the mass of clear evidence of difference and diversity, and the overall scarcity of African NDE accounts. Indeed, the gathering together of relevant material in this chapter may give the impression that NDEs and related beliefs were more common and prominent in Africa than was actually the case, for obviously the numerous cultures in which no relevant evidence was found are excluded. The second factor is the consistency of culturally situated attitudes toward the dead and the possibility of their return, which so neatly present themselves as explanations for the tension between the beliefs and NDEs. In addition, the case presented in the previous chapter so overtly supports a widespread near-death experiential source hypothesis for North America that the contrast with Africa cannot be ignored.

However, none of this indicates that the experiential source hypothesis is irrelevant to afterlife beliefs in African traditional religions. The degree to which experience types are rejected as unwelcome or dangerous, or deemed beneficial or religiously significant, is determined by existing local cultural factors; and in Africa the more culturally relevant experiences tended to more often be spirit possession, dreams, and visions (often involving ancestor spirits), rather than NDEs. Shamanic experiences could also be sources of religious knowledge. In the Nuba mountains of Sudan, "prospective shamans" were identified by virtue of their ability to have meaningful or prophetic dreams and visions of ancestor spirits. Such extraordinary experiences are what set shamans apart from the rest of society. The experiences also played a direct role in socioreligious matters, for communities were guided by such individuals and their visionary experiences (Nadel 1946: 30).

Nor can we conclude that African afterlife beliefs that *do* correspond to NDE phenomenology were not grounded in such experiences, simply on the grounds that there was no explicit indigenous statement to that effect. In some cases where soul and afterlife beliefs were important elements of a religion, NDE-like concepts are present even if a corresponding NDE or shamanic afterlife journey narrative is lacking. For example, the Lozi had fearful attitudes toward death and the dead, a lack of afterlife journey myths or other relevant narratives, a stress on reincarnation into animals, and on ancestor spirits remaining in the grave and continuing to be part of the living community (Prins 1980: 128–9, using late nineteenth-century data; Turner 1952: 54). Nevertheless, Lozi afterlife beliefs also included the spirit traveling towards the sun to realms of the gods. Only those with the correct tattoo or scarification markings were admitted, while the rest were fed flies before being sent to die of thirst and starvation in a desert (ibid. 49–51). Journeying to a light-filled realm of the divine after death, reaching a border, and undergoing some kind individual evaluation are thematic elements consistent with NDEs. Similarly, though lacking afterlife journey narratives, the Luo Adhola of Eastern Uganda believed that at death the body was cast off like old clothes, and that the invisible spirit traveled like wind to the supreme creator deity Were (Ogot 1972: 124–5). The BaManianga (southern Congo) believed that souls of good people left the body at death, and went to a paradise of god-like ancestor spirits (Idowu 1973: 104–5). Despite the Lamba interpretation of return-from-death phenomena in terms of possession, their afterlife beliefs included NDE-like themes such as darkness, ascent, encountering supernatural entities, deceased relatives, returning to the origin point, having a renewed subtle body, and peace and harmony (Doke 1931: 231–2).

As noted in the Introduction to the present chapter, common afterlife conceptions across various African cultures included OBE, journey to another world, encountering deceased relatives, darkness, barriers or borders, personal evaluation of some kind, and dwelling with the divine in a spiritualized state. Such thematic, conceptual consistencies between these beliefs and a particular type of extraordinary experience may indicate that the beliefs were rooted in some distant historical NDEs. Indeed, although they often served to explain why people do not return from death, various afterlife myths and legends concerned people in the past who were able to die temporarily, visit the otherworld, and return. The existence of different versions of essentially the same story (e.g., man taken by lion to underworld), the fable-like element of animal protagonists, and other elaborate, culturally idiosyncratic plot details may suggest that at least some of these narratives were grounded in cultural memory of some original NDE account, which was transformed, adapted to cultural norms, and mythologized by numerous retellings over long periods of time.

Alternatively, it may be that they reflect cultural continuity with similar beliefs found among neighboring peoples that were grounded in some historical NDEs of their own; or indeed that they are the result of borrowing or diffusion from some more distant people (not excluding in at least some cases the possibility of Christian or Muslim influence). While it is impossible to disentangle all the thematic strands of afterlife conceptions in all their varying manifestations throughout the different African cultures—particularly when they occur alongside seemingly conflicting notions such as reincarnation into animals, and spirits remaining on Earth—NDEs at least provide a thematically and contextually stable, relevant experience type that might reasonably account for certain aspects of afterlife beliefs in certain African traditional religions (cf. Shushan 2009: 193ff).

It is interesting to note that the majority of cultures with relevant evidence in the extant primary sources as discussed in this chapter were Bantu-speaking: the Baganda, Bakongo, Chaga, Ekoi, Fang, Kikuyu, Lamba, Luhya, Mbundu, Mbuti, Nyakyusa, Shona, Sotho, Tswana, Tumbuka, Zambesi, and Zulu peoples. They account for the greater number of both NDEs and underworld descent myths. As Werner (1933: 9) observed, Orpheus myths are "found in so many different places that the idea seems to be held wherever a Bantu language is spoken." Furthermore, the Bantu family of languages is itself a subgroup of the Niger-Congo language group, and the second-highest incidence of relevant narratives come from various

Niger-Congo language-speaking cultures: the Ewe, Fon, Ibibio, Ashanti, Akan, Tshi, and Kagoro.[9] It is tempting to speculate that there was some grand diffusion across Bantu-speaking cultures; that is, that there was a single common, originating ancient Niger-Congo protonarrative on which local variations were later based, which spread with the expansions of the original proto-Bantu speaking peoples out of Cameroon beginning c. 1000 BCE. There are problems with such a perspective, however. First, vast cultural and religious diversity makes it difficult to account for the continued transmission of this particular narrative type alone, particularly when the NDE and afterlife journey narratives themselves are highly idiosyncratic. This is in sharp contrast to the far more consistent origin-of-death narratives—notwithstanding variations in animal protagonists (chameleon, tortoise, and lizard; hare, duck, and frog). Second, informants themselves often stated that the narrative was historical or even within living memory. While there may be an element of diffusion, it was perhaps more often in the form of more fluid and flexible general attitudes toward death and the afterlife rather than of a specific narrative. This could account for both the diversity of narratives across the Bantu/Niger-Congo cultural groups, and for their higher incidence of extant relevant narratives than in cultures of other language groups.

Theal (1910: 184) also noted similarities of certain cultural traits and religious beliefs across different Bantu peoples, and argued that their ideas about the afterlife had been introduced by Europeans. This could conceivably account for the greater acceptance of otherworld journey narratives, considering that resurrection (i.e., returning from death) is a hallmark of Christian thought. The Kingdom of Kongo had begun converting to Christianity as early as 1491, with almost total conversion occurring by the early seventeenth century, which is prior to our earliest reports of return-from-death narratives and afterlife beliefs. Nevertheless, despite conversion in the Kongo and elsewhere, local ancestor spirit beliefs and the "basic structure of the original religion remained everywhere" (Thornton 2002: 83, 85, 89)—including vastly different afterlife beliefs both across and within the various cultures. As seen earlier, Kidd (1904: 79–81) characterized Bantu peoples as being unconcerned with the afterlife and afraid of death, though also as having diverse, uncertain beliefs, which sometimes included garbled versions of missionary teachings. Among the various Bantu afterlife-related beliefs are ancestor spirits, component souls, souls emerging from the corpse in the form of a maggot (Willoughby 1928: 6–10), remaining near the body for a period following death, reincarnation, the afterlife being an idealized mirror image of Earth (ibid. 73), underworlds and heavenly worlds, judgment (ibid. 57–61), souls being subtle duplicates of the body (often in miniature form) (ibid. 16–7), and widespread acceptance that souls can live or journey independently from the body (ibid. 10–12; 93ff; cf. Abrahamsson 1951).

Clearly, not all of these beliefs had their roots in European teachings, and it is not possible to state definitively whether or not any particular typically "Christian" belief existed independently in Africa prior to European influence. Rather than being responsible for these beliefs wholesale, it is more likely that Christianity played an important role in facilitating the integration of NDEs (in the rare cases they *were* integrated) and other extraordinary experiences into local worldviews (as seen with Antonianism and other syncretistic movements). In other words, the experiences were interpreted and adapted in indigenous modes alongside Christian influences. Indeed, as Thornton (2002: 87) states, such extraordinary experiences as revelatory dreams, visions, and spirit mediumship actually "played a role in the conversion of individuals." Ultimately, while explanations involving diffusion or Christian influence remain largely speculative, there certainly appears to be some cultural-linguistic significance to the fact that most of the relevant narratives derive primarily from Bantu groups, and secondarily from other Niger-Congo groups. It is also significant that, as Willoughby (1928: 99) wrote, among the Bantu, "hallucinations of the ecstatic and of the entranced are taken as revelations from the spirit-world."

In summary, the fact that NDEs are so infrequently attested in African cultures, alongside a general absence of, or lack of focus on, NDE-like afterlife beliefs cannot be coincidental. On the one hand, we have deep-seated fears of death, and beliefs that it is fundamentally unnatural and related to witchcraft, possession, and malevolent spirits. On the other hand, we have deep-seated acceptance and resignation when death seemed inevitable. Such attitudes were manifested in funerary practices intended to curtail potential negative actions of the dead, a lack of concern for extending the lives of those who seemed certain to die, and a lack of effort expended on attempting to bring individuals back once they had reached a stage of apparent death. These dynamics would do nothing to facilitate the occurrence of NDEs, nor the transmission of accounts of experiences, nor their incorporation into local afterlife beliefs. The dead were not to be trusted, and therefore neither was the testimony of an NDEr, whose very identity was open to question due to possession fears. Contra Zahan (1979: 46), however, we must be careful not to extrapolate from such attitudes and practices a general African "indifference to death and . . . contempt for life." Rather than such negative and judgmental stereotypes, these beliefs and practices are more productively (and neutrally) seen simply as culturally situated ways of negotiating death and the dead. The fact that they may conflict with one's own does nothing to indicate the indifference and contempt Zahan claimed.

Just as there was a general lack of concern for an afterlife in other realms, there was also a lack of interest in the actual experiences of those who had NDEs. The *fact* of their return was the more significant factor, particularly in giving rise to prophets, shamans, and new religious movements, while also reinforcing fears relating to possession and sorcery.

It is also significant that some of the most NDE-like African myths and legends do not involve a temporary death at all, even when describing a journey to the otherworld. Instead, the context was usually a living person following an animal or a rolling nut through a cave or into a hole in the ground (Ga, Ekoi, Efé, Baganda, Kikuyu, Zulu, Bandla). It is tempting to speculate that such accounts were actually based on historical NDEs, but were then couched in more acceptable, culturally relevant, and less dangerous terms.

It should be stressed, however, that the fact that NDEs were sometimes feared in the community does not mean that the experiences themselves were not spiritually or psychologically meaningful for those who had them. Indeed, this was demonstrated by one Tswana and one Zulu NDE, by Fang iboga experiences, and by the modern Bakongo NDErs, including a woman who changed her prior beliefs as a result of the experience. She stated that following her NDE she no longer believed that "the spiritual world was in the sky, as Christianity taught" (Bockie 1993: 94), demonstrating that the experience went against her prior beliefs. Unfortunately, we lack such personal testimonies for earlier examples, so that whatever personal meaning NDEs had for specific individuals is mostly unknown.

While the negative attitudes, beliefs, and practices would not facilitate the occurrence or valorization of NDEs, or even provide an acceptable context for their expression, the significance of NDEs being attested at all in societies with such suspicion, fear, or hostility toward the very notion of returning from death should not be overlooked. Regardless of cultural interpretations or idiosyncrasies of descriptions, the identifiable occurrence of NDEs clearly confirms that the phenomenon itself is not due to prior expectation. Because NDEs would run contrary to religious and cultural norms in many African societies, not only would there be little or no value in relating having had such an experience, but it could also lead to unwelcome consequences.

4

Oceania

Introduction

For the present purposes, Oceania encompasses Polynesia, Micronesia, Melanesia, and Australia. Excluded are regions west of the Wallace Line (Malay Archipelago and Indochina), which traditionally demarcates the boundary dividing Asia from Oceania. Conveniently for the present study, it also happens to constitute a loose cultural boundary, for the western regions saw far more comprehensive external cultural influence from much earlier periods. Hinduism was widespread from the first century CE, Buddhism from the second, Islam from the twelfth, and Christianity from the sixteenth. In contrast, Christian influence did not take root in Oceania until the early nineteenth century, and in some areas as late as the early- to mid-twentieth century (Ernst & Anisi 2016: 591). Nevertheless, by the time of Frederick William Christian (1899: 164), a lexicographer of Polynesian languages, Pacific Islanders were already being characterized as having lost their cultural uniqueness, becoming Christians "of the colorless humdrum order."

Recent genetic evidence indicates that Aboriginal Australians have been on the continent for up to 70,000 years, having migrated from South Asia and with further genetic links to Southeast Asia and to Denisovan people from Siberia (Rasmussen et al. 2011). Polynesians and Micronesians "are strongly related to East Asians, and particularly Taiwan Aborigines." They are almost entirely unrelated to Melanesians, who instead came from Southeast Asia between 30,000–50,000 years BP "and remained isolated for c. 25,000 years" (Friedlander et al. 2008). Settlement from Southeast Asia to Micronesia and Polynesia began as recently as 1500 BCE or later, and New Zealand was not settled until c. 1280 CE. The four areas with which we are concerned thus have distinct genetic and cultural antecedents. It must be stressed, however, that besides Australia, "Polynesia" is the only "truly valid ethnic category, for 'Micronesia' contains at least six widely different ethnic units," and "Melanesia" "contains hundreds." The divisions are to some extent conveniences based on geography (Oliver 2002: 2). Although Dobbin and Hezel (2011: 13) find enough similarity between Micronesian islands to speak in terms of "a Micronesian religion," Micronesia saw less extensive fieldwork than other parts of the Pacific, and evidence from the region is scant.

There are few syntheses of premodern Oceanic religions, and even fewer focusing on afterlife beliefs. Excluding Australia, the Egyptologist Rosalind Moss (1925: v) reviewed Oceanic afterlife beliefs in relation to burial practices, usefully restricting her sources as much as possible to older reports prior to "deterioration by contact with civilization," and to firsthand accounts from "scientific investigators." She found Pacific-wide beliefs "that the dead man may only be in a trance" and could awaken at any time, and that "until the flesh had disappeared" from the corpse, the person was not considered fully dead. Moss (1925: 2–3) also wrote that "speculations about the conditions of life in the hereafter" were more akin to folktales than to matters of faith, though this is contradicted by widespread funerary practices designed to ensure a safe journey and positive outcome for the deceased, and by common general beliefs about the journey of the soul: that it remained for a time near the corpse, departed along a particular route, and underwent ordeals or tests before being admitted to the other world (ibid. 2–3).

It was commonly believed that the underworld was entered through caves, holes, or volcanoes (ibid. 32), and cave burials were common. At the same time, notions that the soul went to the other world via the rising or setting sun were also common, though ascent to a sky-realm was not (ibid. 40). Various guardian figures were encountered on the journey, the most typical being "monster," "door-keeper," "inquisitor," and "judge" (ibid. 112). The other world was commonly seen as a mirror image of this one, where status, rank, and social position were maintained (sometimes resulting in different regions for different levels of society). Admission to the other world was determined variously by rank, wealth, "goodness," mode of death, and/or proper funerary rites. For "less worthy souls" there were less favorable realms or conditions, or simply annihilation. While the association of underworlds with retributive punishment was exaggerated in some reports (e.g., those of the English missionaries William Ellis in Polynesia and Thomas Williams in Melanesia), they were generally regarded as less pleasant than this life, and inferior to some alternative, better realm (Moss 1925: 118–31). Day and night were sometimes thought to be reversed in the underworld, corresponding to the cycle of the sun around the Earth (ibid. 37–8).

A total lack of afterlife beliefs, or beliefs in postmortem annihilation for everyone, were "practically unknown," though ideas of immortality or eternal existence in another realm were also "extremely rare" (ibid. 153). The notion that death was fundamentally unnatural was known in various societies across the region (Karsten 1935: 162–3).

In a more recent overview of precolonial Oceanic cultures (including Australia), Douglas L. Oliver (1989: 132–3) found that beliefs in OBEs during sleep, illness, or even by intention in certain individuals were "very widespread," while beliefs that the soul left the body after death were virtually universal. The "long, adventurous" journey to the other world was typically seen as being "fraught with dangers." The realm of the dead was variously considered to be on a distant island or mountain; or in a lake, an undersea realm, or the sky. It was often described as Earth-like, though there were also concepts of heavenly and hellish fates determined by social status or other earthly conditions, by correct funerary ritual, or by knowledge of how to negotiate the afterlife journey. Often, however, ideas about individual survival after death were of little concern or were simply not subjects of speculation.

Comparatively rare were beliefs that the soul died with the body or lived only briefly after death, that it reincarnated, or that it "returned to the source from which it had issued." Spirits in the other world could be both helpful and harmful to the living, as could those that remained on Earth. People who died violently or in accidents became malevolent ghosts. Some believed that souls of the dead could be simultaneously in the realm of the ancestors and on Earth (usually in animal form). The notion of ultimately merging "into an undifferentiated company of 'ancestors' or some even more inclusive category of spirit beings" was widely attested (ibid. 771).

Polynesia

According to the English missionary William Wyatt Gill (1877: 3), who spent twenty-two years in the Cook Islands, Polynesian "song and myth delight in recounting the adventures of those who have visited spirit-world." The notion that a temporary visit there brought positive fruits and transformation was typical of such narratives. The discovery of fire on a journey to the netherworld was a common mythological theme in central Polynesia (e.g., Tonga, the Society Islands, Manuae, Rakahanga; Williamson 1933: II.190–5, 200), and was associated with the restoration of sight in the blind through a life-giving tree fruit (ibid. 205).

Though Ellis (1829: 396–7) wrote that Polynesian notions of the afterlife were "vague and indefinite," he nevertheless described rather specific beliefs. The soul was seen as having a similar form to the body, as evidenced by appearances of deceased people in dreams. At death the gods sent for the soul and drew it from the body. If not seized by waiting demons, the deceased was then accompanied by "other spirits" to the realm of Po ("place of night"), home of the gods and divinized ancestors. Different elements of the soul would then be "scraped with a kind of serrated shell" by ancestors, before being eaten by the gods. Undergoing this process three times resulted in immortality and divinization. The soul could then dwell in the heavenly realm of Miru, and continue to visit Earth. Souls were also sometimes conveyed to the other world by a ferryman (Moss 1925: 46, 110). Descriptions of ordeals during the journey were uncommon, and differences in social status determined destination: chiefs went to the positive realm of Po "across or under the sea," while others went to a less desirable underworld. Alternatively, it was believed that there was a general afterworld for all (cf. Oliver 2002: 176–7).

Hawaiian Islands

According to the newspaper editor and art collector J. J. Jarves (1843: 42–3), Hawaiian beliefs about the afterlife were revealed in "dreams and pretended visions of the priests." Despite his less than objective tone, Jarves also noted the reception of NDEs and their subsequent elaboration, interpretation, and integration into local beliefs:

> The spirits of the departed were sometimes sent back with messages to the living. These pretended messages were expounded, greatly to their own interest, by the priests, and were received as divine commands by the people.

The converted Catholic Hawaiian historian Kepelino Keauokalini (1860: 48) confirmed that knowledge about the nature of Po came from people "who have been brought back to life from the dead."

Another indigenous author, the last king of the Kingdom of Hawai'i, David Kalakaua (1888: 39), wrote that Po "could be visited by favored mortals, and the dead were sometimes brought back from it to earth." There was even special terminology for NDE-like phenomena, as reported by the American theologian and popularizer of Hawaiian myths Reverend William Drake Westervelt (1915: 248): "The *kino-wai-lua* was a ghost leaving the body of a living person and returning after a time, as when any one fainted." It was believed that life ended when this soul component left the body, and resumed when it returned. This could happen when the spirit was "driven back into the body by other ghosts, or persuaded to come back through offerings or incantations given by living friends, so that a dead person could become alive again." There was also a term for the process of bringing someone back from the dead (*kupaku*) (Fornander 1918–9: II.188).

Through his wide-ranging collection of data, James Frazer (1922: 428–9) also found the belief that "When persons recovered from a death-like swoon, it was supposed that their souls had gone to the underworld and been sent back to earth by Milu," the underworld deity. A family's guardian deity could also "oppose the passage of a soul to the other world, and send it back to life, so that the seemingly dead man recovered." The spirit world could also be visited during dreams. However, according to the indigenous historian and zealous Christian convert Samuel Kamakau (1888: 53–6), "All these stories which are told about people who have gone to get souls and restored them to life are false and lying tales," apparently distinguishing Orpheus-type legends and/or shamanic soul-retrieval accounts from genuine NDE accounts.

The possibility of a recently deceased person returning to life was integrated into Hawaiian funerary ritual: food was left near the corpse in case it revived, and the grave was not prepared until it was certain that the spirit would not return to the body (Green & Beckwith 1926: 181). Deathbed visions were also a known phenomenon, for according to Kamakau (1866–71: 50) it was "a common thing with sick persons while laid low with an illness" to see their deceased parents or grandparents appear before them to help guide them to the other world. Spirit possession typically involved revelations, prophesy, and visionary experiences of other realms.

On the island of Hawai'i at Ka'awaloa village, Ellis (1823: 107) was told by his informants that everything they knew about the afterlife "was from visions and dreams of the priests" (i.e., shamans). According to one shaman, in earlier days the dead would meet their ancestors and "would live again." Two deities, Kaonohiokala ("the eye-ball of the sun") and Kuahairo, would take the souls of chiefs "to some place in the heavens," then later bring them back to Earth to watch over their people. Others said that souls went to Po to be either annihilated or consumed by gods; or to Kapapahanaumoku, the subterranean realm of Akea, the first king of Hawai'i, and his successor Milu. It was a place of darkness where people ate lizards and butterflies, drank from streams, and reclined under trees. Still others, however, told Ellis that they did not know what the other world was like because no one had ever returned from the dead to describe it. Ellis also reported beliefs that the dead could appear to priests in dreams to convey messages from Milu; and conversely that people could visit the realm of the dead during dreams (ibid. 275–6; cf. Jarves 1843: 81).

In the 1820s, the Hapu, or Hulumanu, syncretistic religious revitalization movement was founded after a woman from Puna named Kahapuu visited a heavenly realm during a trance state. She reported that during her experience she learned about prayer, Jehovah, and Jesus, and she returned as a prophet with healing powers. She was said to be "subject to visions and trances" (Yzendoorn 1927: 83–8; Ralston 1985: 324).

Also on Hawai'i, the German ethnologist Adolf Bastian reported an NDE from Kuala in 1833. As Frazer (1922: 428–9) summarized, "The best account of the spirit land was given by one who had spent eight days in it, and on returning to life reported to his family what he had seen." He described the other world as "flat and fruitful," "tolerably well lighted," and "a really delightful place." Milu sometimes "chooses for his consorts the most beautiful of the female ghosts when they arrive in deadland." Souls of the dead maintained "exactly the same state in which they quitted their bodies." Those who died young or in battle were strong and healthy, while those who died of illness remained ill, and those who died of old age were frail and weak.

Bastian also reported a highly detailed Orpheus myth, concerning a chief who traveled to the other world in order to find his departed wife. A "priest" arranged for the deity Kane-i-kou-alii to accompany him, and at "the end of the world" they came upon "a tree, which split open and allowed them to glide down into the depths." Kane-i-kou-alii rubbed putrid oil on the chief's body, then hid behind a rock while the chief proceeded alone. He arrived at Milu's palace, where spirits were noisily playing sports. Because of the stinking oil they believed him to be recently dead, and "turned away from him in disgust and made uncomplimentary remarks on his unsavoury condition." After various games had been played, "the chief suggested that, as a new form of sport, they should all take out their eyes and throw them in a heap." Everyone eagerly agreed, and when Milu took his eyes out the chief grabbed them and concealed them in a coconut vessel. Since the spirits were now blind, the chief could proceed without concern that they would follow. Eventually, the chief successfully bribed Milu—agreeing to return his eyes if he would allow the chief's wife to return to Earth, to be "reunited to her body" (ibid. 430).

From Kona comes the remarkable nineteenth-century NDE of a woman named Kalima. At her funeral, her family and friends sat mourning around her "rigid form and ashen face," when suddenly Kalima breathed and opened her eyes, startling her people "though they were so happy to have her back among them again." It took a few minutes for her to fully revive, and when she was able to speak she said, "I have something strange to tell you." She could not continue, however, and was only able to tell her story a few days later:

> I died, as you know. I seemed to leave my body and stand beside it, look-
> ing down on what was me. The me that was standing there looked like the
> form I was looking at, only, I was alive and the other was dead. I gazed
> at my body for a few minutes, then turned and walked away. I left the
> house and village, and walked on and on to the next village, and there
> I found crowds of people,—Oh, so many people! The place which I knew

as a small village of a few houses was a very large place, with hundreds of houses and thousands of men, women, and children. Some of them I knew and they spoke to me,—although that seemed strange, for I knew they were dead,—but nearly all were strangers. They were all so happy! They seemed not to have a care; nothing to trouble them. Joy was in every face, and happy laughter and bright, loving words were on every tongue.

As if impelled onward, she passed through more villages crowded with happy spirits, and met people she had known in life. She "felt so full of joy, too, that my heart sang within me, and I was glad to be dead." She continued toward Pele's volcano, arriving at South Point, a formerly barren area now "a great village," where she was greeted cheerfully before moving on, feeling "happier every minute." There were few people at the volcano, and they told her, "You must go back to your body. You are not to die yet."

> I did not want to go back. I begged and prayed to be allowed to stay with them, but they said, "No, you must go back; and if you do not go willingly, we will make you go."

She wept and tried to resist, but they persisted and even beat her to force her back the way she had come. Passing through the happy villages again, the people there now turned against her, driving her away. They followed her for sixty miles until she finally reached her home, where she stood by her lifeless body again.

> I looked at it and hated it. Was that my body? What a horrid, loathsome thing it was to me now, since I had seen so many beautiful, happy creatures! Must I go and live in that thing again?

Again she resisted, refusing to reenter the body, but the spirits forced her, "and pushed me head foremost into the big toe." When she "passed the waist" of her body she instinctively knew that it was useless to continue struggling; "Then my body came to life again, and I opened my eyes." Mrs. C. E. Haley (1892: 83–5), who published the NDE as told to her, stressed that Kalima never varied her account "and never ceased to regret coming back to her body." She maintained that it had been cruel to force her to do so, to leave the happiness she had experienced in the other world and the beautiful body she had there (cf. Kellehear 2001).

A myth from Kona tells of how a "priest" advised Hiku to retrieve Kawelu from the underworld by descending on a vine lowered into the sea from a canoe, while his friends waited. The spirits below saw him swing through the entrance, and all wanted to swing, too. When he taunted them they all rushed to the vine for a ride, including Milu, who was holding Kawelu. Hiku asked Kawelu to join him on the vine, though at first she was reluctant due to his bad smell. She agreed when Hiku covered himself, then he tugged on the vine, signaling his friends to pull them back up to Earth. When they reached Kawelu's body, Hiku tried to push her spirit back in through the feet, though she resisted, for the body had begun to decay. After a number of days, Hiku succeeded in coaxing the spirit back into the body and restoring Kawelu to life (Fornander 1918–9: II.186ff).[1]

A narrative from Maui near Lahaina told of a man named Ka-ilio-hae who left his body during a prolonged illness. He exited through his left eye, and when he looked back the body appeared like a great mountain, the eyes like dark caves. Suddenly afraid, Ka-ilio-hae went to the rooftop. The sound of people mourning his death disturbed him and he flew away, impelled toward the spirit world. At the entrance he met his deceased sister, who had "the power of sometimes turning a ghost back to its body again." She took him to her house, but warned him not to enter or eat any food. They proceeded to "the place of whirlwinds"—a hill where spirits were dancing and playing, then passed a house where a party was taking place. Ka-ilio-hae's sister would not allow him to join the revelers, for he would then be unable to return to Earth. She then told him that he must go see Walia, "the high chief of ghosts," and instructed him how to reply to the interrogations of the three watchmen they would meet on the way. The first asked, "What is the fruit of your heart?"; while the second asked the purpose of Ka-ilio-hae's journey. The correct answer to both was "Walia." The third watchman asked Ka-ilio-hae what he wanted, and after replying, "to see the chief," he was allowed to pass. The doorway to "the great house," however, was blocked by "two heads bending together," which threw spirits down to Milu if they did not know the requisite incantations. Following his sister's instruction, Ka-ilio-hae pushed them aside and finally met Walia and his queen. Walia asked Ka-ilio-hae who was the high chief in his land, and he replied with a genealogical history of his people. The king then told him "to go back and enter his body and tell his people about troubles near at hand." If he did not return to Earth, he risked being thrown to Milu. A beautiful woman gave him directions home, and though Ka-ilio-hae was reluctant to leave and tried to hide, his sister forced him. He tried to escape again when he saw his body, feeling "very much afraid," but his sister pushed him in through the foot. Still he resisted, disliking the smell of the body, but his sister ultimately succeeded. When Ka-ilio-hae awoke and regained his strength, "he told his family all about his wonderful journey to the land of ghosts" (Westervelt 1915: 100–7). According to earlier fieldwork at Lahaina conducted by the American missionary Sheldon Dibble (1843: 82), it was believed that the soul remained on Earth as a dangerous presence for a period after death.

It then proceeded to the realm of Wakea (ancestor/sky-deity), a place of happiness, "houses, comforts and pleasures." There the soul remained if the individual had "observed the religious rites and ceremonies" while on Earth. Others were "forced to take a desperate leap into a place of misery below, called Milu."

In a nineteenth-century legend from Oahu, a farmer named Makua was swallowed by a giant fish and taken to the land of Kane, "the beautiful island of deathless people," with abundant fruits, vegetables, and fish. Makua was met by the gods Kane-huna-moku and Kane-huli-honua, who explained that in order to remain there he must undergo a series of trials. At a pair of beautiful houses, two guides identical to the two gods emerged. They told Makua that he could live a life of plenty and leisure in one of the houses, as long as he didn't weep or express sorrow. When Makua began to kneel before them, they stopped him, saying, "You have finished your prayers on earth. Here is only joy." They then departed by growing so high that they disappeared into the sky. Their twin gods then explained to Makua that he, too, would become a god if he passed his trials. If he did not, he would "become a messenger and will tell to men the beauties of this land." Inside the house he was fed a sumptuous feast, and was joined by the spirits of his wife and son, but they departed out of fear that the guards would kill them. Makua followed, refraining from weeping as instructed by the deities. While attempting to swim home, his son was caught by a shark and his wife nearly drowned attempting to save him. Makua pulled her to shore, and believing that she was dead, he was unable to prevent himself from crying. But she revived, and they headed back toward the beautiful house, only to find that it had disappeared. They slept under a tree, and Makua was awakened by someone calling for him. He opened his eyes and saw that his wife was gone, and that eight identical men were approaching. He confessed that he had broken the prohibition against weeping, and "He knew that he must return to earth, and tell his friends there about the beauties of the hidden land and the power of the gods." The gods explained that when he eventually returned to the spirit world, he would not be divinized, though his son would.

> Suddenly a very dazzling light shone. The eight men disappeared. Makua saw that the heavens were open and he beheld two bodies clothed in light and accompanied by many spirits arrayed in glorious raiment, but with sorrowful countenances. The spirits spoke, saying, "Dust to dust," and then the doors of the heavens closed.

Makua wandered into the woods, then was guided to the seashore. The giant fish took him home, and he told his people all that had happened to him (Rice 1923: 126–32).

The American missionary Joseph S. Emerson (1902: 13–4) reported that at Waiale'e, Oahu, it was believed that "sometimes, as if in a fainting fit, the spirit suddenly leaves the body," resulting in a state termed "dead yet not altogether dead" (*make, aole nae make loa*). If the body grows cold in this state (or during trance), "it becomes difficult to force the reluctant spirit to reenter." In such cases, a shaman (*kahuna*) coaxed the spirit back under the nail of the big toe. As Emerson noted, "various accounts have appeared in print . . . of the adventures of spirits, who after a protracted stay among the spirits of the dead, have been forced back into their bodies to resume active life among the living." In one example, a young man named Paele could not be awoken one morning. When he finally returned to consciousness, he told of how he had traveled with his lover to a cliff edge. Spirits there tried to push them off into the undersea realm, but the couple managed to return.

At Waialua, Oahu, Kamakau (1866–71: 47–9) recorded beliefs in jagged cliffs above the ocean called Leiono, from which souls would leap.

> Many people who had died and come to life again had pointed them out; and even some people of this age, who have swooned or perhaps lain dead for a few hours or half a day, have related their experiences in these places. There are many stories from the ancients concerning them, and they have been pointed out by prophets inspired by priests. . . . The reason they were believed in was because so many had died and come to life again and had told innumerable stories about these places.

Sometimes at Leiono, helpful ancestor spirits (*'aumakua*) "might bring back the spirit and restore life to the body, or if not, might welcome it to the realm of the *'aumakua*."

Leiono was said to be guarded on one side by a watchman near a pool, and on the other by a huge caterpillar. If the deceased tried to turn back out of fear, the *'aumakua* urged them onward and guided them to the spirit realm. There was also danger of wandering in the wrong direction and falling into Milu, "the realm of homeless souls." Those who had "no rightful place in the *'aumakua* realm" wandered Earth for a time until they reached Leilono, where a breadfruit tree grew. Spirits who leapt from one branch would fall into "the endless night" of Milu, while those who leapt from the other reached the "*'aumakua* realm and the ancestors." Those who had no friendly *'aumakua* spirits to assist them went to particular realms determined by their island of origin. This account accords well with those of *kahunas* in the 1830s–1870s, though they stated that spirits without *'aumakua* helpers wandered "in some barren and desolate place, feeding upon spiders and night moths," and became malevolent spirits who were dangerous to the living (Beckwith 1940: 154).

The 'aumakua realm was vast and flat, had "many dwelling places," and could be entered by numerous gates. It was ruled by "Kanenuiakea, a single god and many gods in one god" (Kamakau 1866–71: 57), together with a hierarchy of overseers. There was a multitude of heavens in the other world, including the "highest heaven," "heaven of myriads," "cloud firmament," and "the standing walls of Kane" as well as many other places to which the dead could travel, including the sun, moon, stars, ocean depths, and "the pit of Pele." Those who went to the heavenly firmament "had wings and had rainbows on their feet." Souls were "united in thought and all joined together" and "in harmony" with relatives, friends, and acquaintances (ibid. 49–51).

Milu, in contrast, was an "arid," "scorching," "rocky," "evil," "friendless," "terrifying" realm, full of troubles and cruelty, and fires that illuminated the darkness. It was ruled by Manu'a, and by Milu, who was sent there for his "evil and foul deeds" while a chief on Earth.[2] According to one myth, a man named Mokulehua traveled to Milu to retrieve his wife, who had committed suicide and was imprisoned by Manu'a. Mokulehua succeeded in rescuing her with the help of the deity, Kanikania-'ula. Similarly, a man named Malua'e went to Milu to rescue his son Ka'ali'i. After prolonged mourning next to Ka'ali'i's body, he was assisted by the gods who had killed the boy for eating a banana intended for them, but now had a change of heart. They transformed Malua'e "into a spirit form" to facilitate his journey, and gave him a magical cane with which he was able to overcome various dangers. He finally reached "the scorching stratum" of Milu where his son was being held, and brought him back to Earth (ibid. 51–2). In a version told by Westervelt (1915: 15–20), Malua'e underwent perils in the underworld (e.g., battling deceased chiefs), obtained assistance from friendly spirits, transported his son back to Earth inside the magic cane, and forced the spirit back into its body. According to Beckwith (1940: 159), the division of the otherworld into positive and negative regions arose "under the teaching of the priesthood as a means of political power" rather than being an indication of Christian influence, for "There is no evidence that American missionaries dwelt upon the horrors of hell to convert their hearers to seek after the joys of heaven." As seen above, Milu did not have such entirely negative characteristics in some of the earlier narratives from the island of Hawai'i.

Additional Hawaiian beliefs were recorded by the journalist, judge, and ethnologist Abraham Fornander (1916–20: II.573–6), who lived in the Islands from 1844–87. When the body died, "the soul may appear as if in the flesh; then there becomes no more night to the soul, only light." Po was not completely dark, for "there was light and there was fire." It was ruled by Manua, with Milu as his assistant. The souls of chiefs went to a volcano and were served by priests of Pele, who could facilitate visits by the living through chanting. Warriors dwelled in a realm of sports and abundant food. Some believed that those buried near water entered into sharks, eels, or other aquatic creatures, and those buried on land entered owls. These animals then became guardian spirits for the living who allowed themselves to become possessed by them. Others believed that souls took up residence in living persons, or lived on dry earthly plains (Fornander 1916–20: III.337).

There are numerous further examples of myths and legends of "descents and returns to and from 'Po'," often facilitated by deities (Emerson 1902: 66–8, 712–4). Kawelo returned to life after being stoned to death, Mokulehua retrieved his wife Pueo (with the help of Kanikaniaula), and Maluae retrieved his son Kaalii (assisted by Kane and Kanaloa). Other legends told of returns via soul-retrieval (*kupaku*), including those of Eleio, Lohiau, Maluae, Mokulehua, and Halemano. The latter was brought back to life twice by his sister Laenihi's powerful prayers (Fornander 1918–9: II.188). The myth of Pele, volcano goddess and progenitor of the Hawaiian people, included two episodes in which a wandering soul was captured and returned to its apparently dead body (Emerson 1915: 71–3, 138ff). There were also legends of spirits of the dead wandering on Earth who were called back to their bodies, most of which include clear OBE episodes.[3]

These kinds of mythological and legendary accounts generally involved culture heroes from the distant past rather than individuals within living memory. This contrasts with Kalima's narrative, which has more consistencies with NDEs from other parts of the world. Narratives such as those of Ka-ilio-hae and Makua seem to be legends midway between actual NDEs and myths,[4] and suggest a stage in the mythologizing process. The contrasting character of the narrative types, in any case, indicates indigenous generic categories.

Marquesas and Tuamotus Islands

In an account from Fatuhiva collected in 1920–21 by E. S. Craighill Handy (1930: 137), a woman named Taa-po died when two deities, Pa-oo and Te-haa-nau, took her as their wife. Her soul went to the spirit-world of Havaii, where she was told not to enter the house of the deity Ivi-ei-nui, but to remain in the doorway. Taa-po memorized a song that Ivi-ei-nui sang, then Pa-oo and Te-haa-nau decided to take her back.

> So this ghost went up and entered into her body. The people saw the toes and the fingers move. Then the body revived entirely, and the relatives were all very happy. Then Taa-po revealed to them all the things her ghost had seen in Havaii.

She taught the song she had learned there to her people, and to those on the neighboring island of Hiva Oa. A chief who wanted to confirm Taa-po's story asked her if she traveled to Havaii in her body, but she insisted that she had died and was taken "to the threshold of Ivi-ei-nui." This convinced the chief, for "no living man arrives at Havaii" (Handy 1930: 82–4). In another part of the narrative, a man's "ghost" left his body during sleep, saw people and events on Earth, then confirmed them upon awakening (ibid. 81–2).

Various legends from Hiva Oa also concerned visits to the otherworld. A fragmentary narrative told of a man who undertook a voyage to Havaii on a bamboo raft, and returned: "it was as a result of this voyage that the people of Hivaoa knew of Havaii" (ibid. 137). A fisherman named Tue-ato was so filled with grief at his wife Ipo-kino's death that spirits assisted him in bringing her back. They forced her soul into a *tiki* statue, which instantly transformed into Ipo-kino herself. Her soul fled, but was caught and returned (ibid. 113–4). In another narrative, Kena followed his wife Tefio to the underworld. After a long, eventful journey he and his traveling companion reached the entrance to "the fourth Havaii," where giant rocks continually clashed together. After successfully passing through them, Kena found the "chiefess" of the other world, Te-upu-o-Tono-Fiti. She assisted him by having Tefio's spirit bathed in fresh water, and providing her with new clothes and a garland before covering her head with a cloth and trapping her in a basket. Te-upu-o-Tono-Fiti warned Kena not to let Tefio out for any reason. Back home on Earth, Kena let her out in order to sleep with her, and she immediately ran back to the spirit world. He followed her again, and again Te-upu-o-Tono-Fiti helped him trap her soul. This time she told Kena to keep Tefio in the basket for ten days. He obeyed, and when Tefio was finally released there was a great celebration for her return (ibid. 117–20).[5]

In a shamanic narrative, Tiki-tu-ao was taken to a spirit realm in the sky by Taua-te-haka-nau-o-tu, "a deified priest of great power." The priest and his fellow spirits fished with a hook for the soul of Tiki-tu-ao's brother-in-law, who was chanting in a ritual ceremony on Earth. They pulled the soul into the sky "while the body remained chanting with the rest of the men." In a ritual sacrifice, the soul's eyes were plucked out and eaten with kava, an entheogenic plant. Tiki-tu-ao was then thrown back to Earth where the men were still chanting. He told his brother-in-law what he had seen, but was met with ridicule. Soon, however, enemies appeared, dragged the brother-in-law away, and sacrificed him to their deity (ibid. 133–4), validating Tiki-tu-ao's premonitory vision that he would be taken to the land of the dead.

Marquesans believed that the soul could leave the body and travel to other realms during dreams. After death, it remained in the body for three days, until a shaman implored it to depart for the other world. According to the French missionary Mathias Gracia (c. 1843), the dead went either to the underworld of Havaiki or to an upper realm, depending on social status. The French traveler Max Radiguet (c. 1882) specified that the latter was reserved for deities, chiefs, women who had died in childbirth, warriors who died in battle, and suicides. Chiefs and priests were ferried by the souls of sacrificed humans. It was a happy realm where spirits "bathed in rivers of coco-nut oil," as Herman Melville reported, abundant in beautiful women, breadfruit, coconuts, bananas, pork, and fish. The sleeping mats, "plumes and feathers, and boars'-tusks, and sperm-whale teeth" were all finer than those found on Earth. Havaiki "for ordinary human beings" was also superior to Earth. On a perilous journey there, souls traveled in a coffin-shaped canoe via Hiva Oa and Tahuata. Two deities tried to influence the course of the boat into a particular strait, which would result in a second death (Frazer 1922: 352, 355, 363–6).

The French missionary R. P. Amable (c.1847) described Tahuata island beliefs that souls of those who were not tattooed, and who owned "many servants and many pigs and have not been wicked," remained near the body for a time, then gathered on Mt. Kiukiu. When there were sufficient numbers, the sea opened and the souls fell into the realm of the goddess Upu. It was a happy place "planted with all sorts of excellent fruits and beautified by the calm waters of an azure lake." Slaves and the poor, however, went to a dark, gloomy world, where they had only muddy water to drink. After a time, all souls were reborn on Earth, usually as humans but sometimes as animals. The dead could be summoned by "wizards" to provide information to the living, and could visit Earth as ghosts where they were greatly feared (ibid. 367–70).

In the nearby Tuamotu Archipelago on the island of Fangatau, in 1874 the French missionary Albert Montiton recorded the belief that souls could leave the body during illness and travel to the other world. At the entrance they met the deity Tama, "who tried to send them back to their bodies. If they persisted in going on, they found themselves definitely separated from their bodies." In such cases, Tama would help them transition to their new home, advising them not to eat fruit there. If they did, Tama abandoned them to two demonic beings, Tepnamea and Tukihiti, "who hurled them into a terrible pond forever" (Williamson 1933: II.81).

Society Islands

In his vast survey of ancient Tahitian culture, Oliver (1974: 521) found that afterlife beliefs were "continually augmented and diversified through dreaming and trance, either sincere or feigned." According to the British missionary J. M. Orsmond, who lived in Polynesia from 1817 to 1856 and was fluent in the Tahitian language, "Persons in trance were supposed to be dead, and after returning to consciousness confirmed the statements about the Po, which they believed they had seen." He gave an example of a man named Pupu-te-tipa, who "was once taken bodily by the gods down into the Po and kept several days, but at last for the sake of his family was released and returned home" (Henry & Orsmond 1928: 202).

In his journal of 1838–56, George Charter, a British missionary working on Raiatea, recounted the NDE of a woman named Terematai, who had been unconscious for days. When she revived, she stated that she had "been to heaven," where she saw both Raiateans and Europeans she recognized. She concluded, "I wished to remain but God sent me back to exhort my family that they may be saved." According to Charter, she "was in a very happy state of mind and appeared wholly absorbed in spiritual subjects" (Gunson 1962: 218).

From the small island of Huahine comes a mid-nineteenth-century NDE related by the French naval pharmacist Gilbert Cuzent. An elderly queen "visited the other world" while in a cataleptic trance. When she revived, "She told her friends that, when there, she glided about among numerous people whom she had formerly known." They communicated with her telepathically, and they could pass through each other in their "bodiless state." She returned to Earth via a series of islands, for "by order of a spirit she had to enter again into her body, though it was in a state of corruption" (Williamson 1933: I.373). It was believed that decomposition could be stopped if "the soul was allowed by spirits to return to the body" (Oliver 1974: 64).

Robert Louis Stevenson (1891: 215–6) recounted a narrative from 1888, in which a princess died and went to Raiatea. A spirit there forced her to climb trees and collect coconuts for him, but she was aided by a deceased relative who took her back to Tahiti where her wake was still in progress, though her body was "already swollen with the approaches of corruption." When she saw the horrifying sight, she prayed to remain dead, though the spirit compelled her back into the body via "the least dignified of entrances, and her startled family beheld the body move."

In the last decade of the nineteenth century, the American historian Henry Adams recounted a narrative of "the last queen of Tahiti," who returned to her body "many days" after her death, when decomposition had already begun. Upon revival, she described "the departure of her soul through the air to Paradise and . . . its subsequent unwilling return to its putrefying body in obedience to the command of a chief who appeared to reign in the world of happy souls that she had gone to." The chief forced her to return in order facilitate his own forthcoming reincarnation, by becoming her lover. He instructed her not to convert to Christianity, but when she was forced to do by some authority, the chief was unable to complete his reincarnation (Handy 1927: 85–6).

The so-called Visionary Heresy, or Mamaia cult, originated in Papeete in 1826, following the divine dreams of a prophet named Teao. It was maintained by Teao and another prophet named Hue through claims of continued revelations direct from heaven. The movement spread to other parts of Tahiti, with its messages of anti-European revolution, a return to traditional beliefs with an admixture of Christianity, and the practice of extended prayer in order to bring about spirit possession, visions, and divine messages (Gunson 1962: 214ff; 222).

In an Orpheus myth, the spirit of the deceased moon goddess, Hina, was followed to the underworld by her husband, Tafa'i. Assisted by a guardian, he hid behind bushes in order to catch her before she crossed "the last place whence spirits could be recalled to this world." Hina was reluctant to return and tried to escape by ascending to "the happy spirit world." Tafa'i succeeded in returning her to Earth, however, where she "re-entered her body, which was still well-preserved, and opened her mortal eyes" to the joy of her people (Henry & Orsmond 1928: 563–4).

Descriptions of afterlife beliefs also reveal knowledge of NDEs. Souls lingered near the body for three days before traveling "to Tata Hill at Puna'auia, the grand place of assemblage for all disembodied souls in Tahiti." There the spirit would either land on the Stone of Life and "return by powerful attraction to its body," or on the Stone of Death, resulting in the death of the body. Spirits then proceeded to a junction, where one path led to "a lonely hillock" at the center of heaven, and the other to "a cone-shaped heap" at the center of hell. If the spirit had landed on the Stone of Life, the deity Tu-ta-horoa (Stand-to-permit) "would under certain conditions tell it to return to its body to remain a while longer in this life." Most often, however, the god would simply indicate which road to take. Those who took the first path were given amulets by Roma-tane (Voluptuous-man) to be admitted into paradise (Rohutu-noanoa). Those who took the second path descended into a crater to "Great-Ta'aroa-whose-curse-was-death." Earthly rank and status were not recognized, and everyone worked for the gods "according to their capabilities." They then waited in darkness by "the ever-rushing river" until Ta'aroa's cooks "scraped the spirits into a pulp" with a shell, to be eaten by the god then reborn to serve Ta'aroa again. When he grew concerned that people were not happy, they transformed into demigods with the power to visit relatives on Earth, and influence the living in positive or negative ways. For some, afterlife fates were determined by manner of death. Those who died violently remained at the site of death, which would henceforth be considered either haunted or sacred. Those "who committed suicide from disappointment in love or jealousy ever afterward remained with the object of their attachment." Souls of infants killed at birth became their parents' guardian spirits. Infants who died otherwise became shellfish in the waters of the underworld, were eaten by T'aroa, then entered new human or fish bodies on Earth. Older children went to the ancestors (Henry & Orsmond 1928: 199–200).

Captain James Cook (1784: 163–4) reported similar beliefs, with the addition that men who abstained from sex during their last few months of life proceeded directly to the blissful state. Earthly relationships continued in the other world, and couples procreated "entirely spiritual" children. According to Ellis (1829: 244–6), those who could afford to pay a priest to conduct the required ceremonies (mainly chiefs and members of the Areoi secret society) were led by the deity Urutaetae to the creator Oro in Rohutu-noanoa, on the mountain of Temehani. It was a happy and beautiful place where social status was maintained. There was an abundance of food, scented flowers, pure air, festivals, and young beautiful people.

Cook Islands

According to local shamans, sometimes when souls left their bodies at death they would meet "a friendly spirit" who would say, "Go back and live," and send them back to "re-inhabit the once-forsaken body" (Gill 1876: 160–1, 221–4). In a legend from Rarotonga, a woman named Akimano had a sexual experience with the culture hero Moe-tara-uri that "was so potent, that her spirit departed from her body and went up to the god Tiki." When Tiki asked her, "What ails you?" she replied, "I have died from the act of cohabitation." Tiki explained, "There is no place here for those who have died that death; here are places for those who die from acts of jealousy, from slander, from hatred, and from all the ills of which man dies, but that death of which you speak, there is no place for here." He refused her entrance to his realm, made her return to Earth, and "The spirit of the woman returned again to its body and so came to life again" (Savage 1916: 145–6).

In a myth from Aitutaki Island, a man named Tekauae descended to the underworld while near death. The hideously deformed goddess Miru gave him a bowl of live centipedes to eat, but Tekauae had a coconut hidden under his clothes and fooled Miru by eating from it instead. When he did not writhe in agony, leap into a lake, and drown as expected, Miru sent him back to his body on Earth. Though she instructed Tekauae not to speak of what he had seen in the underworld, when he returned to life he told his friends what to expect if they ever descend there. The myth does not explain why Tekauae did not visit Iva, the heavenly realm of pleasure and abundance, ruled by the benevolent Tukaitaua (ibid. 173–5).

In a narrative from Pukapuka, a man named Milimili died and went to Po. His wife and family appealed to the gods to return him, but they refused. Ultimately, he was rescued by "Man of the ocean", who managed to throw his spirit to the family gods, who then restored it to the body (reported 1934–5; Beckwith 1940: 150).

In an Orpheus myth, Kura's sister-in-law, Umuei, pushed her from a tree while she was picking flowers. She fell into a region of Avaiki called Marama, and was caught by ghosts who tied her up and planned to eat her. Meanwhile, Umuei informed her brother Eneene of Kura's predicament. With the help of a god carved from the sacred *bua* tree, Eneene descended to the spirit world, located Kura, and scattered coconut flakes on the paths leading to the house where she was held. This attracted hundreds of rats which distracted the guard, allowing Eneene to lower himself through the roof and rescue Kura. They fled the pursuing "army of Marama," and ascended through a dark chasm and into the daylight (Gill 1876: 221–4).

In a myth of the hero Ngaru, Miru the "fierce she-demon" was envious of his fame, so decided to "destroy him in her fearful, ever-blazing oven" and eat him. She sent her two daughters to lure him to Avaiki, but Ngaru suspected their true motive. While he entertained them, his grandfather, Moko the lizard king, sent lizards to Avaiki to gather intelligence. They reported that Miru used a kava plant to "stupefy" her victims. That evening, Miru's daughters wrapped Ngaru in tapa (bark cloth) and carried him to the spirit world. He heard Moko's voice telling him to return to Earth, but he continued onward, managing to stay alert when the women forced him to eat kava. Once in Avaiki, just as he was stepping into the oven, a rainstorm extinguished the coals and caused a deluge that washed Miru away. Her daughters survived by clinging to Ngaru's legs, and he stayed with them for a time and they taught him a ball game. He then followed a dark tunnel to Tuamareva (expanse), a land of flowers, fruits, and music. There he lived and even married, but was eventually carried by birds back to Earth. In a subsequent episode, Ngaru ascended to the heavenly realm of "sky-demon" Amai-te-rangi (Carry-up-to-heaven), who also sought to cook and eat him. He saw "piles of human bones" along with "beautiful women engaged in ball throwing" (ibid. 228–236). A song version composed in 1815 refers to Ngaru's power, which comes "From the depths of spirit-land; From Vari [mother-goddess] originator-of-all-things, Who sends him back again (to this world)" (ibid. 238ff).

A myth from Mangaia told of Veetini, who died after an illness, went to an undersea realm, and temporarily returned to Earth in ghostly form. He taught his people about funerary offerings, and when they tried to detain him, he insisted on returning to the underworld (ibid. 181ff).

It was believed that souls of the dead traveled westward to a cliff, where a huge wave and a giant blossoming *bua* tree would rise from Avaiki. From there, souls might hear "a friendly voice" sending them back to the body. Otherwise, they proceeded to Avaiki via the branch of the tree reserved for their tribe. Women, children, and cowards were lowered into a net, and submerged in a lake until exhausted. These "weak and feeble" spirits were then fed "red earth-worms, black beetles, crabs, and small blackbirds" before being drugged with kava to prevent them from struggling while being eaten by Milu, her family, and their servants. The souls of warriors who died in battle were consumed by the war god Rongo, but were "eventually disengaged *alive*" from his intestines then ascended to the sky. They remained "strong and vigorous," became immortal, and spent their time laughing, performing war-dances, and reminiscing about their earthly achievements. From their world of light, they were contemptuous of those in dark Avaiki, who were covered with the warrior's falling excrement (Gill 1876: 162–5). However, life in Avaiki was generally conceived as an idealized version of Earth, with an abundance of foods, trees, and arts; though also with continued "murder, adultery, drunkenness, theft and lying." At night "the Sun-god Rā drops down through . . . the edge of the horizon, and thus lights up the inhabitants of the netherworld."[6] Avaiki could also be reached by a road on a cliff above the ocean. Some spirits wandered unhappily along the coast, on a coral outcropping, in a cave, or grassy expanse, until particular groups ascended together with Rā (ibid. 154–9). Souls of those who worshiped the deity Motoro risked being trapped in his house (which they sometimes visited during sleep), swept into the ocean, and then into the spirit world (ibid. 166).

Samoa and Tuvalu

George Turner (1884: 258–9), a Scottish missionary who lived in Samoa for thirty-four years, reported a belief about a tree called the Watcher at the entrance to the underworld: "If a spirit struck against it that soul went back at once to its body. In such cases of restoration from the gates of death the family rejoiced and exclaimed, 'He has come back from the tree of the Watcher.'" Turner also reported a narrative of two "conjurors" who restored a chief to life. Souls of the dead traveled to the underworld of Pulotu by floating on an underground stream, at which stage they could neither return nor swim ashore. Upon arrival in Pulotu, they bathed in "the water of life" to become young, "lively and bright and vigorous." Pulotu was similar to Earth, and was ruled by the human-fish (or eel) deity Saveasiuleo ("Savea of the echo"). Spirits could visit their former homes in the form of "luminous sparks or vapour" (ibid. 142).

According to the English missionary-ethnographer George Brown (1910: 219–24), who lived in Samoa for nearly fifteen years from 1860, local afterlife beliefs were "confirmed by . . . accounts of men going to the other world and returning again to this one." The spirit (*anganga*) was conceived of as an immaterial duplicate of the body that could temporarily separate from it during unconsciousness and in dreams. After death it sometimes appeared to the living, and there was some risk of possession from malevolent ghosts. Souls of chiefs traveled westward to various islands until reaching a "jumping-off stone" from which they dove down to Pulotu, here described as the realm of the gods. It was similar to Earth, and spirits could visit their living families. Everyone else went to the place of "no account," which was mostly "dismal and mournful," though one's conditions on Earth "had an effect on their future conditions." An alternate underworld was Motuononoa (place without conversation), or Sa-le-fee (cuttle-fish). Spirits were blindfolded by gods and taken there through coconut trees, then hit in the chest upon arrival (Brown 1910: 364–5; cf. Stair 1897: 215–7).

In a narrative from 1902, the spirit of a king's daughter was brought back to her body after dying and going to "the ninefold heaven" (Beckwith 1940: 150). On the island of Funafati, Tuvalu, a "spirit-master" (*vakatua*) named Erivara went to the other world in his sleep and encountered "seven spirits who showed him a wonderful object." They instructed him to make a copy of it upon "his return to earth." He did so, and it became a sacred healing object (Sollas 1897: 354).

Tonga

William Mariner (1817: 104–6), a ship's clerk aboard an English privateer, was captured by Tongans and lived with them from 1802 to 1806. He recounted a legend of a canoe that was blown off course to Bolotoo (viz., Pulotu). The crew found that everything there was ghostly and insubstantial, and when they returned to Earth they all died shortly thereafter, poisoned by the air in the realm of death (ibid. 108–9). In a legend reported in 1906, a woman named Sina died, left her body, and went "to the ninth heaven." She was placed in a basket and hung in a house before returning to Earth and coming alive again (Williamson 1933: I.200).[7]

Edward Winslow Gifford (1924: 153) found that narratives of individuals who visited Pulotu were "fairly common." They typically described it as an island realm of gods and spirits located to the northwest of Tonga, reached by a sometimes-perilous journey.

In a myth reported in 1906 by the Catholic missionary Franciscus Dubignon, four earthly deities traveled by boat to Pulotu, reluctantly allowing an old woman goddess to join them. Arriving at the house of the deity Hikuleo, they found it empty and hid inside. When the underworld beings discovered their boat and began searching for them, the four deities transformed themselves into insects and stones, successfully hiding from the search party. Hikuleo implored them to reveal themselves, and when they did he forced them to drink an enormous quantity of kava, questioning whether it was "permissible for gods who are but commoners and fools to come to Pulotu." Hikuleo then set a series of challenges for the Earth-gods, and they triumphed in all of them, killing various underworld deities in the process. Hikuleo finally sent them back to Earth with a certain kind of fish, taro, and the first yams (Gifford 1924: 155–65). Other versions include details such as encountering the eight-tongued goddess Elelovalu, and Hikuleo's house being covered in staring human eyeballs or made of human bones (ibid. 166–73).

The missionary Ernest Edgar Vyvyan Collocott collected a number of relevant narratives in the early 1920s. One myth told of a man named Tui Hattala, who instructed his people not to bury his body, then left it and traveled to Pulotu in order to discover why his sons kept dying. Knowing he was alive on Earth, Hikuleo was surprised to see Tui Hattala in the underworld. He instructed him to bathe, and asked why he had "come to this bad place." Tui Hattala explained that he was there because six of his sons had died. Hikuleo told him that because he had visited Pulotu before the time appointed for his death, he must return to Earth. Tui Hattala did so, only to find that his body had been buried against his instructions. His clothes were still wet from the spring of Pulotu, and when he hung them on a tree the dripping water became a stream. He traveled from place to place and became known by different names on different islands. Because he had gone to the underworld without dying and had returned to find he no longer had a body, subsequent generations could not use his name. The narrative explains that his father (also Tui Hattala) and his mother were the first people to die, and that Hikuleo was his grandfather (ibid. 153–5).

Collocott also recorded a myth in which a young man asked a god to recommend a wife for him. The girl was under guard, however, so the god accompanied the youth to Pulotu to seek advice on how he could meet her. He was told to bathe, then sent back to Earth with instructions to find work near the girl. A ghost gave him a flower to take to her, he did so, and they were married (ibid. 175–8). Visits to Pulotu also occurred in a legend about men seeking a child adopted by Hikuleo (ibid. 173–5). In a reversal of the Tahitian Orpheus myth, Hina traveled to the underworld to find her husband when he was killed by a chief who wished to marry her. Her grandmother, Hikuleo (for the deity could take the form of either sex [ibid. 153]), found the husband and allowed him to return to Earth with Hina (ibid. 183). Another myth tells of Hina's son-in-law, whose spirit was rescued from Pulotu by his uncle who restored him to his body with a "life-affecting fan" (Beckwith 1940: 150).

According to Captain Cook (1784: I.404), it was believed that the souls of chiefs left the body immediately upon death and traveled to Boolootoo (viz., Pulotu), which was ruled by the "personification of death," a "Chief, or god" named Gooleho (viz., Hikuleo). Boolootoo "was never seen by any person," though was believed to be a place of immortality, abundance, and feasting located west of Fiji. Souls of "the lower sort of people" were eaten by a *loata* bird that walked on the grave. Mariner (1817: 117–9) provided additional and alternative details, including that Pulotu was also the divine realm of creation. The souls of the highest nobles had "the power of inspiring priests, and of appearing in dreams and visions to their relatives and others." Lower nobles retained some of their power, and other social classes had "the form and likeness of the body" in spirit form. The lowest classes simply died with the body. There was no war because spirits possessed greater understanding, intelligence, and ability to distinguish right from wrong.

New Zealand

The German naturalist Ernst Dieffenbach (1843: 66–7) recorded Maori beliefs that souls of the living could travel temporarily to Reigna, the netherworld. Te Rerenga Wairua (Cape Reigna, the northernmost point of New Zealand) was the leaping-off place of the "immortal, incorporeal spirit (*waiura*)," which left the body at death and descended to Reigna as a falling star. Concerning the Maori "before they became modified by intercourse with Europeans," the English scholar and linguist Edward Shortland (1856: 150) wrote,

> Often, indeed, it has happened, at least, so it is affirmed, that persons who have died, and actually descended this precipice, have returned again to earth to relate what they had seen below, and lived for many years afterwards.

A man named Te Wharewera told Shortland about his aunt who had died then reappeared a day or two later, beckoning him from the shore while he was out in a canoe. She was weak and close to death, but once she was restored to health she told of how she had left her body and traveled to Te Rerenga Wairua. She descended to a river on a vine, and as she stood on its bank a gigantic bird flew towards her. She fled to an old man who was paddling a canoe toward the shore, and he ferried her across the river. He pointed her in the direction of her family, and on her way she marveled at how similar to Earth everything seemed. When she reached a village she was welcomed by "her father and many near relations formerly known alive." Her father inquired about their living relatives, then said, "You must go back to earth, for there is no one now to take care of my grand-child." He warned her not to eat anything in Reigna or she would be unable to return to Earth. A young man wanted her to stay, but her father rushed her back to the river and ferried her across. He gave her two large *kumara* roots for her to plant for her son, and told her to hurry. As she struggled up the precipice, she was accosted by "two infant spirits" who tried to drag her back, but she threw the roots and the infants leapt away to claim them. When she reached Earth, she "flew back to the place where she had left her body." When she revived and found herself lying in state in a darkened, abandoned hut, she realized what had happened to her—"that she had really died, and had returned to life"—and she crawled out to the beach where her nephew had found her. "Those who listened to her tale believed firmly the truth of her adventures" (Shortland 1856: 150–55).

Shortland (1882: 45) also recounted the NDE of a man named Te Atarahi who died, left his body, traveled to Reigna, and revived five days later. He had lost his hair, and was emaciated, though he returned to normal after being fed and cared for. Once he was well,

> he told how he had been in the Reigna, how his relations came about him, and bid him not to touch the food, and sent him back to the land of Light. He spoke also of the excellence of the state in which the people of the Reigna dwelt.

Nearly forty years later, the scholar and linguist Edward Tregear (1890: 118–9) was told of Te Atarahi's NDE in almost identical detail. He also confirmed beliefs in OBEs during dreams and trance, and that "In illness the soul journeys away and is sometimes on the brink of crossing to Hades, but returns—only a few return." His source explained, "Sometimes the Charon of the death-river drives the spirit back to his friends and he recovers." Tregear concluded, "It is probable that many of the stories told about *Po* and *Reinga* are the dreams of people in trance through illness." The consistency of Te Atarahi's narrative over time, and the fact that it was retold to Westerners on at least three occasions, demonstrates its lasting significance to the Maori. The English missionary Richard Taylor (1855: 104–5) was told an almost identical version, alongside the belief that the journey to Po involved crossing a river called Waioratane. Spirits were assisted by a guardian who would lay a plank across the water. However,

> sometimes he will not do so, but drives [the soul] back to the upper regions, with friendly violence, in order that he may take care of the family he has left behind; so, likewise, if he has not partaken of the food of the Reigna, he may return again to the earth. If a person has recovered from a dangerous disease, or from anything which threatened his life, he is said to have reached Waioratane and returned.

Taylor found "many stories of persons who have descended into the Reigna and returned." In one example, a man traveled to a place beneath the sea "into which the sun shone." He found a door, but when he was unable to open it and his knocking failed to get a response, he returned to Earth. In another narrative a man went to Reigna, married a woman, and brought her back to Earth. She later persuaded him to return to Reigna with her, but after she took the first leap (at his insistence) he decided not to join her after all (Taylor 1855: 105–6). A Christian convert and preacher named Manihera told his gathering that "during the night he had been in the Reigna, and met many of his deceased friends, who told him he should soon be with them." Soon after, he was murdered (ibid. 359–61).

A myth told of how the deity Tawaki was killed by relatives but returned from the Reigna and came back to life. He then ascended all ten heavens to the place where his grandmother lived. It was believed that stars were spirits of the dead, their degree of brightness corresponding to their level of greatness on Earth (ibid. 36-8).

In the legend of Pare, she committed suicide because a married chief named Hutu refused her advances. Her people decided, "Hutu must be the payment" for her death. He agreed, but instructed them not to bury Pare's body until he returned from the underworld. At the entrance, he met the guardian Hine-nui-te-po, who pointed him down the path of dog spirits. When Hutu gave her a green gem, however, she showed him the correct road and gave him provisions so he would not have to eat food of the underworld. At her instruction, he leapt into the darkness and a wind buoyed him to a safe landing. But Pare refused to see him, and ignored his efforts to get her attention by playing games. Eventually he managed to coax her into joining him on a swing he fashioned in a tree. He then used the swing as a catapult to hurl them upward to the mouth of the pit, where they were able to grip the grass growing over the edge and climb out. They returned to their village, and "when the spirit of Pare reached her body, it re-entered it, and she was quite alive and well again" (ibid. 270–72).[8]

The origin of Hine-nui-te-po was told in a myth of how Tane created a woman named Hine-hua-one ("daughter of earth-aroma"), made her pregnant, then married their daughter, Hine-i-tauira. When she discovered that her husband was her father, Hine-i-tauira committed suicide. She went to the underworld, where her name was changed to Hine-nui-te-po ("great daughter of darkness"). Tane followed, hoping to bring her back, but she told him to return to Earth in order to raise their children (ibid. 131–2). In another version, Hine-i-tauira was questioned in the underworld by Hine-a-te-ao ("daughter of the light"), then told to return because Hine-a-te-ao was maintaining the "division between night and day." Tane followed and was also questioned, and though he reached Hine-ata-uira (after passing "Tu the eye-consumer" and "Daughter of the vomiting moa"), he was ultimately sent back to Earth (White 1891: 146).

In the 1860s, an elderly shaman (*tohunga*) named Te Matorohanga recounted two myths of demigods visiting the underworld, Rarohenga. In the first, the sun-conquering "Celestial hero" Maui descended with his companions. They found the guardian Hine-nui-te-po lying asleep with her legs open. With the intention of destroying death, Maui assumed the form of a "hairy lizard" and entered her womb. Hine-nui-te-po became aroused and "closed her parts," strangling Maui (Te Matorohanga & Pohuhu 1913: 174–8). In the second myth, Mataora married a woman from Rarohenga named Niwareka. He beat her while in a jealous rage, and when she fled back to Rarohenga he followed. There he was told, "the under-world is really the world of light," and Earth is a place of darkness. Niwareka and her father agreed that she would return to Earth with Mataora, on the condition that he implement certain moral and ritual practices on Earth: new tattooing, wood-carving, and weaving customs, and not beating women or committing other "evil deeds." It was also decreed that henceforth people could only go to Rarohenga in spirit form (ibid. 183–93).

The German missionary Johan Wohlers (1874: 8-9) recounted a myth of the forest deity Tane ascending to a heavenly realm to see his brother. At each of nine successive levels he asked, "Are there men above?" and was told that there were. He was not allowed to enter any of the levels, however, because one heaven had been "stretched out by Tane," another painted by him, and another had "bounds of which have been fixed" by him (i.e., as the deity who separated heaven from Earth). At the tenth level Tane found his brother, whose gardening added "to the splendour of heaven." They cried together, and after touring other parts of the level, Tane returned to Earth. There he found that his wife had "gone to Po," and he followed.

In another myth, chief Tama was rejected by his wife because of his homely appearance, so he entered into a white heron and flew down to Reinga in order to ask his ancestors to "make him handsome." When he saw how beautiful their tattoos made them, Tama convinced the ancestors to tattoo him. Their first two attempts washed off, because to be tattooed permanently was "as bad as death." It took "many days of painful operation" and healing until he was ready to return to Earth. His ancestors gave him flowers and other gifts, and he was reunited with his family on Earth. Tama ultimately ended up killing his wife, though she returned to life the following spring (Wohlers 1875: 111–5).

A myth of two women told of how they went to the other world and caused "three grey-headed old spirits sitting round a fire" to flee from them. One of the women, "desirous of getting some spiritual fire," took a burning piece of wood and ran away. She was caught by a spirit, however, and when she threw the burning stick into the sky it became the moon (Tregear 1890: 118–9).

The scholar and linguist John White (1891: 145–6) was told by *tohungas* that when souls descended to the first region of Te-Reigna (Uranga-o-te-ra), they were questioned about their identity and occupation on Earth. The soul "replied by giving a history of its life" before proceeding to a river overseen by the ferry-woman, Rohe. "All who recovered from insensibility caused by a blow, or fit, or trance, were supposed to be refused a passage by Rohe and sent back to life."

Elsdon Best (1905: 231–2) also confirmed that Maori afterlife beliefs were "the result of persons dreaming of having descended to the underworld. . . . A person recovering from a trance would be said by the Maori to have returned from the spirit-world." As an example he recounted a double NDE in which Kukia and Toihau, two men of the Ngati-Awa tribe, died and "spoke of strange things" when they revived. Their souls had climbed down a cliff, then over a wall, and they saw "numberless" spirits. Eventually they found their own people, including their parents, who sent them back to their bodies. Kukia and Toihau "said that the spirit-world is a very good sort of place, and not shrouded in darkness, but light like unto this world" (ibid. 231). The narrative was intended to demonstrate that descent to Po was an indigenous belief, in contrast to missionary teachings of ascent to a heavenly realm (Best 1900: 184). The existence of variants of this narrative demonstrates its widespread significance. In one version, Toihau was led to Reigna by an ancestor spirit, who warned him not to eat the food or he would be unable to return to Earth. He was driven back violently by the spirit, then reentered his body, "so that, after being dead for three days, Toihau of the Children of Awa rose from the dead and lived again." A brief narrative told of a woman who was "carried off by spirits . . . and she saw the spirits of all the dead-and-gone people ere she returned here" (ibid. 232).

Best (1900: 3) reported beliefs that the soul could leave the body during dreams, and wander to meet spirits of the dead and obtain clairvoyant information. Visiting the other world and meeting souls there was an experience known as a *Po-mariko*. An invocation for restoring the *manawa-ora* ("life-breath") to a dead person was intended to bring them back to life (Best 1901: 9–10). In a shamanic form of religion (*Mangamangai-atua*) practiced in earlier times, *wairua* spirits would possess individuals as they recited incantations in a state of quivering hands and rolling eyes (Best 1900: 179).

The physician W. H. Goldie (1904: 20) also reported Maori beliefs that souls of the recently deceased could return to the body and bring it back to life. Some were sent back from the netherworld "by its relatives, for the purpose of caring for its children who have been left without a guardian owing to the parents' death." *Tohungas* could also restore souls of the recently deceased.

Despite the claim of Best's informant that heavenly ascent was introduced by missionaries, a heavenly realm for chiefs was cited by Dieffenbach as early as 1843

(66–7, 118). Their souls went there temporarily, leaving their left eye ("the seat of the soul") behind before becoming stars. Consuming the left eye of an enemy in order to incorporate his soul was said to be a common practice. White (1891: 362) likewise reported that priests and chiefs, considered to be partly divine, went to the deity Tawhaki, "up to the heavens, there to exist eternally." Te Matorohanga explained that it was a matter of preference, for "those spirits who have love for the Earth-mother" go by one road to Rarohenga, "whilst those who love the Sky-father proceed forth to the eastern door by way of the Ara-tiatia [via clouds, to the Supreme God Io]" (Te Matorohanga & Pohuhu 1913: 183–93; cf. Best 1926: 6). A funerary recitation for high-ranking individuals of the Takitumu clan referred to the soul returning to the place of creation to be welcomed by the ancestors in "the spaced heavens by which your ancestor Tane ascended to Io-matua [the Supreme Deity]," served by the deity's adoring spirits, and treated like a god (ibid. 10–11). An exhumation ritual recitation recorded c. 1862 mentions ascent on a whirlwind to Rangiatea, "where you will attain peace" (ibid. 18–9).

Po had different regions, the lowest of which was a place of darkness where spirits "would pine away" until they were "finally annihilated" (Taylor 1855: 104–5). Ordinary people "diminished" as they descended to Po, then reincarnated on Earth as worms. Those who rebelled against To, the creator deity, lived an earthly lifespan on twenty successive levels of the spirit world. Souls were considered to be rays emanated from To (White 1891: 360–4), and they could take the form of sun rays or shadows in order to visit Earth. From Reigna—a realm of abundance where life was similar to that on Earth—spirits could communicate with the living via mediums or dreams (Dieffenbach 1843: 66–7). Souls could also return to Earth as butterflies, and could be summoned through incantations in order "to avenge a murdered person or perform some other act." The souls of stillborn children remained on Earth as malevolent spirits, while the fourth heaven was reserved for children prior to being born on Earth. Some believed that the ghost (*kehua*) remained on Earth in a dangerous form until after burial, when it would proceed to the other world (Best 1900: 182, 184).

Finally, it is interesting to compare the above accounts to one from the early 1960s. A woman named Nga, who never converted to Christianity, died from an illness, and her body was taken to be prepared for burial. She revived, however, surprising her family when she sat up and breathed again. She recounted how she had left her body and hovered above its head before leaving the room. She traveled northward over a river, and past various earthly locales to Te Rerenga Wairua. She bathed in "the weeping spring," then climbed a tree and prepared to slide down its root to the underworld's entrance. When she heard a voice, asking who she was and who she was looking for, she stopped and replied that she sought her "old people." The voice told her, "They don't want you yet. Eat nothing and go back where you came from until they are ready. Then I shall send for you." She obeyed, rose from the tree, and returned to her body (King 1985: 87–8; Cf. Kellehear 2001). The account was recently analyzed by cultural psychologist Natasha Tassell-Matamua (2013: 113), who identified numerous points in accordance with Maori beliefs and traditions. She concluded that "the features of Nga's experience are similar to those typically described in other NDE accounts but were explained in a way that made sense to Nga according to the cultural environment she resided in."

Micronesia

In 1700, the French Jesuit missionary Charles Le Gobien reported that prior to exposure to Christianity, the Mariana Islanders believed in paradisiacal and hellish realms determined by mode of death. The souls (*anitis*) of those who died violent deaths went to Zazarraguan, or the "House of Chayasi," a tormenting demon. Those who died natural deaths dwelled in a beautiful underground paradise abundant with sugar cane, coconut palms, and fruits. The dead could visit Earth as malevolent spirits and haunt the living. Communication with spirits of the dead was performed by shamans (*macanas*) (Frazer 1924: 282–3).

In 1888, the Polish ethnologist J. S. Kubary reported that among the Palau Islanders, the appearance of spirits of the dead "in dreams or in waking visions" furnished proof of afterlife beliefs. The soul (*adhalep*) lingered near the body until burial, then traveled by canoe to the invisible spirit realm of Ngadhalok, situated to the south on the island of Peleliu. Ngadhalok was similar to Earth, with much singing and dancing. Shamans could facilitate encounters between the dead and the living (ibid. 234–5, 265). A myth told of the goddess Milad, who returned from the dead (Parmentier 1987: 159).

The most relevant and extensive Micronesian information comes from Waqab (Yap) in the Caroline Islands. Though they had been visited by missionaries and were under German control, William Henry Furness (1910: 11) wrote that the people had nevertheless "retained the greater part of their original primitive beliefs." It was thought that during illness, the soul (*tafenai*, literally "thinking part") was trying to escape, and "when a man is delirious his *tafenai* has left his body and may or may not be enticed to return." Epileptic seizures were thought to result when a returning soul collided with the body after wandering on the winds. The soul also left the body during dreams, "playing all manner of queer pranks" (ibid. 147–51). Mediumistic communication with the dead was also practiced, according to the German missionary Sixtus Walleser in 1913 (Frazer 1924: 170–1).

In 1908–10, German ethnographer Wilhelm Müller-Wismar recounted a Waqab myth in which five sisters, each named Dame Necklace, ascended a tree to heaven. They knocked the tree over to prevent their youngest sister from follow-ing, though a spirit appeared to her and asked, "Are you of good courage?" When she replied in the affirmative, the spirit showed her the way to heaven in return for helping him remove the grass that grew from his body. Upon arrival in the other world, she "hid behind the house of the great god Yalafath in his field of Turmeric." When Yalafath discovered her by her smell, he adopted her. She was then spotted by her sisters at a dance, and they asked her for food. She denied her previous identity, saying "She is on earth, for when she came to the ladder, you had already broken it down." The five sisters then jumped back down to Earth, and were killed (Frazer 1924: 196–7).

Another myth told of how spirits of the dead had been stealing taro from the living. A man named Oayan made friends with one of them, and traded his taro for some fish. When the spirit invited Oayan to go with him to the underworld, he agreed, and brought "poisonous creepers" with him. They visited a friend of the spirit whose entire house was made of fish, but the creepers caused it to "shiver and die," killing the spirit as well. On Oayan's return to Earth, he was strangled by the opening of the underground passageway, turning to stone and blocking the entrance to the underworld (ibid. 201–2).

It was believed that souls of the dead ascended to "a large house known as *Falraman*, and over it presides the creator of the world, who is a kind but rather unsympathetic god." Souls retained their "bodily shape," and once their "mor-tal heaviness and earthly odor" had worn off, they returned to their old homes on Earth where they were invisible. They could also be forced by ancestors to become malevolent to the living, or taken by more benevolent ancestors to the heavenly realm. Some resisted such influence, and remained free to live in heaven or the underworld (ibid. 170–1). Those who cut down trees on another person's land were punished by the deity Boradaileng, "by thrusting them into a pit of fire" (Furness 1910: 11; cf. Christian 1899: 385).

It is also worth mentioning the NDEs of three Chamorra women in Guam, reported by the psychologist J. T. Green in 1984. No sociocultural contexts are provided, and it should be noted that Dobbin (2011: 12) omitted the Chamorro from his overview of Micronesian religions on the grounds of pervasive conver-sion to Catholicism, as well as long-term influence from Spain, the Philippines, and Mexico. Nevertheless, the NDEs feature some elements typical of small-scale societies, most notably walking along a road, and spirit journeys to earthly locales. In these cases, rather than islands or volcanoes, the women visited family members in the United States. This is in addition to elements such as a paradi-siacal realm, deceased relatives, encountering a spirit or diety, being instructed to return (one on the grounds of mistaken identity, another being "not ready to enter"), and a reluctance to do so.

Melanesia

The Melanesian underworld was commonly a gloomy, "empty and unreal" place that "sometimes extends under the sea." It was reached via volcanoes, caves, or other earthly locales (Moss 1925: 42). Entry was determined either by funerary feasts and grave goods that showed the status and "liberality" of the individual; or by "proper qualifications" such as tattoos or other tribal markings, and gifts for the guardian of the entrance. Ordeals such perilous bridge crossings were also typical (ibid. 110, 112).

According to the British missionary-cum-anthropologist R. H. Codrington (1891: 69ff), there was a marked difference between religious orientation in the islands of Vanuatu which were more concerned with nonhuman spiritual beings, and the Solomon Islands and Fiji which focused almost entirely on deified spirits of the dead (ibid. 122). Divination and prophecy via spirit communication were common (ibid. 209ff), as were beliefs in possession by spirits of the dead, and attendant practices (e.g., ritual exorcisms, trance mediumship) (ibid. 218ff).

New Guinea

On Biak Island, myths of "the resuscitation of dead persons through the love of their relatives" sought to explain local afterlife beliefs. Resuscitation was believed to occur through the power of the skulls of ancestors (Kamma 1954: 73–5). During the transitional period of conversion to Christianity, a dying man "dreamt of a golden ladder which took him up to the heavenly house." Such notions were central to Biak afterlife conceptions (ibid. 102).

In a narrative recorded in 1854, prior to the arrival of missionaries, a man named Manarmakeri followed a pig into a cave and heard many voices "laughing and rejoicing." Addressing him as "Not-real-man" they asked, "where do you want to go and what do you wish to take from here?" When he did not reply he was instructed to leave by walking backward, but was told he could see his kinfolk first. Manarmakeri suddenly found himself in a large, beautiful village, where his people sang and danced in the prime of youth. He wanted to stay, but the voice told him that his "time has not come yet" because he was "still in the husk." After his return to Earth he fell into a listless depression. Though only some of his people believed his story, he became a religious leader, teaching nonviolence and a return to a golden age paradisiacal state called Koreri (ibid. 23–5). In a related narrative, Manarmakeri was "given the secret of life and death by the Morning Star," and began teaching his people about resurrection of the dead, immortality, and a golden age of abundance on

Earth. When they failed to understand, he departed for the west to wait for the right time to return (Kamma 1954: 25–36, 40). These narratives were taken literally and were considered historical facts (ibid. 65). Various "Koreri Movements" started when *konoors*, or heralds, had visions of Manarmakeri's return (ibid. 102), demonstrating the maintenance of belief through continued experiential phenomena. In 1860, a missionary from the island of Numfor told of two *konoor* who claimed to have made a five-day visit to a beautiful underworld realm of silver and gold. By virtue of their experiences, they were considered immortal "saints omniscient like God" (ibid. 108).

In the Wandamen area, the Sade Koreri movement began in 1932 after a man drowned and was found alive three days later. He claimed he had been to the underworld, where he met the dead, and thereby became a medium and prophet. He drew large crowds of worshippers to witness a promised return of the dead, and taught that an outbreak of smallpox was punishment for people desiring to change their skin color to white. In another Wandamen account, a man named M. Sobei visited the other realm in a "dream" brought about by "dancing in a completely closed house in the forest during the night and eating unpalatable and nasty things." Upon his return he was able to draw a plan of the other world, where he had learned "ten kinds of medicine" (ibid. 76–7).

Of the forty-six Koreri movements (and twenty-six similar movements throughout western New Guinea) detailed through 1967 by the Dutch missionary Freerk Ch. Kamma, nearly all began with anomalous experiential phenomena, especially "reports of dreams and visions, [and] of persons risen from the dead." They demonstrate that such movements need not be rooted in the threat of cultural or sociopolitical dominance, but can arise in response to other challenges such as disease epidemics. Indeed, anti-European sentiments were not original Koreri features, and only appeared later as a response to negative reactions to the movements from the Protestant mission and government. Though the movements were highly diverse, with varying "intentions and aspirations," all revolved around the "fixed nucleus" of the account of Manarmakeri's NDE (ibid. 278–9). While Kamma (1954: 76–7) wrote that the content of the "dreams and visions" could "be traced back to the existing mythological idea" concerning the land of the dead, it need not be assumed that the experiences were entirely cultural in origin. There are certainly links between NDEs, shamanic activity, afterlife beliefs, and the founding of religious movements; but the structural similarities of the experiences with those in other parts of the world, and indigenous claims that the experiences led to the formation of new religious beliefs and movements, indicate a transcultural component.

Near-death experiences also contributed to the foundation and maintenance of other religious movements. The Baigona cult was founded in 1912 after a man named Maine was killed by a snake, then returned to life with new "magico-medical curative techniques" (Worsley 1968: 54). The Manau cult was founded by a man named Dasiga, "who·dreamed and went up into the sky where he saw God and received from Him certain instructions" related to Christian morality, and "to be more like the missionaries and like the white men" (Williams 1928: 74).

In 1919, in the village of Arihava at Orokolo Bay, Ua Halai became a leader of the so-called Vailala Madness "cargo cult" religious movement[9] by virtue of his NDE. During an illness he instructed his people not to dig a grave for his body and to avoid approaching it too closely, but rather to "wait and see what they would see." After he died, some stood guard over his body watching for signs of returning life. Three days later, Ua Halai revived and began preaching loudly in German. He claimed that he had been to the other world where he was given "warnings against stealing, adultery, etc.," along with plans to build offering temples to the spirits. At these *ahea uvi* ("hot houses"), leaders of the movement mediated between their people and the spirits. Ua Halai arranged to be carried around the village in a litter that he said was "the steamer of Lavara, a legendary ancestress, come back to Papua." Despite Williams's (1934: 390–91) belief that this was "a carefully prepared hoax" drawing on missionary teachings about the resurrection of Jesus after three days (ibid. 393), the local people wholly believed the incident, and pointed to the fact that "Ua Halai was so 'dead' that the rats had gnawed his ears."

In 1935 in the Markham Valley, a man named Marafi founded an apocalyptic, antimission movement after claiming that Satan "had taken him into the bowels of the earth, where he had seen the spirits of the dead who dwelt there." The spirits wanted to return to Earth, but Satan would not allow it unless Marafi's people converted to a "belief in Satan as the Supreme Being." Although Marafi was an opportunist accused of deception and cheating people (Worsley 1968: 101–2), such cases demonstrate the authority that could result from claims of journeys to the otherworld, as well as the variety of reactions to Christian teachings that resulted from accounts of NDEs.

On Karkar Island as late as 1949, a local cult was reinvigorated following the NDE of the prophet and rebellion leader Kaum. He claimed that he had been killed in jail and had gone to Heaven, where he met God who appointed him "Konsel." He also encountered deceased ancestors who were "making Cargo," and he was given a new ritual and a special symbol "by one of the indigenous deities" (ibid. 215). Other movements (e.g., the Taro and Diroga cults) were grounded in ancestral spirit-possession (Williams 1928: 25–6).

According to fieldwork beginning in 1875, NDEs were integrated into after-life conceptions on New Britain:

> They say that when a man dies his soul goes to the spirit-land and meets his friends there, but if they do not want him at that time, they all drive him away, and so he returns to life again. This, also is the explanation they give when a man recovers from a faint or unconsciousness of any kind. (Brown 1910: 190)

In the district of Kininigunan, a man named Warulung "returned from the dead and brought messages to the people from departed spirits" (ibid. 398). Death was thought to be caused by ancestors wanting the person to join them in the other world. Soul-retrieval was practiced on individuals in danger of death after falling from a height, with old men communicating with the spirit until it returned to the body (ibid. 190). A funerary practice involved two men sleeping alongside the corpse in order to accompany the soul to the other world in dreams. They would return with descriptions of "torments inflicted on the spirit, and of some wonderful sights which they witnessed" (ibid. 194). This was "a fairly common custom in Melanesia," and descriptions of the experiences served to prove they had really traveled to the other world (Moss 1925: 104). Indeed, "certain conceptions of the afterlife may have had their origin in some practice of this kind" (ibid. 120–1).

It was believed that when the soul left the body at death it could manifest as a ghost on Earth for a brief period, haunting houses and burial places. Otherwise, it traveled across New Britain, jumping from one hill to the next until it reached a tree on a cliff above the sea. From there it jumped to Mount Balbi. Deceased friends gave new arrivals a betel nut, though to eat it would prevent them from returning to their homes. The other realm was overseen by "the keeper of souls," and had separate areas depending on mode of death. Life was similar to that on Earth, ranging from "dismal" to "beautiful," and economic status was maintained. Adulterers, thieves, the ungenerous, and those who breached customs or etiquette were reborn as animals. When Brown (1910: 192) asked the location of the otherworld, he was told, "if our eyes were turned so that what is inside the head were now outside, we would see that *matana nion* [Place of Souls] was very near to us and not far away at all." The soul did not die with the body "Because it is different; it is not the same nature at all." It could "hear, see, and speak," visit Earth, and enter into the bodies of animals. Those who died violent deaths were malevolent, though in general spirits were helpful and friendly, and could give precognitive warnings during dreams (Brown 1910: 192-6, 210).

In the late nineteenth century, Tami Islanders told the German missionary Georg Bamler that information about the afterlife was obtained by people (primarily women) who were able "to go down alive into the netherworld and prosecute their enquiries at first hand among the ghosts." It was believed that the soul remained near the body for a time after death, then traveled through a cleft in a rock, and embarked on a perilous journey involving a river crossing and practical jokes played by ghosts. Lamboam, the realm of the dead, was a place of fairness and abundance, full of fruits and decorative plants. Earthly patterns of work, marriage, illness, and death continued, though one could choose "the delights of idleness." Souls could visit Earth and protect their relatives. After dying in Lamboam, souls were reincarnated on Earth as "vermin, such as ants and worms," or became mischievous spirits of the woods. The soul also left the body during dreams (Frazer 1913: 291–2, 299–300). Likewise, among the Bukaua of the Morobe region, female shamans descended to the underworld to obtain revelations. It was also believed that the soul could temporarily leave the body "during sleep or in a swoon," and could "appear to people at a distance" (ibid. 257). The Bukaua practiced spirit mediumship, and believed that the other world, situated in the east, was similar to Earth (Lowie 1936: 59, 64).

At Wagawaga on Misima Island, it was believed that the soul (*arugo*) left the body at death and traveled to Hiyoyoa, an undersea realm near Milne Bay. It was "not uncommon" for the souls of "living men and women to journey to Hiyoyoa and return to this world," and most people "fully believed in the truthfulness of those who asserted that they had." Hiyoyoa was seen as a mirror image of Earth where day and night were reversed. It was overseen by the deity Tumudurere, who greeted the dead and assigned them a garden. A man named Tokeri visited Hiyoyoa and claimed to have obtained prophetic information about a giant destructive wave that would hit the area. Though initially believed by some, he became widely despised when his prophecy failed to come true. Another man, Wakuri, was said to have the ability to go to Hiyoyoa at will through the use of a certain "medicine." He claimed to have traveled there many times, and that he even had a wife and child there, but he never ate food because to do so made souls unable to return to Earth. In contrast, at Tubetube, a man named Maritaiyedi claimed that he was able to return from his numerous visits to the earthly otherworld of Beswebo, despite having dined with the spirits (Seligman 1910: 655–7; collected 1898–1904).

People in northern Massim claimed to have visited an afterlife realm beneath the island of Tuma, "and returned to the upper world." According to Charles Gabriel Seligman's assistant and interpreter E. L. Giblin, "There seem to be one or two such visitors in every district" (ibid. 654, n.2). Seligman (1910: 653) believed that such accounts "are probably to be regarded as examples of particularly vivid dreams, partly perhaps the result of auto-suggestion. Dreams have a direct influence on the action of individuals both in real life and in folk tales." In one example, a man named Marogus was in a coma-like state for a week during an illness. His soul went to Tuma and met its ruler, Topileta, "who ultimately sent him back to the upper world." Marogus described Tuma as being similar to

Earth, with people gardening and having children. Eating there would have made him unable to return. Spirits could visit the living in dreams, speaking "in a curious whistling speech, inviting them to visit Tuma and extolling the abundance of its crops and the size of its yams." All shared "equally in the life of the other world," though social status was maintained. Tuma was also the origin point, and Topileta the creator-deity. He had the ability to continually restore youth to himself and his family using a certain medicine (Seligman 1910: 733–4).

In a legend of the Koita people of the Port Moresby area, a man died and returned to his body, though it had already begun to decay. He asked his wife to wash him, though she was afraid and refused. Had she done so, other souls would have been able to return to their bodies on Earth after death. It was believed that sickness or death could occur when souls (*sua*) temporarily separated from their bodies. After death they went to Mt. Idu, taking with them soul-versions of their earthly possessions. They lived a life similar to that on Earth, but for a longer span, then eventually ceased to exist. Spirits could return to Earth to haunt or help the living, appearing mostly in dreams though sometimes also during waking life (ibid. 189–91).

Roro-speaking Melanesians had legends of mortals traveling to an earthly afterlife realm called Ariyo, and returning with plants from spirit gardens. When transplanted on Earth they died, and anything put in their place would grow stunted. On the journey to Ariyo, souls (*tsirama*) were stopped by "an evil spirit like fire" named Boubou, who made sure that anyone attempting to enter Ariyo had pierced ears and nose. He then told the soul which road to take, as determined by mode of death, though all roads led to Ariyo. It was a happy realm with a large garden and an abundance of food. The dead could visit the living for both helpful and harmful purposes (including stealing souls), and could appear to them in dreams (ibid. 310).

The Finnish anthropologist Gunnar Landtman (1912: 71–2) collected "a great number" of Kiwai narratives about people who went to the otherworld of Adiri and returned. He concluded that "dreams" contributed to afterlife beliefs, as they were "believed to describe the real things which the soul sees while roaming about outside the body." It was also thought that the soul could leave the body if a person simply believed he or she was about to die (ibid. 569). In the village of Mawata, a woman named Amara died from an illness "and subsequently returned to life." She described iron bars clashing repeatedly together, blocking the road to Adiri, though they rose to allow her through. She met spirits of the dead, including children who recognized her and alerted her deceased husband to her arrival. He asked "big man"[10] if Amara could stay, and she was allowed one day of dancing and festivities. Her husband then told her that her time on Earth was not yet finished and that she must return. Though she was tempted by the abundant coconut, sugar cane, taro, bananas and other foods, her husband warned her that if she ate anything she would be dead and unable to return to Earth. She was instructed to face the direction she had come, and was given a shove that propelled her back into her body. She surprised the mourners when she revived, for she had been dead a long time. She told them about life in Adiri, its opulence and wonders, and "kept on telling" them (Landtman 1912: 71–2; 1917: 168).

In another narrative, a man named Asai "died, returned to life and told his fellow villagers about Adiri" (Landtman 1917: 167–8). He had traveled there by canoe and was greeted by his deceased father and friends who gathered on the beach, dancing, singing, and playing drums. Asai enjoyed it so much that he decided he wanted to stay. He was summoned by Sido, a trickster deity and the first man to die. Believing he would never return, Asai proceeded through the clashing iron gates. Sido offered Asai a young woman, telling him that if he had sex with her he would forget about home and stay in Adiri. Asai was so taken with his surroundings, however, that he ignored the girl, so Sido kicked him back into his body. When Asai awoke, his mourners told him that he had been dead since the previous day (Landtman 1912: 72–3).

The ghost of an apparently different Asai was seen swimming up from the sea the day after his death. He returned to his body, awoke confused, and was told he had died the previous day. He described how his spirit had traveled westward, but decided to return to his body when he thought of his wife and child. Before doing so, he made a mark on a tree so he could later prove his claim. When his people confirmed it, they believed his narrative. He told them he had not seen any other spirits, and when they wanted him to explain what happens to people when they die, he said he did not know. They concluded that Asai had only traveled on the path toward Adiri but had not actually made it there. But Asai now knew the road, and was no longer afraid to die (Landtman 1917: 171).

A man named Duobe was seriously injured when a pot of boiling fat fell on him, and his spirit went to the other world where he met "dead people who were making a garden." Seeing that he was not a "ghost," they asked him why he was there, and Duobe replied only that he wanted to look at them. They told him to sit while they finished their work, though he mistakenly sat on a pile of human bones. They offered him food, but he did not eat; then a human-pig man asked him if wanted to look like him. Duobe replied that he did not, whereupon the man's pig nose fell off, exposing his skull beneath. Duobe was sent home in a canoe before the man could kill him. "Just as his spirit was entering his body he woke up shrieking," terrifying his wife. He said he had been to "devil-place" (ibid. 170–71).

A man named Ânai fell through a hole in the ground at his brother Kogea's grave. After four days they reappeared together and told of how they had been to the land of the dead, which was very similar to Earth but more populous. They brought back a yam, new medicines, and various agricultural techniques. In another version, one of the brothers refused to speak of his experience, but said that as a result of it "he would not be afraid when he was going to die." From such narratives, "some people concluded that the place of the dead was underneath the ground" (Landtman 1917: 172).

A man named Biri dreamed of waiting on a beach at the border of Adiri, afraid to enter. Some spirits came and asked his name. Biri recognized one of them, and went with him to a house. Inside there were many men but no women. The food cooked itself, and Biri tasted only a bit of banana, being afraid to eat. One of the men grew angry that Biri was there and chased him with a club. He hid under the house, then ran to the beach and escaped. His friend showed him the way home the next morning, and when he saw his house he woke up.

In another afterlife dream, the ghost of Gibuma went to the land of the dead, where he met an old man "who had died long before." The man knew Gibuma did not belong, and asked him why he had come. Gibuma replied that he wanted to see the other world. He asked for his father but was told that he was in another village, too far away to visit. Women came to dance for him, though he was then attacked. He could not move at first but managed to escape into water, only to find he could not swim. When his captors had almost apprehended him, he woke up in his body (ibid. 169–170). Such narratives are of a more idiosyncratic and dreamlike character than other Kiwai examples, and it is significant that they lack NDE or illness contexts.[11]

Other return-from-death narratives lack descriptions of journeys to afterlife realms, though they served to explain the introduction of new rituals, belief, or abilities. A Daru Island man, for example, told of how he was possessed by spirits of his people while fleeing in a canoe from an attack by the Kiwai. His boat capsized and he was washed ashore dead, but revived with information given to him by the spirits on how to summon dugong (Landtman 1912: 74–75). A man named Gabia revived after being killed by a pig, and claimed that while he was dead he met another soul who told him a new ritual for scaring pigs away. A man named Savi was killed by a spirit while bailing his canoe. His bones were removed and replaced with those of a "spirit of a dead person," making him "akin to a spirit." He returned with the ability to "summon the spirits at will" (Landtman 1917: 187–8). Another man returned to life briefly, and gave instructions for a new ceremony (ibid. 343–4). In other accounts, a sorcerer who was menacing children was killed but returned to life (ibid. 264), a woman was resuscitated by the sorcerer who killed her (ibid. 442), a man revived after being carried off by a devil in a burial ground (Landtman 1912: 74), and a man's ghost tried to take his family to Adiri, but when he jumped into a creek they could not follow (ibid. 76–7).

In a myth of Sido, his spirit departed his body while his wife prepared his funeral. With the ability to travel "over wide spaces of water without needing a canoe," he tried to outrun the canoe that carried his corpse. He had various encounters on Kiwai Island, including with a spider, a flying fox, a bat, and thorny shrubs disguised as boys trying to block his way. He eventually met an old man and told him that he did not want "that body . . . that thing" in the canoe, which is "no good" and "dead altogether." On the man's advice, he told "the people in the canoe to throw away the dead body, because his spirit has already gone on its way to Uúo, Sido's home." They ignored him, however, and buried his body. Sido then shape-shifted into a series of different forms, and caused various kinds of mischief in local villages. In one episode, in shellfish form he was eaten by conjoined twins, who became pregnant and gave birth to him. He grew up rapidly and soon departed, but later cleaved his "two mothers" apart with "a sharp wooden tool." Wishing to be rid of his new body, he dug himself a grave and lay down in it, but his spirit could not depart when he was spotted by two boys.

In another version, Sido was buried by his twin mothers and his "soul comes out from the body, and in the dark a light emanates from his disembodied spirit." He proceeded westward along the coast, and at various places was questioned by "legendary beings" about where he was going. At Boigu Island, while he waited "for the new moon for his journey back to Uúo," he was visited by his mothers, who brought him a drink of water in his own skull (retaining the skull of deceased relatives was a traditional custom). This resulted in Sido being unable to return home, and he angrily threw his mothers into the sea. One became a turtle and the other a dugong, and their spirits went with Sido to the border of Adiri. When they arrived in that poor, barren realm they met a man, also named Adiri, and his daughter Dirivo. Sido married her, and during sex he ejaculated on the ground, causing different plants to grow which bore all the fruit he had eaten in his life. In a reversal of the theme of bringing knowledge from the other world to Earth, he gave fire to Adiri and Dirivo, and made them a house (Landtman 1912: 59–66).[12]

The origin myth of the Bugamu and Kunini people also associated afterlife journeys with creation, knowledge, and supernatural power. Javagi, the first human, was born from a kangaroo but accidentally killed and ate her. He died immediately and "his spirit went away and roamed about all over the country" while his body was being eaten by worms. He was brought back to life by a kangaroo spitting "poison-wood" on him, which gave him powers of shapeshifting and "secret methods of killing a man." The myth served to explain why the people do not eat kangaroo meat (Landtman 1917: 83).

In a Ma'o Kiwai myth, the "master of spirits" of Woibu (Adiri) sent a bird to fetch a man named Wiobari. It guided him westward, and when he arrived in Woibu he fell down in a faint at the master's house. He was revived when a female spirit "rubbed his eyes with the string of her grass skirt," and he was greeted warmly by the other spirits. Wiobari chose two wives, who bore him a son and daughter. One day while he was bathing the children, an east wind brought the scent of his birthplace and reminded him of his mother. Though his children cried, Wiobari decided to return to Earth. He was given a choice of various modes of return (canoe made from a feather, bird, etc.), and chose flying bamboo. He returned home and became the founder of the Mao people (Landtman 1917: 165–7).

Spirits of the dead were believed to remain near their homes for a number of days until making their way to Adiri, during which time they were feared because they could abduct the living (particularly children and the ill) (ibid. 303). The journey to other world and the transformations of the soul mirrored those of Sido. They were met by deceased friends in Adiri, and those from the same villages lived together in an idealized version of Earth (ibid. 442). Women who died in childbirth, suicides, those killed by crocodiles, and those who were beheaded remained on Earth as malevolent ghosts, and could be killed a second time (ibid. 176, 179).

There were numerous reports of sightings of ghosts, contact between the living and spirits of the dead, possession, and helpful ancestor spirits (ibid. 181–91; 313). Spirits of the dead radiated light (ibid. 110, 189), as verified by some who witnessed souls leaving the body at death (ibid. 398). Landtman (1917: 558) indexed no fewer than twenty-seven narratives of the dead visiting people during dreams, including some who were summoned. Drug-induced trance mediumship was practiced in order to obtain information from the dead about coming dangers, for healing and agricultural advice, and for details about witchcraft (including identities of murderers) (ibid. 306). Despite such beliefs and experiences, however, the Kiwai believed that "the departed as a rule do not enter into any connection with the living" (ibid. 13). Such experiences were thus indigenously considered to be extraordinary, and were important sources of knowledge. Though Landtman referred to all these narratives as "folk-tales," their content reveals a distinction between genuine myths and what were accepted as historical accounts. Landtman (1912: 71–2) also implied that no distinction was made between unconsciousness and death, though as seen, accounts with NDE contexts differ from dreams.

In the Trobriand Islands, Tuma was sometimes visited by the soul (*baloma*) "of men awake and men asleep, and by those who were almost dead, but returned to life again" (Malinowksi 1916: 154). They would bring back information, songs, and sometimes precognitive knowledge of the death of a family member (ibid. 162). The Trobrianders believed that spirits left the body at death and traveled to Tuma on an "immaterial" canoe. Upon arrival, they would sit on the beach with deceased relatives, lamenting what they had left behind. Souls became invisible by washing their eyes at a well, then proceeded to a place called Dukupuala, where they summoned their ancestors by knocking on two stones. They then met Topileta, who sent souls away if payment (i.e., funerary offerings) was insufficient. In such cases, they were banished to sea to become mythical stingray-shark fish. Otherwise, the deceased were asked how they died, and the answer determined which of three roads was taken to Tuma. New arrivals were assisted in transitioning to their new life by an amorous member of the opposite sex. Life was happy and similar to that of Earth, and spirits could visit living relatives. Eventually the soul died and was reincarnated (Malinowksi 1916: 155–60, 215ff).

The Orokaiva people were also aware of NDEs, believing that "a man may die and come to life again." This could occur when the soul (*sovai*), witnessing the mourning of friends and relatives, was "so affected by compassion as to return; whereupon the corpse is reanimated" (Williams 1930: 269). One narrative told of a man who followed his wife to the underworld and met his deceased relatives (ibid. 282).[13] This conflicted with local beliefs, which did not include an underworld.[14] There is also "a mass of evidence" for dream- and trance- journeys (ibid. 263). A "spiritual substitute" (*asisi*, shadow or reflection) could travel during dreams and commune with others. The soul could appear to the living in ghostly form, or as various animals, vegetation, or some kind of monstrous being. Those who died in fights lived in the air (ibid. 271–2, 274), while others lived in sunny spirit villages without mosquitoes or flies, located at particular hills, rocks, or pools (ibid. 281–2).

In the Wedau and Wamira areas it was also believed that the soul could leave the body during loss of consciousness, and those who came back after "fainting" were said to have died "green" (Newton 1914: 219–20). Their afterlife beliefs were largely consistent with other Papuan peoples (ibid. 228).

Among the Dobu of the D'Entrecasteaux Islands, souls of the dead were not admitted to the other world until their bodies started to decay, so that the guardian spirits there could be certain they were truly dead. The other world could be visited during OBEs, enabling individuals to "hold conversation with the dead." "Magicians" (*tokenobeku*) could do this at will, sometimes for witchcraft purposes. Visitors to the other world could not eat a certain type of banana, for it would prevent them from returning to their bodies. In one legend, a man traveled by boat to the land of spirits where he was greeted by "his brother and sister with their spirit spouses." He saw people build a house, enter it, set it on fire, then ascend to the clouds in the smoke. Before finally returning to his people, he visited various places such as the villages of Those-who-will-do-it-tomorrow, of the People with Sewed-on Wings, and of the People of the Closed up Mouths, who must eat from the tops of their heads. The spirit land was believed to be in an extinct volcano called Bwebweso on Normanby Island, and spirits had to give a betel nut (buried with the corpse) to the guardian couple, Sinebomatu and Kekewage, in exchange for passage. Those who were physically scarred by disease were refused admittance, and instead existed "as monstrous fish bodies with human heads in a swamp at the foot of Mt. Bwebweso." Children were adopted by Sinebomatu and Kekewage, while those killed in battle had their own realm with different guardians (the chief deity Iaboaine and his wife Sinekili). Life in Bwebweso was "conceived as thin and shadowy," or as a reversal of this world (Fortune 1932: 181–2, 186–8).

Concerning the Tanga Islands, F. L. S. Bell (1937: 317–8) reported:

> Where a person, through extreme weakness, loses consciousness for several hours, or, as I know in one case, over a period of days and then regains consciousness, he is regarded as having been dead and refused admittance to the underworld. One of my informants actually attended a case of this nature and quoted it as unimpeachable evidence of the existence of life after death. He told me that the man had been sent back from the underworld because of his youth. His descriptions of the underworld only reinforce traditional beliefs as to the nature of that place and to enhance his prestige among the living.

The account involved a man who was revived by his wife, and described "what he believed to be his *post mortem* emotions and experiences." He was taken by a whirlwind to the land of the dead where bountiful fruit trees grew, and any kind of food "was to be had for the mere asking." People sat around talking and eating betel nut. He met his deceased grandmother, who "told him to go back to his family and his garden," explaining that he was too young to remain with her. Though Bell saw this narrative in terms of wish-fulfillment and merely "a reflection" of local afterlife belief, it actually has little in common with those beliefs, which included the soul leaving the body through the eyes and being guided by the sun to an underworld in the western horizon. The NDE thus conflicted with established beliefs (despite considerable variation between clans and individuals). Bell (1937: 337–8) seemed to contradict his own position when he also wrote, "the conditions of life in the underworld" were known because certain living people had visited it and "have seen how their ancestors are living." It was also believed that a person's soul (*malafua*) could leave the body during dreams; and likewise that the dead could visit the living in dreams and tell "of the advantages of life after death."

It is interesting to compare the above accounts with three early 1980s NDEs from the Kaliai on New Britain. While it is evident in the accounts that the Kaliai have been "at least nominally, converts to Catholicism" since 1949, many

indigenous traditions—particularly funerary beliefs and rituals—have been preserved (Counts 1983: 115–6). In the first example, a headmaster named Frank died
of an illness and met deceased ancestors who directed him to a road. He then
encountered a being of light that he described in Western Christian terms: white
skinned, bearded, and robed. The being motioned to Frank to stop and turn back
(ibid. 118).

In the second example, a young man named Andrew died of an illness,
and returned to report a highly idiosyncratic NDE. He entered darkness, then
emerged into a "field of flowers" and a realm of clarity. On a road he met "a woman
whose death had occurred shortly after his and about which he could have had
no knowledge." He reached a fork, where a man on each path beckoned. The one
he chose led to a village, where he climbed a ladder up to a house. A voice told
him it was not his time to die, and that he should wait for someone to come and
take him back to Earth. Children lying on platforms above the house's doors and
windows helped him down the ladder. He then realized that the house was floating and rotating in the air, and saw people inside building cars and ships. Again
he was told it was not his time to die, and to wait for a return guide. But instead
he walked along a beam of light and down a flight of steps, and found himself in a
forest. He was then told that if mourning for his death had begun he would have
to stay in the other world. He followed the beam of light down a path, and found
himself back in his body. He was reluctant to return, for he had felt happy in the
other realm (ibid. 119–20).

The third Kaliai NDE, reported by an elderly man named Luke, featured similar elements such as ascending a ladder toward a house, and a road with a fork,
revealing cultural expectation/interpretation. This is in addition to more common features such as meeting deceased relatives, and its own highly idiosyncratic
elements such as a row of magnets "like manhole covers" which were scales for
judging sorcerers, according to a voice on a loudspeaker. Luke was motioned to
sit on the scales, though he stood instead, drawing applause from the surrounding
individuals. He then witnessed the judgment of a man who stuck to the magnet
and had to be pried away with a crowbar. His punishment was to be chopped
with knives and his body parts put into a pipe that emerged from the ground,
then boiled and fed to a pig and a dog, which then turned to stone. Luke then
met his deceased father, grandfather, and daughter, who told him to return to
Earth; though a woman with bloody eyes and a lolling tongue tried to stab him.
He ran away, and found himself back in his body (ibid. 121).

The judgment of sorcerers is known also from a Kaliai dream, though
Dorothy Counts (ibid. 129) believes that judgement was a Christian import.
Industrial imagery is also found in Kaliai dreams, and may reflect a "cargo
belief"—that is, that whites might be spirits, and therefore technology is

associated with the spirit realm. Luke's NDE is one of the most overtly dreamlike of any discussed here, indicating a highly enculturated but nevertheless individually unique unconscious imagery.

Solomon Islands

A late nineteenth-century account from the Nggela Islands was reported by Codrington (1891: 256):

> A man not long ago alive at Gaeta once appeared to die, but revived to tell the story of how he had passed with others along the path of ghosts, and had come to take his place in the canoe which came for them at night; but a tall black *tindalo* [ghost] . . . whom he recognized forbad him to come aboard, and sent him back into the world again.

It was believed that the soul (*tarunga*) left the body in dreams, and at death when it was ferried to Galaga on the opposite shore. Only when they landed did souls realize they were dead. A *tindalo* checked to see if their nostrils were pierced by thrusting a rod into them. If so, they could follow the good path to Betindalo, realm of the dead, situated on nearby Guadalcanal. For others the journey was one of "pain and difficulty." Some spirits continued to influence the living and were worshipped, and ghosts could sometimes be seen at Galaga (ibid. 254–5, 249)

In a myth from Santa Isabel, a man named Kamakajaku was swallowed by a fish which took him eastward. Sensing he was near a beach, he cut the fish open and emerged. The sun rose "with a bang" and told Kamakajaku to follow him. He did so, and when they arrived in heaven, Kamakajaku was left with the sun's children. They asked where he had come from, and told him not to go to a certain place. Kamakajaku went there anyway, and saw a hole in the sky below, through which he could see his village. He taught the sun's children how to cook with fire, but refused to eat when they brought him food. When he admitted that he had gone to the forbidden spot, they asked if he wished to return to Earth. He said that he did, so they lowered him down in a house, and when "he came down again from heaven" his friends rejoiced because they had thought that he was dead (ibid. 365–6).

In 1908–9, Gerald C. Wheeler (1914: 111) recorded two legends from Alu Island. In the first, a man who married a ghost descended with her to the underworld along the Path of the Dead. They met the woman's parents, then returned to Earth. The woman gave birth to a child, but had to return to the underworld when her husband broke a taboo on eating breadfruit, which was forbidden to the dead. In the second legend, a man dropped an axe from his canoe and dove into the sea after it. He went to the land of the dead and remained there for two days before returning. Beliefs in OBEs through illness, injury, or shamanic activity were also reported (Wheeler 1914: 87), and knowledge of NDEs was incorporated into afterlife conceptions: when people revived during an illness, it was thought that they had been sent back to the body following assessment in the otherworld (ibid. 98ff).

It was believed that the soul (*nunu*) left the body at death and either traveled on a road or ascended. The Warden of the Road, Uauamai, questioned souls about where they were going. Souls of "good" people who gave the Warden beads or shells were allowed to pass, and were told which path to take. "Bad" souls who offered no gifts were led to a path where they were delayed, lost, or eaten by pigs or dogs and suffered annihilation. Good souls continued to an earthly intermediate place called Dandaronauang, and were told why they died (e.g., murder, adultery, theft). They then progressed through a series of islands and other locales to the volcano Bareka on Bougainville (ibid. 91–6ff), where they were met by ancestors and asked "Who art thou?" Providing identity and clan affiliation were required before being welcomed, bathed, fed, and massaged in order to repair the "body." Life was similar to that on Earth, with hierarchies preserved, though souls were invisible (ibid. 100ff; 110f).

On Buka Island c. 1932, a prophet named Pako returned from the dead after being hanged by the government (Worsley 1968: 118). Another prophet of his cult was "said to have gone to Heaven, where Saint Peter told him that people were to go to church regularly, to abandon their old dances and rituals, and to levy tolls and demand higher wages from the Whites" (ibid. 115). On Makira, shamanic healers undertook trance-journeys to the other world of Rodomana to retrieve souls, even when they were unwilling to return (Beckwith 1940: 150; recorded 1924).

Vanuatu

Concerning the Banks Islands, Codrington (1881: 283) wrote, "At times a departed soul has come back from the *sura* [entrance to the other world] to his body; and the man has revived to tell how he was hustled out of the *sura* by the ghosts, who said there was no room for him, and he must go back." Codrington (1891: 266–7) later elaborated, describing beliefs that when a person fainted the soul left the body and began the journey to the otherworld of Panoi, "but is sent back; the other ghosts hustle him away from the mouth of the descent, or his father or friends turn him back, telling him that his time has not yet come; so he relates when he returns". Reports of such journeys were "by no means uncommon," and afterlife conceptions sometimes derived from them, or were reinforced by them: "The best authority for the state of things in Panoi was a woman who had been down there. . . . She professed herself, but a few years ago, able to go down as she liked, and whatever was generally believed to be there, she declared that she had seen." Souls of the dead were weakened by the journey to Panoi, and rested at the entrance where they were greeted by spirits who asked if they were there to stay. "If he has only fainted, it is then discovered and he returns" to the body. In one narrative, a woman doused herself in perfume infused with dead rat "to give herself a death-like smell," before descending to Panoi through a hole in the Earth in order to visit her dead brother. She was met by deceased friends who were surprised to see her there. When she found her brother in a house, he warned her not to eat anything, and she then returned to Earth (Codrington 1881: 283).

A woman at Vanua Lava "appeared to die" just after the death of her husband. She followed him to a nearby hill, where he was bound hand and foot. The ghosts told her it was because he had not paid his debts. They instructed her to return, and to teach her people, "Pay your debts, don't kill one another" (Codrington 1891: 278).

On Mota, it was believed that at death the soul (*tamate*) would remain nearby for a time, and could be called back to the body. Ghosts greeted the newly dead and conducted them to Panoi through various entrances on different islands. Panoi was a dismal version of Earth, where "all is insubstantial" and people led "empty, aimless" lives. Some believed that "the conditions of rich and poor, great and insignificant, are reversed." Trees had red leaves, and the dead ate excrement. "Stupid, harmless persons" and "young men who had kept themselves chaste" had slightly better lives, and the latter could "dance on moonlight nights." Those who died young lived in a pleasant land filled with flowers and fragrant plants. Some spirits became deified ancestors, and the dead could be malevolent when visiting Earth. It was also believed that the soul could leave the body in sleep (Codrington 1880: 126–9, 133; Codrington 1891: 273).

On Mota Lava, shamans could send their souls to Panoi at will to speak with the recently dead. One escorted a man there, still living and in his body, to see his deceased wife. In order to convince the denizens of Panoi that they were dead, the two men covered themselves in the smell of "putrid black gecko," and rattled dead men's bones as ghosts do. When they found the man's wife, she said she could not return with him. They tried to pull her away, but her hand came off "and her body went to pieces" (ibid. 266–7). It was believed that "according to the character of the man in life," some were allowed to enter Panoi, while others were "sent back to another place," or to wander aimlessly on Earth. Those "of bad character" became "homeless, malignant, pitiable." Those who lived "as they ought" went to an area of Panoi characterized as a joyful, idealized version of Earth, but "hollow and unreal." Some believed that there was a lower Panoi, to which souls in the upper one went when they died to eventually "turn into white ants' nests" (Codrington 1891: 274–9).

On Pentecost Island, when a person lost consciousness then revived, upon recovering "he says he was not allowed to enter" Panoi (ibid. 287). In an Orpheus narrative from Aoba Island, a young man followed his recently deceased wife to the underworld, Lolomboetogitogi, by diving deep under a lake. He was met by a deceased friend and told not to eat, and "to keep by himself." When he discovered that his wife could not see, he ascended back through the lake, taking with him some fragrant herbs from the ghost village. Another man descended along a banyan tree root to Lolomboetogitogi, where he was given old, black bananas, though he did not eat them (ibid. 286).[15]

On Maewo, the soul encountered "the stone of thought" (*vat dodoma*) on the journey to the other world. If a man "remembers there his child or his wife or anything that belongs to him, he will run back and come to life again." He will also return if he fails to successfully jump over a ravine (ibid. 274–5). Healers could visit Malanga, the realm of the dead, in order to rescue the souls of sick children; and "professional dreamers" could dream themselves to the source of a person's illness and negotiate with the malevolent spirit for the return of the patient's soul (ibid. 208–9).

According to a late nineteenth-century narrative from Efate Island reported by the Scottish missionary Daniel Macdonald (1893: 728–30), a man died, went to the undersea spirit world of Abokas, and met his deceased wife. When he tried to embrace her, she turned to dust. Another legend told of a chief named Bau, who went looking for a man named Nabuma Nakabu. He traveled through successive levels of the underworld, and finally found Nabuma Nakabu's bones in the lowest. He took them to the musical area of the spirit-world, and drumming brought him back to life again. Abokas was reached by climbing a tree near the shoreline, then calling for a guide spirit named Tafatokei, who rose from the underworld through the sea and swept away the dead on a wave. At the entrance to Abokas, the deceased encountered four guardians and a giant being named Sara-tau. If the identity of the soul was unknown, the guardians twisted its head around, ripped out its tongue and eyes, and hacked its forehead. If souls were deemed "one of ours" (i.e., a dead person) they were allowed to pass. Chiefs were accompanied by the spirits of sacrificed dogs, which chased away Sara-tau. Death was regarded as punishment, and Abokas was a gloomy, unreal, depressing place with a stagnant lake, and where food transforms into dirt. When souls met their deceased mother, she would show only contempt. The deceased then descended further to one of the five deeper regions of Abokas before eventually disappearing. Those who had elaborate funerals with many offerings (reflecting both their character and wealth) had more favorable afterlives. The "worthless" could eat only a kind of shellfish that tore their jaws. Spirits of the dead could visit Earth, to help the living or cause them harm.

The British navy officer Boyle T. Somerville (1894: 10) reported that on Malekula it was believed that "the sacred men have often been on a visit [to the otherworld], and consequently know all about it." At death, souls went to the underworld and remained in a "semi-corporeal" state for thirty years before dying a second time. Spirits "order the affairs of earth, and punish with death those who transgress," and assist with farming to ensure their own sustenance through sacrificial offerings.

The Scottish missionary William Gunn (1914: 223) reported beliefs from Futuna Island that the soul left the body during illness, injury, or fainting, and only those with special knowledge could call it back. It also left the body during sleep, and its return caused awakening. The afterlife was grim and shadowy: people retained their earthly wounds, ate garbage, and had no pleasure, pain, or even conscious thought. Eventually they descended to a lower realm "and became dead shells." Souls of stillborn babies, however, "became gods with endless happiness." On nearby Ouvéa in the Loyalty Islands, it was a function of shamanic-type healers "to restore souls to forsaken bodies" (Beckwith 1940: 172).

A narrative from Tanna Island relates how a little girl ascended to "heaven" on smoke, and "saw a blind woman feeding a large number of pigs." The woman asked the girl who she was and where she came from, then begged her to remain with her, promising her the freedom to go wherever she liked—with the exception of a doorway in the ground (a dark patch in the night sky, known as the Coalsack Nebula). The girl cured the woman of her blindness by pouring a mixture of fruits and leaves into a pool where she swam. One day she opened the door in the ground, and seeing her family on Earth below, grew homesick. Although the old woman did not want her to leave, she helped her descend back to Earth on a vine rope. Once the girl had safely returned, the old woman lowered pigs down the rope as gifts (Humphreys 1926: 97–8). In contrast to this narrative, the other world was believed to be reached through a volcano. It was seen as a beautiful place similar to Earth but "more luxuriant and fertile" (ibid. 91–2).

Fiji

The English missionary Thomas Williams (1860: 190–4) reported beliefs that the soul could leave the body during sleep and in fainting, and that it could be brought back by calling after it even when one dies. Williams also mentioned narratives from earlier times about people who left their bodies, traveled to the underworld, Mbulu, and returned.

The anthropologist and Methodist minister Lorimer Fison (1881: 146–7) described a Fijian funerary practice in which young people fell into a deep sleep, and their souls left their bodies. In flowing, gliding motions they followed the spirit of a recently deceased chief and watched him ascend the cliffside leaping-off place. There he was met by the soul of a deceased woman of high rank, and when they leapt into the sea together, the sleepers awakened and told their people the identity of the woman. Sometimes sleepers would not awaken and their souls would have to be called back through a long, difficult process. Fison (1904: 139–40) also reported that "Some Fijian heroes are believed to have gone down to Bulotu in the body." Spirits of the dead could be killed again, and thereby suffer annihilation.

The British intelligence officer Basil Thomson (1908: 125, 132; cf. 1895: 355) described a deity named Taleya, "the Dismisser," who functioned specifically to send spirits back to life, and who "sifted out the real dead from the trance-smitten." In the Namata account of the soul's journey, those who died in battle or by drowning were allowed to pass; but to those who died a natural death (which was not considered respectable), Taleya said, "go back and re-enter your body." Being sent back was thus the explanation for reviving from "trance and fainting fits." Some refused to return, however, in their eagerness to reach the spirit path, for "so gloomy and joyless is the prospect of a return to life that the Shades who are offered the privilege by Taleya do not all obey."

A long myth from the Lau Islands, recorded by the British colonial administrator Reginald St. Johnston (1918: 19), contains an otherworld journey section. A man named Tui Liku was being harassed by demons. They were driven away by Ligadua ("the one-armed"), "one of the Lords of Burotu," son of its king, and protector of the people. When Tui Liku wanted to accompany Ligadua to the otherworld, he replied, "If I take your spirit with me it may not be able to return again to its body . . . for no world-man has ever yet come back from Burotu." Tui Liku persisted, and Ligadua relented, warning him that he must follow his movements exactly if he ever wished to return to Earth. Tui Liku's lifeless body washed up on the shore as his soul rode a red wave to Burotu. Ligadua took him to the Council House where they were welcomed by the chiefs of the spirit world, and given a feast. Tui Liku asked if he might take some special red coconuts back to Earth with him, and the King assented, but instructed him not to enter any house, even if invited by one of the "beautiful maidens." Tui Liku obeyed and was thus able to return to Earth with the coconuts. On three subsequent journeys to the Buroto, Tui Liku was allowed to bring back more coconuts, a small bird, and seeds of a special almond tree. On his final return, Tui Liku was "dismayed" to find that a sandpiper had been pecking at his corpse, and had taken out one of his eyes. "I refuse to get into that," he cried, but Ligadua gave him no choice. He went home and was henceforth known as Matadua, "the one-eyed one." The tale explains why sandpipers make the sound *tui liku, tui liku*. St. Johnston (1918: 40–5) wrote that the old man who related the narrative stated that "it was firmly believed in by his fathers, and not a little by himself, as a true story of what actually happened". Though some eighty years following the arrival of Christianity, St. Johnston's enquiries focused on the oldest people of "islands where no resident missionary was stationed."

Fijians believed that the other world was reached by leaping from a rocky outcrop in the west, then crossing a sea or river, assisted by a discourteous ferryman named Vakaleleyaklo. A perilous road journey included dangers at every turn, such as "a Ghost-scatterer, who stoned the Shade, and Reed-spear, who impaled him," a teeth-gnashing goddesses, a "god of murder," and fishers who cast nets for human souls. This meant that only warriors who had died violently were sure to arrive in Bulotu, the origin-point of humans and a realm of abundance (Thomson 1908: 117–8).[16] Other descriptions of the journey to Mbulu involved interrogations concerning the deceased's identity, reason for being in the otherworld, and conduct during life on Earth. The rich and powerful were thrown into a lake and went to Murimuria, "a district of inferior happiness" in Mbulu. The most desirable region was Mburotu (i.e., Bulotu), a realm of beauty and joy. Most of Mbulu, however, was a mirror image of Earth, though everything was larger. Punishments were meted out for those who displeased the gods with offenses such as never having killed an enemy (for which they must "beat a heap of filth with a club" for their misuse of their weapon on Earth), not having pierced ears (for which they had to "carry forever on their shoulder the log of wood on which cloth is beaten, jeered at by all who see them"), or not being tattooed (for which they were scraped with shells and "made into bread for the gods").

Whether souls were immortal was disputed. Some believed in a form of reincarnation, and others simply in annihilation (Williams 1860: 190–4). Fison (1904: 160–4) described the otherworld of Bulu as a happy island realm in the horizon, where the gods drank kava and the healing Water of Life, and sat beneath the "wondrous" Tree of Speech. Bulu was ruled by the evil king Hiku-leo (perhaps Thomson's "Vakaleleyaklo"), who delighted "in tormenting the souls of the dead." Hiku-leo kept watch for new arrivals, and was so "cruel and savage" that he enslaved some spirits and used others "for posts in his out-houses." In fact, he would destroy everything if not for his brothers who kept him tied with an unbreakable rope, one end of which is in the sky and the other beneath the earth.

Also worth noting is the Tuka cult, which originated sometime after World War II. It was led by a man named Kelevi, who "claimed to have visited Heaven and to have supernatural powers" (Worsley 1968: 30).

Australia

In their overview of pre-European Australian cultures, Berndt and Berndt (1964: 256–7) revealed a conceptual link between NDEs and shamanism. Initiates were mourned as if recently dead when entering a trance state, during which they visited the sky-world and had various encounters with spirits. The "return" from the trance state was seen as a rebirth, and the initiate revived with new powers, strength, and abilities obtained from spirits of the dead (ibid. 256–7). This "ritual death, followed by rebirth as a new person" resulted in powers of communication with spirits, telepathy, clairvoyance, invisibility, and shape-shifting. "In all cases there is the assertion, or inference, that he receives this through some mystical experience" (ibid. 259). Eliade (1973: 144–5) similarly observed this pattern of shamanic initiation through "symbolic death followed by resurrection," citing many examples. During these "ecstatic experiences" the initiate "undertakes ascents to heaven and descents to the subterranean world," and returns transformed by the experience and the knowledge received from the "supernatural beings" encountered (ibid. 130).

Part of the initiation for medicine men (*karadji*) among the Kattang-speaking people of Port Stephens involved the initiate being "killed" in a fire. As a result, he "became a new personality" who belonged to the sky-world, and could ascend to the sky in dreams, use sorcery and telepathy, and heal the sick by "catching and restoring the spirit" (Elkin 1945: 91–2). Initiates in Ooldea, South Australia were mourned as if dead while undergoing various trance rituals, including mediumship, having bones broken, and being symbolically swallowed by a snake then reborn. This resulted in the new medicine man (*kinkin*) having supernatural powers such as invulnerability, clairvoyance, and seeing in all directions (ibid. 112–4). In East Kimberly, initiates of the Djerag and Djaru peoples were "killed" by the rainbow-serpent, causing a period of illness and madness, enabling them to visit the dead "by going up to the sky on a string," and conferring various magical and healing powers. A similar pattern is common among many other Australian peoples (ibid. 138–44).

While Berndt and Berndt (1964: 419) found "no single uniform belief about a future life throughout Aboriginal Australia, there are certainly basic similarities." Spirits of the dead could appear to mourners in dreams, sometimes with information on who was responsible for their deaths, or with new ritual songs, dances, or rites (ibid. 391). Though death was considered fundamentally unnatural and generally due to malevolent human influence, it was also seen as a transition in a continual process of cyclical birth and rebirth (ibid. 419). In this transition, a "person passes to another life not entirely unlike the one he has left—even in cases where he is believed to have more than one spirit, or soul." The component souls could simultaneously become trickster spirits, go to the realm of the dead, "return to a nucleus of spirit children awaiting rebirth, merge with the great ancestral and creative beings, and so on" (Berndt and Berndt 1964: 409). Though there were perilous trials in the otherworld, fates and divisions were determined by funerary ritual action. It was important for the living to "sever connections with the spirit and to send it on its way," through mortuary ritual or revenge on the person responsible for the death (ibid. 411).

In a myth of the culture hero Ngurunderi, at the end of his travels he "dived into the sea to cleanse himself of his old life, and went up into the sky: Waieruwar, the spirit world." He decreed "that the spirits of the dead would always follow the tracks he had made, and eventually join him in the Sky-world" (ibid. 204) following a stay on Kangaroo Island. Some believed that Ngurunderi's sons lowered ropes to help raise the recently dead to Waieruwar. Ngurunderi provided the "dazed newcomer" with a place to live and new wives (corresponding to the number left behind). The old became young and the young became old (ibid. 412). In Eliade's (1973: 169–71) summary, the sky-realm was the origin-point and home of the creator deity, and one could ascend there on the rays of the sun, or up a tree. The deceased could be tested by a guardian before gaining entry to the other world.

In contrast, according to the English explorer Edward John Eyre (1845: 356), it was believed that the soul (*itpitukutya*) separated from the body at death and traveled west "to a large pit, where the souls of all men go." Once everyone has died, the souls will return to their graves and ask, "Are these the bodies that we formerly inhabited?" to which the bodies will reply, "We are not dead, but still living." The soul, which is the size of a child, will then become immortal and "live in trees during the day, and at night alight on the ground, and eat grubs, lizards, frogs and kangaroo rats," but no vegetable foods.

The Aboriginal rights activist James Dawson (1881: 58) reported a spirit-healing technique in which a shaman ascended to the clouds, and enlisted the aid of ten spirits who would temporarily accompany him back to Earth. It was believed that souls of the good remained on Earth for three days after death, and were then met by deceased friends in "a beautiful country above the clouds, abounding with kangaroo and other game, where life will be enjoyed forever." Souls of the wicked wandered "miserably" and haunted the living for a full year before descending forever to Ummekulleen, an underground realm of fire where they "get neither eat nor drink, and are terribly knocked about by the evil spirits." There was no marriage, for bodies are immaterial. Children under four or five years old did not have an afterlife, because they did not have souls (ibid. 49–50).

In an account from the Barkindji people of the Darling River area, a shaman named Barpoo visited the other world when he was a young man, facilitated by eating a piece of the thigh of his recently dead teacher (upon the teacher's instruction). Barpoo fell asleep while "his spirit flew away beyond the sky," and encountered a kind and beautiful goddess. She "showed him all the abundance of the joys prepared for his people [after death], game of all kinds, plants, fruits, and fish, so that existence was a perpetual round of ease and feasting." Similar to other revitalization movements, Barpoo taught that there were no white people in the other realm. He was seen as a "scoundrel" by the ruling whites because he refused to work for them or accept their rule, though he was "both feared and venerated" by his own people, some of whom "even believed he had actually visited their heaven" (Newland 1887: 31). Barpoo's teachings contrasted with earlier beliefs, for when the first white people arrived in Australia it was widely believed that they were "returning spirits of the dead." Indeed, words for "white man" (*manakai, markai*) meant "spirit of a dead person" (Landtman 1917: 181).

The Australian anthropologist Alfred William Howitt (1887: 52) reported that "medicine men" could "ascend to ghost-land beyond the sky," and had the ability to see spirits of people "in an incorporeal state, either temporarily or permanently separated from the body." It was believed that the soul could leave the body during dreams, encounter spirits of both the living and the dead, and travel to a spirit world of idealized earthly landscapes. Howitt concluded that "this view of the reality of dreams" enabled the people "to reach, by a natural stage of reasoning, a conception of the individual apart from the body, not only during life but also after death, as an immaterial, invisible being."

The Wotjo and Gunaikurnai (Kurnai) people of the southeast also believed that the soul could leave the body while still alive. In a Gunaikurnai narrative, a man ascended on a rope to the upper-world of spirits, accompanied by the soul of his friend's gravely ill son. There they saw deceased relatives and friends. In another account, before she died, a woman claimed "that she had gone up to the *Nurt* (sky) in sleep, but returned because she could not get through." Spirits of the dead could visit the living, including in the form of deathbed visions (Howitt 1904: 434–7). Berndt and Berndt (1964: 417) mention additional accounts of "living people who have been to the Land of the Dead, voluntarily or otherwise." In one example from the Lower River Murray, a man revived on his funeral pyre and told of his visit to the home of Ngurunderi (cf. Warner 1937: 524–8).

In a Wiradjuri shaman's account of his initiation, he described his father pressing two quartz crystals into his chest, giving him enhanced intelligence and abilities. They ascended together into the sky world, on threads towed by a bird belonging to Baiame, the creator and afterlife deity described as "a very great old man with a long beard." They passed through a rapidly opening-and-closing portal, which would cause sickness and death if touched. They reached Baiame's camp, and found him surrounded by his "boys" and "people, who are birds and beasts." On his shoulders were two giant quartz crystals reaching into the sky (Berndt and Berndt 1964: 405–08). According to Eliade (1973: 154), inserting quartz crystals "into the body of the future medicine man seems to be a pan-Australian practice." They were regarded as "solidified light" "fallen from the vault of heaven," with the power to bring about a "mystical 'transmutation'" or rebirth of the initiate into a supernaturally powerful intermediary between this world and that of spirits (ibid. 157). The Wuradjeri believed that souls of the dead climbed a rope to the spirit world, then passed through a fissure in revolving walls, "revealing from time to time a small aperture." The Moon Man and the Sun Woman sat inside, and souls without fear passed them before encountering further tests: they must not answer when interrogated by the ancestral men Ngintungintu and Gunababa; or smile when they dance and sing humorously with erect penises; and they "must remain unmoved" when women dance erotically. Souls who pass all these tests finally meet Baiami (Berndt & Berndt 1964: 413).

Aranda shamanic initiates went to a sacred cave in order to be "killed" by spirits and travel to the other realm. The spirits replaced the initiate's internal organs and inserted magical stones into the body, which would later be used in healing. The initiate then "comes to life again," and "dwells upon his experiences" for a year while learning the shamanic craft (Spencer & Gillen 1927: 391–2). The Aranda believed that the Kuruna, a reincarnated ancestral soul, split in two at death. One half became a new Kuruna, which left the body and watched over the grave for three days to protect it from malicious spirits. When funerary rituals were complete, it then flew in bird form to the sacred cave to join the other soul, the Arumburinga. The cave realm of spirits, Okalpera, was a place of "perpetual sunshine" and "streams of running water." The Karuna was ultimately reincarnated, and the new person was watched over by the Arumburinga (though it could sometimes be malevolent) (ibid. 421–3). To become a shaman among the Jajaurung people, the initiate also visited the spirit world during a trance-induced journey lasting two or three days (Howitt 1904: 405).

According to the Gunwinggu people in western Arnhem Land, the more powerful shamans "can heal a sick person by following his spirit in a dream, catching it and returning it to his body. . . . Or he may take the patient in a dream to the land above the clouds and heal him there" (Berndt & Berndt 1964: 258). It was believed that when souls traveled to the sky-world (Manidjirangmad), they met a "powerful being" (Gunmalng or Margidjbu) who knocked out their middle teeth. "If the person is really dead, there is no blood," but if the gums bled, the spirit was sent back to the body, which then revived. The truly dead proceeded along a road, startling a cockatoo, which alerted the wife of the guardian of the path. In sympathy, she distracted her husband so souls could pass. Similarly, people eating fish at a village wept when they saw newly arrived souls, distracting a guardian who asked why they were crying. While they replied that they were crying for the fish, souls were able to pass rather than having their legs cut off. At a river, the deceased called for a canoe. The souls of men were beaten by the ferryman throughout the journey to the other shore, though souls of women were treated kindly after paying for their passage with sex. The Land of the Dead was "a large camp, with many people." A component of the soul returned to some personal earthly site, such as place of conception, birth, or ancestral home. There were also malevolent, unpredictable skeletal spirit-components that smelled of decaying corpses (Berndt & Berndt 1964: 414–5).

According to the Yolngu, souls were ferried to the otherworld on Bralgu Island, or traveled there on a path through swamp yams. A bustard bird announced their arrival. Guardians examined the deceased's teeth to make sure one had been removed, and checked that the nasal passage was clear. If not, they were sent back. Otherwise, they continued through further trials (e.g., passing through threatening spears without flinching) before finally arriving at the ancestor spirit community (ibid. 416–7).

In a myth of the Murngin people, a man named Yaolngura took his canoe to the land of ghosts in the horizon, while following a yam to Barnumbir (the Morning Star). When he arrived, he danced for the spirits and they gave him yams and three wives, then asked him to sing for them about his journey. Yaolngura wanted to see Barnumbir and asked its guardian, an old woman named Marlumbu. When she reluctantly showed him the star, Yaolngura saw that it was the same as the one his people used in their Barnumbir ceremony, made of seagull feathers and yams. Eventually, Yaolngura told "the head man of the island of ghosts" that he was leaving, but that he would return with his family. He exchanged his headdress and wand for the head man's headdress and spear-thrower. Marlumbu promised to send the morning star to Yaolngura's people every day, and the ghosts sang a song to ensure his safety on the return voyage. He arrived home with the Barnumbir emblem made of seagull feathers and yams, and food from the island of ghosts. He returned "as a true human being. He was not a ghost." That night, however, his ghost wives killed him while he was having sex with one of his Earth wives—stealing his spirit so he would return to them (Warner 1937: 524–8).

In a Murngin myth explaining why people "stay dead and never come back to life," the Moon offered to give the Parrot Fish his ability to die and return repeatedly. The Parrot Fish declined, however, saying "I want to die and stay dead" (ibid. 523). Death was most often attributed to either sorcery (e.g., soul stealing), possession by evil spirits, or "ritual uncleanliness" (ibid. 193–4). The soul was believed to leave the body during dreams and interact with spirits (ibid. 511–2).

It is significant that the apparently less important soul-element, the *mokoi*, went to the land of the dead—not the *warro*, which was seen as being the true self. The warro became like a fish, lived in sacred emblems in the water, and saved people in danger of being eaten by sharks or drowning (ibid. 445–6). This reflects the fact that Murngin afterlife myths have little in common with NDEs, suggesting that they were not grounded in such experiences. Furthermore, shamanic visionary experiences were not a prominent local cultural feature. Warner (1937: 511), however, wrote of the "spiritualization of the dream to the level of the sacred totemic world," and saw dreaming as an explanation for certain kinds of beliefs, particularly concerning sorcerers who kill by supernatural means (ibid. 513).

Analysis and Conclusions
NDEs and Returning from Death in Polynesian and Melanesian Ritual and Belief

The Polynesian and Melanesian material reveals some shared patterns in the relationships between NDEs, afterlife beliefs, and, to a lesser extent, shamanic practices. In both areas, NDEs were well integrated into funerary ritual and conceptions of the soul's journey to the other world. There were numerous indigenous statements that afterlife beliefs were obtained or validated by people who had NDEs and shamanic otherworld journeys. Even more widespread was the particular belief that people who returned to life after being dead for a time had been sent back by spirits in the other world—effectively using a key NDE feature as an explanation for extraordinary return-from-death events. Also common, particularly in Polynesia, was a concern for "proving" the veridicality of the experience and emphasizing how extraordinary or miraculous it was. Examples of this include claims that the body had already begun to decay when the soul returned, prophecies obtained in the other world, and objects brought back to Earth.

This clear relationship between beliefs and experiences, alongside numerous accounts of ostensibly documentary NDEs, correlates with (1) a greater number of afterlife myths; (2) widespread beliefs in the OBE capabilities of the soul to visit the otherworld in nondeath contexts (dreams, trance); (3) widespread shamanic soul-retrieval practices; and (4) the common occurrence of accounts of deathbed visions. Possession and trance mediumship were also practiced in both areas. Furthermore, though afterlife beliefs varied in many respects between regions, islands, and indeed individuals, they largely correspond to NDE phenomenology on a thematic level. All this indicates a general receptivity to NDEs, together with a high level of interest in ideas about the fate of the soul after death, and phenomena surrounding the notion that it can leave the body and return. The otherworld was also seen as a place where new knowledge and rituals could be obtained, and was often the same as the realm of creation. Detailed examples of shamanic experiences are scarce, and the lack of certainty about their role may be due in part to gaps in the ethnographic record. However, quite a few Orpheus myths, legends, and other narratives have shamanic elements or themes, and some were even related by shamans demonstrating a clear connection.

Polynesian new religious movements founded on NDEs include the Hapu in Hawai'i, and Pako's cult on the Solomon Islands. There are more examples from Melanesia in which return-from-death accounts or NDEs were foundational to the new movement, including the Baigona, Vailala, Tuka, and Koreri movements among others. Such movements were legitimized, promoted, and sustained through the OBEs, visions, dreams of the dead, prophecies, spirit possessions, and visits to the otherworld of their founders, leaders, and followers (Worsley 1968: 20ff, 69ff, 103–4). As in North America and elsewhere, these kinds of movements often incorporated Christian elements with messages of returning to traditional ways of life, bringing about a golden age on Earth, the return of the dead, and opposing Europeans or their cultural influence. Religious movements grounded in spirit possession experiences were also known in both areas, though were more common in Melanesia.

These findings conflict with Oliver's (1989: 770) generalizations, which characterized Polynesia and Melanesia as being on opposite ends of the spectrum of afterlife beliefs. He wrote that the former "professed belief by means of lengthy and detailed accounts" of the spirit's journey to the other world, while the beliefs of the latter "went no further than getting the soul out of the body and into ghost-form nearby." The numerous afterlife journey accounts from throughout Melanesia, some of which are indeed "lengthy and detailed," show this to be incorrect. Oliver (2002: 42) also wrote that Polynesians were unique in the Pacific for their interest in "unseen aspects of their world," though this, too, is an overstatement challenged by the extensive Melanesian material. While it is true that Polynesian societies did focus more particularly on afterlife journey phenomena and narratives, it is also the case that Melanesian societies seemed especially open to all forms of spirit- and afterlife-related experiences, and had an intense interest in the subject overall.

Burial practices varied greatly even across a single region, making it impossible to generalize about their relationships to NDEs and afterlife beliefs. However, there are examples from both Polynesia and Melanesia of funerary rituals intended to allow for the possibility of the soul's return to the body. In the Hawaiian Islands especially, great care was taken to avoid premature burial. The body was periodically checked for a heartbeat, and was not buried for a number of days (Green & Beckwith 1926: 177). On Tahiti, much effort was made to keep alive those in danger of death, and bodies would lie in state for days prior to burial (Oliver 1974: 488, 496). According to the explorer Jules Dumont d'Urville in 1833, Maori burial was performed on the third day after death or later, due to the belief that the soul remained for that long (Frazer 1922: 20). Best (1901: 10) and Goldie (1904: 20) both reported Maori efforts to bring souls of the recently dead back to their bodies. In Melanesia, the Kiwai exposed bodies to decompose before burying the bones (Landtman 1917: 12), leaving ample time for a possible return to life. Similarly, in the Tanga Islands, final burial did not take place until after decomposition (Bell 1937: 321–2). On Mota Lava, attempts were made to recall the soul to the body prior to burial, which occurred at least two days after death (Codrington 1891: 266–7).

In contrast to Best and Goldie, Tregear (1890: 119–20) reported that Maori attempts to revive the dead were rare, and that the sick were often left alone to die. The discrepancy is likely due to local variations rather than to misinformation. In New Guinea and on Fiji, live burial was commonly practiced when it was believed that the individual would not recover, or if there was danger of witchcraft; and indeed it was customary for the sick or elderly on Fiji to request that they be killed (Williams 1860: 144; Brown 1910: 391–2). On Mota Island those dying of illness or old age were buried alive, either at their own request for euthanasia, or if they had become too much of a burden on their families (Codrington 1880: 125). On the Banks Islands, a lack of NDEs and detailed afterlife beliefs correlates with a fear of ghosts and graveyards, and hasty burial practices in which "directly the breath had left the body everyone fled and the grave was deserted." If an individual's dying process was prolonged, he or she might request burial prior to actual death (Humphreys 1926: 166). Death was sometimes ascribed to the malevolent influence of ancestor spirits (Codrington 1891: 194ff).

Melanesian attitudes toward the dead were diverse, marked variously by "affection, respect and fear" (Williams 1928: 25–6, 68). This is reflected in the varying methods of corpse treatment, in a combined interest in both possession and otherworld journey experiences, and in a concern with both benevolent and malevolent spirits of the dead. While there is also variation in Polynesia, it appears to have been more homogeneous. This is unsurprising given Polynesia's greater cultural homogeneity in comparison to Melanesia's "hundreds" of ethnic groups (Oliver 2002: 2). Such distinctions make the similarities in the relationships between afterlife beliefs and NDEs in both areas all the more striking.

Possession, Shamanism, and the Afterlife in Micronesia and Australia

In contrast to Polynesia and Melanesia, Micronesia and Australia share an almost total lack of documentary NDEs, no indigenous statements that afterlife beliefs originated in NDE phenomena, and comparatively few otherworld journey myths or legends. The similarities of the dynamics between these two regions, however, arose from rather different cultural peculiarities.

In Micronesia there was a greater preoccupation with possession and trance mediumship (e.g., Dobbin 2011: 213–4) than with soul travel or retrieval. Religious revitalization movements focused mainly on "ecstatic native dancing and trance ritual" (ibid. 66), apparently lacking foundations in NDEs or spontaneous return-from-death events. It thus appears that the existence of shamanic rituals to bring the dead to the living for purposes of divination obviated the need for the living to visit the dead. Some Micronesian narratives with NDE-like themes describe the deceased remaining in spirit-form after returning to Earth rather than reentering the body. In a Chuuk description from 1835, the deceased ascended to the "Great Spirit" for judgment and was asked "if it was truly the soul of a dead person." It then returned to Earth as an "effecting spirit" with divine powers to help the living (Goodenough 2002: 150).

Another highly significant factor in explaining the lack of NDE awareness was the "Micronesia-wide" concern that the dead leave and do not return—at least not until they have transitioned to the next state of being in the otherworld, and "eventually become a helpful spirit" (Dobbin 2011: 215). Funerary practices such as sweeping the area or placing large stones on corpses were meant to prevent them from rising (ibid. 79). Corpses were often seen as sources of pollution to be disposed of "as soon as possible" in order to prevent the spirit from returning to it (ibid. 155). A narrative from the Marshall Islands told of a young man who died, then made his people ill when his spirit returned to Earth (ibid. 128). Just as possession could be either a danger or a form of invited spirit communication, fears of dangerous spirits existed alongside beliefs in helpful guardian spirits (ibid. 100). This duality reflects the belief that people can be benevolent or malevolent, both before and after death. Nevertheless, while benevolent spirits were welcome to visit Earth, they were not welcome to reinhabit and reanimate their dead bodies.

The dearth of Australian NDEs is somewhat surprising in light of shamanic trance journeys to the other world, involving a symbolic death, rebirth, and return with new supernatural abilities. With but one possible brief exception (the Kurnai woman as reported by Howitt), the experiential accounts that do involve otherworld journeys occur almost entirely within shamanic contexts—especially relating to initiation. Even where we have a religious revitalization movement grounded in an underworld journey, it was in the context of the founder Barpoo's shamanic experience rather than an NDE. Despite a lack of documentary NDE accounts, however, it is nevertheless possible that they were a known phenomenon, and that the shamanic practices attempted to replicate them. The phenomenology and transformative aftereffects of the shamanic accounts are certainly similar to those of NDEs. Perhaps more compellingly, it may be that Australians "discovered" otherworld journey shamanism independent of knowledge of NDEs, and that they naturally became the focus of concerns about the afterlife.

It is worth remembering the general Australian lack of interest in afterlife matters, in favor of a focus "on life rather than on death, on earthly wellbeing rather than on a hypothetical future state, and on the continuity and persistence of the human spirit" (Berndt & Berndt 1964: 278). With this pragmatic, goal-oriented approach, it was the fruits of shamanism that were important, not details about the afterlife or the journey of the soul. Possession traditions were apparently absent, and rather than soul-loss and soul-retrieval, shamanic practices focused on the use of crystals, charms, healing "magic," and discovering who was responsible for an individual's death (Spencer & Gillen 1927: 453).

Burial practices were also a factor in both Micronesia and Australia. On the Gilbert Islands, though bodies were not buried for a number of days in case the soul returned, funerary rituals were intended to drive the soul away to prevent this from happening (Frazer 1924: 43–4). On the Marshall Islands, bodies were eviscerated immediately after death (ibid. 90), while corpses were bound before burial in the Mortlock Islands (ibid. 116–7). No significant relevant afterlife journey narratives were found for any of these islands. The exception that proves the rule in this case is Waqab Island, where much effort was expended on attempting to revive the dying, and the dead were buried only after days of lying in state (Furness 1910: 163–4). Hasty burials were believed to carry a risk of ghosts bringing illness or other misfortune (Frazer 1924: 171–2). This difference is unlikely to be coincidental. Waqab practices that encouraged revival—both before and after apparent death—correspond to their greater number of afterlife journey narratives, beliefs in soul travel and returning to the body, soul retrieval practices, and a greater interest in the subject in general.

In Australia, corpses were regarded "with a mixture of fear, revulsion, and affection" depending on the relationship to the deceased (Berndt & Berndt 1964: 391). The elderly who had become a burden were put to death. Bodies were bound with knees to chest immediately after death, then buried or burned the next day. If the deceased was a chief, the bones of his arms and legs were immediately removed upon death for distribution to close relatives (Dawson 1881: 62). The Dieri people at Blanchwater feared the dead returning to life, and took pains during burial practices "to prevent the body from rising" by tying together the thumbs and the toes (Howitt 1904: 449).

As Aboriginal Australians are perhaps the world's oldest continuous culture, it would be surprising if NDEs were unknown to them. It may have been the case that they were typically interpreted *as* shamanic phenomena (and were reported as such), and that individuals were considered to be shamans by virtue of having had the experience (as seen in many North American examples). However, the almost total lack of return-from-death contexts makes this overly speculative. The lack of Australian NDEs is more likely related to the kinds of potentially preemptory funerary practices outlined above, a general lack of interest in afterlife concerns, and the fact that the benefits of NDEs were reaped instead through shamanic practices.

Burial Location, Migration Memory, and the Afterlife

One structural factor in Oceanic afterlife conceptions is evidently established as historical fact for some cultures. According to Moss (1925: 1, 215), beliefs in island afterlife realms reflected migration memories of earlier times, so that death was a return "home" to the earthly origin-point rather than the more common other-worldly realm of creation. This is partly evinced by funerary practices involving canoes or sea burials. Interestingly, most cultures that practiced such burials did not generally believe in an undersea afterlife realm, but in a distant island one. Sea burials, Moss (1925: 21–2) argued, reflected a desire to save the expense and trouble of a proper funeral in which the body would be sent adrift in a canoe.

While the theory does seem to account specifically for the idea of island afterworlds, Moss's stress on migration is overstated in general. For example, she assumed that a western direction for the afterlife realm reflected western migration, though it could—as with many societies around the world—reflect ideas of the underworld being the place where the sun "dies" at night. Furthermore, the theory is only of limited relevance considering wide diversity throughout Oceania. In the Mortlock Islands, for example, warriors were buried at sea so they could go to "join the sea-god" in the undersea spirit land (ibid.).

In some cases, there was an apparent connection between burial and other-world locations. In the Cook Islands, for example, the practice of throwing corpses "down the deepest chasms" correlates with a subterranean other world (Gill 1876: 152); and cave-burial frequently coincided with a cave entrance to the underworld (Moss 1925: 212). Again, however, such associations are not consistent across so many diverse cultures. In New Zealand alone, for example, exposure, mummification, swamp, sand, and tree internments were among the attested funerary practices (ibid. 49–50), and the Maori had afterlife regions both in the sky and underground. Because other societies also had varying conceptions alongside varying practices (ibid. 229), a one-to-one association between practice and belief should be seen as region-specific tendencies rather than as a rule.

More problematic is Moss's speculation that burial ritual, as dictated by local topographical factors, preceded afterlife beliefs, and that the beliefs arose in order to explain the ritual. Aside from the impossibility of demonstrating this, let alone of comprehensively matching belief types with burial types, the suggestion is not supportable. While this is not the place to rehearse the debates surrounding myth-ritual theory, the notion that the ritual existed at some point in time when the belief did not, and without associated religious underpinnings, is wholly speculative and ultimately unconvincing. It does not explain the existence of beliefs that do not have ritual counterparts, or why and how specific rituals appeared in the first place. Nor does it explain why funerary practices varied so widely when nearly every Oceanic society had access to the ocean, caves, volcanoes, and so forth. A ritual devoid of an underpinning belief is arguably meaningless, and therefore is unlikely to have preceded the myth.

Conclusions

Otherworld journey myths and legends bearing phenomenological similarities to NDEs were found throughout Oceania. Despite a total lack of documentary NDEs in Micronesia, afterlife beliefs included OBE; soul travel to other worlds in a spirit-version of the body; a realm of beauty, abundance and joy; some form of evaluation of one's earthly life; encounters with deceased relatives and with non-human spirit beings; darkness; borders or limits; the afterlife as a place of rebirth and transformation; and the possibility of return. There was only a single, brief NDE from Australia, alongside references that demonstrate some awareness of the phenomenon, and shamanic practices that were highly reminiscent of NDEs. In addition to NDE elements in common with Micronesia, Australian narratives also featured references to light, and were characterized by a focus on the fruits of afterlife experiences in the form of obtaining new powers or knowledge, and transcendent union with the ancestors. In both cases, the similarities may indicate some NDE basis for afterlife beliefs in the remote past, though in Australia shamanic experiences clearly contributed. That they happened to be described in similar terms to NDEs suggests that the two experience types are analogous, and that those who have them are accessing the same "psychic reality." Alternatively, it is possible that the experiences were intended to replicate NDEs, though their scarcity in the historical record makes this speculative.

In Melanesia and especially Polynesia, the relationship between experience and belief is often more explicit, corresponding to numerous historical NDEs and related myths, legends, and experiential practices and beliefs. Moss's (1925: 135–6) contention that the Maori and most other Polynesians showed "a lack of interest in the whole subject" of life after death is not borne out by the findings here— particularly when viewed in comparison with Micronesia and Australia.

While bright light is often mentioned in descriptions of afterlife realms, of all the Oceanic NDE accounts only the modern Kaliai Christian example featured an actual being of light. This suggests that the notion was a foreign import. It is perhaps less likely that specifying the radiance of the entity was somehow deemed unimportant at a pancultural level, so that the detail was not related.

However, beings of light do appear in the Hawaiian myth of Makua, the Maori myth of Tane, and in the Kiwai myth of Sido (alongside beliefs that souls of the dead radiated light). Why they would appear in otherworld journey myths but not in documentary NDE narratives is uncertain. Life reviews were also absent, despite various forms of conduct or status evaluation, tests, or trials. Themes conceptually similar to life reviews appear in the Hawaiian narrative of Ka-ilio-hae, who gave a genealogical history of his people to the king of the underworld; and in the Maori belief that the soul gave a life history to underworld beings before being allowed to proceed.

Though her various ideas often seem contradictory rather than complementary, Moss (1925: 209) ultimately reached a kind of theoretical eclecticism in attempting to explain Oceanic afterlife beliefs. She concluded that ritual and belief were affected by a combination of migration, diffusion, environment, topographical conditions, "ethnology" (presumably meaning cultural idiosyncrasies), and psychological factors such as "the universal tabu-feeling connected with death." Moss also incorporated an experiential source hypothesis into her model, writing that "primitive ideas concerning haunting and the temporary sojourn of the soul . . . are closely connected with dream and hallucinations" (ibid. 210). Such experiences influenced "eschatological belief, especially with regard to the details of the final departure of the soul, the nature and duration of its existence in the afterworld, and the theory of plurality of souls."

In addition to cultural, experiential, and environmental factors outlined previously, there are further considerations drawn from cross-cultural comparisons that help to form a more comprehensive understanding of Oceanic afterlife conceptions. These are discussed in the next chapter.

5

Interpretations, Implications, and Conclusions

Regional Comparison and Analysis

If cultural context does not allow for the expression of near-death experiences (NDEs), narratives of them will be rare. This correlates with a lower degree of concern about an afterlife, as most clearly reflected in the differences between North America and Africa. A general scarcity of NDEs in Africa corresponds to an overall cultural avoidance or indifference to the subject of life after death, to a lack of detailed afterlife conceptions and related myths, and to very few NDE-based religious revitalization movements. This is in contrast to North America, where otherworldly afterlife beliefs were widespread, vivid, elaborate, and explicitly linked to NDEs and shamanic experiences, Orpheus narratives, visionary traditions, and religious revitalization movements. African cultures rarely stated that they based their beliefs on NDEs, while Native American cultures frequently did. Negative attitudes toward the dead and those who apparently returned from death were nearly as prevalent in Africa as the valorization of shamanic experiences and NDEs were in North America.

When phenomenological descriptions of afterlife beliefs and NDEs do occur in Africa, however, they often share general similarities with those known elsewhere. This suggests a basic structural continuity of NDEs, consistent with local afterlife speculations, *when societies choose to make such speculations*. In other words, it is not that such beliefs and experiences were alien to Africa, but that the cultural focus lay elsewhere. Even when there were exceptions (predominantly Bantu), the accounts of afterlife beliefs often accompanied myths explaining why people do not come back to life. As seen, the Ekoi even specified that those who had NDEs in the past were forbidden from speaking about them. In contrast, with the single exception of the Makah, there is no record of such proscriptions, suspicion, or otherwise negative interpretations of NDE narratives in the Native American material. Furthermore, if shamanic otherworld journey traditions are essentially attempts to replicate NDEs (as discussed later), it is not surprising that they would be rare in Africa given attitudes toward the phenomenon.

It is difficult to identify such marked regional consistencies across Oceania, and there are examples similar to both the African and North American models. In Polynesia and Melanesia, there were more statements that the origins of afterlife beliefs lay in NDEs and a concomitant presence of afterlife journey-related myths than in Africa, Micronesia, and Australia; though fewer than in North America. Polynesia and Melanesia also had both highly mythologized and highly NDE-like Orpheus and other afterlife myths, alongside a greater number of documentary NDEs. There was only a single Oceanic myth explaining why people do not return from death, and it was from Australia where NDEs appear to have been virtually unknown despite thematically similar shamanic afterlife journey practices. Shamanic activity ran the gamut from soul-retrieval to possession, mediumship, and other practices.

The comparatively higher incidence of NDEs in Melanesia and Polynesia compared to Africa corresponds with (1) a trend toward less precipitate funerary practices, and greater efforts to keep alive those in danger of death; and the body being allowed to lie in state for long periods while mourning rituals were conducted, thus increasing the chances of revival by a person thought prematurely to be dead; (2) the lack of extensive corpse taboos and negative beliefs about revival from death (despite common fears of returning ghosts); and (3) possession beliefs and practices that centered on divination and trance mediumship rather than invasion by malevolent spirits (e.g., Oliver 1974: 79ff; 1989: 135). This demonstrates receptivity to NDEs, as indeed do revitalization movements with NDE elements—though again, not to the extent of North America. Varying beliefs, practices, and narrative types in Melanesia are reflected in varying methods of corpse treatment and ideas of both benevolent and malevolent souls, so that there appears to have been no normative system. Generally speaking, however, Polynesia and to a lesser degree, Melanesia, conform more closely to the North American model than to the African model.

In Micronesia and Australia, there was a comparative dearth of NDEs and related narratives. These regions bear more similarities to the African model in regard to funerary practices and attitudes toward the dead; though Australians practiced otherworld journey shamanism, while in Micronesia the dead were brought to the living via possession and mediumship. Both lacked the focused preoccupation with witchcraft and sorcery characteristic of many African cultures. Beliefs that death and other misfortunes were caused by sorcery or by malevolent spirits existed alongside more benevolent possession practices. Such practices occupied a similar place that NDEs did in other societies, and fulfilled similar functions, such as the acquisition of knowledge and prophetic information, and interaction with ancestors.

The comparatively few afterlife journey narratives from Africa correspond phenomenologically to NDEs to a lesser degree than in Native America. They often have a more fable-like quality, frequently involving animal protagonists or individuals following animals to the underworld.[1] Nor do such narratives correspond with any consensus about afterlife beliefs (e.g., Zulu), and rather serve to explain certain mythological concepts, particularly the origin or finality of death, strengthening the notion of widespread aversion. Indeed, one of the most common African myth genres served to explain why living people no longer go to the otherworld and return, a form scarce in both North America and Oceania. There are even examples (e.g., Mbuti) of individuals stating that they did not know anything about the afterlife because "the living have not been there." While the reason for returning in Africa was most often due to rejection and being unwanted in the other world, in Oceania and North America it was more often to bring some benefit to the living, to care for loved ones, or simply because it was not yet time for the person to die.

These findings are largely consistent with A. E. Crawley's (1909) review of soul and afterlife beliefs in "pre-scientific psychologies": Native Americans were largely focused on soul journeys in both NDEs and in shamanism; soul-retrieval and shamanic journeys were prevalent in Oceania and NDEs less so; and African religions had more of a focus on possession and ancestor spirits. A lesser interest in the afterlife in Africa, Crawley noted, is reflected in the comparatively few detailed descriptions of afterlife realms and journeys. Talbot (1912: 80) also discerned a fundamental difference between Africa, where possession was common, and "other continents . . . where souls of mystics or sick people, are supposed temporarily to quit their bodies." Similarly, Max Gluckman (1937: 126) observed that in Africa, "cultural attention on the relations of dead ancestors with their living descendants" was often to the exclusion of concern with afterlife journeys and realms, leaving such notions to individual speculation. A dominating belief in the continual presence of spirits among the living community—and indeed not uncommon beliefs in the "spirit world" being in a nearby earthly location— weakened interest in the afterlife, reduced the significance of NDEs, and made shamanic otherworld experiences culturally irrelevant. Gluckman contrasted Africans with Native Americans and Pacific Islanders, who "have an elaborate mythology of the journey to the afterworld and what happens to the ghost there." There is thus "a general tendency for cultural attention to concentrate on one only of several aspects of a phenomenon," which shifts only "when some special situation occurs," such as the belief that those who are struck by lightning go to "heaven" (Gluckman 1937: 133)—or that NDEs were experiences of an afterlife.

Despite regional tendencies, such diversity is also known within North America. Fear of the dead was strong in Navajo and Athapascan cultures, where "the place of death is quickly shunned and every contact with the dead body is avoided." Afterlife beliefs were correspondingly unclear, and most people in these cultures stated "that they do not know what will happen to them after death." While there were "different traditions about conditions in the next life," people were more concerned with life in this world (Hultkrantz 1992: 127–8). The Makah showed fear when Harshlah returned from the dead, and changed their funerary practices to ensure such a thing would not happen again. This correlates with a lack of Orpheus myths, little interest in afterlife ideas, and the notion that exposure to corpses can cause illness or death. Even looking at the dead could bring bad luck, and the rush to get corpses safely out of sight led to a number of premature burials (including that of Harshlah himself) (Swan 1869: 83, 85; Spier 1935: 14–5). There was also a corresponding lack of accepted detailed afterlife beliefs and experiential reports among the Crow, Copper Inuit, and Sauk.

It is also significant that in no case are NDE-like narratives found in a society without beliefs in an afterlife (e.g., the Hadza), suggesting that the phenomenon was unknown. These societies are also exceptions that prove the rule of a correlation between such experiences and beliefs. The alternative—that people do not have NDE narratives *because* they have no afterlife beliefs—is unsustainable on the grounds that (1) it would not explain the cross-cultural recurrence of NDEs or similarities of afterlife beliefs; (2) it denies other indigenous testimonies that their beliefs are based on their experiences; and (3) it needlessly ignores the most relevant type of experiential correlate.

In summary, returning from death is universally seen as extraordinary, and NDEs are thus significant to the NDEr as well as to his or her society. Prior knowledge and cultural acceptance of NDEs in North America, Polynesia, and Melanesia made societies more receptive to the experiences, and thus made individuals more likely to relate them in the first place (and indeed, perhaps more likely to undergo them in the first place). Such a receptive environment was highly exceptional in Africa, where NDEs were also seen as being extraordinary but typically in dangerous rather than beneficial ways. The case was similar, though to a lesser extent, in Micronesia where mediumship and possession were the focus; while otherworld journey shamanism made NDEs largely redundant in Australia.

In addition to funerary and other cultural factors, varying degrees of healing effectiveness might also help to account for the greater occurrence of NDEs in some regions (cf. Badham 1997: 12). While beyond our scope to investigate, it may be that in societies where NDEs were more regularly reported, local

resuscitation techniques were more effective. This was McIntosh's (1980: 7) suggestion concerning disbelief in NDEs among some Papua New Guinea peoples
(Rigo, Kamea, and Elema), despite their acceptance of other types of OBEs.

Near-Death Experiences and Indigenous Revitalization Movements

Religious revitalization movements rooted in the NDEs of their founders are
known from all three areas, again in direct proportion to the level of overall afterlife concern, with North America having the greatest number, Africa very few,
and Oceania in between, concentrated in Polynesia and especially Melanesia (and
none in Micronesia or Australia). The movements typically combined traditional
indigenous beliefs with Christianity, along with new, original teachings, rituals,
and dances reportedly received during afterlife visits. Because there is nothing to
support diffusion of these movements across continents, there is evidently a very
literal revitalization metaphor at work, in which the "rebirth" of the individual via
an NDE is identified with a renewal of indigenous autonomy and traditions. This
may simply be a natural response by one religious culture when threatened with
extinction by another. Alternatively, perhaps there is something inherent in the
combination of existential threat and philosophical reconciliation of indigenous
religions in crisis with Christianity specifically, which results in such movements
on a transcultural level. Regardless, it is remarkable that individuals who made
NDE narratives instrumental to their movements, by interpreting and exploiting
them in similar ways, happened to appear around the world at different times in
response to very similar circumstances.

Some of these foundational experiential narratives were almost certainly fictitious (judging by intertextuality and in some cases by later admission). However,
given that NDEs are also reported in times of relative cultural stability, there is no
reason to assume that all religious leaders who claimed to have them were merely
inventing them for personal or community gain—particularly in light of cross-
cultural parallels. Some may have been NDE-like dreams or visions that mim-
icked earlier successes, arising at times when they were needed. Others would
seem to be genuine spontaneous NDEs for which the experiencers were culturally primed. Indeed, given the similarity of the leaders' teachings across cultures,
it is not surprising that the NDEs of individuals faced with similar threatening
circumstances would incorporate such themes. Populations in crisis would also
likely be more receptive to extraordinary claims, to give them more credence, and
to elevate those who had them to a higher status—particularly when claims of
experiences were accompanied by radical promises that directly addressed their
specific cultural, political, and economic anxieties. Extraordinary experiences

could sanction indigenous religious narratives, reasserting local beliefs through divine commands to return to traditional religious practices. Alternatively, they could sanction and indigenize religious ideas of the foreign invaders through claims of meetings with the Christian god, saints, or Jesus. Rather than accepting foreign teachings as matters of faith, the experiences could validate prior beliefs and generate new ones, providing "proof" of the authenticity of indigenous perspectives, syncretistic or otherwise. There was thus a major sociopolitical dimension to the ways in which NDEs contributed to the formation of religious beliefs, which is independent of their basic phenomenology, and even of their actual occurrence.

Because there was little cultural priming for NDEs in Africa, the phenomenon had nothing like the authority it enjoyed elsewhere. While the act of returning from death held some potency, accounts of journeys to afterlife realms were far less central to prophets' claims. Nevertheless, many African revitalization movements were grounded in other kinds of extraordinary experiences, such as the dreams, visions, and raising of the dead by Simon Kimbangu in 1921. That Kimbangu preached the expulsion of Europeans, a return of the dead in a coming golden age, and the indigenous people becoming Caucasians (Lanternari 1963: 9, 311)—all familiar themes from Native American and Oceanic counterparts—reveals common sociohistorical and cultural crisis contexts of the formation of such movements. Similarly, in the 1810s the Xhosa prophet and military leader Makhanda Nxele started a revitalization movement that combined Christian and indigenous ideas with revelations and prophecies he allegedly received directly from "Uhlanga, the great spirit." While no return-from-death episode is recorded, Makhanda did claim that he would resurrect the dead to fight against the British and usher in a new golden age (Shooter 1857: 195–9). In any case, acknowledging these religions as expressions of "intercultural clash" and an indigenous longing for regeneration, reform, freedom, and salvation does not indicate that the experiences which were so frequently central to them did not actually occur.

While examples of religious revitalization movements can be found that do not conform to this model,[2] a pattern is nonetheless clearly discernable cross-culturally. At least five nineteenth-century indigenous South American examples[3] involved

> shamans with extraordinary powers of clairvoyance, transformation, and curing. They claimed that in visions they ascended to heaven and had direct communication with the dead, with spirits, with saints, and with the Christian God and various indigenous figures . . . who are often identified with him. (Hugh-Jones 1994: 47–8)

All these movements were characterized by the usual themes of expulsion of Europeans, millenarian apocalypse followed by a golden age, and syncretistic beliefs. The "Hallelujah" religion of the Akawaio of Brazil, Guyana, and Venezuela had its nineteenth-century origins in the NDE of its founder, a Makusi man by the name of Bichiwung. The experience itself and the resulting teachings were remarkably similar to some Native American and Oceanic examples, including its subsequent maintenance via shamanic replication (Butt 1960: 388–93, 399, 404).

With few exceptions (e.g., Mooney 1896), in nearly every scholarly discussion of religious revitalization movements, there is an almost total lack of consideration of the role of extraordinary experiences (apart from brief descriptions of their context and content). Without the experiences (or at least claims of them), these movements would not have come into being. Their most indigenously significant factor is thus systematically ignored by most scholars in favor of exclusively sociopolitical functionalist explanations, as if the statements of the very people whose beliefs they are attempting to interpret are irrelevant.

Afterlife Beliefs and the Experiential Source Hypothesis: A Historiographical Survey

In many cultures, accounts of NDEs were often provided as descriptions of afterlife beliefs. This indicates that they were widely considered to be the source and empirical validation of those beliefs. A common concern of spirits and deities in the other world was to convey to the living knowledge of the afterlife or other messages of religious or spiritual import, and they often sent people back to Earth specifically for that purpose.

As noted in the Introduction, the experiential source model has a long and prestigious pedigree across various disciplines,[4] and since the nineteenth century it has even been used specifically to explain similarities between afterlife conceptions across cultures. Giving numerous examples from indigenous societies, Tylor (1871: 2–8, 22–3, 62, 69, 80–1, 85–8) noted the common cross-cultural recurrence of such familiar themes as darkness, realms of light, obstacles, barriers and perils, differing fates based on perceived social or moral worth, and reincarnation. He also cited numerous encounters with deceased relatives and deities, returning to the origin point or creator, intermediate states and experiences, and feelings of joy and happiness. Finding that indigenous people widely believed that the deceased individuals seen in "dreams and visions" were actual souls of the dead, Tylor (1871: 1, 46) wrote "nothing but dreams or visions could have ever put into men's minds such an idea as that of souls being ethereal images of bodies." Indeed, the peoples themselves "claim to hold their doctrines of the future life on strong tradition, direct revelation, and even personal experience. To them the land of souls is a discovered country, from whose bourne many a traveller returns." Along with dreams and shamanic states, Tylor (1871: 48–9) also recognized that afterlife beliefs could be based on experiences in which "men whose spirits, traveling in dreams or in the hallucinations of extreme illness to the land of the dead, have returned to reanimate their bodies and tell what they have seen." He found that such purportedly true narratives were common in small-scale societies, citing examples from New Zealand, Africa, and Finland (ibid. 52). Recognizing NDEs as a distinct experience type, Tylor observed that they are known in both "civilized" and "savage" times, and that some accounts are "no doubt given in good faith by the visionary himself, while others are imitations of these genuine accounts" which themselves were rooted in prior belief. Tylor also drew distinctions between mythological afterlife journey narratives, and those said to recount genuine experiences in which an individual's soul "goes forth, leaving his body behind in ecstasy, sleep, coma, or death." Surprisingly, however, Tylor argued that the experiences are due entirely to individual/cultural expectation (ibid. 49), failing to account for the cross-cultural patterns he made such efforts to reveal,[5] and ultimately ignoring his own inclinations toward an NDE-based experiential source model.[6]

As seen, Tregear (1890: 118–9) similarly concluded that Maori narratives about the other world originated in "the dreams of people in trance through illness." Howitt (1887: 54) theorized that the indigenous Australian "belief in the reality of dreams" of spirit journeys to the other world "gives a key to many universal beliefs which otherwise seem almost inexplicable." Generalizing from his experience with the Saulteaux, Hallowell (1940: 29) argued for the historical authenticity of NDE accounts, concluding:

> Aboriginal beliefs in the reality of a life beyond the grave cannot be viewed as simple dogmas that gain currency without any appeal to observation and experience. . . . Specific individuals are referred to, whose historicity is not in question, however one may choose to evaluate their testimony. When I made inquiries about life after death, it was the alleged experiences of these individuals that were first mentioned. I was not given generalized statements.

Eliade (1964: 504, 509ff) wrote, "In all probability, many features of 'funerary geography' as well as some themes of the mythology of death are the result of the ecstatic experiences of shamans."[7] He regarded shamanism as "primary experience" rather than wholly culturally constructed, and "fundamental in the human condition, and hence known to the whole of archaic humanity." How the experiences were interpreted and evaluated, however, "was modified with the different forms of culture and religion." Eliade's (1964: 34) intense focus on shamanism prevented him from clearly recognizing the NDE as a distinct phenomenon,[8] or even discussing the accounts that appeared in his sources. He did, however, identify the main elements of shamanic journey experiences as disembodiment followed by renewal of the (spiritual) body, celestial ascent and/or underworld descent, encountering and interacting "with spirits and the souls of dead shamans," and revelations "both religious and shamanic." Elsewhere (1973: 170) he described death as being "essentially an ecstatic experience: the soul abandons the body and journeys to the land of its postexistence," just as it can temporarily in "sleep, trance provoked by sickness, [and] shamanistic voyages."

The ethnopsychologist Holger Kalweit (1984: 70) emphasized that when individuals in indigenous societies around the world are "asked about the origins of their knowledge of the Beyond, [they] say they gained this knowledge from the experiences of those who have returned and from shamans." He drew an analogy with modern Western cases in which NDEs lead to new afterlife beliefs. Afterlife myths as well as accounts of shamanic journeys to spirit realms "provide the members of a culture from early childhood onward with psychological guidance and behavioral models which also help the dying to pass safely to a new realm of consciousness." The medievalist N. K. Chadwick (1952: 94) likewise stressed the significance of shamanic journey narratives as a "means of disciplining and informing the flock . . . an initiation into the next life. . . . a kind of spiritual dress rehearsal, a trial trip to Heaven and Hell."

The psychiatrist and philosopher Roger Walsh (1990: 148) similarly concluded:

> around the world people who have never heard of shamanism may be surprised to find themselves having journeylike experiences. These may erupt spontaneously and entirely unsought as out-of-body experiences, lucid dreams, or near-death experiences. Such experiences have presumably occurred throughout human history . . . [and may] have provided a basis for the widespread belief in a soul and soul travel.

Alan F. Segal (2004: 330ff, 335ff, 512ff) similarly suggested that certain Jewish mystical and religious beliefs resulted from "religiously interpreted states of consciousness," including journeys to heaven and OBEs. He also recognized that the experiences and the accounts of them would be influenced by existing religious texts. Acknowledging both differences and similarities between accounts, he concluded:

> If there is a biological basis for these experiences, there surely is also a broad vocabulary of images which the individual mind brings into experience, based on personal history, training, and culture. (Segal 2004: 335)

Further support and cross-cultural evidence for the NDE experiential source hypothesis can be found in Badham (1997), Becker (1981: 159), Collins & Fishbane (1995: ix–x), Kellehear (2001: 34), and McClenon (1994: 151, 172), among others (cf. Shushan 2009: 166ff).

A link between extraordinary experiences and beliefs in dualism and OBEs has also been widely noted. The nineteenth-century polymath Andrew Lang (1900: 105ff, 140ff) argued for the relevance to such beliefs of dreams, visions, possession, and apparitions.[9] The anthropologist Raphael Karsten (1935: 58) similarly contended that belief in the reality of dreams and trance-states worldwide contributed to ideas about the soul and its ability to leave the body. Bourguignon (1973: 11) found that most of the 488 societies she surveyed believed that trance is caused by the consciousness or soul actually leaving the body.

In his survey of 67 predominantly small-scale societies worldwide, the anthropologist Dean Shiels (1978: 697, 699) discovered that 95 percent held beliefs in OBEs, and that they were described in remarkably similar ways across cultures. Many believed that OBEs occurred mainly as a result of illness, emotional stress, trance, narcotic use, and accident (ibid. 729–31). This confirmed Crawley's (1909) claim that almost without exception, each of the numerous worldwide traditions he studied held beliefs in some kind of "soul" that is separable from the body after death, and often before death given certain circumstances (dreams, illness, near-death, sorcery, shamanic journeys). Shiels (1978: 731–4) concluded that the belief must be based on experience: "When different cultures at different times and in different places arrive at the same or a very similar out-of-the-body belief we begin to wonder if this results from a common experience of this happening," meaning that OBEs "are widely experienced among humans." Furthermore, he found "no other culture-trait" to be as "specific and so widely shared among cultures." Shiels rejected social scientific and psychological explanations (e.g., OBE beliefs as a "social control device," or a means of self-empowerment), as well as the notion that such beliefs arose from dreams, stressing that many cultures distinguished between dreams and OBEs. Even when it was believed that OBEs could occur during dreams, not all dreams were considered OBEs. McClenon (2002: 125) also observed that those who have OBEs "generally form the opinion that they have some type of soul that can leave the body, allowing them to experience out-of-body perceptions; the exact nature of this entity (or entities) varies from culture to culture." Given that OBEs are essentially a precondition for NDEs, this wide cross-cultural distribution is highly significant.

From a neuroscientific perspective, Thomas Metzinger (2005: 57) also concludes that beliefs in mind-body dualism cross-culturally originate in OBEs, which "can be undergone by every human being and seem to possess a culturally invariant cluster of functional and phenomenal core properties similar to the proto-concept of mind." Metzinger (2005: 78 n.8) cites other studies that support his experiential source hypothesis, including one (Osis 1979) in which 73 percent of respondents to a survey on OBEs claimed that their beliefs had changed as a result of the experience; and another (Gabbard & Twemlow 1984) in which 66 percent claimed that their OBE caused them to adopt "a belief in life after death." Metzinger's (2005: 78) conclusions here are worth quoting at length:

> For anyone who actually had that type of experience it is almost impossible not to become an ontological dualist afterwards. In all their realism, cognitive clarity and general coherence, these phenomenal experiences almost inevitably lead the experiencing subject to conclude that conscious experience can, as a matter of fact, take place independently of the brain and the body: what is phenomenally possible in such a clear and vivid manner must also be metaphysically possible or actually the case. Although many OBE reports are certainly colored by the interpretational schemes offered by the metaphysical ideologies available to experiencing subjects in their time and culture, the experiences as such must be taken seriously. Although their conceptual and ontological interpretations are often seriously misguided, the truthfulness of centuries of reports about ecstatic states, soul-travel and second bodies as such can hardly be doubted.

Part of the value of the OBE in relation to the experiential source hypothesis is that it is a single, highly specific experience type, rather than a composite one (like the NDE). It is also wholly unambiguous: whatever it is called in whatever language, it is always, by definition, considered an experientially dualistic state in which consciousness is separated from the body. Part of the significance of NDEs, however, is their stable return-from-death context, combined with universal afterlife-related interpretation, and general cross-cultural thematic similarities arising from a complex range of subexperiences.

Near-Death Experiences and Shamanism

A shaman's status was often grounded in some extraordinary experience involving deities or spirits of other deceased shamans. They could be possessed by ancestors, and thus become "spirits" like the dead in order to communicate their knowledge to the living. In North America, the shaman's status was most often based on a claim of a journey to another world. Descriptions of shamanic initiates being temporarily dead, "as if dead," newly dead, in a death-like trance, and so forth, occur repeatedly in some of the most NDE-like descriptions of shamanic journeys. That such experiences were sometimes precipitated by serious illness (Jakobsen 1999: 10; Eliade 1964: 15ff, 32, 82–5) shows that they can have NDE contexts. Thorpe (1993: 26–8, 50) identified this pattern in Native American, circumpolar, and African peoples. While the latter were more focused on mediumship and possession than NDE-type phenomena, shamans were nevertheless commonly selected by spirits on the basis of an illness, prior to gaining their status through dreams or visionary trance in which effective healing information was revealed by deceased ancestors (ibid. 88–9; 104–5, 130).

While some ritual practices such as extended fasting, being clubbed unconscious, burned, or buried alive likely brought about actual NDEs, it is also the case that analogous experiences were brought about by other ritual, psychological, and entheogenic techniques. It is important to remember here that NDE-like phenomena can occur in individuals who were never temporarily "dead" or even near death at all, such as when one merely *believes* he or she is near death (so-called fear-death experiences), or even spontaneously and apparently at random (Van Lommel 2010: 8). This suggests that similar processes are being triggered in the individual during both experiences, so that some shamanic experiences, even when not brought about by physical ordeal, effectively *are* NDEs. Others may be more akin to lucid dreams of NDEs; while still others may have been wholly imaginative, conforming largely to cultural expectations. In any case, a near-death context in conjunction with similar phenomenologies means it is sometimes impossible to tell whether a shamanic narrative indicates an NDE or not.

Nevertheless, shamanic experiences are not spontaneous, and are therefore apt to be influenced to a greater degree by expectation. While it has been shown that ostensibly universal shamanic imagery can be brought about in naïve subjects through repetitive drumming, with the exception of bridges and rivers (thematically borders, transitions, barriers), the imagery is not typical of NDEs (rocky ravines, predatory creatures, and conceptions of three layered worlds) (Rock et al. 2005/2006). This suggests that as products of purposeful induction, many shamanic experiences were also largely products of cultural expectation. This contrasts with NDEs, in which "people never quite find the afterlife to be what they expected" (Wade 2003: 113).

Eliade (1964: 486) suggested that shamanic journeys were intended to replicate some earlier primordial experience from a time when all humans "went up to heaven and came down again without recourse to trance." This was then repeated by "medicine men" and by "the soul of every man after death" (Eliade

1973: 171). Walsh (1990: 148–9) more specifically argued that spontaneous NDEs, OBEs, and lucid dreams "may have provided the inspiration for consciously induced journeys, first in shamanism, then in other religious traditions." Furthermore, "The fact that such experiences can occur spontaneously at first and later be brought under voluntary control suggests that this may be one way in which shamanic journeying was learned and relearned throughout human history" (cf. Green 1998: 209). Stressing the connection between the positive fruits of NDEs and the purposes and functions of shamanism, Walsh (1990: 151) concluded:

> Inasmuch as these experiences may have occurred throughout history and have profound transformative and healing effects, they may well have served as an inspiration for shamans. Indeed, one of the traditional calls to shamanism is unexpected recovery from a near-fatal illness. If some shamans-to-be had near-death experiences, they may well have sought ways to re-create and control similar experiences for the benefit of themselves and their tribes.

Kalweit (1992: 40, 263) also subscribed to the replication theory of extraordinary experiences, writing that people "try to experience them anew through rituals," giving rise to religions. In particular, "Whoever travels in the other world comes back transformed," having gained new knowledge, abilities, and "paranormal faculties." Although contemporary NDErs do not often gain anything like the status of shamans (bestselling authors of personal NDE accounts notwithstanding), positive spiritual changes are common, and there are even claims of paranormal abilities resulting from the experience.

Shamanic attempts to replicate NDEs thus had important individual and community motivations. They were intended not only to recreate the spiritual aspects of the experience (communication with ancestors or divinities, obtaining new knowledge), but also the positive transformations reported by so many NDErs. Both kinds of experiences are often "profoundly meaningful, healing, and helpful," and would thus "doubtless have been valued and sought after." They can improve an individual's psychological well-being with the kinds of "dramatic changes" one would expect from "years of psychotherapy" (Walsh 1990: 150). They were thus beneficial to the well-being of the community, for the individual not only became a model of positive transformation but also provided evidence for afterlife beliefs, conveyed new religious teachings and messages from the spirit world, and became a healer or prophet by virtue of the knowledge and abilities obtained there. As Walsh (1990: 153) summarized,

The techniques and circumstances which favored them would have been carefully noted, cultivated, and transmitted across generations. When these and other skills were collected into a coherent body of techniques and wedded to an explanatory mythology, the core elements of shamanism would be in place and the shamanic tradition would be born or reborn.

Such a scenario could account for the wide distribution of shamanic journey practices around the world, for "If journeylike experiences occurred spontaneously throughout human history, they may have repetitively reinspired and reinforced similar practices and beliefs in widely separated cultures and centuries."

Through attempts to replicate them with shamanic afterlife journeys, NDEs thus had evolutionary adaptational value (as discussed below). In a process of cultural encoding and integration, NDEs led directly to certain types of beliefs and practices. Shamanic journey imagery and beliefs often stemmed from the ritualization and mythologization of NDEs, adapted to sociocultural needs and expectations, presented in locally relevant and valuable terms, and subsequently maintained through experiential replication. The physical ordeals undergone by shamanic initiates could enhance the culturally expected experience, or even cause an actual NDE. While NDE rather than shamanic journeying was most often the primary experience (contra Eliade), it was in some cases brought about through shamanic techniques. Shamans were taught what to expect during their experiences; and members of the society were likewise primed to interpret spontaneous NDEs in terms consistent with shamanic beliefs. Thus, as with experience and belief in general, NDEs informed shamanic experiences and vice versa. Shamanic experiences may thus be seen as being midway along the experience-belief continuum, being products of cultural expectation combined with universal NDE-like characteristics. They are fairly fixed within a given culture, and discussions about them in the secondary literature tend not to be in terms of individual experiences but of what is *generally* experienced.

Of course, such dynamics are only possible where preexisting cultural conditions allow. While this model applies widely to North America, Polynesia, and Melanesia (as well as to Siberia and other world areas not considered here), it rarely applies in Africa and Micronesia, where shamanic journeying was less relevant to begin with and accounts of NDEs were correspondingly rare. Nor should we ignore testimonies which explicitly state that afterlife beliefs arose from shamanic experiences (e.g., in Australia), though these are in the minority and in any case may conceivably have had origins in physical near-death events.

Because spontaneous experiences often hold more authority by virtue of being unexpected and thus particularly extraordinary, they are more likely to generate new beliefs—including in ritual activity designed to reproduce them. A higher degree of culture-specific motifs and literary elaboration not only helps distinguish shamanic from NDE narratives, but also supports the notion that NDEs can better explain cross-cultural similarities in afterlife beliefs.

Cognitive Evolution and Neurotheology

From the perspective of cognitive evolutionary theory, shamanism is seen in terms of its healing and social roles, the adaptive and integrative functions of the human brain and consciousness, and as the foundational experience for religious beliefs. Winkelman (2000: xiii–xiv) states that such experiences provided "a basis for human development in the mythological systems representing self, mind, other, and consciousness." Afterlife-related motifs such as the "soul journey" and "guardian spirits" are seen as forms of "role taking that expand human sociocognitive and intrapsychic dynamics," while the "death and rebirth" motif itself is symbolic of "the death of the old self to permit the emergence and integration of a higher-order self." The relationship between the individual and cultural mythology was "ritually manipulated" in order to "emotionally transform the patient's self and emotions," enabling "shamanic healers to evoke cognitive and emotional responses that cause physiological [healing] changes" (Winkelman 2006: 107; cf. McClenon 2002).

Similarly, McClenon (2006b: 136–7) writes that shamanic experiences "facilitated hominid coping with negative life events. With increasing capacity for symbolization, hominids found that therapeutic rituals based on dissociation were beneficial" (e.g., via placebo effect or hypnosis), for "shamanism provides greater survival advantages to those with genes allowing dissociation, hypnotic capacity, and religiosity" McClenon (2006a: 1). Humans grew increasingly susceptible to such experiences as "rituals shaped human hypnotizability, a genetically based trait correlated with the incidence of certain forms of unusual experiences,"[10] which in turn led to a variety of supernatural beliefs. As seen in the preceeding chapters, the susceptibility of certain individuals to extraordinary experiences was common in all three regions, and many shamans had experiences previous and subsequent to those described. Despite their transformative features, McClenon clarified, "We need not assume that these experiences were valuable by themselves. It seems likely that such perceptions were by-products of the 'cognitive flexibilities' related to dissociation and hypnotic suggestion" (2006b: 136–7).

McClenon (2006a: 1) also saw NDEs in evolutionary terms, arguing that they "have a shamanic basis." The precise role of NDEs is not made clear in his model or in Winkelman's, however, and some apparently underlying assumptions are problematic. First, there is much evidence that NDEs and shamanic experiences are intrinsically beneficial to those who have them, and that their value is not restricted to cognitive factors. Second, the fact that NDEs generally occur near death—and thus presumably when one actually dies—suggests that their origins do not lie in their community functions. The experience in itself does not contribute to society, and any benefit it might have beyond the individual would be determined by local sociocultural factors. The social or functional advantage of having a personally transformative, private experience *at the point of death* is not explained, particularly an experience characterized by themes of renewal, rebirth and "transcendence of ordinary awareness and identity" (Winkelman 2006: 99). NDEs cannot be seen as coping mechanisms, occurring as they do most typically in the dying process when the most advantageous state would be resignation, acceptance, or even a total lack of perception and conscious activity. The relationship to shamanism is also unclear in this context: While the brain may be triggered to have shamanic experiences through various inductive techniques, why would it be triggered in a such a way at death rather than simply losing consciousness? Put another way, why would a dying person (or a person who believes they are dying) have a shamanic-type experience characterized by thematically transcultural afterlife motifs?

Third, if we attempt to explain NDEs in terms of evolutionary biology, this implies that the human brain is hardwired to create specific experiences of OBEs, darkness, light, borders, deceased relatives, divine beings, and so forth, on the off chance that the individual will not die after all, and that he or she will relate their experience upon revival, and that the narrative will lead to social benefit through the development of shamanic ritual practices. Aside from relying on a series of uncertainties, there seems to be no sociocultural *necessity* of NDEs and their specific phenomenology to indicate an evolutionary biological origin. While conversing with ancestors or obtaining knowledge in other realms can confer special status on those who have NDEs, there is usually no external validation of their descriptions of the content of their experiences (other than the apparent fact that they returned to life), meaning that the effect might be the same if the accounts were simply invented. In regard to shamanism, Winkelman (2006: 101) states, "visual symbol systems provide advantages in analysis, analogic synthesis and planning," though such cognitive skills are gained in far more straightforward ways by those who do not have shamanic experiences or NDEs (i.e., the vast majority of essentially every given population group). In any case, the attainment of such skills through extraordinary experience may be unrelated to the *origins* of the experience itself.

Finally, assuming that the individual does relate their NDE to the community, how the narrative will be received varies widely by culture. While in many cases it may be valorized and culturally integrated in such a way as to have social benefit, in others it will be greeted with disbelief, rejection, ridicule, or even violence. As seen, some societies are simply not receptive to NDEs, and indeed relating them can be a danger to the self and to the community, causing fear and hostility that can lead to discord and division. Many NDErs keep the experience to themselves, worried about possible negative reactions from their families and communities. Any social benefit NDEs might have is thus incidental and specific to local circumstances, again suggesting that the origins of the experience do not lie in biological evolutionary adaptation.

The cross-cultural evidence of the present study further limits the force of cognitive evolutionist theories. The fundamental differences in afterlife beliefs between certain cultures, and in the ways NDEs are integrated into belief systems, indicate that neither NDEs nor afterlife beliefs (1) result wholly from neurological activity, or (2) are intrinsically evolutionarily adaptive traits. Cognitivist explanations alone are unsatisfactory for the simple reason that beliefs about and attitudes toward NDEs are not universal. If NDEs were due entirely to the workings of the human brain for a specific function, we should not see such marked variation in content and interpretation; and the ostensibly intrinsic benefits that they are supposed to confer upon a society should not be subject to cultural particularities. The African examples in particular demonstrate that though NDEs share features that are found worldwide, the processing and integration of them are dictated by local cultural and individual factors. Any universalist proposition on its own is inadequate to explain the sheer range of difference and variety of any type of religious phenomena.

Within particular societies, however, shared beliefs and values concerning NDEs and associated shamanic practices likely served to foster "social identity and personhood" as well as physical and emotional well-being, and contributed to social cohesion (Winkelman 2006: 104–6). Such experiences and narratives about them would also stimulate a sense of wonder and ignite the imagination, while encouraging both abstract and critical, evaluative thinking in efforts to understand the experience and accommodate it to local worldviews. However, while there are convincing arguments for social, cognitive, and adaptive functions of NDEs, these functions do not explain the origin or nature of the phenomenon itself. Ultimately, the beneficial aspects of NDEs do not constitute proof that they originated specifically as an evolutionarily adaptive trait.

Finally, the assumption that shamanism is the earliest form of religion is itself extremely problematic. Interpretations of certain burials as being those of shamans, or of Paleolithic rock art as resulting from shamanic experiences or even depicting shamans, are speculative (Kehoe 2000: 4, 72). As Sidky (2010: 82–3) points out, such images are "open to various equally plausible or equally implausible interpretations, for example, hunter in camouflage gear, mythical being, divinity, monster, jester, alien being from outer space, etc., none of which can be tested or falsified." Extrapolating specific beliefs from the archaeological record is largely an imaginative exercise, and even if we do accept prehistoric shamanism (i.e., ritual healing traditions), we cannot know what *kind* of shamanism it might have been, or what beliefs were associated with it. The widely accepted Eliadian paradigm that there are "unique characteristics of 'genuine' or 'classic' Siberian and north and central Asiatic shamanism that are purported to be exclusive to Paleolithic hunting-gathering cultures" (including "transformative initiatory crisis, death-rebirth motifs, soul flight") is simply untrue, as Sidky (2010: 70; cf. Hultkrantz 1989) shows, and as the present study confirms. Thus,

> assertions that shamanism dates back to the Paleolithic period, that it was the foundation of human religiosity, and that shamanistic beliefs and practices survived unchanged into the present on the outskirts of the "civilized" world, become untenable propositions. (Sidky 2010: 72)

Despite the fact that such notions derive from "Eliade's unsubstantiated speculations" (ibid. 78), they are accepted uncritically by many modern scholars of shamanism. Such perspectives are rooted in nineteenth-century cultural evolutionist perspectives that equated "primitive" people with early humans and relegated their religions to a "low" status in contrast to the so-called high religions of "civilized" societies. While such overt claims have been largely abandoned, the ideas are nevertheless embedded in many cognitive evolutionary theories of the origins of religion. Winkelman (2006: 94, 110), for example, searches for the genesis of shamanism in animal behavior, "the paleomamalian brain," and imagined Palaeolithic "hominid ritual."

Both Winkelman (2000: 89; 2006: 92, 98–9) and McClenon (2002: 106, 2006b) also argue that the cross-cultural consistency of OBEs, shamanic experiences, and NDEs is evidence for their neurophysiologic origin. Similarity in itself, however, does not indicate any particular explanation, and indeed can be used to support conflicting metaphysical, diffusionist, or other theories (Shushan 2011). Winkelman's explanation of consistencies across the experience types is that "the core shamanic experience—the soul flight—is an innate psychophysiological structure reflecting neurognostic structures and psychosocial processes." "Neurognostic structures" are "neural networks that produce basic forms of perception and knowledge and the universal aspects of mind . . . as manifested in the shaman's soul journey and other out-of-body experiences." Whether the existence and interactions of such structures have been proven empirically is unclear, however. Kirkpatrick (2006: 161) asserts that "there is no simple one-to-one mapping between the physical organization of brain structures and the functional organization of evolved mechanisms." Experimental evidence does not support claims about a "god module" in the brain that produces "religious" experiences and beliefs: "At most, it appears that brain areas have been identified that are associated with a motley collection of vague feelings and experiences that are sometimes interpreted in spiritual terms—usually by already-religious research subjects." Most crucially, "Even if there are clearly identifiable neurophysiological correlates or causes of a particular pattern of thought, emotion, or behavior, however, it does not follow that the function of the module is to produce those effects" (cf. Kelly et al. 2007). Thus, Winkelman's (2006: 99) claim that shamanism reveals "the biogenetic structuralist foundations of religious conceptions and practices" appears to be a largely speculative oversimplification.

There is also a distinct lack of neuroscientific studies on cross-cultural extraordinary experiences. The notion that findings derived from mainly Western participants are representative of humanity as a whole is problematic. Neuroscientific theories also routinely fail to distinguish between experience types, tending to ignore more complex phenomena such as NDEs in favor of more generalized "mystical" experiences.[11] As Kirkpatrick (2006: 165–6) concluded, "it seems unlikely that any single adaptation could explain the enormous amount of variability in religion across time, individuals, and cultures."

Jesse Bering (2006a) has argued that the common human belief that people survive bodily death is a natural cognitive trait. Being dead is not only beyond our experience, but is alleged to be beyond our imagination. We are thus cognitively predisposed to believe in survival after death. Bering and Bjorklund (2004) found that children's beliefs in life after death are not cultural but intuitive, and that we are naturally inclined to think of people as having souls that represent their uniqueness and personality; and that it is this essential soul-"person" that survives physical death. While the theory does not explain more detailed cross-cultural similarities of afterlife beliefs and ignores relevant experience types, it is in fact complementary to the conclusions here. A cognitive predisposition to belief in souls and life after death would indicate that we are generally receptive to experiences and ideas that seem to validate those beliefs. Kemmerer and Gupta (2006: 479) also made this important corrective to Bering with reference to OBEs, writing that their acceptance by experiencers as a genuine indication of dualism "is consistent with Bering's proposal that psychological immortality is the cognitive default":

> it is not surprising that OBEs have been widely regarded throughout history as confirming the intuition that every human being has an ethereal soul that can literally detach from the physical body, most importantly when that body expires.

More problematic are Bering's (2006b: 129–30) assertions that this propensity for afterlife beliefs can be explained in terms of "'social contract' with the deity," and anticipation of afterlife reward and punishment (cf. Weber 1922: 140–1). Fear of an omniscient observer, he argues, discourages cheating and other negative actions through the threat of retribution, and encourages people "to refrain from social deviance and, subsequently, to preserve their genetic fitness." Besides the fact that suggesting a link between "social deviance" and "genetic fitness" is both vague and controversial, of more direct relevance here is that not all religions feature an omniscient observer, and not all afterlife beliefs involve moral or ethical determination—indeed some are not evaluative at all. If a theory relies on the universal workings of the human brain, it should apply universally.

While there indeed appears to be a cognitive evolutionary component in integrating and maintaining certain religious beliefs and practices, and while extraordinary experiences are clearly central to the development of religions, the more sweeping hypotheses are unconvincing due to their reliance on numerous unproven assumptions about the brain, cultural evolution, and the nature, antiquity, and origins of shamanism. They also rely on unfounded universalizing of beliefs, and diminish or ignore entirely the role of spontaneous, universal, extraordinary experiences such as NDEs; and focus on vague generalities (the *fact* of belief, the *existence* of religion) rather than engaging with the problem of specific cross-cultural differences and similarities. Observations about the functional benefits of extraordinary experiences, and recognition of their component role in the development of particular *religions* (plural), are surely important. However, extrapolating from these considerations that the origins of *religion* per se therefore lie in hypothetical cognitive evolutionary shamanic mechanisms overreaches the evidence.

Conceptual Logic, Myth, and Ritual

The recurrence of certain afterlife mythemes across many societies may be explained simply by "the regularity of the processes by which opinion is formed among mankind" (Tylor 1871: 49); that is, the common cognitive mechanisms of the human mind, resulting in similar modes of logic, information processing, and symbolization relevant to local conditions. For example, while many accounts of NDEs do not refer explicitly to an OBE, this does not necessarily suggest that the individual went to the other world in the physical body, for it may be a detail that was logically taken for granted (Kellehear 1996: 32). The narratives often read as if the sensations and activities are being experienced by an embodied person, and NDE accounts cross-culturally often describe a kind of nonphysical "subtle body." Out-of-body experiences are also implicit in the widespread belief that the spirit remains near the body or in the village for a time prior to proceeding to the other world. Furthermore, simple observation would confirm that an individual's body was still in place during the time he or she claimed to have been having their otherworldly experiences (cf. Hallowell 1940: 29). By implication, the cognitive predisposition for belief in souls that survive death is also an intuitive belief in dualism. This is likely enhanced by the clustering together of our consciousness, primary senses, and phenomenal perceptions of the self and the world, so that our minds seem somehow of a different order than our bodies. As such, it is logical to intuit that they can exist apart from the body, an idea reinforced by experiences of OBE, NDE, mediumship, ghosts, possession, dreams, and so forth.

The notion that the other world is similar to Earth was widespread. Descriptions obviously differed between societies, given that they reflected local topographical, environmental, and sociocultural features. Thus, in agriculture-based societies the other world had a more agricultural character (Hultrantz 1967: 134–5). Afterlife realms were also frequently characterized by themes of creation, abundance, renewal, and rebirth, and the ruler of the land of the dead was often also the creator deity. This reflects conceptual analogies drawn from observations of the death-and-rebirth cycles of the natural world, as well as reports of spiritual renewal and transformation following NDEs. The fact that the other realm was often situated in the west reflects the daily setting ("death") of the sun; though it also recalls NDE experiences of traveling into realms of light, which parallels the sun's journey into underworld darkness and its subsequent rebirth into daylight.

The basis on which one's afterlife fate was determined also clearly reflected local mores. Examples include behavior, wealth, social status, religious or ritual knowledge or devotion, mode of death, age, marital status, and profession. Tylor (1871: 69, 84–96) found that personal merit was particularly widespread, however. This supports Wiredu's (1996: 29) contention that "the principle of sympathetic impartiality" (i.e., morality) is one of the few human universals, despite variations in ethical ideals and social norms (cf. Brown 1991: 139). Even where afterlife fates were determined by factors other than individual behavior, those of higher status were likely considered by their very nature to represent the local ideal for positive conduct. Others deserved a better afterlife in compensation for earthly sufferings, or reward for a noble death.

Love is another cross-culturally occurring theme, especially in Orpheus myths and in reunions with deceased relatives. A homesick Black Elk visited his family during one of his NDEs, as did the Chamorra women. Hultkrantz (1957: 123, 224–5) wrote that love "bursts the boundaries of implacable death," for it is the driving motivation behind those who attempt to rescue a loved one from the other world. It is in recognition of this that the ruler of the realm of the dead allows the protagonist to retrieve the loved one's soul.

Other mythemes may reflect ritual activity. Specific trials and ordeals found in Orpheus myths (e.g., sleeplessness, fasting), for example, likely reflect the initiatory context of a shamanic experience (Eliade 1964: 313). The soul staying in the other world for a maximum of four days prior to return recurs in all three regions, which likely reflects the fact that visible signs of decomposition normally occur three to five days after death, after which point revivification would be impossible. As seen, a Coos NDEr's body had allegedly started to decompose when he waited five days to return. The Tlingit waited eight days before cremation in case the soul came back, reflecting the fact that decomposition would begin later in freezing climates. Waiting periods for funerary rituals in order to allow the soul time to depart were typical in Oceania (Moss 1925: 92, 96), where there were also various claims of souls returning to the body so many days after death that decomposition had begun.

There may also be some correlation between methods of corpse disposal and ideas about the location of the other world. Moss (1925: 15ff, 77) theorized that in Oceania's remote past, funerary practices involved returning the body to the ancestral homeland burial ground. This led to practices of "conveying the soul by means of magical rites and litanies" as a substitute for the long, arduous journey. The ancestral land then changed in conception to a distant spirit world reached by a return to the origin point. While conjectural, this is nonetheless compelling, and could conceivably be relevant to parts of North America. Moss (1925: 54, 56) also observed a correlation in Oceania between simple burial practices characterized by little ceremony or ritual, and beliefs in an afterlife on Earth, alongside a general vagueness and lack of interest in the issue. The case is similar in Africa, where common practices of abandoning the dying or throwing corpses to wild animals reflected local beliefs that spirits remain on Earth rather than going to some other world. However, there seems to be little consistent correlation between burial and belief in an underworld, or cremation and an afterlife in the sky (ibid. 71, 87; cf. Shushan 2009: 179).

Near-Death Experience, Culture, and Social Organization

Some NDE elements are common in indigenous societies cross-culturally, but are not characteristic of NDE reports from state societies. While this suggests some correspondence to social organization or scale, there is nevertheless thematic consistency with familiar NDE elements. Walking along a path or road, for example, is a particular means of conveyance to an afterlife realm, analogous to ascent or traveling through a tunnel or sliding down a mound (as in the Hopi examples). In societies without notions of a heavenly afterlife realm, the lack of an ascent motif is unsurprising. However, conceptions can be deeply culturally embedded as shown by the three 1960s/70s Bakongo NDEs that describe "walking very fast" along a road to the other world, despite the fact that they were Christians and would thus have had beliefs in a heavenly realm (Bockie 1993: 86–95). Counts (1983: 130) argued compellingly that the predominance of earthly-type places (houses, villages, roads, forests) in the Kaliai NDEs suggests a lack of distinction between "empirical and nonempirical" worlds. This is consistent with animistic beliefs that spirits dwell in forests, bodies of water, trees, and so forth, and could apply to many other cultures.

As a form of test or trial, prohibitions on eating food in the other world are a means of judging an individual's character, strength, and worthiness. The theme is often used to explain why particular individuals did not return from the other world, and may be a literary device. Interrogation by guardians, deities, or other spirits may also be seen in this light, as a means of testing whether a person belongs in the afterlife, and/or their level of knowledge and self-awareness. Being questioned or interrogated in the other world, or at some stage on the journey there, was extremely common in narratives from all regions.

Conversely, certain ostensibly "typical" NDE elements appear infrequently in the indigenous accounts. While traveling through a tunnel, for example, occurs in all three world areas, it is not common. Kellehear (1996: 36–7) convincingly argued that the tunnel specifically is merely symbolic of entering darkness and emerging into light—descriptions of which are numerous in indigenous societies. Indeed, many narratives described traveling through dark or narrow passageways leading to brightly-lit other realms. The passageways were variously described as chasms, canyons, trees, caves, houses, forests, or some unspecified "darkness" or "gloom." Furthermore, as noted above in relation to OBEs, some elements may have actually been experienced but not recounted. A lack of description of a particular element may simply mean that the individual did not feel it was a significant enough part of their experience to mention it, or that it would be taken for granted. The relative importance of each element is itself culturally as well as individually determined (ibid. 51). It is not the case, however, that NDEs in hunter-gatherer societies "lack hierarchical social structures" (McClenon 2006a: 4–5), as demonstrated by the presence of various deities, guardians, judges, chiefs, and whatever higher-ranking figure decides fates and sends NDErs back to their bodies. Indeed, social divisions would logically feature in realms seen as counterparts to Earth, and there are many descriptions to that effect.

Life reviews are particularly scarce in the indigenous accounts, and Kellehear (1996: 38–9, 52) correctly predicted that as more NDEs in small-scale societies were found, life reviews would not typically feature in them. He argued that unlike "historic religions" which "link death with conscience, and conscience with identity after death," in indigenous societies individuals would not "review their past personal lives in search of sense of identity." The life review would thus have "little private use or function." However, a sense of personal responsibility and accountability is reflected in descriptions of individual behavior determining afterlife fates, indicating the persistence of both personal identity and conscience after death (cf. Wade 2003: 110). Furthermore, while the prototypical panoramic life review was apparently unknown in all these regions, the theme of being confronted with one's earthly actions occasionally occurs, such as in descriptions of afterlife record-keepers who have accounts of the soul's deeds. This was presumably the meaning of the Tsuu T'ina Book of Life; and of Squ-sacht-un's experience of seeing a photograph of himself with "all the bad deeds of his life." The Ojibwe believed that the spirits of bad people were haunted in the next world by those they injured in this life. In Hawai'i, Ka-ilio-hae gave a history of his people in the other world; and the Maori believed that souls must give a chronicle of their lives before crossing the river to the other side. The Yoruba and Igbo deceased gave accounts of their lives to a deity in the other world. The Fon believed that a record of a person's good and bad deeds was kept in the otherworld, and used in the process of judgment. In a Fang iboga experience, a man saw his history being written by two spirits in the other world. As Kellehear acknowledges, there is evidence (Greyson 1983; Olson & Dulaney 1993; Fox 2003: 304) that the life review occurs primarily in cases of sudden death and is rare when death is expected (e.g., following an illness), which could help account for the general lack of the theme in our sources. There may also be a correlation between life review and duration of the NDE (Sartori 2008: 29), meaning that if they occur at a later stage of "death," differences in medical technology would limit their incidence. This would certainly apply to the indigenous societies, and may help to explain the lack of life reviews among them.

Acknowledging the problem of drawing conclusions from such a limited sample, Wade (2003: 108–9) also noted a common lack of life reviews in the Native American NDEs she discussed. Her other observations of NDE elements missing from indigenous societies, however, are not borne out by the present study. Traveling through darkness is common, for example, and there are descriptions of beings of light in all three world regions. Among numerous examples, the Ojibwe described a being of "mysterious fire," the Greenlandic Inuit described God as "big and shiny as the sun," the Pawnee deity Tirawa emerged from fire that enveloped the NDEr, and the Salish man Squ-sacht-un described a light as "trying my soul." Leaping through some mysterious fire to return to the body was also a common Native American motif. In Oceania, beings of light were described in myths from Hawai'i, New Zealand, New Guinea, and in a Christian NDE from late twentieth-century New Britain. Spirits of the dead were conceived as radiating light by the Kiwai, and in the Cook Islands the sun god illuminated the netherworld on its continual circuit. In Africa, a Chaga narrative described a man going to the sun-god in the other world, and encountering other radiant spirits. A Tswana NDEr also described radiant inhabitants of the other world. In Fang belief, the ruler of the spirit world, Eyen Zame, was a being of light; and in an iboga journey a woman in the moon streamed light from her heart. There are also many descriptions of realms radiant with light in all regions.

Other elements such as "personal euphoria" and "a different sense of body" (Wade 2003: 108–9) are implicit in many accounts, and overt in others. Osis and Haraldsson (1986: 182) suggested that the feelings of joy, peace, and calm the NDEr typically reports were symbolized by idealized mirror-images of Earth, and indeed the NDErs who claimed to have experienced the other world firsthand regularly described it as happy, joyous, worry-free, characterized by singing, dancing, and leisure. Revulsion at one's own body and a reluctance to return to it was most common in North America, Polynesia, and Melanesia, indicating that the bodiless afterlife state was far preferable to the earthly embodied one.

Wade saw similarities between her eleven Native American NDEs, one Hawaiian example (that of Kalima from 1892), and Medieval Christian otherworld journey narratives (Zaleski 1987). These include diverging approaches to the other world (one pleasant and one dangerous), guides who assist in overcoming obstacles, "and a soteriological message that ultimately supports the religious conventions of the day." The latter claim is problematic, for it was actually more often the case that the individual returned from the other world with new religious information or innovations. Obstacles or barriers of some kind seem to be universal, and dual paths are also common (in afterlife beliefs at least) outside the areas Wade mentions (e.g., ancient Egypt and India; Shushan 2009: 152).

Bourguignon (1973: 11) perceived a direct correlation between types of shamanic trance and social complexity. Possession trance corresponds to factors such as larger population, high degrees of hierarchy and social stratification, sedentism, and the presence of slavery. This is typified by sub-Saharan Africa, where possession trance was most prevalent. Societies that practiced "other" forms of trance (a category encompassing a wide range of experiences) had simpler forms of social organization (ibid. 20). However, Bourguignon (1973: 23) also acknowledged that many exceptions to her generalizations can be found. The criteria for a possession trance culture may apply neatly to certain predominantly non-possession-trance cultures in North America, for example. Nevertheless, the overall pattern Bourguignon observed supports the argument here that the importance placed on extraordinary experiences is culturally determined, though the experiences themselves occur across cultures. It is also worth noting Lanternari's (1963: 222) generalization that religious revitalization movements are absent from hunting societies (e.g., Australia) as opposed to agrarian societies (e.g., Melanesia).

Ultimately, while there is some truth in the notion that certain NDE elements are rooted in social structure (Belanti et al. 2008; Kellehear 2009: 135–7), the claim should not be overstated. It is also important to acknowledge that individual factors help to determine the character of an NDE. Even within a single culture (including in contemporary Western studies) no two experiences will be exactly alike. Indeed, certain elements that are typical of small-scale societies, such as food taboos, Orpheus themes, and the motif of "clashing rocks" as an afterlife obstacle, also appear in classical Greek myth (Hultkrantz 1957: 79).[12] It must also be stressed that the cultural dynamics surrounding attitudes toward NDEs and the afterlife are independent of social scale or organization. This is clear from the fundamental differences in the ways NDEs are received across our three distinct culture areas, despite some similarities of social scale and organization.

Diffusionism Revisited

While Christian themes are in some cases obvious (particularly in revitalization movements), any suggestion that external cultural influences could account for all the similarities between the narratives reviewed here across three continents would be wholly unsustainable. The Indologist Michael Witzel (2013) has attempted to trace entire world mythologies from historical periods back to an Upper Palaeolithic (40,000 BP) so-called Laurasian system (Asia and the Americas), the origins of which ostensibly lie in the Gondwana system (Africa, Australia, and New Guinea) when humans migrated from Africa beginning c. 65,000 BP. He further claims to have traced "a few traits" to a yet earlier system dating to "the time of the so-called African Eve of the geneticists, some 130,000 years ago"—which is 126,800 years *before the invention of writing* (and some 90,000 years before the earliest unambiguous figurative art). Witzel's contention that all "major world religions" have been built on Laurasian myth is wildly speculative. Among the manifold conceptual and methodological problems are frequent overgeneralizations based on vague cross-cultural similarities, the possibility of "reconstructing" theoretical past mythologies for which no textual evidence exists, equating movements of prehistoric population groups with diffusion of myths they may or may not have had, and erroneous claims that certain mythemes occur only in certain areas. Witzel's own acknowledgments of the seemingly endless exceptions to the alleged rules of what is typical of each cultural system undermine his own basic claims. Nor can the theory adequately address patterns of cross-cultural differences, such as those revealed in the present study—particularly the scarcity of afterlife journey shamanism and associated narratives in Africa and Micronesia that are common in other parts of the world, including Melanesia; and the ways in which types of shamanism often correlate with attitudes toward death, afterlife, and NDEs. If Africa is the root culture, and if the argument of grand diffusion is based on claims of similarity, such fundamental differences must be explained. Witzel's attempt to explain differences in terms of cultural evolution, characterizing the Laurasian system as sophisticated and complex in comparison to the simplistic and archaic Gondwana system, is equally speculative, as well as wholly subjective and generally dubious (not to mention possibly ethnocentric if not racist). As with most grand diffusionist theories, Witzel's presumes an unlikely continuity of particular beliefs and practices over vast stretches of time, unaccompanied by language or other cultural traits (including names of deities, religious terminology, etc.) (cf. Thompson 2013).

Hultkrantz (1957: 199–206) was also intrigued by the possibility of diffusion beginning with early hunting cultures, spreading throughout Eurasia to "Asiatic-Oceanic" societies and then to North America. He suggested that the wide distribution of intra–North American Orpheus narratives was due to diffusion, and that an even wider distribution (from across the Pacific[13] and Bering strait) was not implausible—particularly in light of similarities between North American, Eurasian, and Oceanic narratives. He did, however, acknowledge problems with his reasoning—including the fact that there were actually more similarities between Greek and North American traditions than between North American and Asian ones. Similarity, he discovered, is not in itself an indicator of diffusion.

As noted earlier, the notion that shamanism and associated beliefs spread from Siberia and Central Asia to elsewhere in the world is ultimately unprovable, if not unsupportable. The earliest archaeological evidence for shamanism in both China and Siberia is from c. 3000 BCE (the earliest textual evidence is from fourth-century BCE China) (Johansen 1999: 46–7; Shushan 2009: 32, 112ff, 171–2), suggesting local independent development. The migrations over the Bering land bridge occurred too far in the remote past to make diffusion of religious beliefs and practices to North America and elsewhere a compelling argument, particularly considering the lack of evidence, and the many differences between Chinese, Siberian, and North American traditions. Common characteristics certainly could have developed independently in Siberia/Central Asia and North America long after the migrations. Links between Siberia/Central Asia and Oceania are weak, despite some distant genetic evidence for Australia. It is possible, however, that elements of shamanism and associated beliefs spread from other areas of Asia to the Pacific islands. Diffusion from Africa to Oceania (and thence to North America) would seem to be groundless speculation, particularly in light of cross-cultural differences.

Diffusionist perspectives discount the possibility of independent invention and ignore the dynamics of cultural interaction, seeing influence as spreading only one way. Sidky (2010: 78) points out that when diffusion does occur, it is generally of single traits (e.g., tobacco) rather than entire cultural complexes. It is not enough to argue that cross-cultural similarities are due to diffusion simply because they are similarities, while differences must be diversions from some hypothetical root culture in the distant, prehistoric past (cf. Shushan 2009: 32f). The cross-cultural recurrence of types of religious practices or beliefs does not indicate global diffusion any more than the cross-cultural existence of mourning, reasoning, agricultural and hunting techniques, social hierarchies, gender roles, and so forth. Conversely, historical connection does not necessarily mean cultural similarity. Despite common origins in the distant past, Siberian and Navajo shamanic initiation practices differed more than those of the Lakota, Shona, and Zulu, who had no such connection (Thorpe 1993: 130).

As Bierhorst (1988: 21) pointed out, "it is well to keep in mind that even the most isolated tribe has, or has had, neighbors and those neighbors themselves have neighbors, and the chain extends through countries and across continents." Varying degrees of diffusion are evident within culture areas as shown by intertextuality of narrative genres (e.g., Orpheus myths), and missionary influence is sometimes clear. At most, however, diffusion can be only a partial explanation and primarily at the intraregional level. Wider-scale diffusion across continents and vast eras of time is in most cases almost entirely speculative. There are good reasons for the fact that, over the last hundred years or so, none of the attempts at grand diffusionist theories have been sustainable and that such theories are largely relegated to outmoded nineteenth-century cultural evolutionist thinking.

Finally, despite consistency between the Classical Greek Orpheus myth and North American counterparts, as Hultkrantz (1957: 184–5, 198) pointed out, the earliest documented Native American example was recorded at a time of scarcely any European presence. It is highly unlikely that explorers or missionaries would devote their time to teaching Greek myths to the people they were trying to conquer or convert—a point that also applies to Africa and especially Oceania. Furthermore, the narratives differ enough to suggest independent invention.

Cross-Cultural Near-Death Experiences and the Survival Hypothesis

Ultimately, the NDE either originates as a neurophysiological occurrence or it is a genuine indicator of the survival of consciousness after physical death (the survival hypothesis). The possibility of the latter has no bearing on the overall arguments of this book, and the experiential source hypothesis makes no commitment to either materialist or survival interpretations. Nevertheless, considering the nature of the subject, this study would be incomplete without considering implications for the debate. As well as the vast majority of NDErs themselves, prominent members of the scientific and medical communities have at least tentatively reached conclusions favoring the survival hypothesis, including, among others, the neuroscientists Mario Beauregard, Peter Fenwick, and Edward F. Kelly; cardiologists Pim van Lommel, Sam Parnia, and Michael Sabom; psychiatrists Bruce Greyson and Ian Stevenson; psychologists Kenneth Ring and Carlos Alvarado; physician Jeffrey Long; biologists Robert Lanza and Rupert Sheldrake; and quantum physicists Amit Goswami and Henry Stapp. Many were highly skeptical of NDEs, and only became sympathetic to the survival hypothesis as a result of their own research. This is in contrast to certain scientists who are critical of survival interpretations (e.g., psychologists Susan Blackmore, Chris French, and Jason Braithwaite; anesthesiologist G. M. Woerlee), despite not having conducted clinical research specifically on NDEs (cf. Greyson 2007: 140–1). In other words, those who investigate the problem firsthand often come to very different conclusions than those who theorize at a distance.

While a review of the arguments for and against a survival interpretation of NDEs is beyond our scope, the most recent surveys of the state of the field indicate that NDEs have not been adequately "explained away" by materialist theories (e.g., Hagen 2017; Greyson et al. 2009; Kelly et al. 2007). In a meta-analysis of four recent studies of NDEs in cardiac arrest patients in Holland, the United States, and the United Kingdom, van Lommel (2010: 156) concluded there was "No physiological or psychological explanation for an NDE," and that the experience occurs *during* cardiac arrest, which "involves a loss of all brain function." The latest international experiment, the AWARE study (AWAreness during REsuscitation) has apparently confirmed that consciousness can persist when no brain activity is detectable, during a period of clinical death prior to resuscitation. This was widely believed to be medically impossible, and has serious implications for the survival hypothesis (Parnia et al. 2014). Nor should claims of veridical observations during NDEs be ignored. Not a few individuals have accurately described events they claim to have witnessed during OBEs (Holden 2009), and some have reported NDEs in which they met recently deceased individuals not known to have died at the time of the experience (Greyson 2010).

These kinds of anomalous information retrieval during NDEs are also attested cross-culturally, as are other "supernatural" occurrences surrounding the phenomenon, and they often convince people of the genuineness of the experience. Such cases are sometimes enlisted to "prove" the veridicality of the experience to others. Among the numerous examples in Oceania, Kawelu (Hawai'i), Ua Halai (New Guinea), and the queen of Tahiti were all miraculously able to return to their bodies even when decomposition had begun. In a shamanic narrative from the Marquesan Islands, Tiki-tu-ao returned from his experience with an ultimately verified premonition of his brother's death; while a Maori Christian had his own impending death accurately predicted by afterlife spirits. In the second 1980s New Britain NDE, Andrew saw the spirit of a woman he knew, unaware that she had recently died. Claims of sacred objects or items associated with food production (e.g., yams, fish) being brought back from the spirit world were found in the Cook Islands, New Guinea, Fiji, and Australia. In Melanesia, the Kiwai man Asai made a mark on a tree on his return from the spirit world in order to prove the story of his journey. In North America, White Bull returned with the knowledge of medicinal roots to cure his illness. Black Elk and Bini both claimed to have brought back information about Christ without prior knowledge of Christianity. In the Deg Hit'an NDE, the girl saw her recently deceased father in the spirit world without previously knowing that he had died. Descriptions of NDEs themselves also acted as proof, particularly if they corroborated earlier NDEs, such as in the case of Don Talayesva. In Africa, accurate prophetic and precognitive information was obtained in the other world regarding marriage (Chaga), the deaths of particular individuals (Mbundu, Tswana, Fang), and the location of missing property (Yoruba, Zulu). An Efé man brought a goat and other gifts back from the spirit-world, a Mbundu doctor brought a bracelet, and a twentieth-century Bakongo NDEr returned with fertility medicine. In the Zulu narrative of Bandla, a spirit scratched his eye to convince people of his otherworld journey. One Sotho man was given the gift of literacy by the Christian god, and another learned about baptism in heaven.

Encounters with deceased relatives were also widely considered to be evidential, and claims that a practice or belief originated in the other world commonly served to legitimize it. As Lang (1894: 345) noted, "if a medicine-man not only went into trances, but brought back from these expeditions knowledge otherwise inaccessible, then there were better grounds for believing in a consciousness exerted apart from the body than if there were no evidence but that of non-veridical dreams." It is also likely that more detailed NDE accounts that incororated elements of established beliefs would have been more compelling, and seen as verifying accepted truths.

Some of the criticisms raised earlier in relation to the various constructivist theories could conceivably indicate support for the survival hypothesis. For example, NDEs cannot be due to cultural expectation because not all cultures expect them. Most cultures nevertheless not only experience them but also attach the same meanings to them, interpreting them as relating to survival. Despite the human capacity for critical thinking, and indigenous distinctions between experience types, it is interesting that the default belief cross-culturally is in the actuality of these experiences, rather than considering them dreams or hallucinations. Nowhere are NDEs interpreted as proving the finality of death. This includes contemporary Western atheistic scientists and philosophers who changed their beliefs as a result of their own NDEs (as discussed in Chapter 1).

As argued earlier, neither our natural predisposition to afterlife beliefs nor any other cognitive evolutionist or neurotheological model has been adequate to explain NDEs in all their manifestations. Nor has a functionalist origin of NDEs been demonstrated, in light of their spontaneous, inner, private nature and the fact that they are associated with the end of life. As Shiels (1980: 739) found in relation to OBEs cross-culturally, none of the usual constructivist social scientific explanations for religious phenomena are adequate to explain them (i.e., "the social control, crisis, and dream theories"). The unique combination of cross-cultural thematic and interpretative *consistency* with culturally idiosyncratic *variation* indicates that the experience can be neither entirely culturally constructed, nor entirely neurophysiological or metaphysical.

Some critics invoke what Karl Popper called "promissory materialism" (Greyson 2007: 142), believing that whatever may eventually be proven by NDEs in cross-cultural contexts will inevitably reinforce a scientific materialist explanation. This is exemplified by Keith Augustine's (2007: 116) statement that if NDEs prove to be universal, they "would be best explained in neuroscientific terms." However, universality does not specify a metaphysical *or* a neuroscientific conclusion. Greyson (2007: 142) argued that models of NDEs as either hallucinatory *or* transcendental create a false dichotomy, for the phenomenology of NDEs suggests "that some NDE features may well be linked to physiological events, some to sociopsychological belief, and others to no known materialist cause." Indeed, as stressed here, any cohesive theory of NDEs must take into account a combination of universal, cultural, and individual factors. While not the most parsimonious approach, as Greyson stated, "a model is not preferable if it achieves parsimony only by ignoring what it cannot explain." It is unsurprising that complex, multifaceted phenomena would require a complex, multifaceted explanatory model.

Nevertheless, accepting NDEs at face value poses challenges for philosophical models of what the afterlife could possibly be like. Once again, the problem is how to reconcile the cross-cultural differences and similarities—specifically, whether the concept of a panhuman afterlife is intelligible in light of cultural, religious, and individual diversity of beliefs and experiences. Critics such as Augustine (2007: 116–7) find cross-cultural difference to be fatally problematic for the survival hypothesis, and believe that in order to be metaphysically comprehensible, any actual afterlife must be the same for everyone. The evidence that NDEs combine thematic similarities with cultural/individual differences does much to address such concerns, however.

The model that best addresses the problem remains that of the Welsh philosopher H. H. Price (1953). He posited a world of mental images, a mind-dependent reality that to the disembodied spirit seems to be just as real as life on Earth. As in dreams, the soul would retain the impression of having a "physical" presence and use of the senses. Indeed, it might be so similar that individuals "would have considerable difficulty in realizing they were dead" (ibid. 5)—a theme reflected in some NDE accounts and afterlife journey myths. The afterlife is a state in which *"imaging* replaces sense-perception . . . by providing us with objects about which we could have thoughts, emotions and wishes" (ibid. 6). Disembodied spirits could interact with each other, communicating telepathically and appearing as "telepathic apparitions" (ibid. 11). Furthermore, like-minded individuals (who share, for example, similar memories, ideas, values, or culture) would collectively create their surroundings, with each soul contributing to the group afterlife while also bringing personal, idiosyncratic features into being. The result would be numerous different shared dream-worlds.

As Price (1953: 16) summarized, "after death everyone does have his own dream, but there is still some overlap between one person's dream and another's, because of telepathy." The way the "worlds" manifest would be determined by the co-creators' "memories and desires." A person's cultural background and individual psychology would thus manifest within the experience. The barriers between the conscious and unconscious minds might dissolve after death, leading to experiences created by states of mind both positive (e.g., love, harmony, unity, wish-fulfillment) and negative (e.g., guilt, fear, anger, resentment) (ibid. 22). Because "the world you experience after death would depend upon the kind of person you are," some individuals would have unpleasant realities (ibid. 21) and experience an "image-purgatory" as the "automatic consequence of his own desires." This corresponds to the NDE theme of evaluation of one's earthly life, and could account for reports of distressing NDEs. The individual's character—with all its internal conflicts and contradictions—remains stable in the disembodied state, and influences what he or she experiences. To some extent, then, altering and improving one's afterlife would involve altering and improving one's character—just as in the present life.

Price (1953: 3) noted parallels between his theory and Mahayana Buddhism, the Hindu notion of Kama Loka ("world of desire"), and ideas formed by the French philosopher C. J. Ducasse and the British parapsychologist Whately Carington. There are also parallels in the Vedas and in the afterlife beliefs of other cultures (Shushan 2009: 188–90). The philosopher and theologian (and Price's student) John Hick (1976: 414) noted consistencies between Price's theory, information allegedly communicated from afterlife spirits via Western mediums, and the description of intermediate afterlife states in the *Bardo Thödol* (*Tibetan Book of the Dead*, c. eighth century CE). In the latter, one has an expected set of intermediate postmortem experiences, though their character is determined by cultural and individual expectation. The experiences include leaving the body, an encounter with a bright light, having a "karmic body" formed by one's "own past and deeds," encounters with good and evil entities (some of whom radiate light), darkness, fear, judgment, and punishment followed by rebirth. Rare enlightened souls, however, will recognize the light as the Clear Light of Reality, merge with it into a state of nirvana, and escape the cycle of rebirth (Hick 1976: 400–3). Similarly, the Buddhism scholar Carl Becker (1993: 82–3, 179–80) saw close correspondences between Price's theories, NDEs, and "both scriptural and experiential accounts" in Pure Land Buddhism. He concluded that the similarities reflect "common religious experience, pointing to a reality envisioned in the West as well: an idealist life after death." He found this notion to be the most reasonable, summarizing, "Since it is the mind or consciousness whose survival we are considering, it need not surprise us that the realms of which it is conscious after the decease of the physical body are also mind dependent" (ibid. 115).

Hick (1976: 270–1) proposed a modification to Price's multiple soul-group theory, in which minds "are pooled to produce a common environment . . . by the cancellings out and mutual reinforcements of the multitude of individual desires," resulting in "a single post-mortem world, formed by the memories and desires of all the human beings who have died since man began." The realm would develop over time, "as new sets of memories are contributed to the common stock" and "the prevailing pattern of human desires changes." Such a scenario, however, might not account for the cultural/individual differences between NDEs; and the idea that there could ever be a universal "prevailing pattern of human desires" seems unlikely.

Another alternative is that the other world is as objective as this one, but that things are only *perceived* differently according to the individual. Perceptions would simply be personal mental interpretations of the structural, thematic "dream" environment—in other words, impressions of objective concepts made manifest by the individual mind. Thus, all may travel to the same spirit village, but the houses will be perceived variously as Fijian *bures*, Sudano-Sahelian adobes, Lakota tipis, and so on. Perceptions could also be shared or even intermingled. As Becker (1993: 121) described, "While some of the scenery and images perceived in such states will be unique to each individual, other features may be intersubjectively perceived by many consciousnesses." As in Pure Land Buddhism, deceased relatives and other spirits would be real identities rather than illusory, and souls of the dead would retain free will and volition rather than being subject to the wishes of others. There would be "various regions suited to certain types of consciousness," while only "minor events" could be altered on an individual level (Becker 1984: 61, 65–6). Becker

(1993: 121) found this model to be the best way to account for both NDEs and Mahayana Buddhist meditation accounts, and it is consistent with the evidence that NDEs themselves are composed of cross-culturally thematically stable features that are experienced in culture- and individual-specific ways. Put another way, the notion of a mind-dependent afterlife helps to illustrate—and perhaps explain ontologically—our model of NDEs. Such a model is also compatible with the many reports of feelings of unity and of having divine-like abilities during NDEs (cf. Shushan 2009: 186–91).

Greyson (2007: 139) similarly pointed out that cross-cultural diversity of NDEs could indicate different perceptions of the same phenomena. Consistent with this model is the suggestion by Osis and Haraldsson (1986: 182) that scenes of idealized earthly beauty are "symbolizations" of the feelings of joy, peace, and calm typically reported by NDErs. The psychologists Adam Rock and Stanley Krippner (2011: 174) outlined a similar hypothesis in relation to shamanic journeying imagery: that the "mental images" experienced by shamans are "real" though essentially representations of the place, object, or entity to which they refer, and experienced according to the individual's beliefs. As they summarized, "while a metaphysical entity exists independently of a percipient, the outward appearance . . . of that entity will be 'refracted' through the percipient's religio-cultural-linguistic lens."

Because individuals remain conscious with the ability to understand and evaluate the NDE in progress, the analogy of lucid dreaming is apt. During such experiences, individuals become aware that they are dreaming, though this does not immediately or necessarily alter other elements of the dream—the landscape, situation, or other individuals involved. Lucid dreamers may, however, achieve a state in which it is possible to change or create dreamscapes with conscious intent and full awareness that they are dreaming. While such control is rare and often achieved only through practice (e.g., "dream yoga" in Tibetan Buddhism), without the confines of the physical brain and the five senses, it is conceivable that the "home state" of disembodied consciousness is something like the creatively interactive state of the advanced lucid dreamer (cf. Badham 1982: 120; Shushan 2009: 186–7). As Becker (1993: 118) speculated, "a radical removal of the limitations of consciousness" might occur as the brain's filters are terminated upon bodily death. In Price's (1953: 7–8) model, an individual becomes aware that he or she is dead as a result of discovering the "rather peculiar causal laws" of the afterlife state, such as the ability to appear in a particular place (or, rather, the mental image equivalent of the place) simply by thinking about it. Similarly, experiences such as being out of the body, communicating with spirit beings telepathically, and encountering deceased relatives are what often cause NDErs to realize they are "dead." The psychologist J. Timothy Green (1995: 53–4) compared the lucid dream state to NDEs, citing common elements such as OBE, darkness, light, feelings of intense clarity, euphoria, and transcendence.

Interestingly, the concept of a mind-dependent afterlife is reflected in the beliefs of some of the cultures discussed here. Oliver (1989: 771) found that the idea of a collective merging with the ancestors or other spirit beings was common in Oceania. In Hawai'i it was believed that souls of the dead were "united in thought and all joined together . . . in harmony" with relatives, friends, and acquaintances (Kamakau 1866–71: 49–51) in the realm ruled by "Kanenuiakea, a single god and many gods in one god" (ibid. 57). There were also different realms depending on one's island of origin or ancestral lineage. In the Cook Islands there was a belief in groups of souls ascending together with the sun-god (Gill 1876: 159). The statement from New Britain that the otherworld could be seen "if our eyes were turned so that what is inside the head were now outside" might also indicate a self-created afterlife (Brown 1910: 192–6, 210). When "the stone of thought" was encountered by the Maewo on the afterlife journey, the deceased's presence of mind and control of memories determined whether they would continue to the spirit world or return to Earth. The Kiwai believed that people from the same villages lived together in the spirit world; while the Aboriginal Australians believed in souls of the dead merging with the ancestors. In North America, A Ho-Chunk shaman recounted the ability to travel anywhere at will by thought alone (Radin 1923: 267), and according to Ho-Chunk conceptions, the spirit must be free of fear and doubt when undergoing afterlife trials, indicating that psychological and emotional factors shaped the nature of the experience. The Plains Cree NDEr could not cross the river to the other world when he recalled his bad deeds; and the Tlingit man could only proceed to the other world when he thought about it. The Wyandot, Ojibwe, and other Algonquian peoples believed in culturally divided realms for indigenous people and Europeans, while the Wyandot also believed in afterlife divisions based on social groupings. The Pawnee believed that each family had their own afterlife village. In Africa, the idea of transcending individuality into "collective immortality" in the spirit world was common (Mbiti 1990: 160). It is typified by the Lango concept of Jok Orongo, the universal spirit of which the soul forms a part.

Mind-dependent afterlife models overcome Augustine's (2007: 117) claim that "the greater the diversity between different NDE accounts, the less credible the NDE consistency argument for survival." The objection, in any case, seems to be based primarily on a preconception of what an afterlife must be like and the rules that must govern it—that it is the same for everyone by virtue of our "common humanity" irrespective of cultural diversity (ibid. 120–1). There is no reason to believe that disembodied individuals would cease to process their experiences in their own idiosyncratic modes, including the use of personal and cultural memory, imagination, and visual metaphor. A metaphysical interpretation of NDEs is not predicated on the negation of cross-cultural difference (Irwin 2007: 160–1; Kellehear 2007: 151). Without a physical body and in the absence of physical surroundings, the default state of disembodied consciousness would likely be to model reality by using the tools of the subconscious, resulting in the creation of an apparently visual, quasi-physical experience. Descriptions of "visual" and "physical" NDE phenomena could be secondary elaborations of an ineffable experience as the individual attempts to make descriptive and conceptual sense of the thematic impressions (cf. Greyson 2007: 138; Kellehear 2007: 149). Kalweit (1984: 64) saw descriptions of afterlife barriers and perils in indigenous societies as "culturally conditioned visions of an ego which is still caught in the grip of social and cultural models of the imagination and has not yet learned to adapt to the new environment." Such experiences are attempts "to make the surviving consciousness aware of the fact that it itself constitutes the world of the Beyond" (ibid. 66–7). Furthermore, just as NDEs are culturally shaped, Kellehear (2007: 148) points out that "supernatural factors may further shape, prompt, or moderate the social and psychological factors" of NDEs, contributing to the symbiotic whole.

It should also be noted that Augustine (2007: 173–4) characterized cross-cultural NDEs as being far less consonant than they really are, sharing only "broadly defined elements that we would expect to see among those who feel that they are dying." As well as being vague as to what constitutes those shared elements, the claim presumes that end-of-life concerns are universal, which is not supported by the evidence. Beliefs in the continued presence of ancestors on Earth, for example, would not prompt an NDE involving going to another realm and meeting deceased relatives. As demonstrated in the present study and elsewhere, Augustine's assertion that elements such as "feelings of peace, OBEs, passages through a tunnel or darkness toward light, and life reviews . . . are strikingly absent from most extant nonWestern NDE accounts" is insupportable. Though life reviews per se are rare cross-culturally, they are at least attested, as are thematic equivalents. The other four elements are some of the most common.

In summary, just as we dream in symbols—giving form and apparent "reality" to fears, desires, worries, hopes, and other abstract concepts without conscious intent or deliberation—it is conceivable that we manifest our afterlife experiences in the same way. In contrast, however, NDEs are nearly universal on contextual, thematic, and interpretative levels, while also sharing highly specific cross-cultural similarities on the symbolic and narrative levels. The most common features can therefore give us some idea of what an afterlife could conceivably be like, including OBE, darkness, light, heightened awareness and emotions, meeting spirits of the dead, personal evaluation, and so on—all given specific form by our individual and cultural particularities (cf. Shushan 2009: 188).

While it is thus possible to accommodate the cross-cultural evidence to a philosophical model of the afterlife, this is very different from claiming that the cross-cultural data actively *supports* such a hypothesis. Arguments that the reality of NDEs is demonstrated by associated clairvoyant or transformative phenomena (cf. Lang 1894: 345) are also problematic. Even if we grant that such phenomena are veridical, they do not necessarily point to an actual afterlife, technically proving only the possibility of clairvoyance and transformation resulting from near-death states. Conversely, if we grant that NDEs *are* evidence for survival after death, that evidence tells us more about a transitional period than about any ultimate fate. Survival itself might be temporary or even brief; a mind-dependent afterlife might be an intermediate state prior to some other state of being (Price 1953: 25) or annihilation. It is even conceivable that different postmortem fates await different people, whether determined by culture, belief, or some unknown factor: a mind-dependent realm; a transcendent, transpersonal state; remaining on Earth in ghostly form; reincarnation; heavens and hells; or simply dying with the body (Becker 1993: 120–1).

Interdisciplinary Models

While many theories discussed thus far have merit, none of them alone can adequately account for all the similarities and differences across cultures, nor for the varying relationships between experiences and beliefs. Some earlier scholars who engaged with these problems also saw the necessity of combining the most persuasive aspects of competing models. Moss (1925: 132) attributed conceptions of the other world in "primitive peoples" to a combination of (1) "The desire for a better existence" resulting in conceptions of the other realm as an "Idealized Continuance" of the present one (following Tylor); (2) "Personal experience" such as "dreams and hallucinations" that underlie "the notion of unreality of the spirit-land where ghosts lead a vague and shadowy existence"; and (3) "A limited mental horizon." Differences are due to "the comparative predominance of one of these factors," together with "such religious or ethnological considerations as funerary ritual and priestly doctrines, ideas of punishment, or of a return to the original home of the tribe." While life in the other world is rarely portrayed as "a vague and shadowy existence," and though we do not subscribe to Moss's racist evolutionism concerning "limited mental horizons," the incorporation of an experiential source hypothesis with a psychological wish for a better world to come, and an acknowledgment of local sociocultural factors, is broadly in keeping with the arguments here.

Perhaps the most useful and sophisticated early interdisciplinary model was that of the American anthropologist Robert Lowie (1936: xvii, 322). While attempting to explain religion per se rather than afterlife beliefs specifically, he noted "the great frequency with which the Extraordinary or Supernatural assumes the aspect of the Holy." He emphasized "the differential response to normal and abnormal stimuli," and the "*spontaneous* distinction" humans make "between Natural and Supernatural" experience. Citing the Crow as an example, he maintained that the most significant element of religion "consists in the memory of an ineffable experience of an extraordinary character: it is the Extraordinary nature of this subjective experience that hallows its objective correlates, lifting them, too, into the empyrean of the Extraordinary." Lowie (1936: 284) further stressed cultural context, and that varying modes of assimilation of an experience are due to local factors, writing,

> the Extraordinary is potentially ambivalent, [and] may be credited with either a mysterious power to confer benefits or a weird tendency to destroy, and which of the alternatives prevails is a matter of chance according to the specific circumstances surrounding the origin of the custom.

This is neatly illustrated by the differences between Native American and African responses to NDEs. Importantly, Lowie (1936: 221ff) also acknowledged the role of the individual in religious innovations:

> The individual is not merged *completely* in his social milieu,—he reacts to it *as* an individual, that is, differently from every other group member. The cultural tradition of his people dominates him, but it is reflected in a distinctive fashion by each psyche. Were it otherwise, novel conceptions could never arise.

Less successful was Chadwick's (1952: 93–4, 104) mix of speculative diffusionism and vague cultural constructivism. However, her acknowledgment of the NDE as a discrete phenomenon that had a role in religious beliefs is noteworthy. She wrote that those who undertake afterlife journeys are often not shamans or other "professionals," and that "Such journeys are everywhere attributed to quite ordinary men and women." She concluded

> that the spiritual adventures of man are moulded by the traditional spiritual experiences of the past. His excursions into the speculative world follow ancient routes, trodden long ago by spiritual thinkers of other religions. Local conditions and personal impulse will prompt and modify and recreate the imaginative effort of a tohunga, or a shaman, or a druid;

but the routes along which his imagination can travel . . . have been determined elsewhere long ago in Erech and in Thebes.

While the attempt at theoretical eclecticism is welcome, this model unfortunately assumes that beliefs are necessarily rooted in previous "other" traditions,
implying that only people in ancient societies had the capacity for extraordinary
experience and that subsequent narratives are a result of intertextuality. Nor does
it delineate the role of cultural construction in relation to diffusion.

More recently, McClenon (1994: 37) noted that many features of extraordinary experiences are to be found in Stith Thompson's worldwide *Motif-Index of
Folk Literature* (1955–58: 38, 184), "suggesting that individual experiences engen-
der certain motifs." The most relevant here include "Soul journeys from the body,"
"Resuscitated man relates visions of beyond," "Dead returns to life and tells of
journey to land of dead," and "Return from dead to teach repentance." Focusing
on Medieval Asian and European NDEs, McClenon (2002: 126–7) argued:

> Although culturally shaped features exist within near-death episodes,
> recurring elements probably contributed to convergence in concepts of
> heaven and hell in Medieval Christian and Buddhist thought. Medieval
> accounts from Europe, China, and Japan are remarkably similar and often
> include narrative features that do not coincide with the prevailing theolo-
> gies of their time. People from all eras found these accounts interesting
> and accepted them as evidence regarding the afterlife.

Relating the experience generated "folk traditions regarding life after death."
McClenon (1994: 184) concluded that the NDE has "primary features that
shaped religious ideologies in a common direction," though the accounts also
"served the didactic needs of the eras in which they were transcribed and reveal
traits associated with the religious imagination." Similarities in the hierarchical systems of afterlife realms reflect "Parallel hierarchical social structures" in
Eastern and Western societies.

The clinical psychologist Gary Groth-Marnat (1994: 11) also concluded
that some features of NDEs "are clearly influenced by culture but there are others which seem universal." He stressed the importance of individual factors, and
advocated incorporating possible "universal/archetypal images as well as biological factors such as the neurological organization of the right temporal lobe."
In their analysis of existing studies of cross-cultural NDEs, Belanti et al. (2008
130) similarly found that

There are aspects of NDEs that are clearly influenced by culture, but there are also features that are universal such as altered states of consciousness and generalized visions. The content and meanings of NDEs may also vary historically, depending upon the level of influence and involvement between religion and society. Although there may be a core component to NDE, cultural influences must be considered when attempting to interpret individual narratives.

Subscribing to a form of theoretical eclecticism, they concluded:

> The variability across cultures is most likely to be due to our interpretation and verbalizing of such esoteric events through the filters of language, cultural experiences, religion, education and their influence on our belief systems either shedding influence as an individual variable or more often perhaps by their rich interplay between these factors. (Belanti et al. 2008: 121)

Kripal (2010: 253) also supports an interdisciplinary experiential source hypothesis, writing that "paranormal phenomena . . . clearly vibrate at the origin point of many popular religious beliefs, practices, and images," including those concerning "the existence, immortality, and transmigration of the soul." To gain a comprehensive understanding of these dynamics, Kripal (2010: 256) proposes research combining neuroscience, psychical research, literary theory, and history of religions.

Summary, Conclusions, and Epistemological Implications

The North America chapter presents a virtual model of the experiential source hypothesis: that NDEs as filtered through cultural/individual layers are commonly the basis for afterlife beliefs. There are nearly seventy narratives describing or attesting to ostensibly documentary Native American NDEs across the continent,[14] dating from the late sixteenth to early twentieth centuries. More than twenty overt indigenous statements testify that local Native American afterlife beliefs, and even whole religious movements, commonly originated in NDEs. Shamanic practices were often intended to replicate NDEs, which provided a road map for the shaman to negotiate his or her culturally situated journey to the other world.

Africa presents a nearly opposite scenario to Native America. From a perhaps even more extensive range of sources from across the continent, scarcely ten NDEs were found, and only two statements that afterlife beliefs originated in them. Such a stark difference can be explained by the crucial role of local sociore-ligious contexts surrounding beliefs in life after death. While there is, of course, a great diversity of cultures and beliefs across every continent, there are neverthe-less some distinctively African regional tendencies very different from those in North America. Generally speaking, African speculations and statements about personal survival and the nature of the afterlife were comparatively rare, as were mythological narratives of underworld journeys and heavenly ascents. Instead, attitudes toward death were more often characterized by high degrees of fear and avoidance, including beliefs in the potentially malevolent influences of ancestor spirits, and that death is fundamentally unnatural and due either to violence or witchcraft. Shamanic-type activities were focused on spirit possession rather than soul travel, and fears of disembodiment were not uncommon. Indeed, most of the few existing African NDEs were related in contexts of suspicion or aberra-tion, with typical reports involving those who returned from death being "killed again," and/or suspected of being possessed by spirits, or of being zombies reani-mated by witches. Corpses were frequently seen as sources of pollution and con-tamination, while burial was often conducted immediately after death while the body was still warm. Clearly, these were not receptive environments for NDEs to contribute to afterlife beliefs, let alone to be reported or to even occur.

This contrasts sharply with North America, where long-standing traditions of otherworldly shamanic practices and visionary experiences undoubtedly meant greater cultural receptivity to the phenomenon. Furthermore, as the exceptions that prove the rule, nearly all the African NDEs were from Bantu cultures, which had a correspondingly greater tendency toward more detailed afterlife beliefs and myths. In short, the differences in orientation of afterlife beliefs between the African and Native American cases reflect different local attitudes toward death and spirits per se. These attitudes, in turn, affected receptivity of NDE phe-nomena, with Africa placing cultural restrictions on them, and North America valorizing them.

Similar conclusions have been reached by the psychologists Natasha Tassell-Matamua and Mary Murray (2014: 22) in their study of 220 NDEs from New Zealand. They found that Maori respondents reported "deeper NDEs" than those of European background, and suggested that they had "greater cultural tolerance and acceptance of transcendental experiences, and supernatural beliefs and explanations for unusual experiences." Cultural orientation thus influenced the content as well as the depth of the experience: "a cultural response affirm-ing experiences such as NDEs may result in less psychological resistance, thus enabling the phenomenology of the NDE to unfold more readily, leading to deeper NDEs." Tassell-Matamua and Murray also concluded that individuals from a culture with more positive attitudes toward NDEs would more readily relate the experience to others, "whereas those from less affirming cultures may downplay their responses."

From Oceania there were thirty-six accounts describing or attesting to historical NDEs, and an almost casual acceptance of them—though they are confined to Polynesia (20) and Melanesia (16). Also from these regions were nineteen overt statements that NDEs were the origin of afterlife beliefs, or that they supplemented or confirmed them (eleven from Polynesia, eight from Melanesia). This is in addition to claims of obtaining specific rituals, instructions, knowledge, or sacred songs and dances in the otherworld. In striking contrast to the preponderance of myths in Africa explaining why people did *not* return from the dead, in Polynesia and Melanesia there was a widely occurring integration of NDE phenomena into beliefs about why some people *did* return from the dead (i.e., that they were sent back by spirits in the other world for various reasons). Indeed, belief in NDEs was more widely attested in Polynesia and Melanesia than documentary accounts of actual incidents. There were also numerous NDE-like myths, demonstrating a strong link between belief and experience. In contrast, while there were examples of knowledge or rituals originating in the otherworld in Micronesia and Australia, they were in shamanic rather than near-death contexts. While shamans regularly practiced the restoration of souls to bodies, however, accounts of shamanic journeys to afterlife realms were rare, particularly in Micronesia. There are no overt statements of afterlife beliefs originating in NDEs from either region, and indeed no unambiguous NDEs.

Oceania also had highly varied attitudes toward the dying. While there are certainly examples of corpse-fear, avoidance, and taboo, bodies were also often the focal point of grief, with mourners weeping over them, embracing them, and even "retaining portions of the corpse as cherished mementoes." While it was often the case that "vigorous efforts" were made to keep an individual alive up to the possible last moment, it is also true that in some societies the dying were ignored, or even abandoned, starved, or buried alive (Oliver 1989: 771). Unlike Africa, however, a specific fear of the dead returning to life appears to have been absent. Generally speaking, these differences were regionally based, and correlate both with local beliefs and incidence of NDEs. Thus, the comparatively numerous NDEs found in Melanesia and Polynesia correspond to funerary practices that facilitated the deceased returning to life, to more positive attitudes toward the dead, and a greater interest in the afterlife per se (bearing more similarities to the Native American model). In contrast, the lack of Australian and Micronesian NDEs reflects funerary practices that carried a greater risk of premature burial, alongside more negative attitudes toward the dead, a greater focus on mediumship and possession (Micronesia) or otherworld journey shamanism (Australia), and a general disinterest in afterlife speculations (relatively speaking).

There is a direct relationship between the occurrence of NDEs, afterlife conceptions that are similar to NDEs, shamanic otherworld journey practices, and indigenous statements that beliefs originated in the experience. Where NDEs are lacking, there were cultural restrictions on their integration into local religions. In such cases, however, there is typically a correspondence between afterlife beliefs and other types of extraordinary experience. For example, OBEs, mediumistic communications, deathbed visions, ghosts, poltergeists, and possession are related to African, Micronesian, and Australian ancestor beliefs. The ethnographic sources themselves indicate that afterlife conceptions were often grounded in conceptually and culturally relevant extraordinary experiences. Considering that the beliefs were never systematized in these cultures and that there was no "orthodoxy," the correspondences between belief and experience are all the more remarkable.

This study has also found that certain NDE elements such as walking along a path or road, earthly locales, and food taboos are cross-culturally common mainly in indigenous societies. Occasional highly specific similarities without NDE parallels are also evident between distant, historically unrelated cultures. The attainment of shamanic status and abilities through quartz crystals being pressed into the chest was common to the Kwakwaka'wakw in North America, and to the Jajaurung of Australia. This is certainly too precise for mere coincidence to be a compelling explanation. Likewise, dipping the hand into one of two pots in the other world as a mode of determining one's return to Earth was shared by the Hopi (red and black pots filled with suds), and the Chaga (hot and cold pots, one containing bangles). Though we may speculate that some other sociocultural features shared by these two societies must have resulted in these particular forms of conceptual logic, for now these similarities remain essentially inexplicable. Parallels with beliefs in ancient civilizations also defy a simple explanation, including the association in afterlife contexts between a sun-god named Rā and his journey through the netherworld in both pharaonic Egypt and the Cook Islands; the motif of the Clashing Rocks in ancient Greece, the Marquesas Islands, and Apache North America; a boy who was killed by his father so he can learn about the afterlife in Vedic India and Hopi Arizona; and the surprisingly common taboo on eating in the otherworld.

All this leads to the following interrelated hypotheses:

• While NDEs are universal, and people commonly base certain religious beliefs on them, they do so only when their cultural environment allows— unless they are innovating away from established tradition. Local attitudes toward death affect receptivity to NDE phenomena.

- In addition to providing a well of symbols with which to express and interpret NDEs, a culture and its environment also impose limitations on such expressions.
- With the exception of certain funerary practices (e.g., the hurried disposal of bodies), existing beliefs and cultural orientation do not make NDEs more or less likely to *occur*, but more or less likely to be expressed and accepted.
- Shamanic otherworld journey practices are often secondary phenomena, contributing more to the maintenance of afterlife beliefs through experiential validation than to their origination. Shamanic experiences vary widely in context (including associated ritual practices and religious beliefs), and therefore vary more widely phenomenologically. NDEs are more thematically stable, and share a universal return-from-death context. Nevertheless, some shamanic experiences may have been actual NDEs, or fundamentally akin to them.
- "Belief" and "experience" can be artificially discrete and even inextricable categories. Indigenous statements about beliefs often referred to an experience not only as the source and authority of the belief, but also as the actual descriptor of it. In some cases, the only statement of belief on record is an account of an NDE, implicitly supporting the experiential source hypothesis.

Evaluating what are normally seen as competing theories from various disciplines, and combining the most cogent and relevant elements of each enables the formulation of a more comprehensive overall theory with the greatest explanatory force. The full range of cross-cultural similarities and local particularities can be most fully understood through a consideration of various factors, which need not be seen as mutually exclusive. Evolutionary psychology helps us to understand why people are willing to accept the claims of NDErs, shamans, and visionaries: contact with ancestors serves a community-binding function, encouraging common beliefs and promoting tradition, social cohesion, and continuity (cf. Hodge 2011), while also sanctioning the NDE testimony. The NDE narratives serve to flesh out and validate our natural cognitive predisposition to believe in life after death, thereby encouraging receptivity to new teachings arising from the experience, and facilitating their integration into local worldviews. The healing and transformational benefits of NDEs and shamanic experiences also help to account for the development and maintenance of religious beliefs and practices.

Some aspects of afterlife beliefs are best explained by psychological factors. Realms of abundance reflect anxieties about having adequate necessities in this life, while providing reassurance of better conditions to come. Political factors include the concepts of postmortem reward and punishment being used as a tool of social control, leading to more elaborate descriptions of rewards and punishments. Though impossible to determine in indigenous societies due to a lack of religious texts that developed over long periods of time, the idea is supported by the fact that a stress on negativity and threat in the afterlife beliefs of early civilizations appeared alongside an increase in more popular religious texts and their accessibility, and were often very clearly manipulations by the elite (Shushan 2009: 175–6). Beckwith (1940: 159) argued that in Hawai'i, themes of reward and punishment were introduced by the ruling elite for political purposes. The relatively rare cases of distressing NDEs (Greyson & Bush 1992) may also contribute to beliefs in punishments and hellish realms, though such descriptions are also comparatively rare in both the beliefs and experiences reviewed here. Another important political factor is the indigenous use of NDE narratives in the formation of religious revitalization movements that reasserted sociocultural power and identity.

Conceptual logic and environmental factors account for afterlife realms mirroring earthly social structures, hierarchies, and local topographical features; as well as notions of rebirth and renewal being expressed in terms of the cycles of the natural and celestial worlds. While there appears to be little correspondence between corpse disposal methods of burial or cremation and beliefs in underworlds or heavens, there is a correlation between complexity of funerary ritual and level of concern with afterlife speculations. This is paralleled in conceptions of spirits of the dead existing either on Earth or in another world, and in degrees of detail in afterlife descriptions. Personal perspective and interpretation also play a significant part, for those who have experiences and codify beliefs are not simply culturally constructed automata, but unique individuals with varying ideas, beliefs, and imaginations.

Nevertheless, the remarkably consistent similarities between afterlife beliefs cross-culturally and their widespread correspondences with NDE phenomenology indicates an integral experiential element. This is supported by the fact that nearly everyone who has an NDE believes in the veridicality of the experience (even where it is interpreted in negative terms by the community, as in some African examples). The fact that such experiences normally occur in death-related contexts makes it unsurprising that individuals would interpret them in relation to that context, and subsequently believe that it was an experience of surviving death in an afterlife state. The numerous examples of NDEs that run contrary to local or personal beliefs demonstrate not only that these experiences are not predicated on cultural expectation, but also that they often lead to a spiritual or religious reorientation. Furthermore, skepticism and reasoning seem to be natural, intuitive human universals (regardless of the cultural parameters in which they exist). As rational beings, we need convincing reasons for our beliefs (Flood 2012: ch. 6), and NDEs offer just such a reason for afterlife beliefs, authenticating and giving form to what we are already naturally inclined to believe. Experiential validation is important to the establishment of new beliefs and the maintenance of existing ones, and is thus itself a factor in the formation of religions.

On a wider theoretical level, the evidence here presents a major challenge to constructivist paradigms that claim that all experience is entirely linguistically and/or culturally created, and that because all religions and cultures are unique there can thus be no cross-culturally common types of experiences on which religious beliefs could be based (cf. Shushan 2014, 2016a). The notion that religious *experiences* are wholly cultural-linguistic constructions conflicts with the widely held perspective that religious *beliefs* are wholly cultural-linguistic constructions. If afterlife beliefs, for example, cannot be objectively and meaningfully cross-culturally similar, how can *dissimilar* beliefs result in cross-culturally *similar* NDEs? If one were to claim that there simply are no cross-cultural similarities of either NDEs or afterlife beliefs, the mass of evidence to the contrary needs to be somehow proven false (cf. Shushan 2009, 2013). Otherwise, if we acknowledge that there *is* a type of human experience that is regularly interpreted in "religious" terms cross-culturally, similarities can no longer be dismissed as theoretically unintelligible Western scholarly subjectivities. We then have a category of phenomena that can logically and generically be called "religious." This could provide validation for the highly controversial concept of "religion" being a category distinct from other aspects of human cultural phenomena (Shushan 2014, 2016a). Kripal (2010: 254) similarly argues that the experiential source hypothesis leads to the recognition of a category of "the sacred"—separate from both faith and reason, suggesting the need for a field that sees "the sacred as the paranormal."

Whatever the ultimate nature of the prompting event (neurophysiological, metaphysical, or something else), NDEs are powerful generators of religious beliefs in an afterlife, both for individuals and in established religious traditions. While not every religious system shares similar afterlife conceptions, and though some have none at all, cross-cultural structural similarities are so widespread that it is tempting to speculate an NDE element for afterlife journey conceptions even in the absence of a documentary example.

The conclusions here have been reached through "inference to the best explanation"—abductive reasoning and rational judgment about the problems in question, the evidence related to them, and the various interdisciplinary models relevant to explaining them. In addition, we have in many cases actual *proof* of our hypotheses in the form of indigenous statements. Our conclusions thus have the advantage of ensuring that the ethnohistorical narratives remain contextually rooted, and interpreted in ways that respect the meaningfulness they had to the people who expressed them to begin with. This ensures our interpretations are consistent with local "religious reasoning" (as per Flood 2012: 134, 146).

This combination of approaches has led to a more comprehensive and satisfying explanation than could be achieved by relying on a single Western social or biological scientific model, all of which have been shown to be inadequate in isolation. Regardless of widespread scholarly assumptions across the sciences and humanities, there is nothing to support any single restrictive and ultimately sterile cultural or biological source theory; and much to support the experiential source hypothesis in combination with various sociocultural, biological, psychological, and environmental factors. The theoretically eclectic model presented here addresses the entire spectrum of similarities and differences in both beliefs and experiences across cultures. In contrast, a cultural source theory cannot be substantiated by reference to diffusion (i.e., to explain cross-cultural similarities), or through a postmodernist-sanctioned denial of similarities on the grounds of prior philosophical commitments. Likewise, a biological source theory cannot account for wide cross-cultural variations of beliefs or experiences. In short, the present study effectively refutes cultural and biological source theories in isolation, and falsifies much of postmodernist doctrine concerning comparison and experience per se, on empirical, theoretical, and philosophical grounds.

Until the late twentieth century, historically and historiographically, NDEs were neglected experiences. Considering the sheer volume of documentary narratives alongside related myths, practices, and beliefs as found in the anthropological record, this is surprising. That NDEs were widely considered on an indigenous level to be key components of philosophical-religious systems is demonstrated both by narratives being repeated over the course of decades in strikingly similar terms (e.g., Maori, Ojibwe), and by the numerous indigenous testimonies that they were the source for various beliefs, rituals, religious innovations, and revitalization movements. What has prevented them from being identified as a discreet and important class of phenomenon by the vast majority of anthropologists and other interpreters of religions? Indeed, what has prevented such a relevant experience type from being seen as a factor contributing to religious beliefs, to the extent that serious arguments to this effect have been isolated, rare, or effectively marginalized? The answer would seem to lie in a refusal to take indigenous testimony seriously, from early missionary astonishment that afterlife beliefs could derive from NDEs, to philosophical and religious denigrations of the authority of experience, to Eliade's determined obsession with universalizing shamanism, to medical and psychological pathologization, to postmodernist fixations on the particularities of culture and language to the exclusion of all else (Shushan 2014, 2016a). All these perspectives deny a voice to the very people whose religions and experiences are being "explained" (or, rather, explained *away*).

The recognition of the significance of NDEs in human thought and experience is long overdue. They can be an empowering force, both on the individual level when we consider the positive life changes experiencers commonly undergo after their NDEs; and on a social-cultural-political level as evidenced by religious revitalization movements with NDE foundations. They can thus be a catalyst for personal or cultural renewal. This helps to explain why at certain times and in certain places, people are more willing to accept the testimonies of those who have such experiences. This applies to the intense popular modern interest in the phenomenon, as exemplified by NDE interest groups in which members seek to renegotiate their spirituality in light of such experiences (e.g., Kinsella 2017). These groups share many characteristics of new religious movements, and elevate those who have had NDEs to a higher, often guru-like status. Near-death experiences provide one way for unaffiliated "spiritual but not religious" people to find a community with certain common beliefs normally the preserve of organized religions. Testimonies of NDErs give comfort to those who grieve the loss of loved ones, and to those who are fearful of death. These benefits come without the attendant commitments and potential philosophical compromises involved in mainstream religious affiliation.

It is tempting to conclude that societies that accept NDEs and lend credence to experiencer testimony enjoy the positive fruits of the phenomenon, as widely described in NDE accounts around the world. Those who pathologize them, silence them, or view them in terms of aberration and danger do not. While individuals are microcosms of their societies, just as in Price's mind-dependent afterlife model, they also contribute to the formation of those societies. The positive fruits of their experiences can thus have a positive impact on their communities.

Notes

1. For example, Sharf (1998: 282–3) uses the evaluative term "tales" when referring to shamanic experiences, questions the credibility of accounts of religious experience, and states that "we are not obliged to accept" them as "phenomenological description." Cupitt (1998: 33) implies that religious experiencers only "pretend to remember" their experiences.

2. E.g., Tylor (1871 68) on Algonquin NDEs said to have occurred before European contact; Rasmussen (1932: 33) on the Copper Inuit; and Courlander (1971: 213) on the Hopi despite acknowledging an almost total lack of influence otherwise.

3. Asia is excluded due to nearly pervasive external cultural influence from Hinduism, Buddhism, and Islam from the earliest records. South America is excluded on the grounds of relatively pervasive early influence from Spain, and to historical redundancy, having been settled by North American and Oceanic peoples. Nevertheless, I hope to produce articles on indigenous NDEs on these continents at some time in the future.

4. As was the case with scholarly characterizations of Sumerian afterlife beliefs as entirely gloomy (Shushan 2009: ch. 5).

CHAPTER 2

1. Cf. Mills and Slobodin (1994), collecting essays on Native American reincarnation beliefs.

2. Cf. Tylor (1871: 21), who argued that reports of human groups who disbelieve in an afterlife should be regarded with suspicion.

3. It is also worth noting the abundance of return-from-death and soul-retrieval accounts outside these narrative streams, which lack descriptions of the soul's journey (Gayton 1935: 283f; Hultkrantz 1957: 22, 165ff).

4. Cf. Wade (2003: 101–2), who found most of these elements in her analysis of eleven Native American NDEs, dating from the seventeenth to the early twentieth centuries. All are considered in this chapter, by reference back to their original sources.

5. These accounts were drawn upon (uncredited) by Captain John Smith in his 1624 *Generall Historie of Virginia, New-England, and the Summer Isles,* and are often thus attributed to him (e.g., by Tylor 1871: 136, n.1). While it is possible that Smith was simply given the same accounts as Hariot, the detailed similarities between the two versions (including the fact that one NDE occurred the year of Hariot's visit) make this unlikely.

6. The specifically Christian form of postmortem retribution did not gain ground until the eighteenth century (Hultkrantz 1980: 163–5).

7. The Wyandot claim of an NDE origin for afterlife beliefs led Brébeuf (1636: 145–6) to conclude that "it is the devil deceives them in their dreams; thus he speaks by the mouth of some, who having been left as dead, recover health and talk at random of the other life, according to the ideas that this wretched master gives them." Interestingly, this conclusion was echoed over 350 years later in the writings of modern-day Evangelical NDE researcher Maurice Rawlings (1993).

8. Neolin's map may be viewed at: http://historytools.davidjvoelker.com/Images/delaware-prophecy.JPG (retrieved November 15, 2017).

9. A nearly identical narrative was related in 1857 by the Belgian missionary Pierre-Jean De Smet (1905: 1047ff), told to him by Father James Bouchard, *née* Watomika, an Ojibwe who had become a Jesuit priest. While either man might have read Schoolcraft without acknowledging him, corroborations between the two narratives may instead demonstrate consistency of Ojibwe narratives and beliefs over time, as well as reliable reporting from two very different Western contexts (a Belgian Jesuit missionary and an American geologist).

10. Again, there is a nearly identical yet uncredited version of this narrative, which appeared just two years after Schoolcraft's (McKenny 1827: 371–2). Cf. Jones (1829: 255ff) for two Ojibwe NDE narratives that may or may not be Jones's own literary elaborations on Schoolcraft.

11. See Jones (1917: 535–47) for a myth explaining the origin of death and the afterlife, containing many of these elements.

12. Jenness (1935: 55–9) also published a long, detailed, Dante-esque account of the journeys of a warrior named Ogauns, during his thirty-year quest for "everlasting life" for himself and his people . Though it has a distinct mythical feel and lacks any near-death context, it nevertheless features various NDE-like themes. Interestingly, however, the narrative is little like that of Gizikkwedanjiani, or like local afterlife beliefs.

13. This is presumably a figure of speech. In the early 1950s, a Tlingit informant similarly stated that the old have trees growing from their heads (De Laguna 1972: 767).

14. For Le Jeune's later elaborations on this report, see Kenton (1927: 321, 378–9).

15. In a somewhat related narrative with no NDE context, a young girl who was separated from her people was rescued by her deceased father. He cared for her in the ghost camp which shadowed that of the living (Opler 1940: 101–4).

16. A similar scenario features in a 1930s narrative about an Oraibi woman named Ruth, demonstrating that it was part of a cultural pattern (or became so after Talayesva's narrative) (Titiev 1972: 104).

17. Seeing people who are still alive is unusual but not unknown in contemporary NDEs, particularly those of children (Kelly 2001: 240, 245).

18. This plot structure is strikingly similar to a series of ancient Vedic Indian afterlife journey narratives (Shushan 2011: 208–9).

19. See Courlander (1971: 101ff) for a nearly identical version collected almost seventy years later. Cf. Voth (1905: 109–14) and Talayesva (1942: 435–6) for similar narratives. The Hopi also had an underworld descent/creation myth involving twins seeking their father and undergoing a series of tests by the Sun (Tyler 1964: 216–7). Though known only in fragmentary form, it is highly reminiscent of the Maya myth of Hunapu and Xblanque in the *Popol Vuh* (Shushan 2009: 124–9).

20. As was the 1886 deathbed vision of the Zuni governor Palowahtiva. During a serious illness he forgot everything and all went dark. When he could see again, he noticed a mysterious bright light entering from the window and everything seemed much clearer and generally better. A "god-sized man"—his "grand-grand uncle" in traditional Zuni clothes—appeared, ready to take him to the other world. An old man then appeared and said it was not yet his time to die, and that he was ill because "One sometimes learns wisdom through great illness" (Cushing 1979: 421; cf. Wade 2003).

21. In an attempt to lend empirical veracity to his visions, Black Elk claimed that he knew nothing of Christianity and "had never seen any pictures of Christ." In fact, he had been acquainted with Christianity while in Europe (DeMallie 1984: 263, n.10, 266).

22. As Wade (2003: 112) pointed out, the fact that Black Elk was feeling extremely homesick at the time is surely relevant to the unusual experience of going home during an NDE.

23. Cf. du Bois (1939) who, charting the dissemination of Wodziwob's movement, cites innumerable examples of dances, dream cults, and anomalous healings that maintained—and sometimes outlived—the main Ghost Dance movement.

24. Cf. Grinnell (1893: 129–30) for a slightly earlier, shorter variation of this narrative, in which the husband convinces the wife to return to Earth without himself going to the land of the dead. A Skidi Pawnee version involves assistance from a rainbow/skunk-spirit, and from the Wind. The spirit woman is reanimated when the protagonist drops lice on her, and her scratching causes her blood to flow again. She

returns with the man to Earth, where they remain happily (Dorsey 1904c: 71–3). In yet another version, a father searches for his deceased son, and is assisted by a divinized leader of a group of men who have been scalped (ibid. 76). Hultkrantz (1957: 18) recounted a 1930s Comanche version.

25. The long, complex myth of the salmon boy bears similarities to the present narrative, though it revolved around the boy following his sister to the spirit world after she laughed herself to death. He met a giant who turned out to be his grandfather, and had various adventures before returning to Earth, where he had been presumed dead. He then ascended to a sky realm for more adventures (Jenness 1934: 99–114).

26. Sometimes transliterated as "Tlebeet."

27. Tlingit beliefs in deathbed visions are also attested: "the dying person often reported seeing the faces of his departed kin hovering over him" (Kan 1989: 105; cf. De Laguna 1972: 779).

28. Cf. De Laguna (1972: 773–5) for further examples from the 1950s, describing spirits playing games in the Northern Lights, the other world being reached via a stairway, and souls being reborn after falling into a river in a "strange land."

29. Interestingly, the Klamath version (Gayton 1935: 279) contained a theme identical to the Aztec *Legend of the Suns* (recorded 1558; see Shushan 2009: 130f), in which the creator obtains bones in the afterlife realms in order to repeople the Earth.

30. The closest I have found is a tale in which a little girl "was taken away by the moon up to his house in the sky," then sent back when the sun grew jealous. The narrative lacks a return-from-death context, however, and rather than explaining afterlife beliefs, "It is from this girl that they know how the moon and the sun live in a double house" (Rasmussen 1932: 33).

31. Some examples were rooted in wondrous journeys that may or may not have been to afterlife realms. The Tsuu T'ina head medicine man Calf-Child (Hector Crawler) described a dreamlike experience of ascending bodily to a mountain where he met the Son of God, radiating light (Barbeau 1923: 113–4). A Nakota (Assiniboine) boy had a dream-vision in which Waktan Tanka instructed him to preach a return to traditional religion and to become a healer (Jenness 1938: 74). Other accounts lack contextual details altogether, for example, the Kickapoo prophet Kennekuk had direct revelations from the Great Spirit which led to religious changes (Mooney 1896: 695ff); and the Apache prophet Nakai-Doklini could reportedly communicate with spirits and resurrect the dead (ibid. 704–5).

32. Cf. Spier (1935), who cites many additional examples of these movements, together with founding myths that almost invariably involve journeys to the spirit land.

33. Found with a number of variations among the Yokut, Chehalis, Haisla, Tlingit, Tsimshian, Klamath, Modoc, Shasta, Pomo, Nisenan, Mono, Mohave, Dakelh, Menomini, and Zuni (Hultkrantz 1957: 62–4).

CHAPTER 3

1. Mbiti (1971: 2) appears to be alone in the perspective that in many African societies, "religious ideas and practices ... are directed primarily to 'eschatological' aspects of life," including beliefs in spirits, the afterlife, and "heaven"—a notion presumably related to his own Christian theological perspective.

2. "They result from a protective cerebellar reaction against a real or anticipated oxygen deprivation, which can be induced pharmacologically in the fastigial nucleus. We presume that cortical influences (the belief that death is impending) may also be a possible cause" (Strubelt 2008: 33).

3. Cf. Baskerville (1922: 12–5) for a slightly different version.

4. Two further Chaga narratives, with overtly fable-like elements (e.g., wondrous animals, magical objects, and transformations), should also be mentioned. The first has no otherworld journey narrative, but involves a girl returning from death after her father killed and dismembered her for allowing his dancing bird to escape (Dundas 1924: 328ff). The second has no overt death or afterlife context, and involves a man ascending to the moon and meeting a race of immortal people (ibid. 330ff).

5. Other ethnographers maintained that the Maasai had no afterlife beliefs (e.g., Fox 1930: 456), or that they believed in "annihilation after death" (Hinde & Hinde 1901: 127). Leakey's (1930: 206) informant told him "that the Masai had no belief in a spirit life after death, or in spirits of any kind," though Leakey was unconvinced, suggesting, "For some reason (probably a restriction with a heavy penalty attached) they were unwilling to discuss this subject." It seems that Merker's long tenure with the Maasai led to his being trusted with privileged information withheld from others.

6. This is not a racial description, for Europeans were locally considered to be red (Willoughby 1928: 100, n.1). It instead seems to be a way of conveying the radiance the informant stresses.

7. Underworld descent and return features in an additional narrative, though without details of the other realm (Callaway 1868: 296ff). Callaway (1868: 331) also related a highly idiosyncratic myth of a woman and her two children who went to another realm when swallowed by an elephant. Inside they found forests, rivers, villages, people, and animals. When they grew hungry, they carved off pieces of the elephant's internal organs to eat. The mother then cut their way out of the elephant, freeing everyone inside.

8. In absence of exegetical works, ethnographic reports, and for the most part documentary material of any kind, this was, by necessity, partly the approach of my book on NDEs and afterlife beliefs in early civilizations cross-culturally (Shushan 2009). While admittedly this made for a somewhat more speculative work, there has been no countering evidence, arguments, or theories to dissuade me from the conclusions I presented.

9. The remaining cultures discussed here are scattered among five other linguistic groups: Ga, Yoruba (Kwa); Lango (Western Nilotic); Nandi, Elgeyo (Southern Nilotic); Efé (Central Sudanic); and Nuer (Nilo-Saharan).

CHAPTER 4

1. See Thornton (1984) for an analysis of three versions of this myth published between 1915 and 1919, in comparison with Maori versions first published in 1855 and 1896 (see p. 161 in this chapter, and n. 8 below) that she believes are actually later.

2. Dorothy Barrére, the editor of the translated texts, believes Kamakau's descriptions of Manu'a and Milu to be reflections of his Christian faith, and "his attempt to reconcile the ancient beliefs with the new" (in Kamakau 1866–71: 60, n.1). That Westervelt also reported such descriptions, however, casts doubt on this assertion.

3. See, for example, Kalakaua (1888: 491–4, 514–7); Fornander (1916–20: I.482–3; II.312); and Emerson (1915: 188–92).

4. Compare, for example, the clearly mythological tale of Ke-au-nini, which included a lengthy, elaborate section about of a boy named Lono-kai who traveled in his body to the underworld to retrieve his grandfather's soul. On the way he encountered a watchman in the form of a giant turtle that made dangerous waves with its fins; then a giant eel; then a beautiful woman who became his bride (Westervelt 1915: 204ff).

5. Cf. the similar legend of Haha-poa and his wife (Handy 1930: 121–2).

6. This is a striking echo of ancient Egyptian belief, even down to the personal pronoun of the deity (see Shushan 2009: 55ff).

7. Cf. Williams (1933: II.148) for a variation on Sina's return-from-death legend.

8. See Hongi (1896: 118–9) for another version in which the female character discovers that the unrequited love interest is her brother Miru. It is otherwise highly similar to the above.

9. Itself grounded in the prophetic trance-vision experiences of the founder Evara.

10. According to the informant, "big man" may have been Sido, who was the subject of his own afterlife journey narratives as discussed later in the chapter (Landtman 1912: 71–2).

11. See Landtman (1917: 93–101) for additional accounts of "Meetings with Dead People in Dreams."

12. See Landtman (1917: 118) for summaries of local variations of Sido's return from death myth.

13. Williams (1930: 282) calls this a "fairy-tale" though does not say if the Orokaiva believed it to be true or not.

14. Nor can the underworld description be accounted for by Christian or other external influence, according to Williams (1930: 262).

15. There also exists what Codrington (1891: 286) referred to as "a sort of parody of the above"—about a man journeying "to the underworld of pigs" ruled by a snake

named Tamatemboe, "dead-man-pig"—presumably related to the human-pig man encountered in the Kiwai myth of Duobe, discussed earlier.

16. For an elaborately detailed and lengthy account from the Namata tribe, see Thomson (1908: 120–31).

CHAPTER 5

1. There are no examples of this motif from North America, and only one from Oceania—the Biak legend in which a man followed a pig to the other world, and only some of his people believed him. In an Australian myth, a man followed a yam there.

2. See, for example, the Indian religious movement of the Munda people of West Bengal in 1895, which was rooted in a theophany of "the Deity" to a young man named Birsa Munda, endowing him with healing powers and spiritual knowledge (Roy 1912: 325–30).

3. The Brazilian Beniwa Indian prophet Venancio Aniseto Kamiko in 1857, the Tukano prophet Alexandre Christo the following year, another Baniwa named Aniseto in 1875, an Arapaco named Vincente Christo in 1878, and the nineteeth century Makusi man named Bichiwung, as described.

4. See also Shushan (2009: ch. 10) and McClenon (2002: 13–4) for reviews of additional experiential models.

5. Just as Zaleski (1985) would do over a hundred years later in her analysis of Medieval otherworld journey narratives in comparison to NDEs (Shushan 2014: 404–5).

6. Considering his engagement with NDEs and shamanic experiences, it is odd that Tylor (1871: 58) also suggested that afterlife beliefs across cultures could be explained by the common human experience of visitations by ghosts, giving rise to speculations about where they might live. Despite his apparent struggles with the problem, he was unavoidably drawn to the experiential source hypothesis, whether concerning apparitions or afterlife journeys, even if he failed to adequately develop it.

7. In an early article, Eliade (1937: 36) cited mediumship, clairvoyance, levitation, firewalking, and other "miracles" as "certain primitive and folkloric beliefs which have concrete experiences as their basis."

8. He did, however, seem to have some inclination that NDEs were something different from shamanic experiences. Regarding the Yupik example recounted earlier, he wrote, "its content extends beyond the sphere of shamanism proper" (Eliade 1964: 292).

9. Like Eliade, given his wide cross-cultural reading, Lang almost certainly would have run across accounts of NDEs, so it is odd that he did not discuss them. This may be because of his focus on the psychical research subjects popular in his day (Lang 1900: 3). Being not yet codified, popularized, or even named, NDEs rarely featured in early psychical research literature.

10. Eliade (1964: 107) similarly noted how shamans are distinguished from the rest of a given society "by their capacity for ecstatic experience."

11. NDEs are scarcely mentioned in the roughly 850 pages of McNamara et al. (2006), for example.

12. In *The Homeric Hymn to Demeter*, Kore inadvertently eats a pomegranate seed and thus has to return to the underworld for four months every year. The clashing rocks were a peril in the punishment underworld of Tartarus, and in other locales in Greek myth.

13. Cf. Hultkrantz (1957: 190ff) on Orpheus-type narratives in later India, China, and Japan.

14. To put this into perspective, prior to this study only thirty-nine accounts of NDEs had been documented from Oceania, Africa, North America, and South America combined (Kellehear 2009: 136); and nearly all of them were of a late twentieth-century date (meaning a higher likelihood of conversion to nonindigenous religions, and more modern, less traditional culture).

References

Abrahamsson, H. (1951) *The Origin of Death: Studies in African Mythology.* Uppsala: Almqvist and Wiksells.

Abramovitch, H. (1988) "An Israeli account of a near-death experience: A case study of cultural dissonance." *Journal of Near-Death Studies* 6, 175–84.

Ackermann, H.-W. & J. Gauthier (1991) "The ways and nature of the zombi." *Journal of American Folklore* 104(414), 466–94.

Andersson, R.-H. (2008) *The Lakota Ghost Dance of 1890.* Lincoln: University of Nebraska Press.

Arbousset, T. & F. Daumas (1852; trans. J. C. Brown) *Narrative of an Exploratory Tour to the North-East of the Colony of the Cape of Good Hope.* London: Bishop.

Audette, J. R. (1982) "Historical perspectives on near-death episodes and experiences." In C. R. Lundhal (ed.) *A Collection of Near-Death Research Readings,* 21–43. Chicago: Nelson-Hall.

Augustine, K. (2007) "Psychophysiological and cultural correlates undermining a survivalist interpretation of near-death experiences." *Journal of Near-Death Studies* 26(2), Winter, 89–125.

Badham, P. (1982) *Immortality or Extinction?* London: SPCK.

Badham, P. (1997) "Religion and near-death experience in relation to belief in a future life." *Mortality* 2(1), 7–20.

Bancroft, H. H. (1875) *The Native Races of the Pacific States of North America, Vol. III: Myths and Languages.* New York, Appleton.

Barbeau, M. (1923) *Indian Days in the Canadian Rockies.* Toronto: Macmillan.

Barnard, G. W. (1992) "Explaining the unexplainable: Wayne Proudfoot's 'Religious Experience.'" *Journal of the American Academy of Religion* 60(2), 231–56.

Barrett, S. M. (1906) *Geronimo's Story of His Life.* New York: Duffield.

Bartram, W. (1789; pub. 1853) *Observations on the Creek and Cherokee Indians.* Transactions of the American Ethnological Society 3/I, 1–81. New York: Putnam.

Basden, G. T. (1921) *Among the Ibos of Nigeria.* London: Seeley, Service & Co.

Baskerville, R. (1922) *King of the Snakes*. London: Sheldon.

Beaglehole, E. & P. Beaglehole (1935) *Hopi of the Second Mesa*. Menasha, WI: American Anthropological Association.

Becker, C. B. (1981) "The centrality of near-death experiences in Chinese Pure Land Buddhism." *Anabiosis* 1, 154–74.

Becker, C. B. (1984) "The Pure Land revisited: Sino-Japanese meditations and near-death experiences of the next world." *Anabiosis* 4, 51–68.

Becker, C. B. (1993) *Breaking the Circle: Death and the Afterlife in Buddhism*. Carbondale: Southern Illinois University Press.

Beckwith, M. (1940; rpt. 1970) *Hawaiian Mythology*. Honolulu: University of Hawaii Press.

Belanti, J., M. Perera, & K. Jagadheesan (2008) "Phenomenology of near-death experiences: A cross-cultural perspective." *Transcultural Psychiatry* 45(1), 121–33.

Bell, F. L. S. (1937) "Death in Tanga." *Oceania* 7, 316–39.

Benedict, R. (1931) *Tales of the Cochiti Indians*. Bureau of American Ethnology Bulletin 98. Washington, DC: Smithsonian.

Bering, J. M. (2006a) "The folk psychology of souls." *Behavioral and Brain Sciences* 29, 453–98.

Bering, J. M. (2006b) "The cognitive psychology of belief in the supernatural." In P. McNamara (ed.) *Where God and Science Meet*, vol. 1, 123–34. Westport, CT: Praeger.

Bering, J. M. & D. F. Bjorklund (2004) "The natural emergence of reasoning about the afterlife as a developmental regularity." *Developmental Psychology* 40(2), 217–33.

Berndt, R. M. & C. H. Berndt (1964) *The World of the First Australians*. London: Angus & Robertson.

Best, E. (1900) "Spiritual concepts of the Maori, Part I." *Journal of the Polynesian Society* 9(4), 173–99.

Best, E. (1901) "Spiritual concepts of the Maori, Part II." *Journal of the Polynesian Society* 10(1), 1–20.

Best, E. (1905) "Maori eschatology." *Transactions and Proceedings of the New Zealand Institute* 38, 148–239.

Best, E. (1926) "Notes on customs, ritual and beliefs pertaining to sickness, death, burial and exhumation among the Maori of New Zealand." *Journal of the Polynesian Society* 35(137), 6–30.

Bierhorst, J. (1985) *The Mythology of North America*. New York: Oxford University Press.

Blair, E. H. (1911) *Indian Tribes of the Upper Mississippi Valley and Region of the Great Lakes*, 2 vols. Cleveland: Clark.

Blowsnake, S. (1909; ed. P. Radin, 1920) *Crashing Thunder: The Autobiography of an American Indian*. New York: Appleton.

Boas, F. (1890) "First general report on the Indians of British Columbia." In *Fifth report of the Committee on the Northwest Tribes of Canada*. In *Report of the 59th Meeting of the British Association for the Advancement of Science*, 801–93. London: Murray.

Boas, F. (1893) "The doctrine of souls and of disease among the Chinook Indians." *Journal of American Folklore* 6(20), 39–43.

Boas, F. (1896) "The growth of Indian mythologies: A study based upon the growth of the mythologies of the north Pacific Coast." *Journal of American Folklore* 9(32), 1–11.

Boas, F. (1898) *The Mythology of the Bella Coola Indians*. Memoirs of the American Museum of Natural History, Vol. II, Anthropology, I. New York: American Museum of Natural History.

Boas, F. (1901) *Kathlamet Texts*. Bureau of American Ethnology Bulletin, 26. Washington, DC: Smithsonian.

Boas, F. (1916) *Tsimshian Mythology*. Thirty-First Annual Report of the Bureau of American Ethnology, 29–1037. Washington, DC: Smithsonian.

Boas, F. (1923) *Notes on the Tillamook*. University of California Publications in American Archaeology and Ethnology 20. Berkeley: University of California Press.

Boas, F. (1930) *The Religion of the Kwakiutl Indians, Part II—Translations*. New York: Columbia University Press.

Boas, F. (1935) *Kwakiutl Culture as Reflected in Mythology*. New York: American Folklore Society.

Boas, F. (1966) *Kwakiutl Ethnography*. Chicago: Chicago University Press.

Bockie, S. (1993) *Death and the Invisible Powers: The World of Kongo Belief*. Bloomington: Indiana University Press.

Bond, G. C. (1992) "Living with spirits: Death and afterlife in African religions." In H. Obayashi (ed.) *Death and Afterlife: Perspectives of World Religions*, 3–18. New York: Greenwood.

Bosman, W. (1704; trans. 1967) *A New and Accurate Description of the Coast of Guinea*. London: Cass.

Bourguignon, E. (1973) "Introduction: A framework for the comparative study of altered states of consciousness." In E. Bourguignon (ed.) *Religion, Altered States of Consciousness and Social Change*, 3–35. Columbus: Ohio State University.

Bourguignon, E. (1974) "Cross-cultural perspectives on the religious use of altered states of consciousness." In I. I. Zaretsky & M. P. Leone (eds.) *Religious Movements in Contemporary America*, 228–43. Princeton, NJ: Princeton University Press.

Bowie, F. (2013) "Building bridges, dissolving boundaries: Toward a methodology for the ethnographic study of the afterlife, mediumship, and spiritual beings." *Journal of the American Academy of Religion* 81(3), 698–733.

Brébeuf, J. (1636) *Relation of What Occurred in the Country of the Hurons in the Year 1636*. R. G. Thwaites (ed. 1897) *The Jesuit Relations and Allied Documents*, vol. 10. Cleveland: Burrows Brothers.

Brown, D. E. (1991) *Human Universals*. Philadelphia: Temple University Press.

Brown, G. (1910) *Melanesians and Polynesians: Their Life-Histories Described and Compared*. London: Macmillan.

Brown, J. T. (1926) *Among the Bantu Nomads*. London: Seely, Service & Co.

Brown, T. K. (2003) "Mystical experiences, American culture, and conversion to Christian Spiritualism." In A. Buckser & S. D. Glazier (eds.) *The Anthropology of Religious Conversion*, 133–45. Lanham, MD: Rowman & Littlefield.

Bryant, A. T. (1917) "The Zulu cult of the dead." *Man* 17, 140–5.

Bulkeley, K. (2008) *Dreaming in the World's Religions: A Comparative History*. New York and London: New York University Press.

Bullock, C. (1950 rev. ed.) *The Mashona and the Matabele*. Cape Town: Juta.

Bunzel, R. L. (1932) *Introduction to Zuni Ceremonialism*. Forty-Seventh Annual Report of the Bureau of American Ethnology 1929–32, 467–544. Washington, DC: Smithsonian.

Burton, R. (1864) *A Mission to Gelele, King of Dahome*, vol. 2. London: Tylston & Edwards.

Butt, A. J. (1960) "The birth of a religion." In J. Middleton (ed., 1967) *Gods and Rituals*, 377–435. Garden City, NY: Natural History Press.

Callaway, H. (1868) *Nursery Tales, Traditions, and Histories of the Zulus, in Their Own Words*, vol. 1. Natal: Blair.

Casalis, E. (1861) *The Basutos; Twenty-Three Years in South Africa*. London: James Nisbet & Co.

Cave, A. A. (2006) *Prophets of the Great Spirit*. Lincoln and London: University of Nebraska Press.

Chadwick, N. K. (1952) *Poetry and Prophecy*. Cambridge, UK: Cambridge University Press.

Chapman, J. W. (1912) "The happy hunting-ground of the Ten'a." *Journal of American Folklore* 25(95), 66–71.

Chatelain, H. (1894) *Folk-Tales of Angola*. Memoirs of the American Folklore Society, 1. Boston: Houghton Mifflin.

Christian, F. W. (1899) *The Caroline Islands*. New York: Scribner's.

Claridge, G. C. (1922) *Wild Bush Tribes of Tropical Africa*. London: Seeley, Service and Co.

Cline, W. (1930) "Religion and world view." In L. Spier (ed.) *The Sinkaietk or Southern Okanagon of Washington*, 131–82. Menasha, WI: Banta.

Codrington, R. H. (1880) "Notes on the customs of Mota, Banks Islands." *Transactions of the Royal Society of Victoria* 16, 119–44.

Codrington, R. H. (1881) "Religious practices and beliefs in Melanesia." *Journal of the Anthropological Institute of Great Britain and Ireland* 10, 261–316.

Codrington, R. H. (1891) *The Melanesians: Studies in Their Anthropology and Folklore*. Oxford: Clarendon.

Collins, J. J. & M. Fishbane (1995) *Death, Ecstasy and Otherworldly Journeys*. Albany: SUNY Press.

Colton, H. S. (1959) *Hopi Kachina Dolls*. Albuquerque: University of New Mexico Press.

Cook, J. (1784) *A Voyage to the Pacific Ocean*, vols. 1–2. London: Strahan.

Counts, D. A. (1983) "Near-death and out-of-body experiences in a Melanesian society." *Anabiosis* 3, 115–35.

Courlander, H. (1971) *The Fourth World of the Hopis*. New York: Crown.

Cranz, D. (1767) *The History of Greenland*, vol. 1. London: Brethren's Society.

Crawley, A. E. (1909) *The Idea of a Soul*. London: A. & C. Black.

Cunningham, J. F. (1905) *Uganda and Its Peoples*. London: Hutchinson.

Cupitt, D. (1998) *Mysticism after Modernity*. Oxford: Blackwell.

Curtin, J. & J. N. B. Hewitt (1918) "Seneca fiction, legends, and myths." *Thirty-Second Annual Report of the Bureau of American Ethnology*, 37–819. Washington, DC: Government Printing Office.

Cushing, F. H. (1979 coll.) *Selected Writings of Frank Hamilton Cushing*. Lincoln: University of Nebraska Press.

Dale, A. M. (1920) *The Ila-Speaking Peoples of Northern Rhodesia*, vol. 2. London: Macmillan.

Davis, C. F. (1989) *The Evidential Force of Religious Experience*. Oxford: Oxford University Press.

Dawson, J. (1881) *Australian Aborigines*. Melbourne: Robertson.

Dayrell, E. (1913) *Ikom Folk Stories from Southern Nigeria*. Occasional Papers, 3. London: Royal Anthropological Institute.

De Laguna, F. (1972) *Under Mount Saint Elias: The History and Culture of the Yakutat Tlingit*. Washington, DC: Smithsonian Institution Press.

DeMallie, R. (1984) (ed.) *The Sixth Grandfather: Black Elk's Teachings Given to John G. Neihardt*. Lincoln: University of Nebraska.

Dennett, R. E. (1898) *Notes on the Folklore of the Fjort*. London: Folklore Society.

Dibble, S. (1843) *History of the Sandwich Islands*. Honolulu: Thrum.

Dieffenbach, E. (1843) *Travels in New Zealand*. London: Murray.

Dobbin, J. & F. X. Hezel (2011) *Summoning the Powers Beyond: Traditional Religions in Micronesia*. Honolulu: University of Hawai'i Press.

Dodginghorse, K. (1875) "The Sarcee Indian prophet." Sarcee Cultural Education Centre, document IH-AS.04. ourspace.uregina.ca/bitstream/10294/2129/1/IH-AS.04.pdf. Accessed December 14, 2011.

Doke, C. M. (1931) *The Lambas of Northern Rhodesia*. London: Harrap.

Dornan, S. S. (1925) *Pygmies and Bushmen of the Kalahari*. London: Seeley, Service and Co.

Dorsey, G. (1904a) *Mythology of the Wichita*. Washington, DC: Carnegie Institution.

Dorsey, G. (1904b) *Traditions of the Arikara*. Washington, DC: Carnegie Institution.

Dorsey, G. (1904c) *Traditions of the Skidi Pawnee*. Boston & New York: Houghton and Mifflin.

Dorsey, G. (1906) *The Pawnee: Mythology*, 2 vols. Washington, DC: Carnegie Institution.

Downes, R. M. (1933) *The Tiv Tribe*. Kaduna: Government Printer.

Drieberg, J. H. (1923) *The Lango: A Nilotic Tribe of Uganda*. London: Unwin.

Du Bois, C. (1939) *The 1870 Ghost Dance*. Anthropological Records, 3/1. Berkeley: University of California.

Dundas, C. (1924) *Kilimanjaro and Its People*. London: Witherby.

Eliade, M. (1937) "Folklore as an instrument of knowledge." In B. Rennie (2006 ed.) *Mircea Eliade: A Critical Reader*, 25–37. London: Equinox.

Eliade, M. (1964) *Shamanism: Archaic Techniques of Ecstasy*. London: Routledge & Kegan Paul.

Eliade, M. (1973) *Australian Religions*. Ithaca, NY: Cornell University Press.

Elkin, A. P. (1945) *Aboriginal Men of High Degree*. Sydney: Australian Publishing Co.

Ellis, A. B. (1887) *The Tshi-Speaking Peoples of the Gold Coast of West Africa*. London: Chapman & Hall.

Ellis, A. B. (1890) *The Ewe-Speaking Peoples of the Slave Coast of West Africa*. London: Chapman & Hall.

Ellis, A. B. (1894) *The Yoruba-Speaking Peoples of the Slave Coast of West Africa*. London: Chapman & Hall.

Ellis, W. (1823; reprint 1917) *A Narrative of a Tour through Hawaii*. Honolulu: Hawaiian Gazette Co.

Ellis, W. (1829; rpt. 1853) *Polynesian Researches*, vol. 1. London: Bohn.

Emerson, J. S. (1902) "Hawaiian beliefs regarding spirits." *Ninth Annual Report of the Hawaiian Historical Society*, 10–17.

Emerson, N. B. (1915) *Pele and Hiiaka*. Honolulu: Star Bulletin Limited.

Ernst, M. & A. Anisi (2016) "The historical development of Christianity in Oceania." In L. Sanneh & M. J. McClymond (eds.) *The Wiley Blackwell Companion to World Christianity*, 588–604. Chichester: Wiley Blackwell.

Evans-Pritchard, E. E. (1937) *Witchcraft, Oracles and Magic Among the Azande*. Oxford: Clarendon Press.

Evans-Pritchard, E. E. (1956) *Nuer Religion*. Oxford: Clarendon Press.

Eyre, E. J. (ed. 1845) *Journals of Expeditions of Discovery into Central Australia*, vol. 2. London: Boone.

Fernandez, J. W. (1982) *Bwiti: An Ethnography of the Religious Imagination in Africa*. Princeton, NJ: Princeton University Press.

Fewkes, J. W. (1899) *Archeological Expedition to Arizona in 1895*. Seventeenth Annual Report of the Bureau of American Ethnology. Washington, DC: Government Printing Office.

Fewkes, J. W. (1924) *The Use of Idols in Hopi Worship*. Washington, DC: Smithsonian.

Fisher, A. B. (1911) *Twilight Tales of the Black Baganda*. London: Marshall Brothers.

Fison, L. (1881) "Notes on Fijian burial customs." *Journal of the Anthropological Institute* 10, 137–49.

Fison, L. (1904) *Tales from Old Fiji*. London: Moring.

Flood, G. (2012) *The Importance of Religion: Meaning and Action in Our Strange World.* Chichester: Wiley-Blackwell.

Foges, P. (2010) "An atheist meets the Masters of the Universe." *Lapham's Quarterly* 8 March. http://www.laphamsquarterly.org/roundtable/roundtable/an-atheist-meets-the-masters-of-the-universe.php

Fornander, A. (1916–20) *Collection of Hawaiian Antiquities and Folk-lore,* First Series (1916–7), Second Series (1918–9), Third Series (1919–20). Honolulu: Bishop Museum Press.

Fortune, R. F. (1932; 2nd ed. 1963) *Sorcerers of Dobu.* London: Routledge and Kegan Paul.

Fox, D. (1930) "Further notes on the Masai of Kenya Colony." *Journal of the Royal Anthropological Institute of Great Britain and Ireland* 60, 447–65.

Fox, M. (2003) *Religion, Spirituality and the Near-Death Experience.* London: Routledge.

Fox, M. (2008) *Spiritual Encounters with Unusual Light Phenomena: Lightforms.* Cardiff: University of Wales Press.

Fraser, D. (1914) *Winning a Primitive People: Sixteen Years among the Warlike Tribe of the Ngoni and the Senega and the Tumbuka Peoples of Central Africa.* New York: Dutton.

Frazer, J. G. (1913, 1922, 1924) *The Belief in Immortality and the Worship of the Dead,* 3 vols. London, MacMillan.

Friedlaender, J. S., et al. (2008) "The Genetic structure of Pacific Islanders." *PLOS Genetics.* http://www.plosgenetics.org/article/info%3Adoi%2F10.1371%2Fjournal.pgen.0040019. Accessed February 1, 2013.

Furness, W. H. (1910) *The Island of Stone Money.* Philadelphia: Lippincott.

Fynn, H. F. (1824–1836; ed. 1950) *The Diary of Henry Francis Fynn.* Pietermaritzburg: Shuter & Shooter.

Gabbard, G. O. & S. W. Twemlow (1984) *With the Eyes of the Mind: An Empirical Analysis of Out-of-Body States.* New York: Praeger.

Gatschet, A. S. (1890) *The Klamath Indians of Southwestern Oregon.* Washington, DC: Government Printing Office.

Gayton, A. H. (1935) "The Orpheus Myth in North America." *Journal of American Folklore* 48(189), 263–93.

Gifford, W. W. (1924) *Tongan Myths and Tales.* Honolulu: Bernice P. Bishop Museum (Bulletin 8).

Gill, W. W. (1876) *Myths and Songs from the South Pacific.* London: King.

Gill, W. W. (1877) "On the origin of the South Sea Islanders, and on some traditions of the Hervey Islands." *Journal of the Anthropological Institute* 6, 2–5.

Gluckman, M. (1937) "Mortuary customs and the belief in survival after death among the south eastern Bantu." *Bantu Studies* 11, 117–36.

Goldie, W. H. (1904) "Maori medical lore." *Transactions and Proceedings of the Royal Society of New Zealand* 37, 1–120.

Goodenough, W. H. (2002) *Under Heaven's Brow: Pre-Christian Religious Tradition in Chuuk*. Philadelphia: American Philosophical Society.

Goulet, J.-G. A. & B. G. Miller (2007) *Extraordinary Anthropology: Transformations in the Field*. Lincoln: University of Nebraska Press.

Green, J. T. (1984) "Near-death experience in a Chammorro culture." *Vital Signs* 4(1/2), 6–7.

Green, J. T. (1995) "Lucid dreams as one method of replicating components of the near-death experience in a laboratory setting." *Journal of Near-Death Studies* 14(1), Fall, 49–59.

Green, J. T. (1998) "Near-death experiences, shamanism and the scientific method." *Journal of Near-Death Studies* 16(3), 205–22.

Green, J. T. (2008) "The death journey of a Hopi Indian: A case study." *Journal of Near-Death Studies* 26(4), Summer, 283–93. .

Green, L. C. & M. W. Beckwith (1926) "Hawaiian customs and beliefs relating to sickness and death." *American Anthropologist* 28(1), 176–208.

Greenbaum, L. (1973) "Societal correlates of possession trance in Sub-Saharan Africa." In E. Bourguignon (ed.) *Religion, Altered States of Consciousness and Social Change*, 39–57. Columbus: Ohio State University.

Grey, M. (1985) *Return from Death: An Exploration of the Near-Death Experience*. London: Arkana.

Greyson, B. (1983). "The near-death experience scale: Construction, reliability, and validity." *Journal of Nervous and Mental Disease* 171(6), 369–75.

Greyson, B. (2006) "Near-death experiences and spirituality." *Zygon: Journal of Religion and Science* 41, 393–414.

Greyson, B. (2007) "Commentary on 'Psychophysiological and cultural correlates undermining a survivalist interpretation of near-death experiences.'" *Journal of Near-Death Studies* 26(2), 127–45.

Greyson, B. (2010) "Seeing people not known to have died: 'Peak in Darien' experiences." *Anthropology and Humanism* 35(2), 159–71.

Greyson, B. & N. E. Bush (1992) "Distressing near-death experiences." *Psychiatry* 55, 95–110.

Greyson, B., E. W. Kelly, & E. F. Kelly (2009) "Explanatory models for near-death experiences." In J. M. Holden, B. Greyson, & D. James (eds.) *The Handbook of Near-Death Experiences: Thirty Years of Investigation*, 213–34. Santa Barbara, CA: Praeger/ABC-CLIO.

Griaule, M. (1938) *Dogon Masks*. Paris: Institut d'Ethnologie.

Grinnell, G. B. (1892) *Blackfoot Lodge Tales*. New York: Scribner.

Grinnell, G. B. (1893) *Pawnee Hero Stories and Folk-Tales*. London: Nutt.

Grinnell, G. B. (1928) *The Cheyenne Indians*. New Haven, CT: Yale University Press.

Groth-Marnat, G. (1994) "Cross-cultural perspectives on the near-death experience." *Australian Parapsychological Review* 19, 7–11.

Groth-Marnat, G. & R. Summers (1998) "Altered beliefs, attitudes, and behaviors following near-death experiences." *Journal of Humanistic Psychology* 38(3), 110–25.

Grout, L. (1864) *Zulu-Land; Or, Life among the Zulu-Kafirs of Natal and Zululand, South Africa*. Philadelphia: Presbyterian Publication Committee.

Gunn, W. (1914) *The Gospel in Futuna*. London: Hodder & Stoughton.

Gunson, N. (1962) "An account of the Mamaia or visionary heresy of Tahiti, 1826–1841." *Journal of the Polynesian Society* 7(2), 208–43.

Gurney, E., F. W. H. Myers, & F. Podmore (1886). *Phantasms of the Living*, 2 vols. London: Trubner and Co.

Haeberlin, H. (1918) "*Sbetetda'q*, a shamanistic performance of the Coast Salish." *American Anthropologist* 20(3), 249–57.

Haeberlin, H. & E. Gunther (1924; rpt. 1930) *The Indians of Puget Sound*. University of Washington Publications in Anthropology 4/1, 1–84. Seattle: University of Washington Press.

Hagen, J. C. (ed.) (2017) *The Science of Near-Death Experiences*. Columbia: University of Missouri Press.

Haley, E. N. (1892) "A visit to the spirit land; or, The strange experience of a woman in Kona, Hawaii." Originally published in *The Hawaiian Almanac and Annual for 1892*. Reprinted in T. G. Thrum (1907) *Hawaiian Folk Tales*, 58–61. Chicago: McClurg.

Handy, E. S. (1927) *Polynesian Religion*. Honolulu: Bernice P. Bishop Museum.

Handy, E. S. (1930) *Marquesan Legends*. Honolulu: Bernice P. Bishop Museum.

Hariot, T. (1588) *A Briefe and True Report of the New Found Land of Virginia*. London.

Hallowell, A. I. (1940) "Spirits of the dead in Salteaux life and thought." *Journal of the Royal Anthropological Institute* 70, 29–51.

Henry, T. (ed.) & J. M. Orsmond (1928; rpt. 1971) *Ancient Tahiti*. Honolulu: Bernice P. Bishop Museum (Bulletin 48). New York: Kraus Reprint Co.

Hick, J. (1976) *Death and Eternal Life*. London: Collins.

Hind, H. Y. (1860) *Narrative of the Canadian Red River Exploring Expedition of 1857 and of the Saskatchewan Exploring Expedition of 1858*, vol. 2. London: Longman Green.

Hinde, S. L. & H. Hinde (1901) *The Last of the Masai*. London: Heinemann.

Hobley, C. W. (1901) *Ethnology of A-Kamba and Other East African Tribes*. Cambridge: Cambridge University Press.

Hodge, K. M. (2011) "On imagining the afterlife." *Journal of Cognition and Culture* 11, 367–89.

Holden, J. M. (2009) "Veridical perception in near-death experiences." In J. M. Holden, B. Greyson, & D. James (eds.) *The Handbook of Near-Death Experiences: Thirty Years of Investigation*, 185–211. Santa Barbara, CA: Praeger/ABC-CLIO.

Hollis, A. C. (1905) *The Masai: Their Language and Folk-Lore*. Oxford: Clarendon.

Hollis, A. C. (1909) *The Nandi: Their Language and Folk-Lore*. Oxford: Clarendon.

Hongi, H. (trans. 1896) "Te tangi a te Rangi-mauri mo Tonga-awhiakau, na Karepa Te Whetu." *Journal of the Polynesian Society* 5(2), 112–20.

Hooper, L. (1920) *The Cahuilla Indians*. Berkeley: University of California Publications in American Archaeology and Ethnology 16(6), 315–80.

Howitt, A. W. (1887) "On Australian medicine men; or, Doctors and wizards of some Australian tribes." *Journal of the Anthropological Institute of Great Britain and Ireland* 16, 23–59.

Howitt, A. W. (1904) *The Native Tribes of Southeast Australia*. London: Macmillan.

Hufford, D. (1995a) "Beings without bodies: An experience-centered theory of the belief in spirits." In B. Walker (ed.) *Out of the Ordinary: Folklore and the Supernatural*. Boulder: Utah State University Press.

Hufford, D. (1995b) "The scholarly voice and the personal voice: reflexivity in belief studies." *Western Folklore* 54(1), January, 57–76.

Hufford, D. (2005) "Sleep paralysis as spiritual experience." *Transcultural Psychiatry* 42(1), 11–45.

Hugh-Jones, S. (1994) "Shamans, prophets, priests, and pastors." In N. Thomas & C. Humphrey (eds.) *Shamanism, History, and the State*, 32–75. Ann Arbor: University of Michigan Press.

Hultkrantz, Å. (1953) *Conceptions of the Soul among North American Indians*. Stockholm: Ethnographical Museum of Sweden.

Hultkrantz, Å. (1957, rpt. 2022) *The North American Indian Orpheus Tradition: Native Afterlife Myths and Their Origins*. Santa Fe: Afterworlds Press.

Hultkrantz, Å. (1967; trans. 1979) *Religions of the American Indians*. Berkeley: University of California Press.

Hultkrantz, Å. (1980) "The problem of Christian influence on Northern Algonkian eschatology." *Studies in Religion/Sciences Religieuses* 9(2), 161–83.

Hultkrantz, Å. (1989) "The place of shamanism in the history of religions." In M. Hoppál & O. von Sadovsky (eds.) *Shamanism Past and Present*, vol. 1, 43–52. Budapest: International Society for Trans-Oceanic Research.

Hultkrantz, Å. (1992) *Shamanic Healing and Ritual Drama, Health and Medicine in Native North American Religious Traditions*. New York: Crossroads.

Human Relations Area Files (HRAF). *eHRAF World Cultures Database*. http://ehraf-worldcultures.yale.edu/ehrafe/

Humphreys, C. B. (1926) *The Southern New Hebrides*. Cambridge: Cambridge University Press.

Hunter, J. (2015) "'Between realness and unrealness': Anthropology, parapsychology and the ontology of non-ordinary realities." *Diskus* 17(2), 4–20.

Huntingford, G. W. B. (1953) *The Nandi of Kenya*. London: Routledge and Kegan Paul.

Huntington, D. B. (1919) "Ute dialect, traditions and legends." In P. Gottfredson (ed.) *History of Indian Depredations in Utah*. Salt Lake City: Skelton.

Idowu, E. B. (1973) *African Traditional Religion: A Definition*. London: SCM.

Ikenga-Metuh, E. (1987) *Comparative Studies of African Traditional Religions.* Onitsha: IMICO.

Irwin, H. J. (2007) "Commentary on Keith Augustine's paper." *Journal of Near-Death Studies* 26(2), Winter, 159–61.

Jacobs, M. (1945) *Kalapuya Texts.* Seattle: University of Washington.

Jakobsen, M. D. (1999) *Shamanism: Traditional and Contemporary Approaches to the Mastery of Spirits and Healing.* New York: Berghan.

Janzen, J. (1978) *The Quest for Therapy in Lower Zaire.* Berkeley: University of California Press.

Janzen, J. M. & W. MacGaffey (1974) *An Anthology of Kongo Religion: Primary Texts from Lower Zaïre.* Lawrence: University of Kansas.

Jarves, J. J. (1843) *History of the Hawaiian or Sandwich Islands.* Boston: Munroe.

Jenness, D. (1934) "Myths of the Carrier Indians." *Journal of American Folklore* 47(184/185), 97–257.

Jenness, D. (1935) *The Ojibwa Indians of Parry Island.* National Museum of Canada Bulletin 78, Anthropological Series, No. 17. Ottawa: Patenaude.

Jenness, D. (1938) *The Sarcee Indians of Alberta.* Bulletin 90, Anthropological Series 23. Ottawa: Canada Department of Mines and Resources.

Jenness, D. (1959) *The People of the Twilight.* Chicago: University of Chicago Press.

Johansen, U. (1999) "Further thoughts on the history of shamanism." *Shaman* 7(1), 40–58.

Johnson, D. H. (1994) *Nuer Prophets: A History of Prophecy from the Upper Nile in the Nineteenth and Twentieth Centuries.* Oxford: Clarendon.

Jones, J. A. (1829; rev. 1830) *Traditions of the North American Indians,* vol. 1. London: Colburn & Bentley.

Jones, W. (1907) *Fox Texts.* Publications of the American Ethnological Society. Leiden, Brill.

Jones, W. (1917) *Ojibwa Texts.* Publications of the American Ethnological Society, Vol. 7, Part II. New York: Stechert.

Kalakaua, D. (1888) *Legends and Myths of Hawaii.* New York: Webster.

Kalweit, H. (1984; trans. 1988) *Dreamtime and Inner Space: The World of the Shaman.* Boston: Shambhala.

Kalweit, H. (1992) *Shamans, Healers, and Medicine Men.* Boston: Shambhala.

Kamakau, S. M. (1866–71; ed. 1964 Dorothy Barrére) *Ka Poʻe Kahiko: The People of Old.* Honolulu: Bishop Museum Press.

Kamma, F. C. (1954; trans. 1972) *Koreri: Messianic Movements in the Biak-Numfor Culture Area.* The Hague: Nijhoff.

Kan, S. (1989) *Symbolic Immortality: The Tlingit Potlatch of the Nineteenth Century.* Washington, DC: Smithsonian Institution Press.

Karsten, R. (1935) *The Origins of Religion.* London: Kegan Paul.

Keable, R. (1921) "A people of dreams." *Hibbert Journal* 19, 522–31.

Keating, W. H. (1825) *Narrative of an Expedition to the Source of St. Peter's River*, vol. 2. London: Whittaker.

Kehoe, A. B. (2000) *Shamans and Religion: An Anthropological Exploration in Critical Thinking*. Long Grove, IL: Waveland.

Kellehear, A. (1996) *Experiences Near Death: Beyond Medicine and Religion*. New York: Oxford University Press.

Kellehear, A. (2001) "An Hawaiian near-death experience." *Journal of Near-Death Studies* 20(1), 31–5.

Kellehear, A. (2007) "Culture and the near-death experience: Comments on Keith Augustine's 'Psychophysiological and Cultural Correlates Undermining a Survivalist Interpretation of Near-Death Experiences.'" *Journal of Near-Death Studies* 26(2), Winter, 147–53.

Kellehear, A. (2009) "Census of non-Western near-death experiences to 2005: Observations and critical reflections." In J. M. Holden, B. Greyson, & D. James (eds.) *Handbook of Near-Death Experiences*, 135–58. Santa Barbara: Praeger.

Kelly, E. F. (2007) "Towards a psychology for the 21st century." In E. F. Kelly (ed.) *Irreducible Mind*, 577–643. Lanham, MD: Rowman and Littlefield.

Kelly, E. W. (2001) "Near-death experiences with reports of meeting deceased people." *Death Studies* 25, 229–249.

Kelly, E. W., B. Greyson, & E. F. Kelly (2007) "Unusual experiences near death and related phenomena." In E. F. Kelly (ed.) *Irreducible Mind: Toward a Psychology for the 21st Century*, 367–422. Lanham, MD: Rowman & Littlefield.

Kemmerer, D. & R. Gupta (2006) "Six feet over: Out-of-body experiences and their relevance to the folk psychology of souls." *Behavioral and Brain Sciences* 29(5), 478–9.

Kenton, E. (1927) *The Indians of North America*. New York: Harcourt Brace.

Kepelino Keauokalini (1860; trans. M. W. Beckwith 1932) *Kepelino's Traditions of Hawaii*. Honolulu: Bernice P. Bishop Museum (Bulletin 95).

Kidd, D. (1904) *The Essential Kafir*. London: Black.

King, M. (1985). *Being Pakeha: An Encounter with New Zealand and the Maori Renaissance*. Auckland: Hodder and Stoughton.

Kinsella, M. (2017) "Near-death experiences and networked spirituality: The emergence of an afterlife movement." *Journal of the American Academy of Religion* 85(1), 168–98.

Kirkpatrick, L. A. (2006) "Religion is not an adaptation." In P. McNamara (ed.) *Where God and Science Meet*, vol. 1, 158–9. Westport: Praeger.

Knapp, F. D. & R. L. Childe (1896) *The Thlinkets of Southeastern Alaska*. Chicago: Stone and Kimball.

Knight, J. (1913) "Ojibwa tales from Sault Ste. Marie, Mich." *Journal of American Folklore* 26(99), 91–96.

Kohl, J. G. (1860) *Kitschi-Gami: Wanderings Round Lake Superior*. London: Chapman & Hall.

Krause, A. (1956) *The Tlingit Indians: Results of a Trip to the Northwest Coast of America and the Bering Straits*. Seattle: American Ethnological Society, University of Washington Press.

Kripal, J. J. (2010) *Authors of the Impossible: The Paranormal and the Sacred*. Chicago: University of Chicago.

Krippner, S. (2012) "The role of spiritually transformative experiences in religious history and the development of a scale to measure them." *Journal of Near-Death Studies* 31(2), Winter, 79–97.

Kroeber, A. L. (1904) "A ghost dance in California." *Journal of American Folklore* 17(64), 32–5.

Kroeber, A. L. (1908) *Ethnology of the Gros Ventre*. New York: Anthropological Papers of the American Museum of Natural History I/IV.

Kroeber, A. L. (1946) "A Karok Orpheus myth." *Journal of American Folklore* 59, 13–9.

Kroeber, A. L. (1976) *Yurok Myths*. Berkeley: University of California Press.

La Barre, W. (1972) "Hallucinogens and the shamanic origins of religion." In P. T. Furst (ed.) *Flesh of the Gods: The Ritual Use of Hallucinogens*, 261–78. London: Allen & Unwin.

Lafitau, J.-F. (1724; trans. 1974–77) *Customs of the American Indians*. Toronto: Champlain Society.

Landes, R. (1968) *Ojibwa Religion and the Midewiwin*. Madison: University of Wisconsin Press.

Landtman, G. (1912) "Wanderings of the dead in the folk-lore of the Kiwai-speaking Pauans." In O. Castrén, Y. Hirn, R. Lagerborg, & A. Wallensköld (eds.) *Festskrift Tillengnad Edvard Westermarck i Anledning av Hans Femtioårsdag den 20 November 1912*, 59–80. Helsingfors: Simelii.

Landtman, G. (1917) *Folk-tales of the Kiwai Papuans*. Acta Societatis Scientiarum Fennicae, 47. Helsingfors: Finnish Society for Literature.

Lang, A. (1894) *Cock Lane and Common-Sense*. London: Longman's Green.

Lang, A. (1900; 2nd ed.) *The Making of Religion*. London: Longmans Green.

Lanoue, G. (1993) "Orpheus in the netherworld in the Plateau of western North America: The voyage of Peni." In A. Masaracchia (ed.) *Orfeo e l' Orfismo: Atti del Seminario Nazionale (Roma-Perugia 1985–1991)*, 447–85. Rome: Gruppo Editoriale Internazionale.

Lanternari, V. (1963) *The Religions of the Oppressed: A Study of Modern Messianic Cults*. London: MacGibbon & Kee.

Leakey, L. B. (1930) "Some notes on the Masai of Kenya Colony." *Journal of the Royal Anthropological Institute of Great Britain and Ireland* 60, 185–209.

Le Clercq, C. (1691; rpt. 1910; trans./ed. W. F. Ganong) *New Relation of Gasperia*. Toronto: Champlain Society.

Lee, S. G. (1969) "Spirit possession among the Zulu." In J. Beattie & J. Middleton (eds.) *Spirit Mediumship and Society in Africa*, 128–56. London: Routledge & Kegan Paul.

Le Jeune (1640) "Relation de ce qvi s'est passé en la Nouvelle France." In R. B. Thwaites (ed. 1898) *Travels and Explorations of the Jesuit Missionaries in New France*, vol. 18. Cleveland: Burrows Brothers.

Le Mercier, F. J. (1638) "Relation de ce qvi s'est passé en la Nouvelle France." In R. B. Thwaites (ed. 1897) *Travels and Explorations of the Jesuit Missionaries in New France* vol. 15. Cleveland: Burrows Brothers.

Leonard, A. G. (1906) *The Lower Niger and Its Tribes*. London: Macmillan.

Leslie, D. (1875; 2nd ed.) *Among the Zulus and Amatongas*. Edinburgh: Edmonston and Douglas.

Levy, J. & Pepper, B. (1992) *Orayvi Revisited: Social Stratification in an "Egalitarian" Society*. Santa Fe: School of American Research Press.

Lewis, I. M. (2003, 3rd ed.) *Ecstatic Religion: An Anthropological Study of Spirit Possession and Shamanism*. London: Routledge.

Lichtenstein, H. (1812, rpt. 1928; trans. A. Plumptre) *Travels in Southern Africa in the Years 1803, 1804, 1805, and 1806*, vol. I. Cape Town: Van Riebeck Society.

Linton, R. (1933) *The Tanala: A Hill Tribe of Madagascar*. Chicago: Field Museum Press.

Loskiel, G. H. (1789; trans. 1794) *History of the Mission of the United Brethren among the Indians of North America*. London: Brethren's Society.

Lowie, R. H. (1909) *The Northern Shoshone*. New York: Anthropological Papers of the American Museum of Natural History, II/II.

Lowie, R. H. (1922) *The Religion of the Crow Indians*. New York: Anthropological Papers of the American Museum of Natural History, XXV/II.

Lowie, R. H. (1936) *Primitive Religion*. London: Routledge.

MacDonald, D. (1893) "Efate, New Hebrides." *Report of the Fourth Meeting of the Australasian Association for the Advancement of Science*, 720–35.

MacGaffey, W. (1986) *Religion and Society in Central Africa: The BaKongo of Lower Zaire*. Chicago: University of Chicago Press.

Mackenzie, D. R. (1925) *The Spirit-Ridden Konde*. London: Seeley.

Malinowski, B. (1916; rpt. 1928) "Baloma: The spirits of the dead in the Trobriand Islands." *Magic Science and Religion*. London: Faber & West.

Mariner, W. (1817; ed. John Martin) *An Account of the Natives of the Tonga Islands*, vol. 2. London: Murray.

Martin, M. (2013) "Bi'änki's Ghost Dance map: Thanatoptic cartography and the Native American spirit world." *Imago Mundi* 65(1), 106–14.

Massam, J. A. (1927) *The Cliff-Dwellers of Kenya*. London: Seeley.

Mayne, R. C. (1862) *Four Years in British Columbia and Vancouver Island*. London: Murray.

Mbiti, J. S. (1971) *New Testament Eschatology in an African Background*. Oxford: Oxford University Press.

Mbiti, J. S. (1990; 2nd ed.) *African Religions and Philosophy*. Oxford: Heinemann.

McClenon, J. (1994) *Wondrous Events: Foundations of Religious Belief*. Philadelphia: Pennsylvania University Press.

McClenon, J. (2002) *Wondrous Healing: Shamanism, Human Evolution, and the Origin of Religion*. DeKalb, IL: Northern Illinois University Press.

McClenon, J. (2006a) "Kongo near-death experiences: Cross-cultural patterns." *Journal of Near-Death Studies* 25(1), 21–34.

McClenon, J. (2006b) "The ritual healing theory: Therapeutic suggestion and the origin of religion." In P. McNamara (ed.) *Where God and Science Meet*, vol. 1, 136–58. Westport: Praeger.

McClenon, J. & Nooney, J. (2002) "Anomalous experiences reported by field anthropologists: Evaluating theories regarding religion." *Anthropology of Consciousness*, 13, 46–60.

McClintock, W. (1923) *Old Indian Trails*. Boston: Houghton Mifflin.

McIntosh, A. I. (1980) "Beliefs about out-of-the-body experiences among the Elema, Gulf Kamea and Rigo peoples of Papua New Guinea." *Journal of the Society for Psychical Research* 50(175), 460–77.

McKenney, T. L. (1827) *Sketches of a Tour to the Lakes*. Baltimore: Lucas.

McNamara, P. (ed.) (2006) *Where God and Science Meet*. Westport: Praeger.

Melland, F. H. (1923) *In Witch-Bound Africa*. Philadelphia: Lippincott.

Merker, M. (1910) *The Masai: Ethnographic Monograph of an East African Semite People*. Berlin: Dietrich Reimer. (HRAF translation by F. Schütze.)

Merriam, C. H. (1910) *The Dawn of the World: Myths and Weird Tales of the Mewan Indians of California*. Cleveland: Clark.

Metzinger, T. (2005) "Out-of-body experiences as the origin of the concept of a 'soul.'" *Mind and Matter* 3(1), 57–84

Miller, J. (1988) *Shamanic Odyssey: The Lushootseed Salish Journey to the Land of the Dead*. Santa Barbara: Ballena Press Anthropological Papers.

Mills, A. (1988) "A comparison of Wet'suwet'en cases of the reincarnation type with Gitksan and Beaver." *Journal of Anthropological Research* 44(4), 385–415.

Mills, A. & R. Slobodin (eds.) (1994) *Amerindian Rebirth: Reincarnation Belief among North American Indians and Inuit*. Toronto: University of Toronto Press.

Moffat, R. (1842) *Missionary Labours and Scenes in Southern Africa*. London: Snow.

Moffat, R. (1951; ed. Isaac Schapera) *Apprenticeship at Kuruman: The Letters of Robert and Mary Moffat, 1820–1828*. London: Chatto & Windus.

Mooney, J. (1896) *The Ghost-Dance Religion and the Sioux Outbreak of 1890*. Washington, DC: Government Printing Office.

Mooney, J. (1900) *Myths of the Cherokee*. Nineteenth Annual Report of the Bureau of American Ethnology 1897–98, 3–548. Washington, DC: Smithsonian.

Mooney, J. & F. M. Olbrechts (1932) *The Swimmer Manuscript: Cherokee Sacred Formulas and Medicinal Prescriptions*. Bureau of American Ethnology Bulletin 99. Washington, DC: Smithsonian.

Morse, M. & P. Perry (1992) *Transformed by the Light*. London: Piatkus.

Moss, R. (1925) *The Life after Death in Oceania and the Malay Archipelago*. Oxford: Oxford University Press.

Nadel, S. F. (1946) "A study of shamanism in the Nuba Mountains." *Journal of the Royal Anthropological Institute of Great Britain and Ireland* 76(1), 25–37.

Nassau, R. H. (1904) *Fetichism in West Africa*. New York: Scribners.

Nelson, E. W. (1900) *The Eskimo about Bering Strait*. Washington, DC: Government Printing Office.

Newland, S. (1887–8) "The Parkengees, or Aboriginal tribes on the Darling River." *Papers Read before the Royal Geographical Society of Australia, South Australian Branch, 3rd Session*, 20–32.

Newton, H (1914) *In Far New Guinea*. London: Seely, Service & Co.

Ogot, B. A. (1972) "On the making of a sanctuary: Being some thoughts on the history of religion in Padhola." In T. O. Ranger & I. N. Kimambo (eds.) *The Historical Study of African Religion*, 122–35. London: Heinemann.

Oliver, D. L. (1974) *Ancient Tahitian Society*, 3 vols. Honolulu: University of Hawaii Press.

Oliver, D. L. (1989) *Oceania: The Native Cultures of Australia and the Pacific Islands*, vol. 1. Honolulu: University of Hawaii Press.

Oliver, D. L. (2002) *Polynesia in Early Historic Times*. Honolulu: Bess.

Olson, M. & P. Dulaney (1993) "Life satisfaction, life review, and near-death experiences in the elderly." *Journal of Holistic Nursing* 11(4), 368–82.

Olson, R. L. (1936) *The Quinault Indians*. Seattle: University of Washington.

Opler, M. E. (1940) *Myths and Legends of the Lipan Apache Indians*. Memoirs of the American Folklore Society 36. New York: Augustin.

Opler, M. E. (1942) *Myths and Tales of the Chiricahua Apache Indians*. Memoirs of the American Folklore Society 37. New York: Augustin.

Osis K. (1979) "Insider's view of the OBE: A questionnaire study." In W. G. Roll (ed.) *Research in Parapsychology*, 50–51. Methuen NJ: Scarecrow Press.

Osis, K. and E. Haraldsson (1986 rev. ed.) *At the Hour of Death*. Mamaroneck, NY: Hastings House.

Parkman, F. (1870) *The Conspiracy of Pontiac and the Indian War after the Conquest of Canada*. Boston: Little Brown.

Parker, A. C. (1913) *The Code of Handsome Lake, the Seneca Prophet*. Albany: University of the State of New York.

Parmentier, R. J. (1987) *The Sacred Remains: Myth, History and Polity in Belau*. Chicago: University of Chicago Press.

Parnia, S., K. Spearpoint, G. de Vos, P. Fenwick, et al. (2014) "AWARE—AWAreness during REsuscitation-a prospective study." *Resuscitation* 85(12), 1799–805.

Parrinder, G. (1974; 3rd ed.) *African Traditional Religion*. London: Sheldon.

P'Bitek, O. (1970) *African Religions in Western Scholarship*. Nairobi: Kenya Literature Bureau.

Petrullo, V. (1934) *The Diabolic Root: A Study of Peyotism, The New Indian Religion, Among the Delawares*. Philadelphia, University of Pennsylvania.

Price, H. H. (1953) "Survival and the idea of 'another world'." *Proceedings of the Society for Psychical Research* 50(182), 1–25.

Prichard, J. C. (1836) *Researches into the Physical History of Mankind*, vol. 1. London: Sherwood, Gilbert, and Piper.

Prins, G. (1980) *The Hidden Hippopotamus: Reappraisal in African History*. Cambridge: Cambridge University Press.

Proudfoot, W. (1985) *Religious Experience*. Berkeley: University of California Press.

Proyart, B. L. (1776; rpt. 1814) History of Loango, Kakongo, and Other Kingdoms in Africa. In J. Pinkerton (ed.) *A General Collection of the Best and Most Interesting Voyages and Travels in All Parts of the World*, 548–97. London: Longman.

Pryde, D. (1972) *Nunaga: My Land, My Country*. Edmonton: M. G. Hurtig.

Quatrefages, A. de (1895) *The Pygmies*. London: Macmillan.

Quen, F. J. de (1657) "Relation de ce qvi s'est passé en la Nouvelle France." In R. B. Thwaites (ed. 1897) *Travels and Explorations of the Jesuit Missionaries in New France*, vol. 43. Cleveland: Burrows Brothers.

Radin, P. (1923; rpt. 1990) *The Winnebago Tribe*. Lincoln: University of Nebraska Press.

Ragueneau, P. (1646) "Relation de ce qvi s'est passé en la Nouvelle France." In R. B. Thwaites (ed. 1897) *Travels and Explorations of the Jesuit Missionaries in New France*, vol. 30. Cleveland: Burrows Brothers.

Ralston, C. (1985) "Early nineteenth century Polynesian millennial cults and the case of Hawai'i." *Journal of the Polynesian Society* 94(4), 307–32.

Rasmussen, K. (1921) *Eskimo Folk-Tales*. London: Gyldendal.

Rasmussen, K. (1929) *Intellectual Culture of the Iglulik Eskimos*. Copenhagen: Boghandel & Forlag.

Rasmussen, K. (1932) *Intellectual Culture of the Copper Eskimos*. Copenhagen: Boghandel & Forlag.

Rasmussen, M., X. Guo, Y. Wang, K. E. Lohmueller, S. Rasmussen, A. Albrechtsen, L. Skotte, et al. (2011) "An Aboriginal Australian genome reveals separate human dispersals into Asia." *Science* 334(6052), 94–98.

Rattray, R. S. (1927) *Religion and Art in Ashanti*. Oxford: Clarendon.

Rawlings, M. (1993) *To Hell and Back*. Thomas Nelson: Nashville.

Ray, B. C. (2000; 2nd. ed) *African Religions: Symbol, Ritual, and Community*. Upper Saddle River, NJ: Prentice Hall.

Ray, V. F. (1936) "The Kolaskin cult: A prophet movement of 1870 in northeastern Washington." *American Anthropologist* 38(1), 67–75.

Reade, W. (1874) *The Story of the Ashantee Campaign*. London: Smith, Elder.

Reynolds, B. (1963) *Magic, Divination and Witchcraft among the Barotse of Northern Rhodesia*. London: Chatto and Windus.

Rice, W. H. (1923) *Hawaiian Legends*. Honolulu: Bernice P. Bishop Museum (Bulletin 3).

Ring, K. (1980) *Life at Death: A Scientific Investigation of the Near-Death Experience.* New York: Quill.

Rink, H. (1875) *Tales and Traditions of the Eskimo.* Edinburgh: Blackwood.

Rock, A. J., P. B. Baynes, & P. J. Casey (2005/2006) "Experimental study of ostensibly shamanic journeying imagery in naïve participants." *Anthropology of Consciousness* 15(2), 72–92 (part 1); 17(1), 65–83 (part 2).

Rock, A. J. & S. Krippner (2011) *Demystifying Shamans and Their World: An Interdisciplinary Study.* Exeter: Imprint Academic.

Roscoe, J. (1911) *The Baganda.* London: Macmillan.

Routledge, W. S. & K. Routledge (1910) *With a Prehistoric People.* London: Arnold.

Rowley, H. (1877) *The Religion of the Africans.* London: W. Wells Gardner.

Roy, S. C. (1912) *The Mundas and Their Country.* Calcutta: Kuntaline.

Ruby, R. H. & J. A. Brown (1989) *Dreamer Prophets of the Columbia Plateau: Smohalla and Skolaskin.* Norman: University of Oklahoma.

Ruby, R. H. & J. A. Brown (1996) *John Slocum and the Indian Shaker Church.* Norman: University of Oklahoma.

St. Clair, H. H. & L. J. Frachtenberg (1909) "Traditions of the Coos Indians of Oregon." *Journal of American Folklore* 22(83), 25–41.

St. Johnston, T. R. (1918) *The Lau Islands (Fiji) and their Fairy Tales and Folklore.* London: Times.

Sartori, P. (2008) *The Near-Death Experiences of Hospitalized Intensive Care Patients: A Five Year Clinical Study.* Lewiston, Queenston, Lampeter: Edwin Mellen Press.

Savage, S. (1916) "The period of Iro-nui-ma-oata and Tangiia-nui-ariki." *Journal of the Polynesian Society* 25(100), 138–49.

Schebesta, P. (1933) *Among Congo Pigmies.* London: Hutchinson.

Schebesta, P. (1936) *Revisiting My Pygmy Hosts.* London: Hutchinson.

Schoolcraft, H. R. (1825) *Travels in the Central Portions of the Mississippi Valley.* New York: Collins.

Schoolcraft, H. R. (1839) *Algic Researches.* New York: Harper.

Schorer, C. E. (1985) "Two Native North American near-death experiences." *Omega* 16, 111–3.

Segal, A. (2004) *Life after Death: A History of the Afterlife in Western Religion.* New York: Doubleday.

Seligman, C. G. (1910) *The Melanesians of British New Guinea.* Cambridge: Cambridge University Press.

Sharf, R. (1998) "Experience." In M. C. Taylor (ed.) *Critical Terms in Religious Studies,* 94–115. University of Chicago Press. Reprinted as "The rhetoric of experience and the study of religion." *Journal of Consciousness Studies* 7(11–12), 2000, 267–87.

Shiels, D. (1978) "A cross-cultural study of beliefs in out-of-the-body experiences." *Journal of the Society for Psychical Research* 49(775), 697–741.

Shirokogoroff, S. M. (1935) *Psychomental Complex of the Tungus.* London: Kegan Paul.

Shooter, J. (1857) *The Kafirs of Natal and the Zulu Country.* London: Stanford.

Shortland, E. (1856; 2nd ed.) *Traditions and Superstitions of the New Zealanders.* London: Longman.

Shortland, E. (1882) *Maori Religion and Mythology.* London: Longman Brown Green.

Shushan, G. (2009) *Conceptions of the Afterlife in Early Civilizations: Universalism, Constructivism, and Near-Death Experience.* London: Bloomsbury. Revised edition (forthcoming 2024) *Near-Death Experience in Ancient Civilizations.* Rochester: Inner Traditions.

Shushan, G. (2011) "Afterlife conceptions in the Vedas." *Religion Compass* 5(6), 202–13. London: Wiley-Blackwell.

Shushan, G. (2013) "Rehabilitating the neglected 'similar': Confronting the issue of cross-cultural similarities in the study of religions." *Paranthropology: Journal of Anthropological Approaches to the Paranormal* 4(2), Spring, 48–53.

Shushan, G. (2014) "Extraordinary experiences and religious beliefs: Deconstructing some contemporary philosophical axioms." *Method and Theory in the Study of Religion* 26, 384–416.

Shushan, G. (2016a) "Cultural-linguistic constructivism and the challenge of near-death and out-of-body experience." In Bettina Schmidt (ed.) *The Study of Religious Experience: Approaches and Methodologies,* 71–87. London: Equinox.

Shushan, G. (2016b) "'The Sun told me I would be restored to life': Native American near-death experiences, shamanism, and religious revitalization movements." *Journal of Near-Death Studies* 34(3), Spring, 127–50.

Sibree, J. (1880) *The Great African Island: Chapters on Madagascar.* London: Trübner.

Sidky, H. (2010) "On the antiquity of shamanism and its role in human religiosity." *Method and Theory in the Study of Religion* 22, 68–92.

Skertchley, J. A. (1874) *Dahomey As It Is.* London: Chapman & Hall.

Skinner, A. (1916) "Plains Cree tales." *Journal of American Folklore* 29(113), 341–67.

Smet, P-J. (1905) *Life, Letters, and Travels,* vol. 3. New York: Harper.

Smith, M. W. (1940) *The Puyallup-Nisqually.* New York: Columbia University Press.

Smoak, G. E. (2006) *Ghost Dances and Identity: Prophetic Religion and American Indian Ethnogenesis in the Nineteenth Century.* Berkeley: University of California Press.

Sollas, W. J. (1897) "The legendary history of Funafuti, Ellice Group." *Nature* 55(1424), February 11, 353–5.

Somerville, B. T. (1894) "Notes on some Islands of the New Hebrides." *Journal of the Anthropological Institute of Great Britain and Ireland* 23, 2–21.

Spier, L. (1930) *Klamath Ethnography.* Berkeley: University of California Press.

Spier, L. (1935) *The Prophet Dance of the Northwest and Its Derivatives.* Menasha, WI: Banta.

Spencer, B. & F. J. Gillen (1927) *The Arunta: A Study of a Stone Age People.* London: Macmillan.

Sproat, G. M. (1868) *Scenes and Studies of Savage Life.* London: Smith Elder.

Stair, J. B. (1897) *Old Samoa.* London: Religious Tract Society.

Stevenson, I. & B. Greyson (1996) "NDEs: Relevance to the question of survival after death." In L. W. Bailey & J. Yates (eds.) *The Near-Death Experience: A Reader*, 199–206. London: Routledge.

Stevenson, R. L. (1891; rpt. 1896) *In the South Seas*. New York: Scribner's.

Strubelt, S. (2008) "The near-death experience: A cerebellar method to protect body and soul: Lessons from the Iboga-Healing-Ceremony in Gabon." *Alternative Therapies* 14(1), 30–34.

Sutherland, C. (1990) "Changes in religious beliefs, attitudes, and practices following near-death experiences: An Australian study." *Journal of Near-Death Studies* 9(1), Fall, 21–31.

Swan, J. G. (1869) *The Indians of Cape Flattery*. Philadelphia: Smithsonian Institution.

Swanton, J. (1908) "Social condition, beliefs, and linguistic relationship of the Tlingit Indians." *Twenty-Sixth Annual Report of the Bureau of American Ethnology*, 391–485. Washington, DC: Smithsonian Institution.

Swanton, J. (1909) *Tlingit Myths and Texts*. Bulletin of the Bureau of Ethnology 39. Washington, DC: Smithsonian Institution.

Swatlzer, D. (2000) *A Friend among the Senecas: The Quaker Mission to Cornplanter's People*. Mechanicsburg: Stackpole.

Talbot, P. A. (1912) *In the Shadow of the Bush*. New York: Doran.

Talbot, P. A. (1926) *The Peoples of Southern Nigeria*, vols. 2 & 3: *Ethnology*. Oxford: Oxford University Press.

Talbot, P. A. (1932) *Tribes of the Niger Delta*. London: Sheldon Press.

Talayesva, D. (1942) *Sun Chief: The Autobiography of a Hopi Indian*. New Haven, CT: Yale University Press.

Tanner, J. (1830) *Narrative of the Captivity and Adventures of John Tanner*. New York: Carvill.

Tassell-Matamua, N. (2013) "Phenomenology of near-death experiences: An analysis of a Maori case study." *Journal of Near-Death Studies* 32(2), Winter, 107–17.

Tassell-Matamua, N. & M. Murray (2014) "Near-death experiences: Quantitative findings from an Aotearoa New Zealand sample." *Journal of Near-Death Studies* 33(1), Fall, 3–29.

Taves, A. (2009) *Religious Experience Reconsidered*. Princeton, NJ: Princeton University Press.

Taylor, R. (1855) *Te Ika a Maui, or New Zealand and Its Inhabitants*. London: Wertheim & Macintosh.

Teit, J. A. (1917) "Okanagon tales." In F. Boas (ed.) *Folk-Tales of Salishan and Sahaptin Tribes*, 65–100. Lancaster, PA: American Folklore Society.

Te Matorohanga & Nepia Pohuhu (1913; ed. H. T. Whatahoro; trans. S. Percy Smith) *The Lore of the Whare-wānanga*. New Plymouth, NZ: Polynesian Society.

Theal, G. M. (1910) *The Yellow and Dark Skinned People of Africa*. London: Sonnenschein.

Thompson, S. (1955–1958, rev. ed.) *Motif-Index of Folk-Literature.* Bloomington: Indiana University Press.

Thompson, T. (2013) Review of "The Origins of the World's Mythologies" by E. J. Michael Witzel. *Journal of Folklore Research.* Review posted on December 5, 2013. http://www.jfr.indiana.edu/review.php?id=1613

Thomson, B. (1895) "The Kalou-Vu (ancestor-gods) of the Fijians." *Journal of the Anthropological Institute of Great Britain and Ireland* 24, 340–59.

Thomson, B. (1908) *The Fijians: A Study of the Decay of Custom.* London: Heinemann.

Thornton, A. (1984) "The story of the woman brought back from the underworld." *Journal of the Polynesian Society* 93(3), 295–314.

Thornton, J. K. (1998) *The Kongolese Saint Anthony: Dona Beatriz Kimpa Vita and the Antonian Movement, 1684–1706.* Cambridge, UK: Cambridge University Press.

Thornton, J. K. (2002) "Religious and ceremonial life in the Kongo and Mbundu areas." In L. M. Heywood (ed.) *Central Africans and Cultural Transformations in the American Diaspora,* 71–90. Cambridge: Cambridge University Press.

Thorpe, S. A. (1993) *Shamans, Medicine Men and Traditional Healers: A Comparative Study of Shamanism in Siberian Asia, Southern Africa, and North America.* Pretoria: University of South Africa.

Thunberg, C. P. (1788) *An Account of the Cape of Good Hope.* In J. Pinkerton (ed. 1814) *A General Collection of the Best and Most Interesting Voyages and Travels in All Parts of the World,* vol. 16. London: Longman.

Titiev, M. (1944; rpt. 1971) *Old Oraibi: A Study of the Hopi Indians of the Third Mesa.* New York: Kraus.

Titiev, M. (1972) *The Hopi Indians of Old Oraibi: Change and Continuity.* Ann Arbor: University of Michigan Press.

Tregear, E. (1890) "The Maoris of New Zealand." *Journal of the Anthropological Institute of Great Britain and Ireland* 19, 96–123.

Tremearne, A. J. N. (1912) *The Tailed Head-Hunters of Nigeria.* London: Seely, Service & Co.

Tremearne, A. J. N. (1913) *Hausa Superstitions and Customs.* London: Bale & Danielsson.

Trowbridge, C. C. (1938) *Meearmeear Traditions.* Ann Arbor: University of Michigan Press.

Turnbull, C. (1965) *The Mbuti Pygmies: An Ethnographic Survey.* New York: Anthropological Papers of the American Museum of Natural History 50/3, 139–282.

Turner, E. (1992) *Experiencing Ritual: A New Interpretation of African Healing.* Philadelphia: University of Pennsylvania Press.

Turner, G. (1884) *Samoa, a Hundred Years Ago and Long Before.* London: Macmillan.

Turner, V. (1952) *The Lozi Peoples of North-Western Rhodesia.* London: International African Institute.

Tyler, H. A. (1964) *Pueblo Gods and Myths*. Norman: University of Oklahoma Press.

Tyler, J. (1891) *Forty Years among the Zulus*. Boston: Congregational Sunday School and Publishing Society.

Tylor, E. B. (1871; rpt. 1920) *Primitive Culture*, vol. 2. London: Murray.

van Lommel, P. (2010) *Consciousness Beyond Life*. New York: HarperOne.

van Lommel, P. (2011). "Near-death experiences: The experience of the self as real and not as an illusion." *Annals of the New York Academy of Sciences* 1234, 19–28.

van Lommel, P., R. van Wees, V. Meyers, and I. Elfferich (2001) "Near-death experience in survivors of cardiac arrest: a prospective study in the Netherlands." *The Lancet* 358, 2039–2045.

Vestal, S. (1934; rpt. 1984) *Warpath: The True Story of the Fighting Sioux*. Lincoln: University of Nebraska Press.

Voegelin, E. W. (1947) "Three Shasta myths, including 'Orpheus.'" *Journal of American Folklore* 60(235), 52–8.

Voth, H. R. (1905) *The Traditions of the Hopi*. Chicago: Field Columbian Museum Anthropological Series Vol. VIII, Publication 96.

Wade, J. (2003) "In a sacred manner we died: Native American near-death experiences." *Journal of Near-Death Studies* 22(2), 83–115.

Wagner, G. (1954; 2nd ed. 1998) "The Abaluyia of Kavirondo (Kenya)." In D. Forde (ed.) *African Worlds: Studies in the Cosmological Ideas and Social Values of African Peoples*, 27–54. Oxford: James Currey and International African Institute.

Wallace, A. F. C. (1969) *The Death and Rebirth of the Seneca*. New York: Vintage.

Walsh, R. (1990) *The Spirit of Shamanism*. Los Angeles: Tarcher.

Warner, W. L. (1937) *Black Civilization*. New York & London: Harper.

Weber, M. (1922) *The Sociology of Religion*. London: Methuen.

Weeks, J. H. (1913) *Among Congo Cannibals*. London: Seeley, Service & Co.

Weeks, J. H. (1914) *Among the Primitive Bakongo*. London: Seeley, Service & Co.

Werner, A. (1925) "African." In L. H. Gray (ed.) *Mythology of All Races VII: Armenian, African*. Boston: Jones.

Werner, A. (1933) *Myths and Legends of the Bantu*. London: Harrap.

Westervelt, W. D. (1915) *Legends of Gods and Ghosts*. Boston: Ellis.

Wheeler, G. C. (1914) "An account of the death rites and eschatology of the people of the Bougainville Strait (Western Solomon Islands)." *Archiv für Religionswissenschaft* 17, 64–112.

White, J. (1891) "A chapter from Maori mythology." *Report of the Australasian Association for the Advancement of Science* 3, 359–64.

Williams, F. E. (1928) *Orokaiva Magic*. London: Oxford University Press.

Williams, F. E. (1930) *Orokaiva Society*. London: Oxford University Press.

Williams, F. E. (1934) "The Vailala Madness in retrospect." In E. E. Evans-Pritchard, R. Firth, B. Malinowski, & I. Schapera (eds.), *Essays Presented to C. G. Seligman*, 369–79. London: Kegan Paul.

Williams, T. (1860) *Fiji and the Fijians*, vol. 1. New York: Appleton.

Williamson, R. W. (1933). *Religious and Cosmic Beliefs of Central Polynesia.* 2 vols. Cambridge: Cambridge University Press.

Willoughby, W. C. (1928) *The Soul of the Bantu.* London: Student Christian Movement.

Winkelman, M. (2000) *Shamanism: The Neural Ecology of Consciousness and Healing.* Westport, CT: Bergin & Garvey.

Winkelman, M. (2006) "Shamanism and the biological origins of human religiosity." *Shaman* 14(1/2), 89–116.

Winkelman, M. (2013) "Shamanism in cross-cultural perspective." *International Journal of Transpersonal Studies* 31(2), 47–62.

Wiredu, K. (1996) *Cultural Universals and Particulars: An African Perspective.* Bloomington: Indiana University Press.

Wiredu, K. (1992) "Death and the afterlife in African culture." In K. Wiredu & K. Gyeke (eds.) *Person and Community: Ghanaian Philosophical Studies.* Washington, DC: Council for Research in Values and Philosophy.

Wissler, C. & D. C. Duvall (1908) *Mythology of the Blackfoot Indians.* Anthropological Papers 2(1). New York: American Museum of Natural History.

Witzel, M. (2013) *Origins of the World's Mythologies.* New York: Oxford University Press.

Wohlers, J. F. H. (1874) "The mythology and traditions of the Maori in New Zealand." *Transactions and Proceedings of the Royal Society of New Zealand* 7, 3–53.

Wohlers, J. F. H. (1875) "The mythology and traditions of the Maori in New Zealand, Part III: Maori mythology—miscellaneous tales." *Transactions and Proceedings of the Royal Society of New Zealand* 8, 108–23.

Worsley, P. (1968) *The Trumpet Shall Sound*, 2nd ed. New York: Schocken.

Wren-Lewis, J. (n.d.) "The dazzling dark: A near-death experience opens the door to a permanent transformation." *What Is Enlightenment?* http://www.nonduality.com/dazdark.htm

Young, D. E. & J.-G. A. Goulet (1994) *Being Changed by Cross-Cultural Encounters: Anthropology of Extraordinary Experience.* Peterborough, ON: Broadview.

Yzendoorn, R. (1927) *History of the Catholic Mission in the Hawaiian Islands.* Honolulu: Honolulu Star Bulletin.

Zahan, D. (1979) *The Religion, Spirituality, and Thought of Traditional Africa.* Chicago: University of Chicago.

Zaleski, C. (1987) *Otherworld Journeys: Accounts of Near-Death Experiences in Medieval and Modern Times.* New York: Oxford University Press.

Index